THE AVATARS OF BHUJANGAIAH

The sculpture reproduced on the endpaper depicts a scene where three soothsayers are interpreting to King Suddhodana the dream of Queen Maya, mother of Lord Buddha. Below them is seated a scribe recording the interpretation. This is perhaps the earliest available pictorial record of the art of writing in India.

From : Nagarjunkonda, 2nd century A.D.
Courtesy : National Museum, New Delhi

THE AVATARS OF BHUJANGAIAH

Alanahalli Sri Krishna

Translated from the Kannada Original
C. P. RAVICHANDRA

Sahitya Akademi

The Avatars of Bhujangaiah. An English translation by C. P. Ravichandra of Alanahalli Sri Krishna's Kannada classic *Bhujangaiahna Dashavataragalu*. Sahitya Akademi, 2010, Rs.180

First Published, 2010

SAHITYA AKADEMI

Rabindra Bhavan, 35, Ferozeshah Road, New Delhi 110 001

'Swati', Mandir Marg, New Delhi 110 001

Regional Office

Central College Campus, Dr. B.R. Ambedkar Veedhi,
Bangalore 560 001

4, D. L. Khan Road, Kolkata 700 025

171, Mumbai Marathi Grantha Sangrahalaya Marg,
Dadar, Mumbai 400 014

Chennai Office

443, Guna Buildings, Anna Salai, Teynampet, Chennai 600 018

Rs. 180

ISBN : 81-260-2785-1

Cover design : P.S. Kumar

Typeset by Arjun Printers, Bangalore and printed by Keerthi Printers, Bangalore

FOREWORD

A translator's lot is an unenviable one. Whereas 'creative writers' consider him/her a second-class citizen of the literary world and patronizingly allow him/her to exist on the rim of the literary circle, critics love to fault him/her for omissions and additions in relation to the SL text. However, people continue to translate and readers continue to read such translations. Maybe, the urge to communicate, to share with others what he/she enjoys in a particular text, is as strong in a translator as in any other writer. One such translator, who has an irrepressible urge to communicate is Dr. C. P. Ravichandra.

Ravichandra, a well-known critic (and the awardee of the coveted 'Northrope Frye Award for the best critical article of the year), is a Professor of English in the University of Mysore, and, by vocation, a translator of Kannada works into English. He has already published some of his translations of Kannada saint-poets into English; but, I must confess, what he has undertaken to do in this work is really challenging –challenging for two reasons: the novel, *Bhujangayyana Dashaavataaragalu,* is quite voluminous (running to some 500 pages), and it is written in a caste-region-specific dialectic variation of Kannada. Anybody would think twice before venturing into such a task.

Srikrishna Alanahalli, the author of this novel, was a highly promising *navya* (Modernist) writer in Kannada, who, before his untimely death (at the age of 42), had written three collections of poetry, two collections of short stories, and three novels. While his short stories showed him treading a new path, his first two novellas

Kaadu ('Forest') and *Parasangada Gendethimma* ('Gendethimma the Raconteur') caught the imagination of readers to such an extent that they were immediately translated into English and most other Indian languages, and later were turned into very successful films also. (Girish Karnad directed *Kaadu* which won the President's gold medal and in which Amarish Puri, the famous Hindi actor, took the lead role.) *Bhujangayya* was Alanahally's most ambitious novel.

The present novel has a two-fold objective: to document the very process of an ordinary man of flesh and blood slowly ripening towards an extraordinary person who renounces the world, and, through him, to capture the ethos of a stagnant life, gradually and unwillingly, shaking itself out of stupor. Bhujangayya, the character around whom the novel revolves, is a man of steely will and astounding self-confidence; and the novel, in a leisurely manner, records the many twists and turns of his life. A small farmer in the beginning, Bhujangayya, in course of time, turns into a smalltime hotelier, a shopkeeper, a contractor, and finally a blind mendicant. His knowledge of curing persons from snakebite becomes the cause of his death in the end; with the full knowledge that his attempts to save one more victim of snakebite might lead him to death, he succeeds in bringing the victim back to life, but meets his own death as a result.

What the novel emphasizes is that each new turn, new twist in his life, makes Bhjangayya more and more introspective regarding the meaning of life and living. Also, importantly, every new attempt on his part to rise from ashes like phoenix (the name of a successful story by the author), also involves Bhujangayya's crossing the traditional caste-community barriers on the one hand, and, on the other, losing interest in earthly possessions like land, money, and physical pleasures.

Alanahally, who spent his childhood in a small and remote village of Karnataka, had a penchant to record, authentically, the tumultuous changes ushered in the Indian society by a complex set of causes in the pre- and- post-independence India. He attempts to register in his novels the very pulse-beat of a people, caught in the vortex of sudden changes brought in by urbanization, industrialization and modern education – in short, 'Bharat' that was painfully transforming itself into a modern 'India.' In the course of events unfolding in this novel, we see how each avatar of Bhujangayya introduces a change –resented initially and finally accepted: a 'high-caste' man opening a hotel, getting into a second marriage with a 'low-caste' woman, setting up a grocery store, digging up a tube-well in his land to make his dependence less on the whims of the Rain God, and finally, knowingly, giving up his life to save one who had violated his wife. (Incidentally, it is fascinating to study the motif of 'hotel' as a leveler of castes and classes, a recurring marker of modernity in Kannada fiction from Shivarama Karanth to Devanuru Mahadeva.)

* * *

As a translator, Ravichandra's accomplishment is enviably brilliant. He has perfected a style in English that is concise, precise, and forceful. More importantly, he appears to have found almost a perfect balance between the Text's demands and the Reader's expectations. Hence, reading his translation is a real pleasure.

However, to do justice to the amount of dedicated labour he has put in as a translator, backed by a meaningful ideology of translation, I want to be more specific about Ravichandra's translation. Let me consider now the three categories which distinguish one translator from another: a) culture-region-specific terms; b) expressions of abuse; and c) proverbs and adages.

a) Regarding culture-region-specific terms, Ravichandra usually searches for the most appropriate term in English (if any); for instance, milk-hedge for '*kalli beli*'; fickle mind for '*tikkalu swabhava*'; spell for '*modi*'; white-blossomed Babool tree for *biliya jalada huvina mara;* and such. Most translators would have italicized these terms and glossed them in detail at the end.

   When he doesn't find such suitable equivalents, he uses the term and explains it unobtrusively in the text itself: 'propitiatory para,' 'Kesaribhat, a sweet dish made of semolina,' 'the unaging tree of plenty, Kalpavruksha,' 'for binna, the holy alms,' etc. Owing to this technique, not only the reader understands the text immediately, but the glossary (considered an absolute necessity in a translation) becomes redundant.

b) Abusive terms and expressions are language-culture specific, and as a rule 'indecent'; normally, in the name of 'taste' and 'decorum,' most of the translators either avoid them or use euphemism. But, Ravichandra translates them literally so that the readers of the translation are as shocked as the readers of the SL text. Consider these expressions:

"Now, shut your ass and behave like a responsible man"

"Should we then, merely, sit here and shave pubic hair?"

"You lousy son of a bitch!" "You son of a whore, who husbands his mother" "You son, born to my husband's second wife"

c) Similarly, regarding proverbs and adages, Ravichandra opts for literal translation. For instance,

"The horse laid eggs when the perilous day dawned"

"To drink empty the seven ponds"

"He plants the sacred shrub at home, though indulging in acts of immorality"

"When advised 'unlearn your trait shrew,' she said, ' I may leave my husband but not what I have learnt"

"A beggar grown suddenly affluent will open the parasol under the full moon"

Such literal translations of abuses and proverbs help the TL reader to recognize both the norms and their violation in an alien social system in the form of abuse. (For instance, I am sure the phrase '*Widow's son*' will not be taken as a terrible curse or abuse in any but a Hindu society.) Ravichandra here has worthy precedents in Chinua Achebe and A. K. Ramanujan.

* * *

A translator's task is a tight-rope-walking in which even the rope is prone to break at any time. On the one hand, there is the SL text, which is a network of language-culture-specific assumptions and connotations, demanding of the translator total loyalty to it; on the other hand, there is the TL reader, who comes to the text with his own 'horizon of expectations' constructed by his own literature, language and culture, demanding of the translator to cater only to his needs; and, obviously, both these demands are so opposed to each other that it is almost impossible to meet both. Hence, A. K. Ramanujan exclaims in one of his articles that the translator's task "more often than not... like Marvell's love, is begotten by despair upon impossibility."

Still, A. K. Ramanujan himself continued with his commitment to translation and introduced Kannada and Tamil mystic poetry (besides Anantha Murthy's novel *Samskara*) to the readers of English; and, since times immemorial there have been translators, struggling in their own way, to bridge two languages, two peoples, and two cultures. It is to this dedicated group of bridge-builders that Ravichandra belongs. We need today, more than at any other point of time, such bridge-builders.

- C. N. Ramachandran

ACKNOWLEDGEMENT

I wish to acknowledge my indebtedness to Shaashi Ramesh who helped me prepare the entire draft of the translation by painstakingly copying the manuscript and Dr. Kikkeri Narayan, who sympathetically read the translation and offered many an insight into the complex world of Bhujangaiah during the translation.

Ravichandra P. Chittampalli

CHAPTER - 1

Parvathy woke her husband up at the first cock crow and went out into the backyard. Bhujangaiah, who sat up, muttering at his obdurate wife, had little desire that day to hitch the plough ahead of the village, as was his wont. So, getting up he continued to squat on his haunches for a while, though troubled. He realized he had never felt thus in all his life. Three days had passed since the performing of the propitiatory *Para.* He was worried that it hadn't rained. When last year too the monsoon had slipped past them, Bhujangaiah had taken the lead in performing the rites, not just once but thrice over. Varuna, the rain god, had not blessed any of the *Paras.* Though the rains had failed time and again, the people of this village had an unflinching faith in *Para.* They wouldn't have argued if Bhujangaiah had advised performing it thrice as in the previous year. Bhujangaiah had laughed in private at their uncommon faith and patience.

When Parvathy found her husband smirking, squatting as at the open, she was consternated for a while, No! Her husband had never remained thus after rising. Why did he sit still though every one in the village went about getting their plough ready? Parvathy approached him,

"What's with you? Why do you sit so? Aren't you feeling well?" Bhujangaiah stood up and stretched. His wife queried persistently,

"The entire village is readying the plough, why won't you?"

In response he went out to hitch the ploughshare mumbling all the while, "I cannot see why I should get the plough hitched every day. There is no happiness to be gained by it."

Parvathy's heart missed a beat at her husband's speech. He had never talked thus from the time when she stepped into that house as the daughter-in-law. He had never ignored his profession. "Hadn't he himself said that they who were born to live by labour would destroy themselves should they learn to laze about?" Parvathy was troubled. It was always so with her, growing anxious over the silliest of events. She finished tidying and lit the hearth deciding to inquire into her husband's troubles when she took him his lunch. The children had not risen yet. She shook them awake not heeding the old crone of a mother-in-law's advice to let growing children sleep late. Her little daughter woke up sounding like a hautboy. The peeved mother-in-law wondered why at all she had to speak out knowing well her words were so much garbage. Her daughter and son-in-law on the other hand were compelling her since three months that she moved in with them at their village Kallalli. Everyone there showed such concern for her! Unlike her daughter-in-law here, they wouldn't neglect her.

Yet, how could she leave the house that she had illumined in spite of all the comforts in the other place? Can she possibly live away from her delightful grandchildren who wouldn't bear to be parted from her even for a moment? Would gods ever approve of such an act? Tche! Feeling wretched for having ever thought of such a thing, she buried herself in routine tasks while praying to her family deity Hulikanthyappa, the God who rode the tiger.

By the time Bhujangaiah reached his cornfield where the fig tree stood and hitched the oxen to the plough, the farmers on the adjacent fields had already run three furrows. They too had noticed his unusually late arrival. Bhujangaiah was always at the forefront of any task in the village. He was forever eager to have the tasks performed at their appointed time whether it was ploughing, sowing, or weeding. But today it seemed as if his fealty by Mother Earth had slackened ever so little.

More than a month had elapsed after Ugadi, the New Year Day. They should have had rains by this time - at least three good showers; but not even once had it rained. If it had showered they could have had their fields cleared of the stubbles and readied for sowing. Apparently, it was a week since it began raining heavily in Kodagu. When he was young, why, till a few years ago, the rains would arrive on the back of Ugadi filling the ponds and dikes. Whoever knew what had gone amiss now? The villagers too, like him, could not help watching the sky every passing day. It was probably true what someone had said: "The rains had stopped once the forests of Kote were felled!" He seemed to remember having read some such thing. The woods that surrounded his village were but a memory now. People hadn't spared even the roots as they transported timber to Mysore. Now, one had to walk ten miles for firewood.

Bhujangaiah gazed at the many trees that verdantly fringed his field. He felt glad for a while. Even as he was relieved that those at least were spared from danger he grew aware of the plough turning once more in the same furrow.

"Tche! What's wrong with me today? Nothing is going right since morning."

He wondered how many times he had fallow ploughed the field. Perhaps ten times, at the least? He was tired of ploughing the same ground over and over again. But if he sat idle people might laugh. As the day progressed the sun grew into a burning ember. Even the dust grew hot. The ochre cloud that rose from the plough stuck to his body drenched with perspiration, making him look like one who had daubed the make-up for the Grand Drama for the festival. This would be the last time. He decided not to hitch the plough again unless it rained, and goaded the oxen to step faster so that he could be done with ploughing that field.

Each day grew unbearably hot. The village folk too, like him, had misconstrued the heat for the precipitation before rains. If a fiery sun spewed heat the entire day, with the approach of evening a cool breeze would get up bringing overhead the clouds that refused to set their feet on earth but vanished floating away into the distance. Only the peasants, having dreamt of fruition in them and in their descent to earth, would grow anxious. The season that should support their lives the entire year round would soon be past if a few more days were to go by in such fashion. One had to then sit putting one's trust in the North Easterly, the Kharif. But, there was no believing that it at least would serve them well. If the Kharif too were to fail then theirs would be a dog's life. The labourers had no such worry. They migrated to Kodagu whenever famine struck. The rich too knew no anxiety. They all had cultivated some paddy in the rice fields adjoining the stream. But then, what about people like himself who had put their trust in the clouds, depending solely on an earth fit only for termites? Of course, one did manage to grow a little, as if to prove the proverb, "Those who put their trust in mother earth would not be fed with dust by her". But of what earthly good was that? It was a state where if you had something to eat you had nothing to wear; if you had something to wear you had nothing to eat. Was there no relief from such a fate? When the irrigation canal arrived at the fields of Gaddige, people of his village did not heed his advice to buy lands there. And the Tamils had arrived and settled on those very same fields. They were all living in comfort now. They did not share the anxiety of his people. If it were to rain over there in Kodagu, their rice fields near Gaddige here would float in water. The Tamils really were blessed. It looked as though what he and the others had asked for from the heavens was mere suffering.

Bhujangaiah was preoccupied. If only those who believed that his furrows were as straight as a tautly drawn string were to see them today their opinion would've altered drastically. Today, the furrows that normally resembled neat waves of stacked betel leaves were in disarray. Why should he strive so hard who had known no happiness? How long should he waste his life in this fruitless physical labour, unmindful of the heat and glare like an ox at the grind? Sure, Basavanna had said that to work was to attain Kailasa. But, shouldn't the body possess some little strength to work? What can a body do if one were feeble? One could strive without getting vexed if only there were the promise of an abundance of crop as in the past. But their fate had been to suffer the agony, which the clouds floating overhead forced them into, in the stinging, thorny game of hope and despair. If such state of affairs prolonged they would be left with no option but to migrate with their families, even as the labourers did, either to Kodagu or to Wynad. Bhujangaiah's resolve dissipated envisioning that scene. "No! He shouldn't despair thus. If he should lose courage, then what would be the state of those who were in direr straits? Shouldn't he try and fill them with some hope once more? Another *Para* should be performed. Hulikanthyappa, the village deity, would certainly open his eyes. The lament of his children would not fail to move him. What if he were God? would not their curse touch him if he should shut his ears to them?"

Bhujangaiah's train of thought was interrupted by Parvathy's arrival. She who carried his lunch in the blistering sun put down the laden basket under the tree and called out to her husband. Bhujangaiah's stomach oblivious of hunger all this while began to smart. Even the oxen were breathing hard in the heat. He brought the plough under the shade so that the beasts too could rest. He perfunctorily washed his face and limbs with the little water his wife had brought and sat down to pray to Lord Shiva, smearing vibhuthi, the holy ash, on his forehead. From the day he began wearing the Linga, his faith in worshipping Shiva had grown. He never touched food without praying first. But then, on his visits to Kote or Mysore whenever he failed to find a hotel managed by Lingayats, he had perforce to eat without worshipping at hotels managed by Brahmins, not without a feeling of guilt. However, he had gradually grown free of such qualms.

Parvathy set down a rimmed bronze plate for her husband and served Ragi mudde, made of millet flour and poured on it the spicy gruel made of horse gram. She had also brought for a side dish some sauted peas and fried chillies marinated in yoghurt. Though Bhujangaiah owned half an acre of rice fields next to the village pond, he couldn't grow paddy as the pond had received scant water the previous year. The paddy he had bartered for ragi after harvest was gradually being used up during festivals and other religious occasions. Parvathy would cook a fistful of rice every day to serve her children and husband. Bhujangaiah was partial to rice from the beginning having been raised in the tradition of eating "a stomachful of ragi and a mouthful of rice".

Partvathy noticed her husband's unusal conduct of silently swallowing *mudde* that day, instead of talking incessantly to her while ignoring his food the instant he saw her. She watched intently the lump of food slowly going down his gullet every time he swallowed. Why had her husband's behaviour altered since morning? Parvathy gave vent to her thoughts forcing him into speech. Bhujangaiah's answers to all her queries were monosyllabic. Fed up by his disinterest Parvathy flared up, "Why can't you blabber out what the problem is? Will your tongue shrivel if you speak?" When Parvathy got enraged the hue of her speech too altered drastically. There were times when Bhujangaiah trembled with fear listening to the pearls of wisdom gushing forth from her lips. Though he was a peasant, Bhujangaiah was one of the few in Madalli who had some education. The slang of Parvathy's village Jakkalli, was notorious in the entire district of Kote. The language of her village had naturally accompanied Parvathy. Though thanks to Bhujangaiah she had managed to keep it in check, it would rage forth unbridled on occasions when she lost her temper.

Bhujangaiah who had known this other face of his wife unburdened the weight of his silence and in clear tones began to share his anxiety with her. Parvathy burst into laughter. She found his speech frivolous. "Now tell me, what's this madness of yours? Is it in our hands to make it rain or to beget children? It can only happen if God opens his eyes, is that not so? We shall do as the village does. In what way are we *pesal?*"

Bhujangaiah laughed out loud. The newly added word "Special" to his wife's vocabulary had transformed into "pesal". Overcoming his reticence, Bhujangaiah now asked his wife jocularly, "What did you say? Did you say that it is god who brings rain and children?" Partvathy countered, "Then what?" and looked at her husband believing that there could be nothing wrong in what she had opined. Bhujangaiah reiterated as he laughed. " Look, was your having two children due to God or me?"

Though Parvathy felt like giggling at once she made a show of anger and added shyly,

"Thu! Enough of your madness! What if somebody should overhear? It looks as if you are growing younger by the day." Teasing her further he said, "All right then, it wouldn't be wrong if I marry again."

Parvathy for a moment felt as if a thorn had pricked her. The suspicion whether that were really her husband's deep-seated desire began to worry her. Bhujangaiah attempted cajoling his wife who had suddenly grown sullen. Though Parvathy was no great beauty, she had been fair and supple when she arrived in Madalli as a bride and was attractive enough for others to wish taking a second glance at her. But the chores at Bhujangaiah's home and the children had already tired her out. Parvathy who had borne two children in the five years of her marriage was again into the third month of pregnancy. There was now a renewed freshness dawning on her cheeks. Bhujangaiah who noticed it gently massaged her abdomen not wishing the baby in her womb to be affected. Parvathy, afraid that some one may notice their intimacy covered his act with the top end of the sari, her *seragu,* and drew his head on to her lap with the apparent intent of searching for lice in his hair. In the cool shade, even as her husband's finger excited her gradually overcoming her shyness, the searing thorn that had embedded in her mind slowly dissolved. His wife's pleasant touch dispelled the nagging headache about the fate of crops that clung to Bhujangaiah like glutinous leaves.

Farmers in the adjacent fields had already begun to till their lands after lunch. Parvathy gently pried her husband's hand from her sari and stood up, mindful of the neighbours noticing them. Though Bhujangaiah was disappointed for a moment he began to plough happily like one who had regained a zest for life. The furrows now began to form regularly, in straight lines.

***

CHAPTER - 2

As he woke up, something formless and inscrutable seemed to penetrate his mind and disturb him that morning. Though he had felt happy at having spent a few moments with his wife who had brought his lunch, oblivious of everything, his mind gave into anger as the sun ascended the roof. Everything began to get addled up in his brain; nothing took a definite shape. Though the others around him had already unhitched their ploughs, Bhujangaiah alone continued to plough. If he tilled a few more rounds his field would be thoroughly ploughed. Aware of his resolve not to plough again till it rained, he shouted at the oxen spurring them. The beasts foamed at the mouth, tired of their arduous task under the fiery sun. After unhitching the plough he turned towards the village. Even the thirsty beasts, which waited for that moment, stepped briskly. When Bhujangaiah arrived at the junction it was already time for the bus from Kote to Mysore. There were, however, a few villagers waiting for its arrival. The people of Madalli referred to the big tamarind tree at the junction as the Tree of the Goddess. A strange fact about the tree was that though the tree was burdened by blossoms beyond its strength, it had never ever yielded fruit. If there were an occasional fruit it would invariably be fallow. It was attributed to the fact that the tree was haunted. But then there was not a single traveller from around that place, who was ever troubled by the spirit of that tree.

Harlequin Ajappa whose fields bordered the tree used to say that the ghost appeared either on the full moon day or on the new moon day. Many were the times when he, sitting at the entrance to the village, narrated stories of his conversation with the ghost. When the villagers surmised in sarcasm that he must possess ghost-eyes to have seen the ghost which none else saw, he would feel proud. Basalinga and Cennamalla materialized from nowhere as Bhujangaiah took out a bundle of beedies pulling his oxen under the tree. Even before they could ask, Bhujangaiah tossed them a beedi each and lit his own, pulling on the halters of his impatient animals. Both Basalinga and Cennamalla, who had arrived to join him after unhitching their ploughs, used Bhujangaiah's beedi to light their own. When Bhujangaiah spotted Mahadeva, the boy from Basalinga's house, he called out. "Lo, Mahadeva, come here, hold the oxen for a while." Basalinga at once offered, "He's going to the village, if you so wish he can drive them to your house." Bhujangaiah handed the reins over to Mahadeva and said, "Look, you unhitch the plough at home and secure the oxen in the shed, and tell my woman I will follow at once." He sat relaxed with his companions and began to enjoy his beedi.

In a short while a few more people arrived to wait for the bus. They sat down with sighs, overcome by the summer heat. Many were familiar faces. Every lip had the same prayer on it; anxious tones of what the rains had in store for them that year too. Basalinga asked, "Why, brother? Aren't you hitching the plough again in the evening?" Bhujangaiah declared in a manner that would inform everyone around of his decision not to plough the fields till it rained. Though many thought him sensible, one or two wondered, "How can one sit with folded hands even if it did not rain?" Both Basalinga and Cennamalla found Bhujangaiah's resolve after their own heart. The countenances of those who argued certainly did not reveal them as those who ploughed their fields under the hot sun every day. Cennamalla was not as free as Bhujangaiah even though he voiced his approval, "What you said is right brother! I do not see why we break our heart tilling this dry, dusty field over and again". He breathed a long sigh at his fate of having to work under duress of his father and elder brothers at home. How nice it would have been, he wondered silently, if he too, like Bhujangaiah, had none to obey.

The bus was inexplicably late in arriving. Undone by the heat some of the travelers who awaited the bus were already dozing off. A few others overcome by thirst, though knowing fully well there was nowhere they could get a little water, queried, merely to satisfy a need "Is there some water to drink anywhere here?" They then fell silent. Everyone knew well that there was no water to be had anywhere around. One of them, thirstier than others, spoke harshly,

"I have never seen such a place as this, not even the graveyard, where you cannot get a drop of water to drink."

"There are hotels to be found in all sorts of places, why shouldn't somebody start one here? So many people come here every day. Even if they drink a cup of coffee each there is bound to be good business!"

Bhujangaiah's ears pricked up. There was sense in that traveler's speech. He looked at the speaker curiously. The traveler was glad that his words were having an effect, "Look the junction of Madapura too was like this one here before someone arrived, put up a shed and opened a hotel there. None can match up to him today. He has grown rich in just two years. You should hear about his house and his hotel. I was there only the day before. The owner himself told me that he bought four acres of rice fields. Even if we struggle day and night, without enough respite to scratch our ass, our earnings wouldn't suffice to provide food and clothes. I wonder what sort of life this is."

Bhujangaiah felt as if a divine revelation had come to him. What he felt since that morning seemed suddenly to find a form now. The source and the means that he was searching for seemed to reveal themselves before his eyes. Though, from the very beginning, he had felt an uncontrollable desire to do something different from farming to improve his lot, it was never very clear to him what he should do. But he now found a model to his future plans taking shape, complete in all its details.

By then Bhujangaiah had smoked through four beedies. The bus must have broken down on the way. For, it should have by then according to schedule reached Mysore. One among those who waited for the bus left for Madalli to drink water, unable to bear his thirst. Followed by Basalinga and Cennamalla, Bhujangaiah accompanied the traveler. They found it strange Bhujangaiah had fallen silent. They had heard similar speech, which the traveler had made, a number of times earlier. Though on occasion such comments had fallen on Bhujangaiah's ears too, in the past, the words had not left such a deep impression as they had done now.

When Bhujangaiah, unable to control the wish that arose in his mind, confessed to his friends finally, they laughed in derision and said, "Why did you get such an evil thought brother? Should we Virashaivas wash the tumbler from which all castes drink? You are an only son. The property which your father has left behind should do by you."

They had deliberately undermined the very foundation of Bhujangaiah's wish. Their opinion could not be ignored. He too had eight acres of corn field and half-an-acre of rice field below the pond. Not half the village had so much property. Yet, he was not affluent enough to employ a couple of labourers. He had to struggle alone though, and perhaps his children too, after his demise. His father and his grandfather too had lived thus. Things never improved to six nor waste to three. None escaped the fate of scratching at the termite-infested field. If a bus had plied then when he was young as it did now, or if his father were to have a couple of acquaintances in the city, he too could have attended school and taken to a profession. The son of the elder of Sargur the neighboring village, who was of his age, was now a Shekdar, a revenue officer, somewhere. His father now owned half the village. He seemed to give his father thousands of rupees whenever he visited. If only such fortune were his!

Even as they reached the outskirts of the village, Bhujangaiah's friends turned in another direction. The thirsty traveler sought water at the first house he came to. The woman of the house enquired about his caste and his religion before bringing a vessel full of water and poured the water asking him to cup his palms. Bhujangaiah found the scene funny. There was more water being spilt on the ground than what the man drank.

Parvathy had started bickering even before he entered the door. Overcome with thirst, Bhujangaiah flared in anger, "Hey, give me some water to drink first, and then you howl as much as you please!" Parvathy retorted, "I howl, do I? I am no dog come from a pauper's house to howl. Do you realize that even now my father feeds all those who approach him begging?" She banged the vessel of water in front of him and went in. The fairly comfortable situation of her parent's house was the source of her arrogance. Bhujangaiah had never stretched his hand for help in all those five or six years of his marriage, however well situated Parvathy's parent was. He had never thought of anything that may have undermined his dignity.

Bhujangaiah grew introspective once more, paying scant attention to Parvathy's ranting. Would his setting up a hotel be proper? Would that lead to a situation where he may have to walk with his head bent low in society? There would be talk only if he should wash the plates and tumblers used by other castes. He could employ a boy for that, though. Having sipped some more water he reclined with his arm for a pillow on the *jagali*, the raised platform at the entrance to the house, and began to ponder. Parvathy, disturbed once again by her husband's incongruently idle behaviour, approached him and inquired gently. Bhujangaiah told her of his resolve in definite tones and delved into his plans silently, turning a deaf ear to her words. Parvathy went in as if she had stepped on a burning ember, saying, "This does not appear like coming to much."

Bhujangaiah who lay motionless, suddenly rose as if he remembered something and rushed to the house of Shastri situated on the Last Lane. There were already a couple of people waiting to have their fortunes read. On seeing Bhujangaiah on this rare visit Shastri welcomed him with due deference, "What is it Bhujangaiah? Did you come to ask about the rain like everyone else or do you wish to ask something different?" Bhujangaiah laughed, "Why did we have to live thus if it rains by the predictions of your almanac?" Shastri rebuked him, "Look! You should not speak thus. As long as this world exists, the almanac, which has come down to us from thousands of years, will without fail exist. It will matter because of its relevance. You and I are insignificant beings who live today only to depart tomorrow. It is because of our fate that the rain has failed. The age of Kali, of vice and contention, is growing in decadence. Let that be, your visit now is about...?"

He looked at Bhujangaiah questioningly. Bhujangaiah removed a quarter from the pocket of his shorts and placed it on the betel leaves in front of Shastri. Shastri removed the cowries from the box and rolled them thrice, did some calculation on a piece of yellowing paper and finally spoke, "What you wish for will transpire. But there are some hazards for which you must propitiate." He sent Bhujangaiah thus assured.

Bhujangaiah went in search of Harlequin Ajappa. Having learnt that he was at the liquor shop with Siddappa of the Idiga community, he went there. The entire village talked ill of Ajappa, who was born into the caste of the faithful of Lord Shiva, for having entered into partnership with Siddappa of the neighbouring village in his liquor business. Yet, none had the guts to confront him with it. That was because everybody needed the help of Ajappa through whose hands money flowed eternally. Ajappa who sat at the counter welcomed Bhujangaiah. Though he could barely stand the odour of liquor Bhujangaiah masked his emotions, entered and sat by Ajappa's side. People sat in a row holding scoured coconut shells or scooped gourd. They were all familiar faces. A couple of them poked fun at Bhujangaiah, "Taste some Bhujangaiah!" Ajappa grew furious if anyone spoke slightingly of liquor. He never ever touched liquor himself though he would say, "what do you know you sons of country mongrels? It is the Goddess of fortune, a veritable Lakshmi".

He had hired Chikka of Parivara community to serve liquor. Bunde Sidda of the fisherman community who had downed many a gourd of liquor by the time Bhujangaiah arrived stood up unsteadily singing, "Mother Goddess of the palm tree reveals Kailasa, the very heaven, to those who can afford it." Admist all the commotion Bhujangaiah told Ajappa of his plans. Ajappa was not a person to ever dilly-dally. He promised to lend Bhujangaiah some money and immediately agreed to let Bhujangaiah put up a hotel on his plot at the junction. Of more consequence was his driving home to Bhujangaiah that there was nothing evil in running a hotel, quoting innumerable instances of people having done so. He thus dispelled the nagging doubt in Bhujangaiah's mind. when he said that he would take Bhujangaiah with him to Mysore not merely to show how many of their own caste had moved up in life by running a hotel but also to show how they were shown due respect by the Swami of the Main Mutt, Bhujangaiah's resolve to set up a hotel shored up.

As soon as he returned home Bhujangaiah began to organize the wood, the palm fronds, the straw, and other essential materials to build a hotel that was to begin its existence from the very next day. Manchachari, the carpenter promised to have the doors and windows ready in the next couple of days. Kencha and Cheluva of the Madiga community assured to raise the mud walls in a week's time. His close friends promised to help in thatching the roof with palm fronds and straw.

In an instant the news of Bhujangaiah setting up a hotel spread through the entire length and breadth of Madalli. His wife Parvathy and his mother Deviramma began to wail, beating their chests. The children who couldn't understand the cause of their grief joined them vociferously. Much as Bhujangaiah, nauseated by their stupidity, attempted to silence them, their wailing grew more and more in intensity. He walked towards the village assembly away from home. He was surprised that he had already become an object of criticism for many people. His friends were of mixed opinion about the propriety of starting a hotel business. Because of all this Bhujangaiah had reached a mental state wherein he felt it impossible to live without his setting up a hotel.

***

CHAPTER - 3

The construction of the hotel at the Crossroads of Madalli progressed speedily as a testimony to Bhujangaiah's irrepressible energy and adventurous spirit that paid scant attention to the problems and obstacles which anyone might pose. Though this new foray of Bhujangaiah was subjected to a variety of reaction, it appeared to be an excellent venture to those who arrived at the Crossroads to wait for the bus. They were pleased that at last the weary traveler could now quench his thirst. Many showered a rain of praise in his presence. But Bhujangaiah, not allowing their accolades to swell his head, said with due deference, "If your blessings are with me, what I have ventured into will succeed. Your good wishes are necessary." He had already begun to practise a novel manner of speech that well suited his new business.

There were still four days for the auspicious hour fixed by Shastri for the inauguration of the hotel. Though almost all the tasks were taken care of, Bhujangaiah was far from satisfied. He went about as if nothing had been done. Since work started on the hotel it had become the focus of attention for the curious villagers. Each one had a suggestion to offer. If one wondered, "The roof is a little high, what if it lifts off in the wind?" Another opined, "The door should have faced East. It's now to the North. That's not proper." Having been preoccupied with one chore or the other since morning, without breaking off for meal, Bhujangaiah now grew aware of the rumbling in his stomach. There still remained a mountain of tasks to be assigned to the labourers. He had to fence the shed where the hotel was to be housed. He asked the workers to stack the chopped firewood neatly in a corner. He instructed Basava of

Madiga community to firmly lay the split sticks of bamboo over the straw that covered the roof and to secure them with rope so that the wind wouldn't drag them. He wanted Manchachari who was planing the benches, "Look Achari, the benches should be smooth. If you leave them rough, I shall strip the knickers off you and plane your ass on them!" Achari too could not help but join Bhujangaiah in the laughter.

That evening he had to leave for Mysore in order to procure the necessary provision for the next morning. If Ajappa should also accompany it would be a help. He was jotting down the things he had to remember. As he spoke to Achari he recalled that he needed a tin of paint, which too he listed.

As he turned towards the village, reminded of his growing hunger, he was stopped by the racy speech of Halegowda alias the Beard, nicknamed thus because of the beard of Kyatanahalli village who had appeared from nowhere. The speech of Beard was a feast to those who heard him. Each one of his utterances dripped with mirth. Even as his words fell on the ear, Bhujangaiah became oblivious of his hunger. Beard began to examine each detail of the construction. Even before he began to actually see, a plethora of invaluable suggestions began simmering in his head. In deference to Bhujangaiah's suggestion that they start from the inside, all of them trooped into the shed. Bhujangaiah pointed out to the large area where the customers would be seated, where he would now arrange the six benches and later, when he could afford, the tables. Beard approved and instantaneously dealt a proverb, "You first sit down before lying down." He continued, "Look brother, Bhujangaiah, there is a fine Jack tree in my village. It can be had for a good price. I can strike a bargain for you. That one tree should do to crowd your hotel with furniture." He shot an arrow into the future too. Bhujangaiah replied, "Let's see." He led him through the kitchen, the room out front meant for a shop and another room adjacent to it where he could sleep if he needed to stay over. Beard who inspected everything now seriously advised, "That's all fine, but get a cot made for your room." Bhujangaiah laughed, "Yes, of course there is an urgent need for that now!" Beard averred, "No brother, if there is a cot a mattress will arrive, when the mattress comes then the other too will follow." He helped ease Bhujangaiah's mind with his libertine speech.

Though Bhujangaiah was not the man for such affairs, when he caught the import of Beard's words he could not help but laugh, however much he desired to control his reaction.

Bhujangaiah remembered that he himself had to fetch another cask of water after lunch and so took leave of Beard who had latched on to him like the saturnine planet, Shani. He reminded the workers to fill some more red earth for the flooring. He returned to the village assuring that he would fetch the water cart on his way back from lunch. When he reached home, the by now week old silence and stillness still reigned. His mother was not home. She must have been out grazing the buffalo. Parvathy who was feeding the cattle with hay stacked in the backyard saw her husband arrive and brought a vessel of water to him and laid the plate in the hall. Silence ruled between them. Both refused to open their mouths. All tasks were performed through signs. Bhujangaiah, who perfunctorily went through the ritual of eating, led the oxen out to hitch them to the water cart. Only the previous week he had got Manchachari to repair the wooden cask that lay in a corner of the *jagali* by the door, and had loaded it on the cart. As the cask had not been properly seasoned, the joints were quite leaky. Parvathy who had happily presumed that the arduous task of drawing water every day from the well had ended hissed in fury on realizing that the cask was meant for the hotel.

As he was about to hitch the oxen to his cart, Bhujangaiah noticed his wife's father arrive. He hitched the oxen to the cross bar and welcomed her father. Bhujangaiah had a mixture of fear and respect for his father-in-law. Parvathappa of Jakkalli was a well known name in that region. His body, as his name implied, was as enormous as a mountain. His upturned moustache suited his stature. He wore ear rings inset with rubies close to the lobes; his feet were adorned by leather slip-ons, which sounded like a mewling bitch that had just littered. As he entered the verandah with his father-in-law, he ordered his wife to fetch water for her father, forgetting his vow of silence. Parvathy had lost all her fears at the very sight of her parent. She served food to her father certain that he wouldn't return without curing her husband of his craze for the hotel. Bhujangaiah who sat in the verandah guessed that inside the hall both father and daughter were engaged in some conspiracy.

After his meal Parvathappa made his son-in-law sit next to him and reminded him that running a hotel by people of their stature and to wash dishes used by low castes would drag to dust their honour and reputation. Yet again, wouldn't people talk, if a son-in-law of his, who was known as the master of the house with the raised verandah in seven villages, were to run a hotel? Parvathappa tried convincing his son-in-law in very many ways, as one would teach a parrot.. He also poured on him in the manner of the swami of the mutt the libation of knowledge of sin and virtue. Whatever he said or did, Parvathappa couldn't shake ever so slightly what had firmly taken root in Bhujangaiah's mind.

Parvathappa lost his temper at his son-in-law's stubbornness. He had never known his plans to fail thus. He simmered in anger. The hotheaded nature, which had been kept under control all this while, began to manifest at last. "What people had said before the marriage is true then! Perhaps you remember the time when you absconded from home and lived off by licking the discarded leaves of left over food. Now shut your ass and behave like a responsible man. Do not get into such screwy business and get spat upon by everybody."

So saying he climbed down the steps of the house and left without waiting for his son-in-law's reactions. Nor did he in his anger bid his daughter good bye. Bhujangaiah was disgusted by his father-in-law's speech. After witnessing his father-in-law's real colour and having heard his language Bhujangaiah who had believed him to be a man of worth walked out as if to throw to the winds the regard he had for him. When Parvathy followed him trying to put the fear in him by emulating her father, threatening that she too would leave the house, Bhujangaiah struck back like an injured snake, "Get lost you bitch." Parvathy was taken aback. She had never seen her husband in that incarnation. Parvathy who realized that if she should so much as twitch her lips he would stomp her down, retreated into the house, swallowing the pearls of wisdom of Jakkalli that were dancing on the tip of her tongue.

The main reason for Bhujangaiah's rage was the fact of his leaving home in anger at his father, which his father-in-law had referred to so derisively. Why should he be touched to the quick when somebody talked about it? Bhujangaiah appeared oblivious to all as he drove the water cart to the pond. He had never tolerated insult from anybody. He had walked out of his house unable to put up with his father's abuse. He had wandered for many days till in the end he had found a job at a hotel in Mysore. Somebody from his village who noticed him there had forcibly brought him back home. His father had compelled him to take an oath that he would never leave the house. All those scenes flashed across Bhujangaiah's mind's eye. The person who had brought him back had talked about the job he had professed in Mysore to the entire village. Because of that his father had taken him to the Mutt and had him first undergo the rites of absolution and then got the swami to perform the ritual of adorning Bhujangaiah with the linga. Yet, people had refused to marry their daughters to him till in the end Parvathappa of Jakkalli had agreed. It was not that the story of his wandering the world had not reached Parvathappa's ears. All the same, he had with an open mind said, "A bad moment can force anybody to act in strange ways." He had given his daughter Parvathy in marriage to him.

Even as he lifted pot after pot of water to fill the cask on the cart his mind delved in to the past. When he was employed in the hotel, his companion - what was his name? He couldn't recollect now - had taken him, a couple of times, to a whore.

Bubbling up in him now were memories of how he had run away in fear after having stepped into that house. Back at the hotel, his friend had taunted at night, "What sort of a eunuch are you!", challenging his very manhood, till one fine day, he at last had picked up enough courage to sleep with a whore. In the meanwhile no one noticed him filling an already overflowing cask. Bhujangaiah, ashamed of his idiotic act hooked the pots on the peg and hitched the cart.

At the hotel, he poured the water on the earth-fill. When the floor dried a bit he called a worker and asked him to tamp the floor with the tamper, which they referred to as "destroyer". In the kitchen, Dasapa, the mason was laying the hearth. The grinding stone essential for the kitchen was yet to arrive. Peera of the Vadda community from Shindenahalli, who had been paid an advance, was to have delivered it that day. He sent one of the workers to check on him. If he left now for Mysore he would return only the next evening. He drove home to the workers the importance of all the tasks to be completed before his return.

The shopping list for purchases in Mysore grew long like the tail of Hanuman. The money he had saved and the interest free loan that Ajappa had advanced were together enough to take care of all his needs. While he debated whether to have a thatched front, Manchachari revealed his sense of aesthetics saying, "Without the thatch the hotel wouldn't look good".

Bhujangaiah shifted the responsibility on Manchachari's head for organizing the palm fronds, bamboo and poles for the thatch to be erected. Shouldering it half-heartedly Manchachari said, "When you return tomorrow bring some jelly paper and tinsel." Though Bhujangaiah pulled his leg, "Are you working on a marriage hall?" he decided to fetch what was asked for.

Leaving by the evening bus Ajappa and Bhujangaiah were in deep consultation over naming the hotel till the bus reached Mysore. Though Bhujangaiah had a strong desire to name the hotel after his family deity "Hulikanthyappa", the little education he had stopped him from finding it pleasing. In the end Ajappa suggested "Kendaganna Swamy", the Lord with the blazing eye, the other name for "Hulikanthyappa". Bhujangaiah did not find it too bad. The first thing to be done was to place an order for the sign board to be painted. They got off the bus hoping that by the time they were ready to return the next day, the paint on the signboard would have dried properly.

***

CHAPTER - 4

On Monday morning the immortal hands of Shivarudraswamy, the astrologer of Madalli, inaugurated Bhujangaiah's Crossroads hotel, which was since a fortnight a subject of curiosity, at least for a few in the neighbourhood of Madalli. Bhugangaiah performed all the rites and propitiations insisted upon by the Shastri. As advised by the astrologer he tied an ash gourd, which the Shastri had blessed. He fixed the signboard in such a manner that the gourd tied to ward off the evil eye was completely hidden from view. The invitees looked upon the board in red, white and blue with awe. Those who could read did so over and over again. In the entire of Madalli a board such as this had never been put up, anywhere. At the top was written the holy "Om" and under it was printed in red letters "Blessings of the Lord with the Blazing Eye". The second line read in bold blue, **"Verashaiva Snacks Center"**. Among those who could read, some could not grasp the meaning of "Snacks". At one of the corners at the bottom of the board was the legend "Madalli" and at the other end was the legend "Pro : Bhujangaiah". Bhujangaiah explicated to those who would inquire that "Pro" was the abbreviation for proprietor. He had himself learnt it from the painter of signs. On the inaugural day Bhujangaiah served all those who visited a ladle full of "Kesaribath" a sweet dish made of Semolina. The villagers bowled over by its delicious taste could not help but wish for a second serve. Children from Madalli, Kottegala and other villages attending the Middle School at Kyatanahalli had to pass by the hotel. Those of them who had left for school early had been waiting expectantly for the distribution of *kesaribath* and now began to run as it was getting late for the school. The

Crossroads which was deserted for most part of the day excepting when the bus arrived was now invested with a new life. As for the school children, the hotel was a transmogrified reality. Earlier, on days when the school broke off late they would shiver in fright as they approached the haunted tamarind tree. Having heard talks of the tree being haunted, they prayed to god with eyes shut till they passed the tree. They wouldn't have such trouble any longer. Bhujangaiah's hotel was adjacent to the tree. No more fears! Bhujangaiah had hired a boy from Mysore to prepare snacks for a few days. He too was a Lingayat. He was well known to Ajappa since he had worked as a supplier at Gurumalla Hotel, in Agrahara, in Mysore. They had somehow inveigled him. He was an expert at delicacies like kesaribath, karabath, rave unde, kara sev, vade and bonda. And the kesaribath he had prepared on the first day had made everybody's mouth water. Having decided on a menu of idli, vada and rice in the mornings and karasev, bonda etc.., in the evenings from the very next day, Bhujangaiah began to get things ready. The stone grinder too had arrived by then.

Pundri and Kariappa, the confidants of Bhujangaiah in Madalli, who had no significant responsibility of their own, promptly arrived to help him. They too billeted with Bhujangaiah on the first night at the hotel. There was now a new place for Pundri's tales to grow limbs and a few more ears to listen to them with curiosity. Pundri's real name was Puttaswamy, though everyone called him Pundri. No one knew, including Pundri, how the acronym stuck to him. Bhujangaiah was restive throughout the night. His head was full of the many tasks yet to be attended to. There was an urgent need for a glass display case for the sweets and the fried savory, *karasev*. But he could not afford to get that made just then. All his money had gone. What he had earned from the week's business was needed for fresh purchases. What would be the profits? How would the business run? He must contrive to have the passengers from Kote to Mysore stop over for breakfast at his hotel. If he could impress Victor the driver and Subbanna the conductor, he was certain to have a business of at least twenty rupees every morning. The same bus arrived four times a day at the crossroads. "Lingajamba Motor", the only mode of transport on that route between Mysore and Kote was owned, he had heard it said, by someone of his caste. Occasionally, the owner too traveled. Bhujangaiah decided to welcome him cordially.

From the day he set up business Bhujangaiah had changed not only in the manner of his dress but also in his speech. Harsh words grew strange to his tongue and he began practising a gentle manner of speech that would be appreciated by all. Victor who stopped at Madapura gate for breakfast began to stop the Lingajamba bus now at Bhujangaiah's hotel. Though he used to get free breakfast at the gate's hotel too it was hard to eat that early. The bus reached the crossroads at a decent hour. A majority of the passengers adjudicated that halting at the crossroads for breakfast was the proper thing to do. Moreover, Bhujangaiah served a fairly hygienic food. His business shored up beyond his expectations. Apart from those who traveled by the bus, people from Madalli and nearby villages too grew to be his regular clientele.

Though the news of her husband's success spread throughout the village, Parvathy alone averred. She did not approve of it in the least. The stench of a fresh fear began to rise in her mind, "What if her husband should sit at the hotel allowing the fields to grow fallow, while the entire village took up sowing in case it rained now? Wouldn't the villagers speak ill of them?" She should confront him when he arrived home for supper. If she thus remained mute like a dumb woman, he would certainly grow wild, unbridled. Why should he find it hard to live like the others? She busied herself with the chores around the house wondering when god would bless him with sense. Parvathy who had assumed he would not arrive for lunch as on other days was surprised to see him. That day too Bhujangaiah had brought some eats for the children, as was his wont. Only, his mother protested every time. "You keep bringing stuff for them to eat everyday and they'll grow up spoilt." He would laugh saying, "No, instead you give them the sooty food and horse gram to eat." He would then force the delicacies he had brought on his mother too. Only Parvathy had not given up her resolve. She never allowed a morsel of it to touch her lips despite her mother-in-law, nor did she deign to address her husband directly. Bhujangaiah asked his little daughter to fetch him some water. It was an indirect injunction to his wife. Parvathy too asked him to sit down for food through the child. Such was their daily routine for a month now. They would normally make the presence of their son or the aged woman the agent of their conversation. Only, today they were both away from home. The four-year-old son or the aged woman could understand what went on, but the daughter, hardly in her second year of life, looked askance, not comprehending.

That day, all the snacks prepared had been sold before ten. When Bhujangaiah instructed Manja as to what to prepare, he had volunteered, "I shall make *raveunde*". As soon as Bhujangaiah acquiesced, Manja began to prepare the sweet balls of semolina. When he brought the fresh, hot ball for Bhujangaiah to taste it just melted in his mouth. "Hey, Manja! Where did you learn to cook so well?" Manja was delighted at his master's praise. Bhujangaiah had brought home those steaming balls. Even before his daughter, who looked expectantly at her father's hands every time he arrived, could stretch forth her hands, he handed her a *raveunde*. The child broke the ball into pieces on the dung-plastered floor and began pecking at the pieces. Bhujangaiah left the packet of the balls on the stand in the hall where the framed Gods were arranged. After prayers he got up for his meal. Of late, he was irregular in his worship of Shiva. His mouth, which had relished the *raveunde*, could hardly find the meal of ragi and horse gram gruel palatable. Incapable of wasting what was served he began to force the food down his throat. Finding it an appropriate moment Parvathy leaned against the doorframe and enquired about the work to be done at the field. Bhujangaiah slowly turned to face his wife, lifting the vessel of water in his hands as he felt the food getting stuck in his throat. Parvathy stood like a question mark in the dimly lit hall. Bhujangaiah stared at her perplexed as though he had not entirely grasped the import of her query. Parvathy repeated her question. Bhujangaiah felt happy at his wife's concern for his family. He had not bothered about sowing, weeding, and such other tasks. What if it rained now? Happy at Parvathy's good sense in having warned him in time, he assured her that he would try and contract somebody to work from that very day. Parvathy at once ululated, "What the servant does is what turns to ruins! If you should rest depending on them......" Bhujangaiah retorted, "Why, am I paralyzed and confined to a corner that I cannot supervise?" Parvathy responded saying, "Thu! Do not speak ill." She served him the rice that she had made for the children. She would cook some more rice later for them.

Not having spoken directly to each other for all these days, they now began to converse intimately with the screen of disagreement torn between them. Bhujangaiah brought the *raveunde* and forcibly fed his wife though she feebly attempted to resist. Even she found it delicious enough to wish eating all of them. But she stopped herself thinking of her children and her mother-in-law. It had been ages since she had been fed thus by her husband. Bhujangaiah too resolved to take good care of a pregnant Parvathy from then on and went towards the village assembly. It had been a long while since he had sat and gossiped there. He had forgotten all about performing *"Para"* in the business of setting up the hotel. The people there were reminded of it at the sight of Bhujangaiah and began to collect ragi flour, rice, jaggery etc., from that very evening, having arrived at a consensus to perform another *"Para"*. Even amidst this sudden responsibility Bhujangaiah managed to meet Shaggy Sidda who was the Village Attendant and talked to him of his need for a labourer. Shaggy Sidda said, "Why should you look for somebody Bhujangaiah? My son is good at ploughing. I will send him. If there is more to be done I am myself there to help." Bhujangaiah had not thought his problem would be solved that easily. Even that year the monsoon appeared to have failed. Knowing it fully well, Shaggy Sidda, not wishing his son migrate to the hills of Kodagu so that his child would remain within his sight, had agreed to send him for work without even talking of wages. When Bhujangaiah offered a certain amount over and above his food and clothing, Shaggy Sidda agreed without murmur. The *"Para"* fell on Monday, two days hence. That was also the day when Bhujangaiah had planned to visit Mysore to procure provisions. When he arrived at the hotel wondering how he would manage, he found Pundri, Cennamalla, Kendaganna, Kariappa and Guard Nagaraja. Though Nagaraja never ever entered the services of the Forest Department, the title "Guard" had somehow been prefixed to his name. They too wondered at Bhujangaiah arriving so late from the village. Even before they could open their mouth he told them of all the arrangements he had made for "Para" and said, "Now you go and organise some more ration and firewood." They all stood up to leave", They made a show of protesting, "Oh, that is not necessary brother". However, they had sat down again with alacrity. Bhujanagaiah knew it was no loss to offer them tea occasionally, as they faithfully carried out the odd jobs he entrusted them with.

After his cronies left, Bhujangaiah began to weigh the consequences of his intended visit to Mysore on Monday. It wouln't do to be absent from the place where *"Para"* was performed, whatever the excuse. He couldn't go the next day to Mysore. It being Sunday all the shops would be closed. If he should send Manja then the hotel had to be closed for the day. As if to break his reverie the Lingajamba bus arrived on its second trip to Mysore. Bhujangaiah had not realized that it was already four in the evening. Every time the bus reached the Crossroads Victor and Subbanna had to take a break for a cup of tea. Their friendship with Bhujangaiah had grown as the days passed by. They shared a joke occasionally. Today, as soon as they stepped inside the hotel, Bhujangaiah offered them a *raveunde* each. Victor, who was genuinely bowled over by its flavour, recommended it to all the travelers who had come in for tea. Curiosity made one of them order for it. After eating it he ordered for another again. The desire to eat *raveunde* grew contagious. There was not a single ball left when a passenger arrived late. The balls had all vanished like the heap of ladus in front of Ghatothgaja, in the movie "Mayabazar".

The travelers began boarding the bus. Bhujangaiah stepped outside with Victor and told him of his problem. Bhujangaiah felt a heavy load lift off his head when Victor volunteered, "List all that you want on a piece of paper and I shall bring them for you". When Bhujangaiah asked, "Shall I send a boy to fetch them to the bus? Victor rebuked, "Why, is there a dearth of porters in Mysore?"

He jumped on to his seat. Subbanna began to crank the shaft. The bus began to emit poisonous fumes and started with a terrible din.

***

CHAPTER - 5

On the very day the *"Para"* was performed it rained heavily in Madalli. Curiously, not only did it rain in the village that performed "Para" but in all the villages from Kote to Mysore, breaching ponds and dykes. Victor had safely brought back the rations even in such heavy downpour, without them getting damp ever so little. Bhujangaiah was at a loss not knowing how to thank Victor enough. He felt deeply obliged.

It was as though the village had not slept on the rainy night. As the season for sowing was over by then, one could only sow for the returning Monsoon. The village was desperate for seeds. Only a few families shared what was left. Bhujangaiah who had three sacks full, kept what he needed and distributed the rest among those who were despondent for the ragi seed. He asked Amase, the son of Shaggy Sidda, who had begun to work for him of late, to sleep at his house, as Amase would find it hard to rise up early enough to go for work from his own house. Bhujangaiah's mother filled the basket with seeds of Jerusalem peas from the granary for sowing. Parvathy too had the firewood removed from the backyard to the kitchen so that she could start cooking before the break of dawn. Such chores had grown lighter since Amase's arrival. Bhujangaiah slept at home once again. He had forgotten the hotel for the time being. If it had only rained thus a month earlier, he would not have dreamed of setting up a hotel. Bhujangaiah gently ran his hand over the soft swell of Parvathy's womb while consoling himself with the thought that whatever happened had happened for the best. Having been cheated of the comforts of even a touch for a month now, Bhujangaiah found Parvathy's body to be like a warm blanket on a bitingly cold day.

The entire village sat up in the nippy pre-dawn hour. Even before the day broke the ploughshares were ready in the fields. The sowers began sowing along imagined lines. Though it had rained rock solid, the earth was not damp enough. Yet, the streaming rain had cooled the very depths of earth which this long had stood hungry under the sun. Bhujangaiah too began sowing, as Amase readied the plough. He felt like he was treading on butter as he stepped on the deep furrowed soil. The earth was fragrant in the morning breeze. How long had it been since such aroma had reached his nostrils? The earth, which had drunk water, hid the falling grains in its sillions and promised to perform the miracle of life in a couple of days. The joy of life, which had disappeared from the eyes of the villagers, would resurrect the moment they witnessed the shoots spring. The anxiety and the agony of all these days would subside even as the burning earth cooled down.

Bhujangaiah had finished sowing even before the sun could traverse three yards. Only, Amase had not ploughed even a quarter of the field. Bhujangaiah's mother was sowing the Jerusalem pea in the wake of the plough as Amase progressed, furrow after furrow. Bhujangaiah had been unaware of her arrival as well as her beginning to work. He now approached Amase and urged him to plough faster. But the oxen wouldn't heed Amase's voice. Finally when he himself took the plough and raised his voice did the oxen step briskly frightened by the new voice.

Having yielded the plough to his master, when Amase went to sow not knowing how else to occupy himself, Deviramma chided him, "Leave it alone, you wouldn't know enough to sow properly." Amase stood confused. Finally, he settled down to separate the pebbles and stones in the field and collect them in heaps on the edge of the field. Bhujangaiah, oblivious to it all, was engrossed in the act of ploughing. With the rains, the readied field seemed in heat yearning for the plough. As the ploughshare moved from one wave to the next the earth seemed to draw the plough deep into itself.

Parvathy, having prepared the meal, unable to sit at home, lifted the laden food basket to her head and her daughter to her arm and wended her way slowly to the field, though she well knew it was not yet lunch time. Her son Soma trailed her, sucking his thumb. Nothing could cure him of that good habit. Parvathy put the basket down under the tree and sat with a sigh presuming on her husband noticing her. But, only when Soma ran up to him and put his hand on the crossbar of the plough did Bhujangaiah grow aware of his wife bringing food. After ploughing four more rows he called Amase, handed the plough over to him and walked towards the tree. Parvathy's face was suffused with a strange glow. The inexplicable joy and involvement, which he had felt while ploughing the field, came back to Bhujangaiah as he gazed at his wife. Parvathy grew shy as her husband watched her as though he were seeing her for the first time. She began to lay the plate. She called her mother-in-law too who had left for work without eating a morsel that morning. It had of late grown rare that the family sat thus together in one place. If Soma sat by his father to share his food the daughter went to her grandmother to share from her plate. Bhujangaiah would certainly have invited Parvathy to share the food from his plate if only his mother were not there.

Bhujangaiah lit a beedi after his meal and thought of ploughing the stubbly field on the morrow. If that too had been ploughed and readied he could have begun to sow ragi. But he consoled himself knowing well he could only do so much with a single plough. He decided to procure a second plough before the next season. He needed at least three ploughs for the land he possessed. But if the rains did not arrive in time how was he to maintain the oxen and servants all through the year?

Having smoked the beedi he sent Amase to eat and began to till the field once more. Soma walked next to his father holding on to the crossbar, as if his legs would never tire. With the sun growing intense, the earth too grew humid. The soil began to pant as though the heavy rains had yet left the earth insatiate. The earth in a renewed thirst seemed to moan spreading itself open to the imminent inebriating rain.

Bhujangaiah wondered if he should hire an extra plough. But it would not be easy to find labour now that it had rained. He finally decided to entrust the task of hiring a plough to Shaggy Sidda. He wished to produce a good harvest especially as a slap on the face of his father-in-law and such others who were on their toes to deride him for neglecting his fields for his hotel business. Sidda would pull a mountain down if he were given a gourd of liquor. If he couldn't find a plough any where he was certain to bring his own oxen. It would help to send his own plough to till Sidda's lands one of these days. Once the stubbly fields were ploughed, he colud weed it and sow the ragi. There was enough time still. He must now look for ten cart loads of compost manure for the rice fields down the ponds. If he could adequately manure the rice fields he could grow more than sufficient rice for them to eat throughout the year. As the single rain had brimmed over the pond, it wouldn't pose a problem to grow a single crop that year. As Amase returned to take over the plough Bhujangaiah instructed, "You unhitch after ploughing the entire field. I've already sown the ragi." He walked in under the tree. Parvathy sat playing with her daughter as if she did not wish to return home. Her husband too joined, joking and laughing. Sowing was in progress at a fast pace in the adjacent fields too. Bhujangaiah saw that the sun had almost reached the zenith. He stood up, "I have not stepped in the direction of the hotel since morning. Manja is alone. I wonder what's happening."

Parvathy did not contort her face as usual when her husband mentioned the hotel. Bhujangaiah too did not fail to notice the change in his wife. Parvathy walked towards the village via the hotel. She had not deigned to turn her face in that direction from the day the hotel was opened. On a couple of occasions Bhujangaiah himself had taken his children to the hotel.

Bhujangaiah arrived with his family at his "Kendaganneshwara Prasanna Hotel". It was almost empty. Because of the sudden rains people were busy with cultivation and had no time for the hotel. The only customer present was the "Tampura Ayya" from Hampapura who visited Madalli every week, without fail, for holy alms, and Shetty, the bangle merchant from Mysore. As the hotel was situated at the Crossroads leading to Kothegala, Kyathanahalli, Hosalli and Saragur, the two had to pass by it every time they visited one village or the other on their regular circuit. Bhujangaiah's hotel was a rest house to such wandering souls. Again, their taste buds too found their delight at the hotel. This was the first time they were visiting after Bhujangaiah had started the hotel. He welcomed them heartily. Though Manja assured him that they already did have some tea and paid for it too, he wouldn't hear of it. He served tea personally once again and insisted on their drinking it. The three began to gossip.

Parvathy scrutinized every portion of the hotel, engaging Manja in conversation. The one thing that came under harsh criticism was the grinding stone in the kitchen. Manja supported her, "Mother, by the time the dough for idlies can be ground my body would be fit to be carried to the grave.". He used his Mysore dialect. The cup was bigger than the pestle. Peera of the Vadda Community had worked rather hastily on it. The result was they were ill fitting. Parvathy was upset at not finding a single picture of any of the gods. She who believed firmly in god and religion couldn't tolerate such a lapse on her husband's part. She called him into the kitchen and took him to task. She suggested that he bring a picture of god from home for the time being and put it up. Bhujangaiah too was contrite and expressed his appreciation for the timely warning. He made up his mind to get some nice pictures of Gods on his visit to Mysore next week. He recalled the framed pictures of Basavanna the Treasurer of Devotion, Akkamahadevi the supplicant of Lord Shiva, who clothed her nudity with her long tresses that kissed the ground, Siddalingeshwara of Yadiyur who sat in the centre surrounded with pictures of his miracles, and more than all the portrait of Mahadeshwara of seven hills, riding the tiger. He promised his wife to put up the pictures by next week. She suggested that he bring a picture of Shiva and his consort Parvathy riding the bull Nandi, who together were the fountainhead of all those Gods, in the heavenly abode of Kailasa.

The children had by then struck friendship with Manja and were eating till their stomach would burst. Soma had filled the pockets of his shorts with *kharasev* as if what he had already eaten were not enough. Bhujangaiah noticing it seemed to defend his son, "Manja, today the business has been dull. The customers from the bus too were few. Whatever was prepared has not been sold." He sat in conversation with Shetty and Ayya after instructing Manja, "There is no need to make anything in the afternoon. If a customer should arrive he can be served with whatever is left." Parvathy walked home with her children.

***

CHAPTER - 6

The business at the hotel, which had suffered some for the past few days, picked up beyond his expectations after the rain. Each day brought new customers. The children from Madalli who frequented the hotel unknown to their elders in the early days began to arrive now without fear. The trellis of palm fronds erected in the backyard for the scheduled castes was also not in disuse. It too began to get crowded till in the end it could hold no more. Among the scheduled castes too there were two groups. The tumbler used by the "Left handed" was never used by the "Right handed" and vice-versa. Though they had separate seating arrangement, very soon it would all get mixed up leading to confusion. whatever it was, Bhujangaiah prospered.

The hotel had grown into the unaging tree of plenty, the Kalpavruksha, probably due to the auspicious moment of its inauguration. The respectable citizenry of Madalli who had poked fun at him were now secretly jealous.

It was almost a month, since Bhujangaiah opened the hotel. If it were not for the rains and their preoccupation with cultivation, they wouldn't have hesitated to hoist the owl, the bird of ill omen, on his head, thus attributing the bad season to his having set up the hotel business. Bhujangaiah, heedless of the opinion of others began to practise to the letter, Basavanna's exhortation, "Work is redemption". In his view no profession was lowly as long as it was not unethical. Such a principle was not new to him. He had always tried his hand at many jobs with professionalism. He would go to the palm grove, bring bundles of palm leaves, split them, and weave them into baskets. People liked the baskets he made, as they were sturdier than other baskets. He kept what he needed and sold the rest. He stored the fronds in the buffalo puddles or the village pond, rotted them in order to draw out their fibers to make varieties of rope. The ropes could be used for the plough, to draw from the well, as halter for cattle, etc.... . More than all, Bhujangaiah deserved the affection of the village lasses and was the object of immense wonder of little children due to his expertise in diving. He would dive like a Brahmini duck, impervious of the depth of the wells and retrieve the vessels lost. He never took money for this service of his. Bhujangaiah would salvage the vessels for many a daughter-in-law, who had lost her vessel, even before her mother-in-law chastised her. Apart from this he had made enough name with his expertise in cooking on community occasions like "*Para*", "the festival of the village deity," as well as during marriages and on death anniversaries.

For the children of Madalli there couldn't be another person as lovable as Bhujangaiah. He would make tops for children, and play with them unmindful of what people may think. He thus involved himself in one activity or another, despising laziness. His natural propensity was to be engaged in some activity all the while.

Though the elders of Madalli praised him, "He is truly the Kalipurusha, the man of our times"; they did not desist from opining, "The horse laid egg when the perilous day dawned." They were critical of his running away from home as well as of his opening the hotel. The hotel business strengthened his trait of working constantly, neither gloating under praise nor growing depressed under criticism. Nothing was dearer to him than encountering new faces each day and listening to conversation. As a result, he grew worldly and began to develop a personality that would soon make him important in his village.

Bhujangaiah's hotel grew so very popular that even those who took the bus at Kote for Mysore said "We can eat at Madalli". Even Victor encouraged the passengers half in jest, "Indrabhavan of Madalli has arrived, get down! get down!". Bhujangaiah started growing "civilized" under Victor's encouragement. He started wearing dhoti instead of his knickers all the time. Though he never shaved even once a month earlier, he had now ordered Sanjeeva, the barber from Hosalli to visit him every week without fail. Of late, he never left for the city on his purchases without a shave. His children too began to dress different from the rest of the boys in the village. Only, his wife and mother did not alter in any way that the village would notice.

The hotel, which improved by the day brought the Crossroads a new face lift. Madalli began to grow addicted to tea. The villagers experienced some sense of loss if they should miss drinking tea on a particular day. Bhujangaiah too found it difficult to manage with just Manja and started looking for an extra hand. He could not find in Madalli another boy of is own caste, though there was no dearth for unemployed youth. But the parents believed that it was beneath them to allow their children to work at the hotel.

It was Beard of Kyathanhalli who finally ferreted out a boy from nowhere. Though Bhujangaiah could see at once that the boy would be of no help in handling the grinder or chopping firewood he still engaged him as he might help in dish washing. With the boy's arrival, Manja too felt relieved of some of his burden. Bhujangaiah did not feel entirely relieved. There were many more jobs to attend to. Before the incessant rains began in the season of Ashada, between July and August, he had to store at least five cartloads of firewood. He had purchased the Jackfruit tree, on the advice of Beard. But now, it had to be logged. He had to first find the woodcutters, have them saw it so that Manchachari could be asked to make tables and, what was most urgent, a display case to keep the sweets.

Bhujangaiah had not ignored Ajappa amidst this busy schedule. When he visited him to pay the monthly instalment on the loan Ajappa had said," I am not in any financial strait! You can pay back after four or five months." He had inquired about his business and the profit he had made. Bhujangaiah had not hidden anything from him and had confided the profit and the loss he made in his new profession. Bhujangaiah had scrupulously maintained a daily account of his business in the Kalanidhi Pocket calender diary, which he always carried in his pocket. It was Ajappa who had instructed him to be as diligent with accounts as the care he exercised in preparing the delicacies. Ajappa patted Bhujangaiah for having carried out his advice as if it were a sacred task. He gave him a few more business tips. Bhujangaiah, astounded by Ajappa's business acumen, wondered at the people of Madalli who ridiculed him by calling him a harlequin. Perhaps, it was to hide this ability of his from them that he pretended to be one! What else would have made such a wise man to behave so ridiculously?

Shiva was the name of the boy who had newly taken up employment with Bhujangaiah. He was emaciated with scant food to eat in the village. The vestiges of a knicker and a shirt that scarcely hung from his body did for his raiment. Bhujangaiah added two pairs of clothes for Shiva to the list of purchases to be made this time. Bhujangaiah cared for Shiva, as he appeared to be sincere.

Only when he scrupulously went through his accounts with Ajappa's help did Bhujangaiah realize that he had made a profit of almost three hundred and fifty rupees in the one month of his business. He had not seen such a whopping profit in a year as a farmer since the demise of his father, in spite of his striving hard through the dark and the night. This was a miracle. He at once thought of replacing the smoky, black, wooden box of his grandfather's time with an iron almirah, but was ashamed. He consoled himself not to desire for too much at once and decided to wait for a few more months before thinking of improvements. He counted the money he needed for purchases on the morrow and gave the rest to Parvathy for safekeeping in the old box. All that money had been secreted in the inner pocket of his shirt all these days. Parvathy felt the very heavens shake and fall on earth. She had never seen so much money in that home, let alone handle it! Not daring even to count, she secreted it in the box, locked it and lit an incense stick. When there wasn't much of an income that one could speak of, her husband who did manage to somehow save a bit, never trusted her with the keys to the box in which he kept the money. But this day, his act of not only handing her all that money, but also the key had astounded her. She began to see her husband as a veritable god and found nothing wrong in his starting a hotel. What should it matter if people talked? No one was going to either help them or care for them if and when they were to lose all their possession.

If only she had known there would be such profit in running a hotel she wouldn't have quarreled with her husband in the first instance. She could have avoided sending for her father and him arriving to break off their relationship, never ever to be reconciled. Bhujangaiah could sympathize with Parvathy who stood silent as if her mouth were locked. Yet, not finding it necessary to comment on it he merely told her, "Warm up some water for the evening. I must leave for Mysore tomorrow".

Parvathy sat dumbstruck. She felt small in front of her husband's generosity. He hadn't uttered one harsh word in spite of all that had transpired. She had belittled him at every opportunity. She had pestered him with very little reason. She was not even fit to be the dust under his feet. Yet, she had the arrogance rooted in her parent's affluence. If her husband continued earning thus, she had no need to bow her head to any body. She need not wait at anybody's door. Instead, people would come to them. They wouldn't dare talk lightly of them. Even as she realised her folly, Parvathy felt that her father too would one day or the other realize his mistake. She checked the lock on the box one more time before getting up to fill the cauldron with water from the cask for Bhujangaiah's bath. Unmindful of the fatigue after drawing water, she left for Karigowda's house on the outer street, with her daughter in her arms. Gowda was the most affluent man in the village. His wife Kalavva was a saintly person. One couldn't find another woman like her in the entire village. There was a large backyard to their house of twin courtyards, where a few drumstick trees, curry leaf trees, and hog plum trees grew. Gowda neither flaunted his riches nor looked down on others. Troubling others was never a part of his life.

Parvathy's main reason for the visit was the drumstick leaves. Her husband thought no end of the broth made from it. Even as she approached the doors of Gowda's house, Sakamma, Gowda's eldest daughter-in-law welcomed her with a smile. Kalavva called the pregnant Parvathy on her rare visit to sit next to her and enquired, "How many months is it now Parvathy?" Parvathy answered shyly, "Must be the fourth or the fifth month now aunt." She had addressed Kalavva in the manner which all the young used towards their elders in Madalli. After exchanging the glad and troubled tidings of life Parvathy confessed to the purpose of her visit. Kalavva at once summoned a servant and asked him to fetch some drumstick leaves for Parvathy. She said, "You are pregnant now. If you should desire for anything at all just send word. Don't hesitate."

Parvathy arrived home to prepare the water for his bath, and entered the kitchen. She felt ineluctably festive as though the burden of her womb too were eased. The Jerusalem pea seeds left over after sowing was put on the boil, as it added a flavour to the leaves. Parvathy gazed into the flame squatting in front of the hearth. The Acacia wood burnt well in spite of being damp.

When Parvathy emerged from the kitchen, the night was already descending. She lit the lamp and burnt the frankincense sticks to gods as well as to the box. Amase had secured the oxen in the shed and was feeding them grass. Parvathy who heard him took a vessel and stepped out to milk. Amase was taken by surprise to hear her address him, "Amase, free the calf , I'll milk the buffalo." It was the old woman who milked the buffalo every day. And it was not milking time yet. Wondering at this novel event he unhitched the calf. Parvathy watching the buffalo yielding in a trice squatted to milk. When she put her hand to its udder the buffalo kicked about scaring her a little. Even the animal must have realized through scent and touch that it was a stranger who sat to milk her. But in the end it stood uncaring as if to say. "How does it matter who milks?"

***

CHAPTER - 7

Having made Madalli woebegone by playing truant, it was raining heavily since the last four days. A new fear of floods assailed the villagers who reeled under the unrelenting rain. Though such rains were a rarity now, Madalli was not new to the experience, having once bordered a dense forest. Let alone people, not even cattle dared to venture out. One stepped into puddles everywhere. The fields were all inundated. Though more than a month had passed after sowing ragi for the summer, the shoots couldn't be bunched for the second weeding. Though the crop was good, due to rain-chill the ears were turning yellow. If the rains ceased and the skies cleared for at least a week the crop would break through the fungus to turn dark. If not, there was the danger of it rotting due to the chill. The peasants were once again troubled. Though the dead leaves rotted, the tender blades of grass shot up to laugh without a care. The beds that were once sere had now grown all green. In another week the verdure of Sravana period, between August and September, would cover with moss even the paths through which people walked. Even the manure pits drew attention with colourful weeds growing as tall as a man. Excessive rain brought excessive weeds in the fields. However, there was no dearth of labour for weeding. As most fields lay uncultivated, with very little winter ragi sowed, the problem of labour would never arise. Though the peasants did not visit their fields they were busy on the *jagali* of their huts in tasks such as making a rain cape or braiding a rope.

Only the hotel hummed with activity like a beehive even in that devilish rain. The tamarind tree whined like a scabby dog whose tail was caught in a cleft. The hotel roof weathered the roughest of the winds. The heat from the kitchen kept the entire hotel warm. The dripping water from those who walked in out of the rain turned the dung treated floor damp and squishy. Bhujangaiah thought of a new plan to get the floor mortared or even concreted. It would help avoid such slush. It would then be easy to clean the least of dirt. On the other hand, even if he should have the entire flooring treated with dung it wouldn't dry in this rain. However, he decided to let things remain until after the rains. The room meant for a shop had remained tidy as it was locked, and so Bhujangaiah hadn't any problem sleeping there at night. Manja, Shiva and Urupa who had of late taken to staying permanently at the hotel joined benches together to sleep. The trellis in front of the hotel needed proper mending. Those who wished to get out of either rain or sun could find shelter there. Then the customers wouldn't be at a loss for space to sit. A number of thoughts crowded Bhujangaiah's brain even like the rain. The roof leaked at a couple of places. It too needed repairs, once the sun shone. As soon as he made a mention of such little tasks Urupa would attend to them. Though he never got paid for his troubles, his face already as wide as a town would further expand in glee when offered an occasional cup of tea and the leftovers. Urupa earned some money whenever the bus arrived. Apart from lending a hand in loading and unloading, he now helped in cranking the engine every time Lingajamba bus had to be started. Subbanna, the conductor, happy to be relieved of the task, readily compensated Urupa with a little money. Urupa who dreamed of becoming a cleaner on the bus performed whatever tasks that Victor or Subbanna assigned him without a murmur. He was a tall youth. There was always a bruise or two to show on his knees or elbows. He used to stick them with the phosphor paper from the sides of a box of matches or else with crushed leaves of some weed. Though his name was Chandrashekar Achar, because of a permanent pale sheen on his limbs and face he was called "Urupa". Occasionally, when irritable he would object to people addressing him thus, "Why brother, haven't my parents given me a name?" Yet, he would on other occasions give his name as Urupa to those who enquired. His unique trait was to do whatever one asked him to. But one had to invariably warm his palm first. It was enough if it were a mere coin of three *kasu*, with a hole in it. Urupa had in fact strung round his waist such coins worth two rupees. He would exhibit his affluence to children by jingling them. The most he was ever paid for jobs done was one *anna*. One day when Subbanna gave him a quarter in a good mood Urupa had promptly given it to his mother, not spending any of it, thus causing her anxiety whether he had stolen it. In the past, Urupa had tried his hand at petty thievery on occasion.

Though the hotel had by now three employees on a permanent status, including Urupa, it did not stop Pundri, Kariappa, Guard Nagaraja and other guests who visited the hotel at least once a day from offering their essential services, in the manner of the legendary squirrel which carried pebbles for Rama's bridge to Lanka, as though the hotel was their own. Now that a violent rain battered the village they took root at the hotel. Bhujangaiah had no need to dirty his limbs for any of the tasks. It was enough if he merely sat at the cash box. But he never forgot to personally ensure the comfort of his customers. He was from the beginning a generous man. Ajappa had tried telling him it was not a trait that a businessman should possess. Though Bhujangaiah would tighten up a bit whenever he remembered Ajappa's timely advice, in the next instant he reverted to his normal self. With a firm belief that god blessed when the time was propitious he never saw money to be more than a necessity. That was the reason why many had been impressed by him. None of his friends would double deal with him. They wouldn't touch a morsel without Bhujangaiah first offering it. They too would stay back on nights when Bhujangaiah rested at the hotel. Pundri would, on such occasions, recount juicy tales or gossip that never let any one shut eyes. Urupa found Pundri's tales irresistible. He would sit on his haunches, open mouthed, listening avidly, throughout the night. Pundri would somehow learn in full detail, every single incident that transpired in the village. Pundri enacted and narrated with gestures the secret liaisons of those respectable men in the village, their discomfitures when found out, or what woman slept with whom in the village, and the result thereof. Bhujangaiah saw in him a prodigy.

The one misfortune, which marked such a sensuous person as Pundri was that his first-born was a hermaphrodite. The child who was the butt of ridicule and an object of pity for the entire village was brought to the mutt to be an acolyte, a "mari", when he was six years old. Pundri had thus washed his hands off the child. One by one all the customers had left. The Tampura Ayya and the bangle merchant had not paid a visit due to the rains. That day the rain did not show signs of letting up though it was nearing nightfall. As all the snacks prepared were sold Bhujangaiah instructed Manja to make some *uppittu* with Semolina and gathered with his friends in the room meant for the shop. He shut the door so that their conversation would not reach the ears of his employees who were all still very young. His exclusion made Urupa feel as though he was at once lifted and thrown down the chasm of disappointment. Yet, he chose to sit close to the shut door hoping to catch a few words that may filter through the chinks. He was further disappointed. He cursed Manchacnari roundly for having joined the panels without leaving the slightest of gaps. Totally at a loss he finally rose to join Shiva and Manja who were busy preparing *uppittu*.

The recent sexual exploits of Madalli, which Pundri had either heard of or had seen, began to unravel behind the doors, as soon as they gathered in the room. Though Bhujangaiah at first pretended to be nonchalant, he soon grew excited enough to make his hair stand on end even in that cold. Of all the incidents narrated by Pundri, Gundappa the village clerk's affair with Cheluvi, the daughter of Kali was quite titillating. The whole of Madalli had known about Gundappa's affair with Kali. Many had spied them lying behind the milk-hedge or in the fields of standing jowar crop. A few vagabonds had followed them in secret, as soon as they crossed the village, and had with glee watched them making love. Kali was proud of her affair with the village clerk. He had managed to allot her four acres of revenue land, in appreciation of her satisfying his needs, whenever he had the urge, in the Masanakuppe survey zone, which was the tract on which once, long ago, a village had flourished. Though she was willing to surrender everything she possessed, the village clerk had preferred her daughter Cheluvi. In fact he had a daughter older than Cheluvi. He had searched all over the countryside for a groom for her. Though by then the stench of the relationship between Vanajakshi his daughter, and Narayana, the youngest son of Karigowda had spread throughout the village, for some reason the details of the affair had not as yet been recorded in Pundri's life. In Pundri's broad view, the Monsoon rain that year had done a grave disservice to the "whoring thieves". If only it had rained on time, the jowar crop in the fields around the village would have by now stood a head tall wherever one turned ones eyes, concealing inside them many a sexual escapade. But now, those who met secretly had to seek shelter behind the milk-hedges. Though it was common knowledge that the sap from the hedge would burn the skin, people ignored it.

Pundri described the many love affairs on the evidence of such burns. He would say that those who lust after flesh were oblivious to fear, terror, honour, disgrace, cold, wind, fire or heat. To them, even to think of the right and the wrong of an act was a grave sin. Pundri illustrated it with the story of the affair between the village clerk and Cheluvi. He ruled that it was no sin to make love to anyone as long as it was with mutual consent, as if his was the final word on the ethics of love.

The last words of Pundri stirred and raked up strange memories in the minds of his friends leaving them confused. Their suppressed desires woke up, ready to rush forth. But by then *uppittu* was ready and Urupa banged on the door. His frustration was vented through the act of knocking hard on the door. He couldn't stop knocking till the door was opened. Bhujangaiah wished he could kick him. He rebuked him in anger, "What's with you? Do you have the fits? Is that the way to knock on the door?"

Urupa stood in dismay like an erring cur. After feasting on Uppittu, they all assembled again in the room. Their body and mind were all ears to Pundri's tales of sexual exploits while the rain kept time. Only Urupa was disappointed again.

****

CHAPTER - 8

When Bhujangaiah emerged from the hotel, rubbing his eyes, the rain that had haunted like a spirit from the dead had abated. The sky was clean like a washed plate of blue, with the clouds all melted. Beyond the eastern hills the sunrays shone and the rain-washed trees and plants danced. Earth reveled like a woman luxuriating in the sun after a bath. Bhujangaiah thought of Parvathy. She would leave for her parent's in a month or two having advanced in pregnancy. The house would be empty without her. Children too would leave with her for Jakkalli. Because Soma had joined school he couldn't be sent. He would stay with mother. Bhujangaiah was both surprised and glad to note his mother looking as strong as tamarind fibre in spite of her advanced years. Because she managed affairs with such care life went on without a hitch. Though there were occasional jousts between the mother-in-law and the daughter-in-law, his mother with her childlike heart soon forgot all that transpired. It was his wife who was a little obdurate. Though she still retained a little of the arrogance inherited at her parental home, her exaggerations of it had reduced in contrast to a pride that she had begun to develop, that there were no wants at her husband's home too, especially after he began to give her the money from the hotel business every month, without fail, for safe-keeping. She used to belittle her mother-in-law, whenever angry, saying, "I wonder to enjoy what fortune I arrived here!" She could not say so any longer, if the hotel were to do business with the same pace for a couple of years it was not impossible for them too to become one among the rich in the village. Parvathy prayed to Basappa of Pond to keep her husband's fickle mind firm. After Hulikanthyappa the only other influential god in Madalli was Basappa, the Bull of the Pond, down the embankment of the village pond. Because of the big pond next to his shrine people called him Basappa of the Pond. The priest of that shrine was Bhujangaiah's cousin. The shrine did not boast of regular worship. Muddubasava, the priest, who was always unkempt would occasionally look clean. On such days, the people of Madalli knew that a worship had been performed at the shrine. For generations Muddubasava and his family lived on the more than five acres of temple land. When Muddubasava's father had been alive not a day had passed without flowers being placed on the crown of god. It was during his time that the *jagali* around the Bael tree in front of the shrine was built with mortar. It was still sturdy. The Oleander and the mountain ebony trees that he had planted, watered and nursed, provided flowers today for all the homes where Lord Shiva was worshipped in Madalli. In his childhood, accompanied by his mates, Bhujangaiah had gone there every day at the hour of the cock's crow, climbed the tree to fetch flowers. His father never worshipped without those flowers. But now, his son Soma was never up at that hour. He himself did not care for the flowers to worship Shiva. That day, inexplicably, even as he woke up, Bhujangaiah was nostalgic about his childhood "Oh, how wonderful were those days? Each day dawned differently." He recalled the punishment they were meted out by Subbaraya who used to come from Magge to teach them on the wide *jagali* of Gowda's home. Their village did not have a primary school then. Those who wished for education had to seek private tuition. By the time he had finished his schooling Kyatanahalli had a Government Primary School. Today's kids didn't learn at middle school what he had been taught by the teacher at home. Though they couldn't master the alphabet, yet, they advanced to higher classes in Mysore. Who knows what they'd come to?

After the morning chores and tea, as Bhujangaiah surveyed his hotel for damages, he began to reminisce. He was always ahead of the rest at tuitions. Even the passers by stopped for a while to nod in appreciation as he read aloud the *Amarakosa*, and *Bharatha* musically, emulating Subbaraya. He had learnt to recite the Puranas from Marideva alias Cedimari, who would visit from Devanur, rest at his home and recite in the evenings the *Miracle of Prabhulinga* and the *Purana* of *Cannabasava*. But his desire to excel in recitation gradually waned as the interest among the village folk in listening to them also faded. But even now, occasionally, in Madalli, the recitation of Purana was performed if someone, who could read hours at a stretch, or who took part in a discourse, or those who would sit and listen could be found. However, the recital was performed without fail every year on Basavajayanthi, the birthday of Basavanna. Cedimari of Devanur had stopped visiting for the recital. The villagers had presumed that he had grown one with Shiva. Cedimari was an expert in conducting the obsequies as well as in reciting the Purana of Basava, Though he was from Devanur, he camped at Mysore almost all the time. As times changed, the traditions practised among the urban Verashaiva community declined and they searched for a person who knew the intricacies of their religion only when someone amongst them died. At such times as though he descended from the sky Cedimari would present himself, god alone knew from where. The spoor of death of a Verashaiva devotee would invariably reach his nostrils wherever he was. He had not grown one with Shiva as the people of Madalli had assumed. He had met Bhujangaiah once on the latter's weekly visit to Mysore at the Gurumallu Hotel in Agrahara and had promised to visit on the next Shivaratri, the holy night of Shiva. Though he had grown feeble under the onslaught of time, his voice hadn't grown weak. When Bhujangaiah told him of his starting a new business, Cedimari who followed with unquestioned faith all the edicts of the Verashaiva religion, ruled that it was not wrong to run a hotel and assured him that it too was a kind of devotional act, a "Dasoha." Bhujangaiah compelled him to visit Madalli that very day. Cedimari, who could see Bhujangaiah's problem, had offered an invaluable suggestion, that was to invite to Madalli the Swamy of Devanur Mutt. If Bhujangaiah were to perform in the holy presence of the Jagadguru certain propitiatory rituals like the worship of the divine feet, the offer of a thousand Bael leaves, the ablution of Rudra, then all his problems would be resolved. But it was not normal for the Jagadguru to visit his house or his hotel and bless him with the dust of his feet.

If such an event should transpire then there certainly would be a change in his stature from that very day. Though the suggestion of Cedimari was a marvelous idea it was not possible to invite the Swamy without notice. There was no predicting the rain. What if there was a downpour on the day of the visit? His plans would fail. All the Verashaivas would certainly throng like the very floods from the nearby villages, hoping for a glimpse of the Jagadguru. The crowd shouldn't be cheated of an opportunity to witness all the rituals that would be performed. Deciding to fix a date for the event after the rains, Bhujangaiah asked for Cedimari's permanent address. But today, Bhujangaiah felt that he should invite the Universal Mentor without further delay. It would take three to four months for the rains to let up entirely. By then Parvathy would have delivered.

How could he organize such a special occasion in the house without her? Whatever happened he should set the date for the last Saturday of Shravana. He would visit Mysore the day after tomorrow, that is on Monday. Today was the first Saturday of Shravana. He should leave for Mysore tomorrow evening, look up Cedimari, and go to Devanur to get the Swami's concurrence, He presumed that it would all take a fortnight to accomplish. He noticed the bundles of firewood stacked in lots in the backyard of the hotel growing wet in the rain. He called out to Urupa. Not getting an answer from that worthy he came round to the front of the hotel when he saw Urupa gossiping with the boys who attended the middle school in Kyatanahalli. The ritual markings of ochre and the "U" lines in white on the forehead of a few boys testified to it being a Saturday of Shravana. Urupa who had heard Bhujangaiah calling him broke his conversation with the boys, for the time being, and jumped like a monkey to stand bent at the waist, with arms folded like Hanuman waiting for his orders. He asked, "Why did you call, brother?"

Bhujangaiah too joined Urupa in the task of removing the firewood and spreading it in the backyard to dry. Even before they were through with half the lot, Bhujangaiah was shocked to see Urupa jumping away suddenly, shouting, scared for his life, "What happened? What is it?" Urupa trembled, pointing his finger at the stack of firewood, "Snake...look, look at its tail there!" Bhujangaiah was not scared of snakes. He would catch them alive, pull out their fangs and play with them. However dangerous a King Cobra might be, he wouldn't leave it alone even if it should enter its hole in the anthill. He would drag it out and put an end to its tale. The reason why Bhujangaiah's name was popular in half the surrounding villages, not only in Madalli, was his ability to treat snakebite, which had saved innumerable lives. Bhujangaiah carefully watched the spot, which Urupa pointed out to, and after making sure it was really a snake's tail, he approached the spot gingerly. Urupa moved further away and watched with all attention. He was all eyes. Bhujangaiah suddenly caught hold of the snake's tail and pulled on it as he would a rope. He managed to hold its hood and brought it to the front of the hotel. Urupa was stupefied. He was amazed to see Bhujangaiah pressing the snake's mouth in a vice like grip, with a strength that seemed magical, before it could raise its hood. Bhujangaiah had pried open its mouth and pulled out its fangs with the help of a knife even as he watched petrified, expecting it to strike out any moment.

Manja, Shiva, and a few customers who had stood at a distance all the while, scared enough even to breathe, now drew closer. The snake had coiled around his upper arm and writhed. When Bhujangaiah pulled it off and threw it down on the ground, it sizzled like a thunderbolt, raised its wide hood and leapt almost its entire length up into the air to strike back at Bhujangaiah's palm. As if it sought to avenge the tortures meted out to it, the snake fought Bhujangaiah with a terrible rage. But he continued to tease it without exhibiting even the slightest sign of fear; as if it were a normal game of fun he indulged in. By then a large crowd had gathered. However, none of them dared go anywhere near the snake. In the gentle morning sun, the wheat brown skin of the cobra shone. The snake having regurgitated all its futile rage, tired out finally and closing its hood attempted to escape in surrender to Bhujangaiah. Some among the crowd advised that he kill it while others suggested he remove the snake to a distance and free it. Bhujangaiah, paying scant attention to them called out to Shiva for a gunny sack with the intention of playing with the snake for a while longer. He tied up the snake in the sack and ordered, "Hey, Shiva, throw this in a corner." Shiva refused to follow his master's order, trembling in fear. "Thu! You cowardly offspring of a widow", abusing him, Bhujangaiah himself leaned the sack with the snake against the wall of the hotel. The snake was writhing in the sack. Its enraged hiss could be heard. None could fathom his purpose of incarcerating it inside the sack. Having instructed Urupa not to tell anybody that the sack contained a snake, Bhujangaiah asked for some water and washed the knife as well as his hands clean, pleased as if he had performed a ritual. The customers who had rushed out of the hotel could hardly guess whose plate was which absorbed as they were in the spectacle. They ordered for fresh snacks now that their earlier order had grown cold. Even Manja had lost track of what they ate, but billed them through sheer guesswork. The customers who had witnessed the flow of blood and the whitish, mucous like secretion from the snake's mouth could hardly relish what they ate.

It was almost time for the bus to arrive. With new customers entering those who were already present left one by one. Urupa wanted to show the snake to those who arrived. But as his orders were to the contrary he writhed suppressing his desire even like the snake under Bhujangaiah's magical spell writhed inside the sack. Soon, the bus arrived, Urupa now began to grow restless as though it were impossible to remain without narrating the marvel, which had transpired, to Victor and Subbanna, who were not merely his well-wishers but also his friends. Bhujangaiah assigned a task to him as soon as the bus arrived thus forcing him to remain inside the hotel. The regular customers finished eating. With the rains having abated and the sun shining, the bus was crowded. As only a limited quantity of snacks was prepared fearing rain, it was all over in one go with the hotel receiving an unexpected number of customers. Manja had taken care to save a second helping for Victor and Subbanna. When they were drinking coffee Bhujangaiah told Victor, "Victor, brother, I've bought a chicken, a layer for you today." Victor was surprised. It was true that he thought the life of a layer. Yet, he could not remember having ever asked Bhujangaiah, who was nauseated at the very mention of meat, for one. He asked in disbelief, “Really?” Bhujangaiah answered, “Have you ever found me lying to you?” He pointed to the sack next to the wall. Victor went out with his coffee to see. He began to believe in Bhujangaiah when he saw the sack move. “ If you tie up the hen in the sack would it not die?” He called out to Urupa, “Hey, Urupa! First undo the sack and tie the legs of the chicken. Keep it next to my seat,” Urupa looked at Bhujangaiah in alarm not knowing what he should do. Bhujangaiah came to his rescue; “He is busy slicing onions for Uppittu. And then he is a Lingayat, he cannot touch chicken. You do that yourself,” Victor could not have asked Subbanna who was a tamarind curry eating Brahmin. In the end Victor put his coffee cup down and approached the sack to open its mouth. Bhujangaiah followed him silently. Victor, as he bent down to untie the string binding the sack, grew suspicious. The snake sprang out hissing even before he could undo the knot fully. Victor jumped back as if he were struck by a jolt of electric current. Bhujangaiah supported him before he tumbled down. “My God! What a miracle is this? The hen has turned into a snake!” Bhujangaiah stepped back, dragging Victor with him, as if he too were scared. The snake, confused by the noise of the crowd stood with its hood raised. The hotel had by then emptied out. Everyone stood at a safe distance scared of the snake. Bhujangaiah pretending ignorance ran up to the reptile, caught it by its tail when he saw the snake trying to slither away towards the backyard. The snake, in a terrible rage, spread its hood and struck its tormentor repeatedly. The gathered crowd grew agitated for a moment. Victor too felt his heart stop for a while.

Urupa realized it was to play a joke on Victor that Bhujangaiah had incarcerated the snake. After the bus left Bhujangaiah asked Urupa to break a stick from the Solanum bush. While breaking the stick from the hedge row bordering the path, knowing that the snake’s end had approached, Urupa noticed somebody approaching on the Madalli road. It was the bangle merchant with the bangles in a cloth sling on his shoulder and behind him a girl carrying a basket of bangles. Urupa deliberately delayed fetching the stick wanting them too to witness what may happen next. Urupa joined them and narrated the story of the snake as they approached the hotel, all the while stealing glances at the girl who was visiting for the first time. Bhujangaiah began teasing the snake wanting the merchant too to have some fun, before he killed it. The girl trembled with fear at the sight of the snake. The merchant placed his bundle down inside the hotel and helped lift down the basket from his daughter Sushila's head. He now stood childlike watching the snake. He had, while walking from Madalli, told his daughter that snakes never attacked unprovoked, but they struck only when they were teased, or if stepped upon accidentally. Sushila had wondered, that morning, as soon as they left Karigowda's house in Madalli, taking the path that lead to the Crossroads, "Father, what if there are snakes on this path?" He had then warned her to be careful while walking such paths. They had continued to walk still talking about snakes. It all seemed strange to them now. He too, like his daughter, had been shaken for a moment, when a real snake suddenly confronted them. This was the very first time that Bhujangaiah had seen the merchant's daughter. This must be the snake that Sushila had thought of then. The thought had come to her probably as a prelude to the actual sighting. Sushila stared at Bhujangaiah who stood holding the snake, Though short, he was well built. His face had a childlike innocence though just now he seemed capable of mesmerizing, standing there with the snake in his hand. On seeing them, he had brought the snake over to show them. When he narrated how he had removed its fangs and forced its mouth open, showing, "Look, this is the snake's venom duct", Sushila had leaned forward in curiosity. Although she couldn't tell the difference between the duct and the tongue and wanted to know, she had for some reason felt shy and held back.

One day, the bangle merchant had said while conversing at the hotel, that he was on the look out for a suitable boy for his only daughter, whose mother had died a few years ago from tuberculosis. He had remarried, and the incompatibility between his second wife and daughter had resulted in some quarrel or the other every day. He had said that it was difficult to find boys in his community, and rare to find suitable ones as those who made money from business surely would indulge in vices. Each day they were in a new town. Who is to say what they had been upto? And he had little choice. His daughter was a petite girl of sterling qualities. She took after her mother both in speech and manner, The merchant's eyes welled up with tears by the mere thought of his dead wife, while he spoke of his daughter. He had also talked of his second wife's irritable nature and of how she ill - treated his loving daughter. The snotty merchant grew snottier when anguished. The people of Madalli called him the "Snotty Shetty" behind his back. Bhujangaiah wondered how such a man could have fathered such a comely daughter.

Bhujangaiah was stunned for a moment, when he saw Sushila. Her wide eyes and sensuous figure had distracted Bhujangaiah at the very first instance. Though scared, when Sushila came close to the snake with an uncontrollable curiosity to see it, something electric had passed through Bhujangaiah's body. His body had risen in goose flesh. Though he had wished to invite her to touch the snake, he had been hesitant to ask. The hour of the snake's death that had temporarily been postponed with Sushila's arrival, had now neared. Seeing the Solanum stick in Urupa's hand Bhujangaiah asked him to kill the snake. Urupa shook in his pants. "No brother, don't you know it was because my father killed a cobra that I got this sheen? That's why I won't kill snakes." He had suddenly recollected what he had been told a long time ago in order to show a girl like Sushila he was not really scared of killing snakes. Bhujangaiah laughed, "You cowardly son of a widow! Aren't you ashamed of saying you are scared?'" "Upon my head brother, it is true. Ask my mother if you wish." Urupa tried hiding his defeat in front of the strange woman. In truth, he felt like pissing in his shorts at the very sight of a snake. Knowing it was useless to ask him, Bhujangaiah crossed the fence and killed the snake with the stick. "Lo, Urupa, you could at least bury the snake.' When Bhujangaiah ordered him, Urupa left to bury the snake.

Though her father urged her to eat something, Sushila followed Urupa to look again at the now dead snake. Urupa opened a pit in a trice, digging at the earth loosened by the rain. Though the snake's head had been crushed to death, Urupa while lifting it at the end of a stick felt it roll and dropped it suddenly. When Sushila, watching his fear, burst out laughing, Urupa shrank in shame. However, he gathered courage to throw the snake into the pit with the stick. The snake had not been killed entirely. Bhujangaiah had merely crushed the head and had not injured any other part of the snake. While shoveling earth into the pit Urupa grinned, "Sister, you are the merchant's daughter!" Urupa resembled the orangutan that Sushila had seen in the Zoo- unkempt hair, long limbs, flattened nose, black face, and shining, broad teeth. There was a sort of imbecile look on the face. "Yes, I am the merchant's daughter. What's your name?" Urupa felt he was blessed by her mere addressing him. Swallowing the answer, which had danced on his lips, Urupa lifted his head like a garden lizard and uttered "Chandrashekarachari". Sushila, who did remember he being called "Urupa" by the man who killed the snake, did not inquire further.

Sushila entered the hotel with her father, who still stood at the door, to eat snacks. Urupa attempted to escape leaving the shovel at the door, scared that Bhujangaiah may again say something that would belittle him in front of this strange woman. But as soon as Bhujangaiah asked "Whereto Urupa?" he stood comically, caught like a thief, and said in confusion, "I am going to the field." Bhujangaiah cursed him in his normal fashion, Thu! Useless fellow, you know only to shit and to eat" but was contrite at having uttered such words, when he saw Sushila, wondering what she might think. He then began to expand on his adventures as to how many varieties of snakes he had caught, and how many he had saved from snake bite. Sushila, who listened to him intently, was bewildered by the very manner of his narration. The people of Madalli had seen many a time Bhujangaiah capture a snake, pull its fangs out, and play with it. After Manga, the outcaste had died, it was Bhujangaiah alone who administered medicine for snake bite in Madalli. It was believed that Manga had taught none but Bhujangaiah the chant and the knowledge of the herbs for snake venom before he died. Bhujangaiah collected the herb once a year, dried, powdered it and stored it in a couple of gourds. He never sucked the venom out like Manga used to. Manga would suck and spit the venom out, if the poison had spread too far. Though Bhujangaiah wished to follow suit his caste would come in the way. How could he who was of upper caste put his lips to the leg of a victim to remove venom if he were of low caste? Even if he were to do so would the others of his caste in the village let him rest in peace?

Once, when Bhujangaiah had absconded from home each one in the village had a different story to tell. If one said that he had joined the snake charmers, another believed that he had gone off with the marionette troupe that visited the village. That worthy had asserted he had spied Bhujangaiah with a woman of the troupe in the garden behind the shrine of Basappa of the Pond. His mother too believed that someone had cast a spell on her son and lured him away. Though she had visited a number of necromancers to ward off the spell, her son had failed to return by the promised hour. In the end, a person said to be from Kollegala had arrived in the village. He had announced a prize of Rs.100/- to anyone who challenged him. That had attracted a man from Kote who belonged to the Kadu Kuruba tribe. The Kadu Kuruba was accompanied by his wife. The stage was set up in front of the village office. On either side of the stage the villagers erected a trellis of beech leaves. The shepherd succeeded in removing one after another all the spells cast by the man from Kollegala. People not only from Madalli but also from nearby villages had poured into the village. They had climbed on to the roofs of the houses in search of vantage points. In the end, there was but a final spell that the sorcerer from Kollegala was left with. It was to break a coconut with a machete. The sorcerer announced victoriously that should the coconut be broken the head of the shepherd too would split. The crowd had their testicles knocking. The shepherd squatted in the center of the stage ready for such an eventuality too! His wife brought a black blanket and covered her husband with it. She drew a circle around him with the bone of a human hand, which she held. She then drew with the same bone a wider circle around the enchanted coconut placed by the sorcerer from Kollegala. She now invited him to exhibit his magical powers. The sorcerer drew blood from his palm and made an offering to his personal deity consecrated in front of the trellis. But, for all his efforts, he could not enter the circle. He offered blood once more to his deity. Though he could now break into the circle he could hardly lift the machete to break the coconut. However, each time he brought down the machete the coconut would shift. Finally, the sorcerer who failed in his attempts directed his baleful gaze at the shepherd's wife. She went and removed the blanket covering her husband. The shepherd stood up and announced that he would give up his wife if the sorcerer could get out of the circle drawn by his wife. Everybody was filled with great excitement at that. The sorcerer's companion tried his best to extricate him futilely, The sorcerer sank foaming at his mouth inside the circle. He screamed, complaining of a burning sensation. The helper ran to the shepherd's wife and fell at her feet begging her to save his master. She then erased the circle. The sorcerer stood up, accepted defeat, presented the shepherd the prize money, which he had announced in front of everybody and left the village at once. The villagers greeted the Kuruba with awe and respect.

Bhujangaiah's mother believed that her son returned to the village thanks only to the Kuruba's magical prowess. On the very evening of sorcery, Bhujangaiah's father invited the Kuruba home, in deference to his wife's wish, and told him of his son's leaving them. The Kuruba had assured that he would perform a ritual in the woods outside the village, a week after which their son was certain to return from wherever he was. The couple had spent every moment of that week in anxiety after the shepherd had left sacrificing a black ram and performing a complex ritual. On the last night of the promised week when they opened the door on hearing a knock they had found their son standing as tall as the door. The mother wept embracing her son who seemed to have been cast in self-determination. The son too had promised his mother he would never ever leave the house again and had stuck to his words. That was a long while ago. But that night was imprinted strongly in the eye of memory.

After that incident the villagers attributed all that he did to what he had learnt when he ran away. The villagers never tired of recounting the story of the sorcerer's defeat. Having heard the tale so very often, Bhujangaiah had almost begun to experience the event unfolding in front of his eyes, though he refused to share the mother's belief that his return was due to the magical powers of the Kuruba. The reason for his unavoidable return was different altogether. He couldn't divulge it to anyone. The memory of that incident would throw his body and mind into confusion. That memory was for him both an indescribable pleasure and a nightmare. The event was as significant for him as the sorcery was for his village folk. He should have left Mysore on the very day of the incident. But not knowing where to go his mind had rambled like a mangy dog to finally hide in the very hotel, where he had sought shelter when he had left home. Yet there was an indescribable anxiety. Within a day or two a person had seen him from his village and when told by him to return home Bhujangaiah had obeyed without a word.

Though he had started a hotel and was old enough now, with that incident too growing less intense in its force, it still bothered him every time he visited Mysore. He could not, even now, dare visit the ward of the city where the bungalow stood. Today, at the very sight of Sushila he suddenly was reminded of that incident. Bhujangaiah went home to celebrate the Saturday of Shravana wondering how strange it all was. He would bathe, perform a special prayer and eat a meal cooked exclusively for him at home, This was a custom observed from the time of his great grandfather.

***

CHAPTER - 9

Bhujangaiah's wilting life, caught in the battle for bare necessities, had begun to take on a new dimension. Though he was yet to be considered a man of consequence in the eyes of Madalli, a few envious members of the village ridiculed him, "He has found fortune washing dirty plates." The hallmark of Madalli was that whoever was affluent was also considered the wisest. All contentions in the village had to be resolved in their presence. None dared cross the line drawn by the rich. There were half a dozen such rich men in the village, and each had a history behind his affluence. Yet, there were amongst them one or two such as Karigowda who had remained respectable from the very outset without causing any one trouble. Others like Patel Rudrappa, Chairman Mudappa, Kempegowda of the Lower House and Eregowda had come into property through their criminal ways and ruled the village. They were either at the law courts or at the revenue offices every day at dawn fleecing all who approached them while pretending to be veritable Dharmarayas in their speech. The poor people of the Madiga community, who had borrowed some little money from them when they could find nothing to eat, had lost whatever little ancestral land they held, caught in the whirlpool of compounding interest. They were now slaving away like oxen, never enjoying the joys of a single festival throughout the year, believing that slavery was what God had writ on their forehead.

Such affluent people would wait like the proverbial crane for some poor person to commit the smallest of mistakes to finish him off. No one in the village had the guts to question them about their misdeeds. Once when Bhujangaiah stood up to question in the assembled court, Sannappa, the rich man had brayed like an ass, "Hey, sit down! Are you a noble man to deliver judgment? If people who wash dirty plates start delivering justice should we then merely sit here and shave pubic hair?"

The other crooks too had supported Sannappa and had insulted Bhujangaiah to his face. The ember that had touched his dignity to the quick that day was still smoldering. Though he was needed for all the "Para" and festivals that were performed in the village, why was he not required to decide on what was right in the village? Though he could speak with intelligence, in a more balanced manner than others, why didn't they give him an opportunity? Though there were many who had assembled there why even one of them didn't stand up to speak for him? What was the conspiracy behind all that? Bhujangaiah's mind was preoccupied with such questions. Once, when he had confessed to it to Sannaputtappa, who was both an elder and a venerable man, that man had revealed his helplessness, "what you say is true, But son, the times belong to them, why should you box the air and sprain your fist? Children of the poor should live by their fate."

Though he hadn't bothered to interfere in the adjudications of the village from then on the confidence that the days were not too far off when he would be asked to sit at those judgments grew stronger after he started the hotel business. He had grown wise to the harsh reality of money buying everything in Madalli. His resolve to make enough fortune was spurred by the steadily increasing clientele. The fact that the Swami of the Main Mutt had accepted Bhujangaiah's invitation and would visit Madalli had not only gladdened the caste people but had also spurred the envy of many. He was to visit on the second Monday of the month of Bhadrapada, between September and October, after the Ganesha festival. The Swami whom he had met thanks to Cedimari's influence had acquiesced to his desire and had granted his wish. Cennamalla and Pundri who were close to Bhujangaiah had spoken of the visit at least ten times at every home in the Lingayat street and extended the invitation. Except for a few, all others in the village counted the days when the great Swami would arrive on a rare visit, so that they too could be absolved by the wash of his holy feet. Patel Rudrappa was irked when he learnt that the Swami was visiting at the behest of Bhujangaiah. The previous year when his father had died the Swami had refused to be present on the eleventh day, in spite of his inviting him thrice, wishing to perform the holy ritual in his divine presence. Now, did the Guru value the words of Bhujangaiah who, till recently, roamed about like a vagrant water carrier? Or, was it all Bhujangaiah's exaggeration?

Though there were still several days for the visit Bhujangaiah busied himself with preparations as if the Guru were arriving the next morning, not bothering about what people said. He got the main temple of Basaveshwara and especially the shrine of Basappa of the Pond white washed at his own expense, in deference to his wife's wishes. That act confirmed the event to those who as yet entertained some doubt. They requested Bhujangaiah to bring the Swamiji to their house for the worship of his holy feet. Rudrappa saw red at this. Bhujangaiah began sprucing up his house as though a momentous event of historical significance was about to transpire. Dasappa the mason estimated at two cartloads of lime to have the flooring of cow dung properly mortared. That very day the required amount of lime was procured from Saragur. He did not have to worry about sand as it was the rainy season. He got all the four walls of the house, and the dung firmed floor from the times of his grand father, mortared within the week. It did not cost him even two hundred rupees. The platforms on either side of the front door were painted over by Dasappa's artistry. The villagers were astounded. Not even three months had passed since he started the hotel. Where did he get all that money from? Though Parvathy did not approve of the extravagance of her husband at this particular juncture, she consoled herself as there was still some money left in her trunk from what he had saved. And then, what woman wouldn't like to have her house spruced up? The one worry that constantly nibbled at her mind like the borer insect was whether her father would visit them for the worship of the Swami's holy feet. The link with Jakkalli had been severed after the quarrel with her husband that day. Parvathi had waited for a moment when her husband was in an expansive mood and said, “Whatever happened did so at a poisoned moment, please go to Jakkalli personally and invite everybody.” Bhujangaiah had refused as intractably as breaking a stick. Finally, when Parvathy had wept saying, “If you are vengeful in god’s work it will never do us good.” Bhujangaiah mellowed a little and asked Parvathy to visit Jakkalli with the children. Parvathy left for Jakkalli a week before the visit of the Swami and after much beseeching with her father prevailed upon him to return with her mother and younger sister, Chinnamma. Moments before they left for Madalli thanks to some god who must have changed his mind her father had given one hundred rupees to Parvathy as his offering for the occasion and had volunteered, “I will try to come on the day of the worship if I find time.” Parvathy had hesitated to tell her husband of the money, but finally had given it to him so that he learnt of her father’s generosity. Bhujangaiah would perhaps have uttered something perverse if his in-laws were not around. He silently slipped the money into his pocket for now.

It was a week after Sravana. The month had brought happiness to the village. Bhadrapada too had stepped in with the arrogance of thunder and rain. But it would rain heavily though intermittently, with the sun emerging occasionally, thus not proving a bother. The cattle of Madalli that had grown emaciated, without proper feed, now grazed well enough to fill their famished bellies. People were busy sowing subsidary grains, manuring, ploughing and preparing the rice fields for transplanting as the pond had already brimmed to the full. Bhujangaiah too was busy cultivating his fields not ignoring even a single plot of it, whatever his other preoccupations were. The resolve to raise a better crop than others had not weakened. His mother stayed the whole day at the field with precise instructions to Amase to do what had to be done at the proper time. With the work on the ragi fields taken care of, the crop now stood dark. The chilly and castor planted on a spare acre too had yielded rich. By evening the heavy clouds of Bhadrapada would envelope the sky scaring the villagers and when the village grew dark with night there would be the sudden onslaught of rain in a cloud burst accompanied by thunder and lightning. Who knew from where such clouds arrive? It was a matter of immense wonder for the villagers.

Come morning, the sunrays would start raining like gold gilting the green treasure of the village, brimming Madalli time and again with the joy of life. Though most of them lived on a single meal, the thought of future days of happiness made them go about with a pleasant countenance borrowing from the affluent to eat well. The village had pawnbrokers too. At such times, the loan sharks were generous with their loans without taking up issues with their debtors. The poor people, emaciated, had no thoughts of tomorrow. They would suffer only on the day when the major portion of their crop for which they had laboured day and night would be adjusted towards the interest owed to the loan sharks. Till then they were not worried. However good the harvest, their situation did not change for the better. Who knows when they would witness the times that would yield the proper fruits of their labour?

Bhujangaiah sitting in his hotel began to assign his close friends various responsibilities to be shouldered on the day of the Swami's visit. He requested guard Nagaraja to go to Hosahalli to engage the band to play in the procession welcoming the Swami with horns and trumpets. Pundri volunteered to organize the erection of a trellis at the entrance to the village. Cannamalla anxiously waited for Bhujangaiah to assign him some task. When he was asked to manage the kitchen with Kariappa for the Feast of the Followers, the ganas, he felt let down. For, it meant he couldn't stir out of the kitchen from the moment the Guru arrived till the function was over. He had wished to drive the processional cart, which was to carry the Swami. By Bhujangaiah's estimate, the expense to be incurred on the Feast of the Ganas was more crucial than any other. He had to merely hint at it and people would compete to provide. But he could not bring himself to do so. As he did not have that much stock, he wondered whom to ask. Finally, he thought of Karigowda who had never said no to him and emerged from the hotel.

The Feast of the Ganas and Dasoha, the holy meal, had to be organized meticulously. Bhujangaiah who walked towards the village discussing with Kariappa what he may need allowed his gaze to take in all he could see. Mother Earth was smiling, swathed in a rich green sari. Gowda wouldn't refuse if he promised to return what he borrowed by next harvest. Even he wouldn't find it hard to pay back at the harvest. He should borrow on the higher side. If it did not rain, people from the near by villages could be expected to arrive in hordes. If the victuals were not distributed properly all his efforts would come to waste. This occasion by itself was enough to instil an attitude of respect towards him among his caste in the village as well as in the neighbouring villages. He decided not to cut corners when putting his hand to such a mammoth task. He was unhappy that Ajappa his well-wisher was not in the village at such an important moment.

The sky was placid. The clouds floated in places like silver foam. The goddess of vegetation, darkly green, shone enchantingly and filled Bhujangaiah's mind with a pleasant sensation. Bhujangaiah who had vowed to make offerings to God if it did not rain on that day till after the Swami's visit, remembered people saying that he had great powers and grew calm consoling himself that if the Swami minded no such disaster would take place. When he met a few persons like Sannaputtappa who were dignified and did not know what prevarication was, and requested them to perform properly and ritualistically all the events of that day, they gladly agreed believing that it was because of Hulikanthyappa's blessings that they were chosen for such an august task. Though astounded for a moment by his virtue, they judged that it was unlike what they had thought and that he truly deserved. From that very day they too were prepared to lend whatever help they could in welcoming the Swami. Madalli began to take on a festive atmosphere. It was the first visit after the Swami ascended the seat. His predecessor, the Guru who had merged with the Linga, had paid a visit once so long ago that its memory was faint among the people. But when that Swami surrendered to God, in the flood of devotees that had flowed to the Holy Mutt the people from Madalli too were present. They had seen the heir apparent that day. They had surrendered to the new Guru's eminence when they had visited the mutt again on the occasion of his anointment, which ceremony had taken place in the grand manner befitting the status of the mutt. It was no common event that the swami who had come to power in such a grand manner was visiting their insignificant hamlet! However, the preparations for the religious event that was about to take place, in a week's time, began infusing the static life of Madalli with a new spirit.

The Tampura Ayya of Hampapura who visited Bhujangaiah's hotel was overjoyed when he learnt of the visit of the great Swami of the Main Mutt, especially on the invitation of Bhujangaiah, whom he held dear. Ayya who visited the holy mutt once every three months never got tired of extolling its greatness. The daily distribution of food for the devotees was a miracle in itself. Ayya found it a great mystery, the source of rations for the mutt to cook such large meals every day, throughout the year. He having extolled the mutt began to sing the verses of the Wisdom of Eternity to the tune of Tampura. Bhujangaiah was not at the hotel then. Among the customers present were the bangle merchant and his daughter Sushila. On hearing the mellifluous voice of Ayya those who wished to leave also sat down again. The meaning of his songs touched the listeners to the core.

Ajappa, titled harlequin, who wished from the purest of his being the success of Bhujangaiah, learnt of his eminent disciple's recent adventure only when he boarded the bus at Mysore. While traveling on his liquor business some divine intervention had brought a change of heart in him. He had impulsively continued on a pilgrimage to Basavana Bagewadi, Srishyla, etc., in the very clothes he was wearing. His wife and children did not have to worry because he had sent words through an acquaintance about his change of plans. Now, there was this auspicious tiding as he returned at the right time. He went in search of Bhujangaiah, talked to him, and decided to hold the worship of his holy feet at his house too. His starting the liquor business was a crime ten times more heinous than Bhujangaiah opening the hotel, in the eyes of the villagers.

Most of the families in the village looked down upon them, bringing tears to his wife's eyes. Realizing that this was an opportunity to redeem himself from the low esteem of the villagers by earning the merciful blessings of the Swami with Bhujangaiah, he volunteered to bear half the expenses of food. The two friends grew busy refusing to relax even for a moment.

***

CHAPTER - 10

Sri Sri of the Main Mutt visited such an insignificant village as Madalli in deference to Bhujangaiah's wishes. He purified it with the dust of his holy feet, graced the populace with his presence fulfilling its long cherished desire, spending the entire day shriving the disciples with the wash of his holy feet, blessing every body, including children and women. He finally visited Bhujangaiah's hotel before leaving, blessing him in his novel endeavour. Everyone, including Parvathappa of Jakkalli, the father-in-law, who had belittled him because of his starting the hotel business, was filled with wonder. A big crowd had assembled to see the Swami off in front of the hotel. The Swami was to return to Mysore by the evening bus. Bhujangaiah fell at his feet, boarded the bus ahead of everyone and got an entire row of seats vacated for the Swami. He spread on the seat the deer skin which he had procured through Beard of Kyatanahalli a week ago, touched the Guru's feet once again after the latter sat down, received his blessings, and joined his voice to the chorus of praise shouted by the crowd, as he got off the bus.

The visit of the Swami to Madalli was like the floods having come and receded. Even after a week everyone spoke of the visit. What an extraordinary splendor! The measured gait, the calm countenance, the gaze pregnant with something inscrutable ! Bhujangaiah, though for a day, was deeply affected by the proximity of the Swami. He was absorbed by the gestures and gait of the Swami from the moment he had entered the village, as though he were drawn by a great force. His eyes held the images of the Swami's walk, his speech, his gaze, his posture, his majestic excellence and his composure. What really impressed him most was the Swami's address. As he listened to the discourse on sorrows that result from hatred and desire, he was filled with a righteous disgust. The Swami had pointed the way out. True, the corporeal body subject to the tongue that tasted salt and vinegar forced one into wrong doings. But if one did not exert control on the body how was one different from beasts? The Swami's utterances were as precious as pearls. Bhujangaiah had grown meditative as long as he was in that august presence. He had taken care to assign various tasks to his friends, which they had seen through admirably without a hitch during the Swami's visit. Once all relatives and friends had left it was decided that Parvathy need not visit her parents for her pregnancy. Instead her sister Chinnamma was requested to stay back to help her.

Bhujangaiah's mother was once more filled with vigor having met all her relatives on the pretext of the Swami's visit. Though glad to be free again, having finished his tasks, the very depth of Bhujangaiah's conscience was disturbed by the Swami's words. He was preoccupied, as he sat for a meal with his children. The mirror which the Swami held upto them had reflected his wish to be a person of consequence, the momentary distraction at the sight of the bangle merchant's daughter, Sushila, his impatience when people spoke touching him to the quick. Bhujangaiah felt humiliated. He should henceforth never live his life vainly in an unintelligent manner. How many were the problems he had to face when he had run away from home? Bhujangaiah suddenly felt an ache in his heart and grew scared. Parvathy was surprised at her husband's silence. There were times when her husband sat in confusion thus. He would be oblivious even though the very rafter was to collapse on his head. But she could not put up with this silence of his. Lovingly she admonished him. Bhujangaiah went through his meal as if he woke up suddenly, threw a blanket over his shoulder, and walked towards the hotel clutching a torch. When he reached the path beyond the village, there was not a flicker of light any where. Though the clouds had gathered like herds of elephants, there was still a star or two twinkling from afar. The ceaseless flow of the noisome cicada assailed the ears. Bhujangaiah recalled how he had caught one of the cicadas when a child. How strange! Would it never grow short of breath making such incessant noise? None had provided him with an answer though the constant drone of the insect seemed to attempt to convey something significant to him.

Bhujangaiah almost stumbled as he entered the hotel when he saw those who sat in the light of the petromax lamp, It was the merchant and his daughter. Sabi of the whip, and Nazir, his servant who had begun to frequent his hotel were seated in the corner next to the door. Though Bhujangaiah's hotel was a "snack" room, it would also turn into a "meal house" for those who arrived late at night. Manja cooked *rice* and *saru*, the yellow lentil gruel for himself and Shiva. He cooked for others too if someone happened to arrive, His kitchen duties were unfinished as yet. The petromax lamp had dimmed. Bhujangaiah took it down to stoke. Soon it began to burn bright and noisily, Sushila watched Bhujangaiah intently. He appeared disinterested. He began to converse casually with the merchant after lighting a beedi. In spite of all his efforts his mind seemed to weaken. It desired to watch what it should not. It seemed as though this woman had suddenly descended from somewhere in order to test his resolve. Why did he have to return from home? Bhujangaiah stepped into the kitchen as though he recalled something and spoke to Manja. He wondered why his friends had not arrived yet. It would do if that good for nothing Pundri did not turn up. He came with a hundred tales ensnared in his black blanket. Pundri too had heard the Swami from the front row that day. Presuming that even he would have been similarly affected, Bhujangaiah ordered, "Manja, hurry up and serve them some food." He went out and spoke to the merchant, "where will you sleep tonight?" The merchant replied that he would rest at Karigowda's as usual. The wife of Gowda invariably forced him to eat there. But the merchant found it embarrassing to do so every time, but on rare occasions accepted a meal and slept on their *jagali*. He praised the generosity of Gowda's wife. Bhujangaiah recalled that his wife too had on many an occasion praised Kalavva. Manja spread the leaves and served food for the four customers who waited. Bhujangaiah, considerate of Sushila's diffidence in having to eat in his presence, got up and went into the shop front. Shiva lit the tall glass lamp, which was meant for the hotel at first. There was enough light in the room. There were a couple of calendars on the wall of what was Bhujangaiah's private quarter for the time being. One of them was of some film actress. He now grew uncomfortable with guilt looking at the half-nude picture of the woman. He should take it down in the morning. Pundri had smacked his lips describing every little detail of the picture the very day he had seen it. What was strange, Pundri who talked so much about sex had never touched another woman in his life. As the merchant made ready to leave, Bhujangaiah handed him a torch sounding a warning against the darkness outside. The merchant who left with his daughter warned her to remind him to fetch a torch the next time, Sushila murmured in assent as she briefly stopped at her father's back to throw a backward glance. Bhujangaiah standing as if to watch them leave felt foolish and guiltily turned back in haste to enter the hotel. Soon enough Pundri and his company arrived conversing loudly. Bhujangaiah had already permitted Sabi of the whip and his servant to sleep at the hotel. Pundri's crowd had not arrived empty handed. They had brought a big jackfruit. Pundri, who saw Kendaganna standing still, thin as a stick carrying the fruit, ordered Kariyapppa, "Hey, adiya, help him lift the fruit down." Kariya the adiya, the tribal from the plains, after helping Kendaganna, asked Shiva to fetch a knife and a cup of oil as he squatted down to cut open the fruit. Pundri quietly observed, "Who knows where this son of a widow had been. He had said he wouldn't come here today. I don't know how he sniffed out the fruit. He has arrived like a wild dog!" He started guffawing in his characteristic manner. Kariyappa was older than Pundri. He had already performed his daughter's marriage. His son too had come of age and now taking care of cultivation. Only, Kariyappa had not outgrown his prankish nature. Pundri watching the manner in which Kenda and Nagaraja were separating the fruit from the rind said, "Thu, you are squeezing it like babies squeeze shit." He took a portion of the fruit and demonstrated how to do the job delicately even as he abused them " Watch! You children of a widow." Kenda complained in good humor against his friend and teacher, "Unless you find fault with a job however well done it may be, you cannot digest your food. You are a pest!" Whether he wished to or not Bhujangaiah too was forced to eat the fruit. The entire hotel was filled with the fragrance of the fruit. After everybody had eaten, Urupa tidied the place up where the fruit was cut. He had polished off more of the fruit than anyone else. He hadn't returned for a long time after having left with a burp. When Manja called out to Urupa, Pundri himself had answered, "Where will he be? He ran in a hurry to empty his bowels". Kariyappa was still busy trying to wash off the sticky milk of the fruit from his hands. Bhujangaiah sat leaning against the wall with legs out stretched. Pundri, who wouldn't allow anyone to sleep began to bluster as if he couldn't rest without gossiping about the village, especially about the Swami's visit. He had not yet finished talking about it. Pundri had keenly observed the Swami during the entire visit. When the Swami left Ajappa's house after the worship of his feet, and had walked past the bush he had accidentally stepped on shit. Though others too like Pundri had noticed it they hadn't spoken out of trepidation. Just before the Swami visited the next house, Pundri had stopped him and had poured a large vessel of water on his feet, It was only then that the Swami too had realized that he had stepped on shit, the stench of which had now risen to the nostrils. Pundri had subtly observed that the Swami too had crinkled his nose in disgust. Before the worship of the feet at that house, the Swami had insisted on going to the bathroom to soap his feet and wash. None of his disciples had observed it very closely. The picture had been etched in Pundri's retina. Only Pundri had not touched even a drop of the holy wash from that house. Inexplicably the jackfruit smell had reminded Pundri of that incident. Even Bhujangaiah couldn't help laughing as he listened to Pundri's tale. He experienced a lightness of being even as he laughed unrestrained. Pundri in the meanwhile felt an urgent need to recount another incident. It involved Puttabasavi who had a regular affair with an elder of irrefutable reputation in the village. He had felt like laughing at the sight of her pumpkin like breasts when she had touched the feet of the Swami like a great woman of virtue, with her forehead smeared with vermillion, and her torso covered by the *seragu* of her sari. As he recounted how he had secretly laughed to himself, Urupa had run out of the hotel fearing Bhujangaiah's ire, unable to check his laughter. How low could Pundri get? Though Bhujangaiah thought of him as the most dastardly of rascals for having thought of such things in the presence of the Swami, he could not prevent himself from laughing. "Hey, Pundri, what a lousy son of a bitch you are!" He had answered, "Do I lie? Should 1 hide things because Puttabasavi is of my caste?" Who in the village does not know her lifting her legs indiscriminately to the aged as well as to the young?" He had challenged Bhujangaiah.

The effect of the Swami's preaching which had troubled his mind since supper slowly diminished and he realized that Pundri was time and again digging up and encouraging the desires which he had pushed deep down. He wondered if he would ever be free of Pundri's association.

***

CHAPTER - 11

As was guessed Ajappa and Bhujangaiah had not heard a single jibe about their professions after the Universal Mentor's visit to Madalli. But that did not preclude fools who talked behind their back. Patel Rudrappa alone had venomously uttered in front of a few, "whatever you may say, the present Swami has not got the austerity of his predecessor. What a stern person he was! He wouldn't brook the smallest of offence against dharma. But this one visited a liquor vendor today. Tomorrow he may very well visit the house of Racha the cobbler." But his talk made no impact on anybody in the village. For every one believed that even to think lightly, let alone speak thus, of their mutt was a great sin.

As days went by, with improving business, one after another vices too began to find room in Bhujangaiah. He furnished his hotel better. He got made tables for the hotel, a chair and a cot for himself in the shop room from the Jack tree that Beard of Kyatanahalli had chosen for him. The room was a shop only in name and was never commissioned. If enquired, Bhujangaiah would reply that he was not interested in opening the shop as the business from the hotel was good and managing the shop was a problem. His two vices were reading the daily "Tainadu" and playing cards. Forester Rajappa of the Madalli Forest Gate, the bangle merchant, Sabi , who dealt in cattle, and Singri the lame, who would come from Kyatanahalli, were the other card players. As the game was played in the shop room it did not affect the hotel business. It was Victor who introduced Bhujangaiah to the habit of reading the newspaper. Though they played Rummy invariably, occasionally they tried a hand at a game of three cards too. Bhujangaiah, who had heard of people losing all they owned because of the game seldom allowed it to be played. Sushila was the one person unhappy because of her father neglecting his business. Though many a times, she decided never to step towards the hotel something forced her to accompany her father without so much as a murmur of protest. There was an added novelty in Bhujangaiah's hotel now. It was a gramophone that he had bought to entertain the customers. Manja was in love with it. He had learnt all the songs. He had also begun to throw glances at Sushila who too enjoyed music. She did not take kindly to his staring at her like an animal, She showed her displeasure towards Manja by pointedly asking Shiva for whatever she needed. But an unfazed Manja would himself do whatever it was she asked Shiva for. Thus, the hotel which caught the scent of a female only in the tales of Pundri, began to quicken to the touch of a woman on Sushila's occasional visits.

Bhujangaiah had taken to staying long hours at the hotel now. His wife had delivered a baby boy. Her mother had arrived to nurse her. At times Bhujangaiah had both lunch and supper brought from home to the hotel. As expected the North East monsoon had served well this year. The rice fields below the pond swayed festively with heavy ears. The crop in Bhujangaiah's field was better than in all others. He had used a sack of fertilizer from Mysore. The villagers expected him to harvest in half an acre what others harvested in one acre. Ragi, chili and corn too had yielded well. Bhujangaiah's mother summoned him one day and took him to task for sitting at the hotel all the time neglecting mother earth. A recalcitrant Bhujangaiah without as much as a word left for the fields to inspect. Chinnamma, who had carried the baby out for her brother-in-law to see and to take delight in, turned back disappointed when she saw him leaving without stopping even for a moment. After the child was born, Bhujangaiah had visited the narrow room only a couple of times to look at as yet an indistinctly formed child, in the lamp light. He couldn't bear the acrid smell of the post-partum room. They had seen to it in that cloistered room light did not seep through either the window or even the tiles.

The cane cradle at home had been woven for his first child. It had reared two children and was rocking the third now. The child had not been named yet. Chinnamma, his sister-in-law had apparently suggested one. But it wasn't what they could call the child by. As they were devotees of Shiva, it was imperative that the name was an attribute of Shiva. The gowdas had no such qualms. They could name their children either after Shiva or after Vishnu. Bhujangaiah chose a name wondering about the pointless restrictions of his community. It was both an attribute of God and novel too. He decided to tell his sister-in-law of his choice after going round his fields once.

Ragi would be ready for harvest soon. In the chili field too the crop was turning red. The castor had grown luxuriantly and it hung in bunches. Bhujangaiah surmised that they'd have enough oil to last for the next four years. He walked towards the pond. It was brimming. If only the great mother water would always bless thus, Madalli too would for ever enjoy good harvest. He could get two harvests a year in his half an acre alone and eat comfortably through the year. Bhujangaiah now wished to buy the half acre of rice fields owned by the village clerk, adjacent to his. The village clerk possessed on the other side of the pond, next to the vent, a couple of acres of rice field. However, his cultivation was not anything to talk about. He should find out.

Bhujangaiah walked acrobatically on the bunds of the rice field. The crabs slithered away splashing into the water at his approach. He recollected how he used to catch them with a forked stick and tease them under the russet blossomed Neep tree upon the banks of the pond. When the crab caught hold of the stick with its pincers he would lift the stick high and the crab would fall with a splash. When it fell on its back, he would lift its shell to witness the innumerable young ones. Cheluva the Madiga called it *Gunguru*. He would roast it on fire and eat it smacking his lips all the while saying that it tasted like butter. He would tease Bhujangaiah singing,

"The Silver at dawn,
The crab on the bund,
Your wife is innocent,
Hold her tight,
Or you can't catch the thief!"

The tragedy was that Cheluva, who was of his age, had separated from his wife who was living with another man in Thippur. Cheluva had married again. There were many changes in the village since his childhood. A cool breeze began to waft across. The rice fields ready for harvest bent their heads as if they were saluting Mother Earth. Suddenly there were a variety of bird songs emanating from afar. As he began to walk towards the village, after washing his limbs in the pond, Bhujangaiah saw Karigowda approach.

Karigowda owned a large property. It was a single plot of thirty acres. If it rained well it would yield hundreds of tons of ragi and jowar even if the seeds were strewn with the left hand. He had three sons, all of whom were married. Narayana was the last. The villagers opined he was no fit son for Karigowda. Gowda had got him married out of fear that he might take to wrong ways. One of Karigowda's brothers lived in Muddaiana Hundi which was on the other side of the pond of Madalli. The Hundi was a small hamlet. It had eight or ten homes. Karigowda had large holdings there too which was enjoyed by his younger bother, Muddegowda. He was named after their grandfather. Because it was he who built the first house there, the place came to be called Muddaiana Hundi. All of them were gowdas at the Hundi. Each one of them was rich. If in Madalli it was Karigowda's house that was known for generosity and morality, in Hundi it was Muddegowda's house. His wife Puttavva was a veritable goddess of kindness. None had returned empty handed from her. During famine, even the Lingayat children went to her house for food, unknown to their elders. Bhujangaiah never approached his own caste, whatever his trouble was. He went straight to Hundi and got whatever he needed from Puttavva whether Gowda was present or not. He had never returned without drinking a brass tumbler of milk.

When Bhujangaiah had said he would pay back the grocery borrowed from Karigowda for the Swami's visit soon after harvest, Karigowda had gently rebuked, "What is this Bhujangaiah? Did I ask you for it? Have you got plenty to give me?" He had enquired after his business. When Bhujangarah confided that he had little money left, Karigowda had advised, "Look, times will not be the same ever. Whoever knows when Goddess Lakshmi visits and when she leaves? Buy some property when you have some money." When Bhujangaiah immediately broached the issue of the village clerk's field he promised, "Wait, I'Il personally find out from him." Bhujangaiah recalled how his own people were enemies of his good fortune as he mulled over the good advice of Karigowda. As there was much time for sunset, Gowda invited him, "Come if you are free. We shall see how well our Hundi fields are cultivated." Bhujangaiah accompanied Gowda without saying a word even though the temptation of the game of cards drew him.

Unlike those of Madalli the fields of Hundi were mostly in the valley. As everyone possessed cattle, apart from milk, people had enough manure for their fields, the year round. As they entered the village half a dozen dogs began barking. Because of them, strangers were scared of setting foot in the village. Though they tucked their tails at Karigowda's voice they hesitantly barked at the unfamiliar scent of Bhujangaiah. At the sight of Karigowda, the women sitting on the *jagali* of the house got up at once. When they approached the house of Muddegowda, Puttavva who sat sifting ragi with the maids stood up, welcomed and said she would heat up the milk. Bhujangaiah replied that he would first visit the fields and then return to drink the milk before leaving.

Theirs was the last house in Hundi. The field stretched into the distance beyond. Bhujangaiah felt that compared to these, the crops of his village were nothing. The Ragi fields were in plentitude. The rows of sesame bloomed with golden flowers. One couldn't get tired of watching. How rich the crop! The crop stood filling the farmers with confidence, promising it would take care of Hundi though the entire country may reel under famine. Before the duo could go half way round the spread, the sun had dipped behind Andanamallappa Hill. They returned knowing they wouldn't be able to complete their inspection. When Karigowda enquired "Where is your Gowda?" having met the servant Nanja on the way, the later had replied, "He has gone to the rice fields near the pond of Pura, Gowda." The entire acreage below that pond belonged to the cousins of Gowda. When asked, "How's the paddy there?" Nanja answered enthusiastically, "Such yield has not been seen in our neighborhood. It dazzles the eye as one gazes."

When they returned to Hundi. Muddegowda too had arrived. The milch cows and buffaloes were tethered in a line in front of the house while the bullocks were hitched to the pillars of the platform. Recently bought at the Chunchankatte fair, they sparkled silvery like a rupee coin. Two servants were busy feeding them with the jowar stalk. Muddegowda came to his feet at the sight of his elder brother and Bhujangaiah approaching and asked them to sit on the mat. Puttavva who knew of their visit had already swept the platform and spread the mat. There were only two boys who went to the school in Kyatanahalli from Hundi. They were Puttavva's son Raja who was already in the eighth standard and Thammanna the son of their cousin Boregowda. Raja who had already returned from school brought milk for his uncle and Bhujangaiah. Bhujangaiah asked, "What class Raja?" Raja replied, "Eighth, brother" "But you haven't shown your face even once at our hotel!" Bhujangaiah now turned towards Karigowda, "If the road can be repaired some how we can have the bus run upto Kyatanahalli. It'll save the school children from walking everyday." Gowda sipped his milk noisily saying, "Whatever needs to be done has to be done by Kyatanahalli."

Bhujangaiah entered the house after drinking his milk. Puttavva asked him to sit on the cot on the verandah and enquired after Parvathi. She said, "I haven't had time to come to Madalli. I must visit once at least to see the child. Our Raja says your hotel is doing grand business." Bhujangaiah answered humbly, "It's all because of your....." Before he could complete Puttavva said, "God shall bless when the time is ripe. It is enough if one has gratitude.

By the way, I hear that Raja's teacher frequents your 'otlu. Please ask him to look after our Raja," Even as Bhujangaiah got ready to leave, a servant brought from the backyard some drumstick leaves and a fan full of aubergene which Puttavva packed in a bag and handed over to Bhujangaiah.

Bhujangaiah's heart brimmed over. He hadn't been used to such affection. Mother never ever sent him empty handed. For all that, he neither belonged to their class nor to their caste. They never needed his help. Moreover he was not even an important person. And yet why such concern? Puttavva was kind hearted. If there were mothers like her who all the time wish for the village's prosperity no famine would ever afflict them. It was because such truth and dharma had grown rare that people suffered, caught in the grip of famine every other year. Bhujangaiah's eyes brimmed with tears as his soul was overcome with emotion. As he emerged with the bag Gowda too rose to leave. Both reached Madalli discussing the rain and the harvest.

Deviravva was glad that her son had visited Hundi after visiting the fields. She knew that over there both Muddegowda and Puttavva would have advised him to pay good attention to cultivation. She had talked to Muddegowda about her son when she met him near the pond the day before. Because Bhujangaiah was with his brother Muddegowda had desisted from advising. Though Bhujangaiah had walked so much he had not forgotten about the naming of the child. He called his sister-in-law and whispered in her ears the name he preferred. Chinnamma too had liked the name. She immediately advertised to everyone that the child had been named Umashankara. Parvathy too found the name endearing. But Bhujangaiah's mother was disappointed. She had wished to name the child after his grandfather. Bhujangaiah, on seeing his mother's lack of response, tried to console her. "Mother, this too is the name of your Hulikanthyappa." The old woman retorted with impatience, "I do not know what would have gone wrong, if you had named the child Madappa." Chinnamma immediately said, "Who names a child Madappa these days grandmother?" The old woman was a little irritated. Her husband's name too was Madappa. Bhujangaiah who subtly noticed the twinge of pain on his mother's face tried changing the subject, " It's all right. The child has been named something now. Come let's all sit down for supper," When Chinnamma said they should have a naming ceremony for the child, Bhujangaiah could find nothing wrong with it. But, Parvathy did not agree to that. While no one in the village observed such ceremonies, they themselves had not done so for the first two children. Parvathy was scared of festivals. It meant expenses. Added to it was the jealousy of people. They would not rest without saying, "A beggar grown suddenly affluent will open the parasol under the full moon." Bhujangaiah's mother too thought it improper when Parvathy opined that such extravagance was not for them. Bhujangaiah left for the hotel as soon as he finished his meal. He had not touched cards since that afternoon. A game was in progress for the past three four days without a break. Day by day the game grew intense. Apart from the regulars, night would bring a few others too. The middle school teachers of Kyatanahalli were addicted to the game. What a strange game it was that involved them so much throughout the night without letting them so much as wink their eyes? What else had such attraction? Bhujangaiah's mind began to ponder intensely about it. When he reached the hotel the game had heated up as expected. They were all engrossed in their game of cards scarcely breathing. The merchant was there but not his daughter. Of late, the merchant had taken to leaving his daughter at Karigowda's home after supper at the hotel before returning to the game in the night. There were times he would sit for a game early and ask Urupa to escort his daughter. Urupa used to perform his task as if it were a sacred duty. He had something or the other to learn from her whom he deferentially addressed, "sister Sushila". It had grown certain to Sushila's mind that her father would never prosper unless he stopped visiting that hotel. Why should she not talk to Bhujangaiah one of these days? What if he said it was none of her business?

***

CHAPTER - 12

Bhujangaiah began to feel the dizzy passage of time, whether he was busy or not. Unlike in the past, when each day was one of anxiety and expectation, wishing under stress for that day to pass, the present had grown sweet filled with new desires unfolding each day. Whatever he saw appeared beautiful. It was an easy and uncomplicated life. But the life that was used to living by labour from childhood found it embarrassing to eat in indolence. Bhujangaiah stopped thinking of the future, consoled in the thought that carrying on business under the shade too was labour. Quite a few of Madalli were his customers and used to ask for credit when they had no money to pay for their snacks. Thus being obliged to him in a way, they readily did whatever he asked for.

That year's agricultural tasks such as harvesting and stacking of hay went on smooth. Though he did not personally oversee any of it, his mother's care had ensured that there was no hitch. Deviramma had reached the conclusion that it was no use talking to her son about cultivation, fed up after her repeated attempts at scolding and advising him. It was fine as long as she were alive, thereafter what? Though Parvathy too was as keen about farming what could she do without a man's support? Deviramma knew she was growing old. She was strong all these years and therefore had laboured. How long could she go on? If once she lay down on the floor her story would end. Though there were many who were of her age in the village none had her resilience. They were all confined to their corners. Even now when she kneeled down for weeding, the villagers watching her race ahead of even the young women would comment in appreciation, "Mother, you are a strong woman". Who had the guts to question her if she should sit back at home today? But she could never do so. She had to go round the fields once a day at least, and clear a few thorny bushes. If not she felt she had failed in her duties. It was a habit grown since she had arrived as the daughter-in-law. How many quintals of ragi had her husband grown on the very same plot! The large granary pit in front of the village court that was allotted to them was never full after his death. It was a joy to open the pit and draw the ragi to transport home every time when he was alive. Where are those events now? What was grown hardly sufficed to fill the bushels at home. If one grew in excess of bare necessity it had to be sold at Mysore to provide for clothing and other imperative. Deviravva's hair had turned gray. Though her skin had creased and folded and old age had ravaged her, her eyes were yet lucent. Though her teeth were blackened brushing with coal dust, they had not yet fallen. The news of her son planning to add half an acre to their existing rice field filled her with happiness. Her husband hadn't bought any new property. The satisfaction that at least their son was doing so had increased her desire to live longer. It was only the day before that Karigowda had given her the news on his way to the fields. When she had complained of her son's disinterest in cultivation she had been greatly surprised by his words, "What are you saying mother? Your son is planning to buy the village clerk's paddy field. I have taken the responsibility of striking the deal," When she enquired about it her son had smiled," Who told you mother?" When Muddegowda of Hundi came looking for Bhujangaiah, the latter was getting Sanjiva to shave him under the tamarind tree. Bhujangaiah couldn't rest without getting a shave at least thrice a week. He was uneasy with stubbles on his chin. Victor shaved everyday without fail. Unless he was indisposed he never even washed his face without a shave. He too should buy a razor. After Sanjiva shaved with his razor one felt the itch. Though he honed his blunt razor on the whetting stone, stropping at least twenty times, it never stopped making a dragging noise. In Mysore, the barber shops were decorated like palaces! If they sat on the revolving seat, they were done shaving before you realized. They applied scented snow and powder after the shave. But Sanjiva, he lathers the beard of a hundred people with a small piece of toilet soap. Though Bhujangaiah began to have reservations every time he sat down for a shave he would soon forget them all. Sanjiva too performed his task for a mere cup of tea and the lentil patties, *vade*. Bhujangaiah who was inspecting himself in a small mirror, which Sanjiva handed him, observed in the reflection Muddegowda approach form behind. He asked Shiva to fetch some water and washed. He served a cup of tea to Muddegowda and sat conversing, sipping tea. When Muddegowda hinted at the private nature of his visit Bhujangaiah took Gowda to the shopfront.

The village clerk had no intentions of selling his land yet. He had not yielded to Karigowda. Karigowda had wondered why he should not get Bhujangaiah the fields of Singari which were adjacent to his own till such time the village clerk grew amenable. Singari had left the village to enter bonded labour in Saragur. Though fertile, his fields were fallow. Because of its proximity to the Gende pond, the soil retained moisture. He had approached Karigowda offering to sell the fields on a couple of occasions. He had not wanted it being content with what he had. Now, when he had sent word thinking it good to have Bhujangaiah for a neighbour, Singari had sat down at once saying, "I cannot find time to visit again, if possible finalize the deal today." Not wishing to do the deal in Madalli, he had taken Singari to Hundi and had sent words through his brother to Bhujangaiah and to bring him if he were interested.

Bhujangaiah accompanied Gowda without a word. As they approached the embankment of the pond, Raja was seen going to the school with Thammaiah. Bhujangaiah was reminded at once of what the Kyatanahalli school teacher had said only the previous night when he had come to play cards. At his enquiry the teacher had praised Raja unreservedly. He had assured that Raja would stand first in his class that year. Bhujangaiah happily informed Muddegowda of Raja's progress and broached the issue, "As soon as he passes his eighth standard you should send him to Mysore for further studies." Muddegowda had complained, "I do not understand this business of being first. Will it be easy to send him to Mysore for studies?" Bhujangaiah laughed, "Tell me, how can somebody as affluent as you be scared of expenses? What is it that God has denied you?" Bhujangaiah decided that he would look for a room on lease for Raja in Shivarampet at the house of his acquaintance and planned to visit Raja once a week when he visited Mysore for groceries. Bhujangaiah's words delighted Muddegowda and he began to dream of his son studying in Mysore.

When the two reached Hundi, Karigowda and Singari were waiting for them. At their arrival another round of milk was served. Karigowda took Bhujangaiah in, and as the custom of the village demanded talked about various things before broaching the main issue. Bhujangaiah nodded his head like an obedient student to everything that Gowda said. There after they went out and asked Singari to quote a price straight away. Singari had already decided to demand Rs.4,000/- for the four acres. Karigowda averred, "That will neither catch fire nor shred the cloth. The land is not cultivated in any sense. Mention a price that one can afford friend." Singari fell silent. Karigowda probed again. Singari did not respond. Gowda said, "come on say something." Singari uttered in a measured speech how people had bought lands in the village at a price of Rs. 1,000/- to Rs. 1,500/- per acre already. Gowda pretended impatience, "Hey, those are the lands at the entrance to the village and cultivated from ages. They shine like mirror. How can you compare your land with those?" Singari replied, "You quote a price." But Gowda refused to be drawn in, "How can I? Why don't you mention another price? Singari haggled for a long while before saying, "Brother, I'll let go Rs.100/-." Gowda appreciated Singari's shrewdness. But he wouldn't yield, "If you quote so high we cannot afford it." Gowda fell silent now. Singari looked at Gowda and said, "Why don't you quote your price then?" Gowda refused to comply, "Is it a child's game? One can quote respectably if one can approximate what is expected. How can I talk to you if you sit high in the attic?" Realizing that his cereal will not cook in Gowda's fire Singari at once reduced his price by another hundred rupees, Gowda growing wise to Singari coming round to their way, at once fixed his gaze on both Singari and Bhujangaiah and said, " Look, Singari, if we go on haggling the deal cannot be clinched even at the end of the day, I will quote a price and you both should abide by it." Though Bhujangaiah's countenance revealed his acquiescence, Singari laughingly refused to be bound by it, "Ask brother, let me see." Gowda said in serious tones, "We will give you Rs. 1,500/-. Both will share the expenses of stamp paper and registration. Singari grew firm as if refusing to deal any further, "It is not possible."

Again both of them resumed like two expert wrestlers attempting a hold and breaking the hold till a decision was arrived at. Finally, the deal was to be clinched at Rs.2,000/- but both Singari and Bhujangaiah haggled over who should bear the expenses of registration, etc....

Muddegowda who had sat silently all this while said finally, "It's all right Bhujangaiah, you shoulder the expenses. He is however the loser. You are the buyer. Mother Earth will not impoverish you." Bhujangaiah agreed without another word. Muddegowda himself paid an advance of Rs. 100/-. It was decided that the papers would be drawn the next day and the deal to be registered at Kote the coming week. Puttavva brought out the beetle leaves and areca nut. Bhujangaiah placed the money on it and handed it over to Singari. While Singari was receiving it Karigowda exclaimed, "We met at a propitious moment". Puttavva brought them a vessel of water to wash and announced food was ready. As Bhujangaiah would not eat supper at their place, she had prepared *uppittu*. Puttavva addressed Bhujangaiah, "You run a hotel, I wonder if you like the *uppittu* I make." Bhujangalah asked for a second helping, "It is delicious. How can you say such a thing?" For him more than the *uppittu* being good, whatever one ate from the hands of Puttavva was like the ambrosial Amruta. He lifted the vessel, drank the water deep and burped in satiety.

The village learnt of Bhujangaiah acquiring Singari's lands only after the deal was registered in Kote. Though it had been agreed upon to have the papers made the next morning, fearing mischief, Karigowda had got both the papers and the registration made on the same day. Madalli had people who destroyed homes by hurling stones at good events. They could not wag their tail once everything was over. Bhujangaiah had borrowed from Mudddegowda when he fell short of the amount. From that day it was clear to Bhujangaiah that it was the Gowda's family that could be depended upon at times of need and not people of his own caste. Though they could not buy the clerk's rice field the fact that they now owned property large enough to support a family made Bhujangaiah's wife and mother very glad. Parvathy had emerged from the post-partum room that day and had offered a special puja. Coming by such property was not a small matter. One had to deserve that. Bhujangaiah had acquiessed when Parvathy suggested that they should go to Gaddige to perform a holy ablution, believing that such luck had come by her husband because Hulikanthyappa had deigned to bend his eyes towards them. He said he would take his mother, child and his sister-in-law to the temple by bus the next day. As Parvathy was still in the post-partum care, she could not venture out. She felt that all this good fortune was thanks to the moment which brought the birth of her youngest son. Deviramma began to address the child as the "fortunate one".

***

CHAPTER - 13

The eyes of men considered prominent among Madalli's Lingayat community began to see red at the good fortunes of Bhujangaiah. Their actions seemed to confirm the fact that it was man's natural trait to be jealous without cause, though Bhujangaiah had not harmed anyone. The news that he had bought property had not only confounded them, but also had made them jealous to an abnoxious extent. Not having new barbs to hurl at him, they were playing the old tunes again and again. There was yet again another significant reason for their heartburn. It was Bhujangaiah growing respectable in the eyes of the poor among the Lingayat and the other communities of Madalli. A few days before, when the village attendant had gone to request Karigowda's presence at a dispute, the latter had insisted in everyone's presence that Bhujangaiah too should be invited. Bhujangaiah, who had kept aloof, not wanting any part of the village politics, had gone to the village court with surprise. Excepting a few of his own community the juries too had welcomed him. They sat with a stern face. In fact, what Bhujangaiah, who was much more sensible than the others there, had appealed to all the communities present. From that day Bhujangaiah grew popular enough for people to say that there was no justice without Bhujangaiah. Sannappa, who had once in the past insulted Bhujangaiah into silence, now sat quiet.

That night, at the hotel, the coterie of Bhujangaiah was unrestrained in its joy and happiness. Thanks to Bhujangaiah, the disaster that would have been caused by the so-called elders had been averted. The details of the dispute were not merely ridiculous but nauseating to hear, Doddathamma of Parivara community had raised the dispute. It concerned Karisiddi, the widow of Chamanayaka whom he had accused of having an incestuous relationship with her brother-in-law Bettanayaka bringing disrepute to the entire community. As he was the only person among his caste who had learnt to speak in public, they respected him. Whether Karisiddi had an affair with Betta or not when Doddathamma had made overtures to her she had spurned him. He had lost face when Sannappa and Rudrappa had ditched him after having promised to support when he had come with a couple of false witnesses who stood like clowns unable to answer Bhujangaiah's questions. No evidence could be produced to show Karisiddi had sex with Betta. At least if she were pregnant it would have been possible to find her guilty. Bhujangaiah used it for a strong argument to assert that Doddathamma who had dragged Karisiddi, who had never appeared on the street after her husband's demise, to the court should be made to pay a fine. In the end, Bhujangaiah's stance found much support and Doddathamma had to pay a fine to the Panchayat. If the "rogue elders" were distraught at not having protested out of fear, realizing that their prominence would rupture if they allowed Bhujangaiah's tongue to wag as it did today, others went paying tribute to the points, "lawyer punts", that Bhujangaiah had made, convinced that he should have been a lawyer. To those who were Karisiddi's well wishers he was a veritable God appearing at a moment of tribulation.

That night Pundri was unrestrainedly happy. He narrated a very interesting tale about Doddathamma. They were both very close. Their friendship was engendered by the cattle business they partnered. They earned commission on trading oxen. Once on a business visit to Bilikere, he had taken Pundri to the Parivara street. Finding that all the male members were away from the house he intended visiting, he had returned and asked Pundri to wait for him at the peepul tree, on the spillway of the dyke outside the village, saying, " Please wait for me here, I'll be back." He then went back, Pundri had grown impatient waiting when at last Doddathamma had arrived in an inordinate hurry urging, "come, come, let's go." Till they had passed Dallalu village, he had not opened his mouth. He had been looking over his shoulder all the while. By then Pundri too had begun to entertain doubts about him. Finally, as they neared Chikka Beechanahalli, he had confessed.

The woman whom he had visited was from his own lane in Madalli. Having made sure that she was alone he had left Pundri on the embankment of the dyke and had returned to renew his old affair. He had lifted her in his arms and had walked into the room as soon as she had eagerly bolted the door. In a short while, when there was a knocking on the door he had got up in a hurry and had tried to pull on his knickers discarded on the floor. He had struggled in the process finding the knickers a little too tight. He had pulled hard, clenching his teeth cursing, "Thu, this mother........." He had succeeded in pulling on the knickers, but could not walk. In his anxiety, he had put both his feet through the same leg. Even under those circumstances the woman had laughed at his plight. Now then it was harder to take it off. The knocking on the door hadn't ceased. As he tried pulling it off hard, the knickers had split. When he opened the door, having somehow managed to hold the knickers together and wrapping his dothi, he had found the woman's mother-in-law standing there. She had been transfixed at his sight, and before she could open her mouth he had made his getaway, and reaching Pundri he had dragged him hurriedly homeward. Doddathamma had lifted his dhoti as if to reveal all that he had related was no fiction but what had really transpired. A portion of the knickers had split. When Pundri saw that the laughter that had hardly been kept in check during the narration of the incident had welled up to burst forth. He had laughed till his sides hurt and had to sit down for a while to rest before returning home. When Pundri finished telling the tale everyone had laughed till they grew tired.

When Pundri had begun his tale everyone, including Bhujangaiah, had listened avidly to him forgetting the game of cards they were playing. Fortunately, the bangle merchant was absent. If he were to be present, and had listened to the tale, who knows he pehaps would have hesitated bringing his daughter to the hotel from the very next day. Pundri wouldn't rest without blurting out what he felt like saying unmindful of who was present. Because of the game of cards the hotel had grown to be the center of attraction for Pundri. Though he was ignorant of the game he still sat and watched till his eyes grew tired. He himself couldn't explain what pleasure he derived out of that.

On a day Victor failed to bring the "Tayinadu" newspaper, which spurred Bhujangaiah's curiosity every day, he felt as if he had lost something precious. Of late, yet another person who had grown venerable for Bhujangaiah was Mahatma Gandhi. He had learnt quite a few things about him from the school teacher from Kyathanahalli. He had seen while in Mysore, the police dragging away all those who shouted Gandhiji's name. He had himself run away. Those days he had merely heard Gandhiji's name and had seen his photograph. The School Teacher had wept while narrating how a man called Godse had killed Gandhiji a year ago - killed such a great personality because of whom they had regained their country and self-rule. Bhujangaiah too had inexplicably felt like crying. The School Teacher while playing cards on innumerable occasions used to recount many incidents such as Gandhi's love for the poor and the suffering.

One day, the teacher had lifted his gaze while at breakfast to be stunned by what greeted his sight. Next to the pictures of Gods arranged on the wall of the hotel was a framed portrait of 'Grandfather' Gandhi, toothless, kissing a child. Bhujangaiah who adored individually each picture of Gods, worshipped Gandhiji's portrait too. He had deified Gandhiji. Looking at Bhujangaiah's interest, the master had lent him Gandhiji's autobiography. Bhujangaiah began reading it whenever he found time. What had stoked Bhujangaiah's curiosity was that Gandhiji, who had desires like all else, and who had committed wrongs, had grown into a Mahatma in the end, to whom all folded their hands. His suspicion that Gandhi must be a greater soul than even the Swamiji of his own mutt had found substance gradually. It was said that there were many such universal mentors as his. But how many could be Mahatma Gandhi? The teacher had said: "Such a Mahatma had never been born in our country in the past and will never be in the future." He would assert that such a man was unique to the entire universe. Though he had died, not a day passed without his name being mentioned in Tayinadu. If nothing, there would be printed at least a single line of quotation from him, Bhujangaiah on many occasions would wonder if it were ever possible for somebody like him to live by Gandhiji's tenets.

It had grown of late increasingly difficult to walk in Madalli, especially through the street of his community. When he had just enough for food and clothing there was then a sense of participation in each other's sorrow or happiness. It seemed as if such cordiality had evaporated. There was either envy or doubt now. Not just adults, even children looked at him as they would when strangers passed by. They did not anymore come in a rush to mount an attack of affection when they heard him approach, He had never in the past admonished them, even if they were to sit on his head, Why had they all distanced themselves from him now? No! No! He perhaps had grown different from them. All three times of the day he was either busy with his hotel, in his game of cards or in unproductive gossip. Somehow all his earlier interests were waning. He had not paid proper attention to Puttavva's son Raju, who trudged past the hotel every day. Bhujangaiah decided to call him and offer some snacks while he returned from school that evening. He instructed Shiva to call him when the children went past, if he himself should forget while playing cards.

Raja, while returning, as was his wont, in the company of a large group of boys was surprised when hailed by Bhujangaiah. Even he knew that his headmaster frequented that place for a game of cards. But he wouldn't be there at this time of the day. He arrived only after school. Bhujangaiah invited Raja and placed some *raveundes* packed in an old Tayinadu newspaper. Raja found the gesture strange. For, once before when he had asked for a *raveunde*, Manja had replied that the money that Raja possessed was not enough to buy one. Bhujangaiah hadn't even lifted his head.

Raja couldn't comprehend why so many so many undes were offered that day. After crossing Madalli, he took out the packet, removed one to share it with Thammanna. He wanted to eat all of them at once, but desisted, deciding to do so later at home.

"Thammanna, have you seen Bhujangaiah diving into the well," The latter had replied, "Of course, yes. He dived in our well at Hundi once and retrieved a vessel." Raja tried to recollect his first meeting with Bhujangaiah. Once, when a cobra had crept into the chink between the bamboo poles that were part of the roof of his uncle's house in Madalli, Bhujangaiah had come to catch it. It was on that day that Raja had come to know him well. Bhujangaiah was a Merlin as far as Raja was concerned. Raja's fear would grow seeing Bhujangaiah diving into the wells however deep they were, staying for interminable moments under water. Whenever Raja swam in the pond of Pura, unknown to his elders, he would attempt at diving, only to be scared to death even by the briefest of submersion. Water entered his nostrils discomfiting him for long. How did Bhujangaiah manage to stay under water so long? Raja was reminded of a specific incident. Some years ago, Madeva, who would rant about his visitations, had once jumped into the pond next to the shrine of Basappa while performing *Para*, after having stood trembling as though he had a visitation. When those who knew Madeva shouted that he couldn't swim, Bhujangaiah had dived and pulled him out by his hair. Madeva's belly had already swollen. Bhujangaiah had rolled him on to his stomach and had pressed his back to expel the water, Madeva had sat up opening his dead eyes. He, who had bit the silt, would have by now joined the crowd of ghosts in the woods of Madalli adjacent to the pond if it were not for Bhujangaiah.

Raja was also amazed at Bhujangaiah's alacrity in catching a snake as well as at his expertise in curing snakebites. Raja fervently wished to see Bhujangaiah's palm as every one said that he was born with the line of the eagle. He had heard that Bhujangaiah had once joined the snake charmers. The story went that it was with them that he had learnt the charms for the snakebite. However, Bhujangaiah had always asserted that it was Manga of the outcastes who was his guru. Raja had shivered in his testicles at the very mention of snake. It was said that a teased serpent would wait twelve years to seek revenge. Bhujangaiah not only played with such snakes as though they were merely strands of ropes, but occasionally was seen putting them round his neck as though they were stoles. These were enough reasons for Raja to admire Bhujangaiah.

Bhujangaiah was the *boondi* maker for marriages of Raja's community. He would begin preparations a week before the marriage. He made sweet *boondi* as well as spicy *boondi* with chickpea flour. He seldom desisted making jokes when children gathered round him. Though he was like a hero of some adventure tale for Raja, what endeared him most was the immense regard Bhujangaiah had for Raja's mother. He addressed her as "Puttakka", the elder sister. Every time Bhujangaiah visited Hundi on some errand or the other, he never failed to ask Raja's mother at least for a glass of butter milk to drink. The affection and respect Raja had for Bhujangaiah doubled when the latter started a hotel, invited the chief of all their gurus and played cards with none other than his headmaster whom he feared most.

Raja took to visiting the hotel whenever he wished. Both Manja and Shiva had grown friendly. Raja would sway his head to the music as he watched Manja play the gramophone. He would hum a few lines of some song or the other whenever alone. He was fascinated by the singing machine. He had queried his headmaster about it once. The headmaster too had grown pleased for a moment at his question before answering vaguely. Raja, whose curiosity was not sated, thought that he would find answers to such questions only if he went to Mysore for his studies and so began to dream of Mysore. Bhujangaiah encouraged his dreams by constantly urging him, "Finish your school this year, your father will send you to Mysore." On occasions when Raja visited the hotel he would find Sushila sitting and listening to songs. Raja would blush whenever Bhujangaiah praised him in her presence. Though it filled him with pleasure to watch Sushila looking at him with appreciation he was shy meeting her gaze. Sushila visited Hundi on rare occasions. She had personally adorned his mother with bangles. His mother had appreciated her expertise in sliding the bangles skillfully over wrists without causing the slightest of pain. Raja was surprised that Sushila had grown close to his mother in such a short time. His mother was by nature cordial. The bangle merchant and his daughter Sushila both used to stay at his uncle's home whenever they visited Madalli. Raja too occasionally stayed over in Madalli. On such occasions he felt sorry for them when he saw the merchant and Sushila sleeping on the *jagali*. His mother would have never allowed them to sleep thus. It was all right for men but how could a woman be allowed to sleep on the *jagali*? When he had told his mother about it she had sympathized, "Tche? The poor souls." He hadn't forgotten that.

A certain incident which Raja had witnessed had filled him at that very moment with strange emotions. One day, Raja returning from school had seen Manja intently watching something through the gap between the ceiling and the kitchen wall, oblivious to his query as to Bhujangaiah's whereabouts, when Raja hadn't found him either in the hotel or among the card players. Raja too had climbed the grinder pedastal and had spied Bhujangaiah and Sushila standing near the tall row of hedge laughing and whispering. Manja had returned to his senses only when Raja had jumped down noisily feeling queasy. He had been alarmed and guilty and had brushed aside Raja's protests to ply him with snacks and had prepared a cup of "Pesal" tea for him.

The incident had upset Raja a little about Bhujangaiah. From then on Raja, who had never thought ill of Bhujangaiah, began to doubt him. Though he had wished to tell his mother of the incident he had refrained from doing so. But, on a Saturday, returning home after school, when he found Sushila sitting with his mother in conversation, he had shown his displeasure by refusfng to return Sushila's affectionate greeting. He had refused to even look at her. Raja had run off not to return home till she had left. Raja could not understand why he had behaved thus.

***

CHAPTER - 14

The Tampura Ayya from Hampapura was one more soul who wished for Bhujangaiah's well-being and the prosperity of his house. He invariably performed worship at Bhujangaiah's house before setting out on an alms tour in his saffron robes and saffron turban with a bag slung across his shoulder, singing the Songs of Morals as he strummed the tampura with one hand and clacked the castanet stringed with bells with the other. Those who heard him sat still as a stone, mesmerized. He had taken to sleeping at Bhujangaiah's house of late, as there were too many people crowding the hotel at night indulging in a game of cards. Parvathy too was fond of listening to devotional songs. She used to sit listening, with the baby in her lap, far in to the nigtht till sleep overcame her.

The Ayya's name was Mahantadeva. Bhujangaiah's mother addressed him as " Mahantappa.' The rest of the village called him "Ayya". He was unlike other beggars. He visited once a week. He would finish his alms tour of Madalli, Kyatanahalli, Sargur, Hundi and Hosalli over a few days and leave for Hampapura cross - country on foot. No house sent him without first offering a handful of grains at least, if he should stand at the door singing. The one weakness he had was his need for tea at least thrice a day. The other vice was smoking marijuana. It had to be a necessary adjunct to every visit of his to Bhujangaiah's hotel.

There were some who arrived from the village especially for that. The marijuana stock in the box secreted in Ayya's pocket was perennial. A pipe was stuffed with the leaves, a piece of white cloth was tied around the butt and the smoke would emanate from mouth and nostrils. The eyes of the smokers would grow bleary. The pipe was passed around till the leaves were all burnt. Ayya would then empty the pipe, refill with fresh leaves, wet the cloth once again, readying the pipe for the devotion of the oversoul. The children of the village loved watching it.

Though Ayya of Hampapura owned lands and had a wife and children, the tradition of begging for the "alms of Shiva's mercy" had been handed down to him from the times of his grandfather. He did not consider it belittling. He knew hundreds of songs. He had visited all the important mutts of his caste. The one desire he had was to visit the holy place of Srishyla before he died. Bhujangaiah had promised to take him there. Bhujangaiah too had been influenced by the tale of Akka of Uduthadi who having refused to consort with mortal men had fallen in love with Lord Shiva and had grown one with him. Ayya who believed that the portals of Bhujangaiah's fortunes had opened due to his devout nature had of late grown sorry at his succumbing to the vice of gambling. Still more, he did not approve of his placing Gandhiji's portrait along with those of the Verashaiva gods, "Whatever Gandhi maybe to the country he certainly did not belong to the Verashaiva community. After all, he was a mortal. Would Shiva approve of it? Bhujangaiah had laughed when confronted once. Who knew when Bhujangaiah would grow free of this Gandhi madness with which the Brahmin School Teacher of Kyatanahalli had touched him? None of this will ever come to good. But such is Lord Shiva's will. Our task is merely to perform his dictates. When ordered we must needs stop and heed his summons leaving all that we possess. Our life is but a three-day long game." It was already sunset when Ayya reached the hotel after his alms round in Kyatanahalli wondering about God's design. There was not a single customer at the hotel. What surprised him most was none had assembled to play cards. The flower for God's crown may perhaps be forgotten of late but the game of cards at Bhujangaiah's hotel was not to be missed out ever. Ayya questioned Manja after lifting his bag and Tampura down in a corner, Manja too had been surprised by his master's behaviour. After the travelers had arrived by bus for breakfast, Bhujangaiah had suddenly got up from the counter, taken out the pack of cards from the shop front and thrown it into the kitchen fire. He had asked Shiva to sweep and wash the room tidy. He had got the floor mortered laid at the hotel when renovating his house. When Shiva swept the room he had collected half a winnow full of burnt matches and beedi butts. The gamblers had not risen for three days. Manja had caught Shiva whispering into his master's ear as he played the previous night. The latter had left the game in the middle to go out and converse with Sushila, who had already eaten her supper, under the tamarind tree. His master's face revealed sadness when she had left for Madalli with Shiva for escort. He had been morose the next morning too. He had asked all those who had riveted themselves to the floor to leave on the pretext that the bus would arrive any time then. When the players returned after their morning rituals, long after the bus had left, Bhujanagaiah was not around. The shop front had been locked. Manja had announced his master's decision not to allow gambling anymore. When Singri the lame, who was addicted to the game of cards remonstrated : "All right, give us the cards at least. We'll play under some tree or the other." Manja had informed that the God of fire had already fed on them and burped. Singri the lame had felt the earth giving under his feet. He had lost much money to Rajappa the forester the previous night. His desire to somehow win back the money, even if it meant playing the three-card poker, had died like a layer hen with a broken neck.

He had left without even drinking tea cursing Bhujangaiah under his breath. The others too had left, one after another, disappointed when they realized they had nothing to show for their effort saying Bhujangaiah had grown insane.

Ayya who listened to the tale from beginning to end breathed a sigh of relief. At last God had given Bhujangaiah good sense. It was not easy to predict the workings of men's mind from moment to moment. If it were not God's design what else was it which made Bhujangaiah who used to sit gambling oblivious of his home and his religion suddenly cut adrift of his vice? There was no vice worse than gambling. The Pandavas had grown wretched due to gambling. Not satisfied at losing all that they possessed they in the end lost the wife who had accepted their hands, the entire universe knew the story. The worry that the vice which had reduced even those such as the Pandavas to a sorry state may wreck Bhujangaiah had niggled at him. How can one guess at the divinity's maya? How else can one explain the change in Bhujangaiah, which had come about as casually as one turning over in sleep? When he had striven to advise Bhujangaiah, as one would teach a parrot to speak, had he not refused to heed?

However, Manja had entertained his own doubts. He had grown curious from the very day he had caught sight of Sushila. Though she had shown her disgust when she saw his desire for her and had pointedly ignored him, a beastly lust for her had grown in Manja. He had known his master's attraction for her. Manja had looked upon Bhujangaiah as a godly man who never uttered a harsh word to hurt him since he began working for him. But now that he had become his adversary, Bhujangaiah's very sight gave rise to an unpleasant experience in him. Sushila was a haughty woman. However delicious his snacks were she never ever praised them. Why was it that he never found favour with her? She must have called the master out that night to complain. It was because of what she had said that the master had stopped the game of cards, which he loved so much. Many a time Sushila had quarreled in anger with her father when he lost all his business earnings at the game. She had made him take a vow that he would never step inside the hotel. But all her efforts had met with failure. She had to once ask Bhujangaiah, though reluctantly, for money when they did not have enough to replenish the stock. Bhujangaiah, by nature generous, had obliged at once. He too like Shetty had suffered losses many a time. He was yet to repay the loan he had taken from Muddegowda when he bought lands. Though he would often make up his mind never to touch cards again his resolve melted as soon as he saw a pack of cards.

But yesternight Sushila had wept saying her livelihood would be destroyed if the gambling at the hotel did not stop. When she revealed that she had little money to buy her stock of bangles Bhujangaiah had once again lent her all the money in his pocket without even counting. He had promised unhesitatingly, "I shall stop the game of cards tomorrow itself and lock up the room." Sushila had left with her father by bus the following morning. Manja could not guess why Sushila had grown so dear to Bhujangaiah. Both Victor and Subbanna thought well of her. She too addressed them as "brothers". Victor always took care to place their basket of bangles next to his seat out in the front. The chances of the bangles breaking were more if they were placed at the back or on the top of the bus. Only God knew the travails of a bangle seller. Whatever care one took many a bangle was lost due to breakage. And even when one managed to transport them with great difficulty, without a breakage it was certain that many bangles would be lost in the act of sliding them on the hands of customers. The village folk wanted perfect fit. If the size were to be ever so slightly large they would refuse to buy. Though she too had striven to learn the skill of adorning without breaking the bangles like her father, success hadn't come to her easily. Of late, rubber bangles had entered the market. Only children wore them. The villages around Madalli were regular customers of her father for a long time now. He was content with the business. Yet, now that his daughter accompanied him, his business had extended to Maranahalli and Muddanahalli on the bus route and to Gaddige where people congregated for the weekly worship. The business had grown to his satisfaction but then because of the vice of gambling which stuck to him like Shani they could not visit all those villages regularly.

It was a week since the gambling had stopped. The hotel, which buzzled with people, if not with customers at least with gamblers, was now empty once the customers left. Whenever Bhujangaiah was tempted by the sight of his empty hotel he would either take to reading "Tayinadu" or visit the granary, which was getting cleaned to stock- pile paddy. Sankranti, heralding the summer solistice, arrived. In a week's time people would begin storing paddy. Each granary would wear a festive look brimming with joy. For the peasants there wasn't a happier event, which equaled that of bringing home the gathered fruits of their year long labour. Sankranti meant everything to them. The chariot of their life rolled by that measure alone! The harvest alone had to provide for all their contingencies: the seed to sow, the grain to eat the year long, and the money to fend for other needs. It had been a good harvest for everybody this time. But then what if the market fell? Those who were well to do could afford to store and sell when the prices improved, but what about the poor? They had to pay back the loans, buy for their wives a sari at least to protect their honour, buy clothes for their children who had this long marked time in patched rags. And one cannot begin to talk about the plight of those who sharecrop or work the fields on weekly contract. They had to make good to the owners who would not agree to accept even a gram less, half the yield of their year long labour of blood and sweat. The owners were deaf to the sharecropper's cries of hunger.

Bhujangaiah had finished gathering the harvest, which had exceeded his expectation. Before transporting the grain home he reserved a small portion to celebrate the abundance. His mother disapproved his extravagance of reserving so much grain to distribute among the poor of the village who went from granary to granary after harvest. They would be able to happily eat well at least for four days from what they collected. Bhujangaiah spread his palms generously this time to distribute grain among the destitute. Those who had received a good harvest filled their granary pit with grain. Bhujangaiah had not harvested enough to fill his pit. He made up his mind to grow enough the following year so that the pit that had been dug long ago could be opened. If only he had grown crops on the fields he had bought that year he could have had the pit filled up then itself. If only the rains would oblige the coming year too his long cherished desire would be fulfilled. The poor who received Bhujangaiah's generosity praised and blessed him wishing that God might provide him better. Bhujangaiah measured the amount of grain he had borrowed from Gowda on the occasion of the Swami's visit and carried the sack to Gowda's home. When Gowda jested, "What is this? Would the grains have refused to remain in your home if you had asked them to stay at least for this day?" Bhujangaiah had replied, "It had to be returned someday or the other. Therefore I thought it better done today." Gowda was happy at his promptness. On returning home Bhujangaiah asked Amase to fetch his father to whom he made adequate recompense. When Shaggy Sidda protested, "Why give so much?" Bhujangaiah had replied, "Do not mention it. Isn't that what your son cultivated with his sweat?" Sidda had decided to allow his son to continue on labour at Bhujangaiah's for four more years. Deviravva unable to control herself at her son's largesse finally lost her temper. Parvathy too supported her mother-in-law and protested against her husband. But Bhujangaiah had refused to heed their advice. After happily eating his meal he left for the hotel, en route met Nagaraja and asked him to bring the rest of their friends. Nagaraja, who presumed that there must be some special reason, collected all of Bhujangaiah's companions and arrived at the hotel.

Bhujangaiah who averred that there was nothing important to talk about finally disclosed a plan that had formed in his mind while he was having his meal. It was to produce a drama. Pundri was elated at the very mention of a play. He would begin getting busy from the very next morning. It had been three years since a play had been performed in Madalli. He decided in accordance with Bhujangaiah's wishes to call a meeting of all those who would take part in the play in the house where "Para" had been performed adjacent to the temple. Pundri began singing as if to remind the others that he had not yet forgotten the role he had performed a long time ago. Though his voice was passable he said, "My voice has gone a little hoarse because of the dust while collecting grain," Manja too was drama mad. His ears too had pricked up at the news, Pundri refused to do the female part protesting against his lot at having to play the part every time. When Bhujangaiah said, "When we haven't as yet discussed whether a play should be put up he is already worried about his role!" Pundri had looked at Bhujangaiah and said, "Who else needs to accord permission? If you have taken a decision it is done then. Do you wish to know how I'll summon people tomorrow? "We are performing a drama, those who wish to take part come, that's it!" Bhujangaiah felt a sense of pride at Pundri's speech.

As soon as the people of Madalli were free from the tasks of harvest they had begun to rehearse the play in the House of

Para. Having searched high and low for a "master" to direct the play, they had learnt that Govindaraju, the headmaster of Kyatanahalli School was the right choice and had persuaded him to accept the responsibility. In a couple of days everyone had learnt, to their surprise, how good a director Govindaraju was. He had a resounding bronze-like voice. His manner of teaching, which made learning easy couldn't be quantified. Bhujangaiah wondered why he had looked for ghee all over the town when he had butter at home. Govindaraju had in just four days assigned the roles. At the very outset he had made clear his rules. He once more told sternly what role each one had been assigned according to the timbre of voice, appearance and the physique of each person. Pundri was assigned a female role this time too. He had accepted it without a murmur. There were some in the village who did not like the idea of a drama being staged under Bhujangaiah's leadership. Though this had kept a few from taking part there was no dearth in Madalli for boys who wished to take part in the play. When Bhujangaiah wished to include Raju the son of Muddegowda of Hundi the master had refused, pointing out that his examinations were fast approaching. And Ajappa had refused to accept even the smallest of roles in spite of Bhujangaiah's efforts.

The rehearsal went on full steam. Manja too had been assigned a role. Bhujangaiah had refused to accept any role. But in the end, in deference to the master he had agreed to play the "Sutradhara", the prime mover of the play. Every day people began to crowd the House of Para. It had been three years since any one had heard the sounds of harmonium and tabla, when they had staged "Basaveshwara, the Light of Universe". Though some had suggested staging that very play Bhujangaiah was firm that they should rehearse a new drama. The master had narrated the tale of "Shiva and Jalandhara". Every one had liked the theme and had begun rehearsing. Bhujangarah had insisted that not a single day of rehearsal was to be missed by any one.

That rule had put Bhujangaiah himself into difficulties. He had to take to sleeping at the hotel. Though Shiva was not a part of the play he went to witness the rehearsal every single day without fail. The Ayya of Hampapura had begun to rest at the hotel again. Whenever Ayya was around Bhujangaiah would stay back at the rehearsal till the very end. Occasionally the master too would stay overnight at the hotel. But normally he returned to Kyatanahalli every day escorted by Pundri and friends. They would return to sleep at the hotel. There were days when the rehearsals went on well past midnight. The villagers would everyday sit through the rehearsals right to the end, listening to the same dialogues day after day without boredom. The dialogues were on the lips of even children who grazed cattle.

Madalli which seemed to have suffered from a stupor in the past was now filled with gaiety; a new rhythm could be heard everywhere. There was still a month to go before the drama could be staged. Though the actors had begun to spend time on memorizing the dialogues at least three times a day, they in their anxiety made mistakes in front of the master. He did not let them off easily as they stood rather foolishly becoming the butt of everybody's taunts. He wouldn't rest till they were corrected and till they delivered their dialogues properly. Bhujangaiah had given Pundri the responsibility of collecting money from those who had volunteered for the drama. Pundri had promptly begun to collect from the very first day of rehearsals. He was much more interested in performing such tasks than donning a role in the play.

***

CHAPTER - 15

Sushila had been greatly delighted that her father's addiction for the game of cards, which had proved a headache for her, was cured by a mere word from her to Bhujangaiah. Her esteem for Bhujangaiah had increased as a consequence. Her father's interest in his business revived. Once their earnings grew respectable both father and daughter were free from the abuses of her father's second wife. Sushila would have jitters at the very thought of her stepmother. Sushila, cheated of a mother's affection, had found it safer by a thousand times to wander bracing the weather with her father than to remain home with her stepmother. Whenever Kalavva, Karigowda's wife, spoke to her kindly and served her food generously Sushila's eye's would brim with tears. Why was she not born to such a woman? But Kalavva's daughters-in-law were unlike her. They would stare at Sushila enigmatically. Sushila felt uncomfortable at such times. That really was the reason why she had begun to frequent the hotel for her meal.

There was a fresh danger that of late confronted Sushila. Narayana, Gowda's son, had taken to staring at her as if he would maul her. Everybody in the village knew of his character. He followed around any good-looking woman as a pie dog did. That had led to several incidents in the past, which had forced Gowda's head to bow in shame. Gowda, aware of his son's weakness, had wished many a times to warn the merchant not to stay at his home with his grown up daughter. Sushila was charming enough for anyone to get distracted. Her youth, which was blossoming in her body of late, had cast a spell even on Bhujangaiah. It was therefore, no wonder that Narayana too, who was at the prime of his exuberant youth, was affected. Sushila seemed a rare thing with her alluring body. Though her roaming in the sun had dulled the colour of her skin the colourful saris and blouses she wore made her look attractive. What drew Narayana were her full breasts, which belied her tender youth. Though she took care to cup them in brassieres under blouses finely textured, her breasts distracted all those who saw her. Narayana's wife had caught her husband waiting for the moment Sushila lifted the basket of bangles on her head, with his mouth drooling. That was the reason why she had begun to ill treat Sushila.

Narayana was scared though he intensely desired to accost Sushila. What would be the consequence if she should reject his advances? She was close to his mother. What if she should complain to his family? Shushila's familiarity with his family and her staying over at his home both proved obstacles to Narayana. If only she had stayed over at some other family he would already have attempted to seduce her. Whenever he attempted, on occasions, to begin a conversation with her, either his wife or one of his parents would arrive on the scene. At night Sushila's father was never far from her, even for a brief moment. On those few nights she slept without the father being around, his mother had made Sushila sleep next to her on the *jagali,* foiling his designs. Even so, when one day, his mother had stayed over at Hundi, Narayana's wife had refused to close her eyes the entire night as though she had guessed at the attempts he might make on Sushila. She had thus reduced to naught all his intentions. That was when his wife had decided not to allow Sushila to sleep over at their place any more and had subtly warned her mother-in-law. But Kalavva could not find any fault in Sushila's behaviour. She would believe that all that was white to be milk. She never looked at anybody with suspicion. She was that innocent. The villagers had attributed Gowda's affluence to her pure character. Sushila had found her mother in Kalavva. She never failed to bring betel leaves, areca nut and powdered tobacco for Kalavva from Mysore. Kalavva accepted what ever Sushila brought with love. She had known Sushila's temper whenever she had attempted to refuse her presents. Though Sushila would arrive after a meal at the hotel there were times when Kalavva would force her to a second meal.

Occasionally, out of boredom, the merchant too went to witness the rehearsal. On that particular day, Kalavva too had gone to the rehearsal to listen to her second son sing. Narayana seeing his mother at the rehearsal had returned home after a while. The people in the village never used to lock doors while going out late not wishing to disturb the others who slept. Narayana had pushed the door noiselessly and had entered on silent feet like a thief. The doors of his own room and that of the elder brother's were both shut. The inner courtyard was awash with moonlight which spilt like milk. Narayana had seen Sushila sleeping on her back on the verandah, Her high breasts rose and fell, Narayana had felt the blaze of fire in his veins. He had approached stealthily and had squatted next to her. What deranged him was the sight of her legs exposed to her knees by the sari in disarray. He had trembled touching her. Sushila had started for an instant but had continued to slumber deep. Narayana touched her again. Sushila did not stirr; Narayana felt triumphant. He gently slid his hand up. As he progressed beyond the knee and touched her thigh, Sushila had cried out "who is that?" and sat up. Narayana too stood up at once. His wife too had woken at Sushila's cry. When she opened the door, Narayana stood there. Strangely, his speech had died.

Sushila had sat trembling, as if she had trodden on a snake. Afraid that his wife might take him to task in the dead of night Narayana had held her in his arms saying, "I stepped on her leg accidentally." He had drowned in the pleasure that had cheated him a moment ago. But Sushila, who was still shivering, had not shut her eyes. Who knew when her father would arrive? Each passing minute had seemed like an age. Sushila having escaped an incident which she had for long suspected may take place had been filled with disgust at Narayana. She had resolved then never to sleep there even for a moment. "How could a divine mother like Kalavva beget such a son? What people said of him was no lie. Why did he possess the mind of a dog in spite of a sterling wife?"

Sushila had been filled with revultion recollecting his touch on her thigh. Once before, when she slept, Subba, her stepmother's younger brother, who had stayed over, had thus touched her. She had slapped him in terrible anger. Since that incident he had not set foot in their home. Sushila could still recall his sad face as he had left. She had taken to a boy herself. He had never misbehaved. Sushila had felt a loss for a few days when he had married some time back. Sushila who had sat on her haunches without shutting her eyes had stood up when her father had arrived with Kalavva. When she had gone out and talked to her father about leaving at once, the merchant had been taken aback not knowing for a while where to seek shelter at that hour. When he consoled her, whispering and patting her, he had learnt the reason for her distraught condition. He too had thought of leaving at once. But then the bundle of bangles and the basket were inside the house and he had not known what reason to offer if Kalavva were to inquire. Sushila too had not wished to hurt Kalavva. Though Sushila had agreed to their spending the rest of the night on the *jagali*, the merchant had thought better of it. He had entered the house, removed the basket and the bundle and had said before Kalavva could ask, "we have to leave for Maranahalli tomorrow. We'll be late waiting for the bus. We do not wish to disturb you as we will be leaving at the hour of cock's crow." Kalavva had not said a word in reply.

Both father and daughter sat on the *jagali* for a long time. Sleep eluded them. At last, the merchant shouldered the bundle and helped his daughter lift the basket to her head and walked away. Sushila followed her father silently. The merchant went straight to Bhujangaiah's hotel. Sushila shuddered thinking suddenly of the snake. Yet, her fervid mind found the memories of the hotel cool. When they arrived at the hotel it was silent. Everybody was sleeping after returning from the rehearsals. When the merchant called out. Bhujangaiah himself opened the door. He was surprised to see them at that late hour. The merchant sought to sleep there without offering any reason. Bhujangaiah lit the lamp. He woke Pundri who was sleeping in his room and offered the room to the merchant and Sushila. Pundri curious, yet uncomprehending, couldn't keep his eyes open. He went out and stretched his body on a bench in the hotel. Bhujangaiah too lay down on another bench. He shut his eyes thinking to enquire in the morning. Sushila slept consoled.

When Manja awoke in the morning he was surprised to see his master too, like him, sleeping on a bench. Only when the drama master stayed back was Bhujangaiah's cot taken by a stranger. But, Pundri and he had escorted the drama master within sight of Kyatanahalli before returning to sleep. Manja peeped in through the door left ajar. The cot was empty. But he felt strange seeing the merchant and Sushila sleeping on the floor. Everybody woke to the sound of Manja and Shiva starting on their chores, Urupa had left for the pond having risen earlier than others. In his urgency he had run without having noticed anything. When he returned he saw Sushila rolling the mat. He inquired with his face opening wide and with a grin that revealed his chisel sharp teeth," Sister, did you sleep here last night?" Sushila murmured a yes. Why did she who normally slept at Gowda's sleep here? Not knowing the answer, he asked foolishly, "Will you be sleeping here henceforth?" Bhujangaiah who heard his indiscreet questioning called out to him and ordered him to transfer water from the cask. Urupa emptied the cask in no time and reported back. When Bhujangalah asked him to fetch water from the pond Urupa replied with alacrity as if it were an easy task, "I shall fetch water at once."

The merchant took Bhujangaiah out after breakfast and told him of what had transpired the previous night. He requested him not to divulge it to anybody. The merchant was concerned about his daughter's reputation. Bhujangaiah felt sorry for the merchant. It was proved now that Narayana was a scoundrel. He sympathized with Sushila. She sat arranging the rows of bangles in the basket. She placed them in loops inside the basket. In the center went the rubber bangles tied in bundles with strings.

Sushila was ashamed to see Bhujangaiah's face after having noticed her father narrating to him the previous night's incident. Bhujangaiah welcomed them to rest at the hotel henceforth, whenever they visited the village. But the merchant resolved to return to Mysore by the evening bus from then on whether he did business or not. He was determined to get Sushila married that very year. It was not proper to take a daughter come into her youth from village to village thus. Yesterday was bad enough. Who's to say what may transpire tomorrow? Days do not roll unaltered. Even the hotel was bound to have boys in their youth. What if something should happen? The merchant was caught in the whirlpool of worry. The whole day the merchant advised his daughter as they went around on their sales. In the evening they left by the last bus to Mysore. The merchant's mind was busy weighing things. Having decided not to take Sushila on the sales trips any more the merchant started searching for a suitable boy among his relatives wishing to marry her off that very year, even if it meant raising a loan. At the end of a round of search for a bridegroom, to the neglect of his business, the merchant had decided on a boy who lived in Nanjangud. That very evening the boy too had met Sushila and agreed to marry her. But when the families sat down to negotiate the dowry, the conditions which the boy's father put unnerved the merchant. The only property he had possessed was the small nest of a house. Even if he should contemplate selling that house it was beyond the merchant's means to enter into an alliance with the family from Nanjangud. Sushila's stepmother began to spew forth her hymnals faulting Sushila's cursed fate for the breaking up of an alliance that had almost been through. Having witnessed the manner in which his wife tore into Sushila in his very presence, the merchant, fearing for his daughter's fate in his absence, once again began taking her with him. When they arrived at the bus stand Victor inquired why they were not to be seen for a week. The merchant offered some lame excuse. Ajappa and Pundri were on the same bus and said that they were returning from Mandya. The father and daughter learnt that the duo had visited Mandya in search of costumes for the drama.There were still twenty days left for the staging of the drama.

When the bus reached the Crossroads Pundri announced, even before Bhujangaiah could ask, as though he had won a conquest, "we managed to get the costumes from Kalappa the butter vendor of Mandya". He would have Manja bring tea even before stepping into the hotel and then discourse on his adventures! But Bhujangaiah interrupted. “Pundri leave that for later. Come here first and serve tea to the customers.” He forced Pundri to serve the tea Manja had made. Manja and Shiva who had been to Madalli had not yet returned. Sushila’s arrival by the same bus had infused Bhujangaiah with vigor. When the father and daughter had not visited for a week after the unhappy incident at Karigowda’s, Bhujangaiah had thought that they might never return to his village. In spite of the rush hour Bhujangaiah went out frequently to catch a glimpse of Sushila. As the hotel was crowded, Sushila had preferred to remain outside talking to women from Kyatanahalli, who had got off the bus. Beard had appeared as though he had fallen from the sky soon after the bus had left. Bhujangaiah realised that Sushila had been speaking to Beard’s wife and sister-in-law as they entered the hotel. He ordered snacks and tea for them too and went out knowing they would be shy to eat in his presence. Beard’s wife never failed to welcome him with a brass vessel full of milk or butter milk to drink whenever he visited them in Kyatanahalli. Beard joined Pundri and Ajappa with his tea as they stood talking with Bhujangaiah. Ajappa was talking about the agreement made in Mandya. Beard warned Pundri: “It won’t be easy Pundri. You country boys have to drink empty the seven ponds before you can get every villager to appreciate you.”

Beard announced that he had made it known to every one that it was Bhujangaiah his friend who was the motivator of the drama, which had generated enough curiosity in all the neighbouring villages. When Sushila said that they could go with Beard’s family to Kyatanahalli for business, the merchant got up without another word. With Beard accompanying them, let alone the two miles, they wouldn’t even know if they walked twenty miles. Beard had made Sushila too partisan to his chat by colourfully interjecting with due respect every time, “Was there anything wrong in what I said mother Sushila?” A week had gone by since they had visited Kyatanahalli. It was evening by the time they finished selling bangles there. And they had not yet covered the Sheperds’ Street. They decided to visit there the next day. It was already sunset by the time they left for Madalli, and the Schoolmaster of Kyatanahalli joined them. The merchant had known him well from the days of playing cards. The master spoke to them about the drama all through the journey. When they reached the Crossroads night had already stretched its legs.

***

CHAPTER - 16

It was that time of the year when spring was about to set foot after winter. The biting cold had yet retained its sharp teeth. Sushila who slept in Bhujangaiah's hotel, in her special room for the past three days, woke up and sat stretching her limbs. Her father was already sitting outside drinking his tea. Sushila wished she could sleep longer. The past three nights had brought her sweet sleep. It had of late grown difficult to sleep well because of her wanderings. When she slept on the *jagali* of Gowda she had to be up before the villagers began to appear on the street. But at the hotel one could sleep as long as one pleased. There was no hurry. But the problem was of not having a private toilet. Sushila found the life in the village funny. Everybody built a large home but none had a toilet. The women folk of the village had to wait for darkness to use the field. Even she was getting accustomed to that, after beginning to visit Madalli. Though one squatted in the dark one was anxious. The fear that somebody might notice was ever present. In contrast, however small a house one had in Mysore, every house had a toilet. If they in the city, like in the village, were to have a large backyard and fields all around the house they wouldn't have needed toilets. Sushila smiled thinking of the women of Madalli squatting on the edge of the road or in narrow lanes at night. She felt pity for them when she saw them stand up abruptly whenever a male passed by and then sit again.

When Sushila emerged from the hotel she saw a few people drinking tea even as they gave up their bodies to the tender sun. Bhujangaiah too sat there in front of Sanjiva the barber for a shave holding a tiny mirror in his hand. Sanjiva was honing his razor noisily on the whetstone. Sushila watched curiously. Sanjiva was engaged in his task with an uncommon involvement. Sushila felt like laughing finding the entire scene ridiculous, that of Bhujangaiah lifting his arms one after another to get his arm pits shaved, and Sanjiva stretching his body erect like a leech from where he sat, to shave. Sushila felt strange when her father too went and sat in front of Sanjiva who was packing in his tools signaling that his task had ended. On her father's face too was a three-day old stubble of grey and black. When Bhujangaiah stood at the door of the hotel asking Shiva to bring water Sushila took a surreptitious look at his face from behind the door. His face was smooth. But there were drops of blood resembling the tiny seeds of scarlet rosarypea in many places on his cheek and chin. She at once recalled her father shaving with a razor and wondered why Bhujangaiah too should not posses one. If he had one he could shave before washing his face every day. She decided to gift him a razor set from Mysore the next time.

Bhujangaiah had many times decided even as Sushila had done now, not to have Sanjiva shave him, when his cheeks and chin sizzled, nicked by the razor of Sanjiva. Once the burning stopped he forgot about it. Bhujangaiah went through perfunctorily the motions of washing his face in the glass of water which Shiva brought to him and entered his room wiping his face with the towel on his shoulder. Bhujangaiah carefully inspected his face in the tiny ancient mirror, which seemed to suffer from lukoderma, as it hung on the wall in a corner. In the vague reflection of his face he could neither witness Sanjiva's skill nor his fault. He took his comb out of his knickers pocket and began to comb. The comb would bend like a bow when it emerged after combating his hair, which resembled a blackberry bush. Bhujangaiah would straighten it and transfer it back to the bush. Though each time he passed the comb through the hair it would turn into a bow and he would straighten it. For all the effort his hair got disheveled more and more as he combed, resembling a large thorny bush. Sushila watched his adventure silently, without as much as a blink, from a corner of the room. She found the scene funny. Bhujangaiah seemed to remember something all of a sudden and called out to Shiva to bring him another glass of water. Bhujangaiah's bushy hair, which sponged all that water, finally had begun to take form forcing Sushila into a peal of laughter. Bhujangaiah was startled and felt idiotic for not having noticed her presence in the room all this while. He went out after throwing a stupid smile at Sushila. Bhujangaiah found her laughter puzzling. They were shy speaking directly to each other as though they were trying to hide something from one another.

On reaching home, when Bhujangaiah informed Parvathy that he would leave for Mysore straight away, she asked him to bathe first. Bhujangaiah normally bathed in the evening. It was not an easy job to rub his body with a rough stone to remove the dirt. If only the scented soap could cleanse his body it would prove an easy task. Parvathy had unwittingly heated water not knowing that Bhujangaiah would be visiting Mysore that day. Though Parvathy was still in the early period of her post-partum condition she had already begun to take care of easy tasks moving about the house. Though Chinnamma had wanted to return, her sister and brother-in-law had prevailed on her to stay till the play was staged. Everyone from Jakkalli would anyway be arriving for the play. She had agreed to stay knowing that she could return with them. In the meanwhile they had sent back her brother who had come to escort Chinnamma back giving the drama for an excuse. Chinnamma's voice was louder than her sister's. Amase would shiver in his testicles whenever she shouted in anger. Bhujangaiah, while thinking how his sister-in-law who was loud mouthed even in his presence needed a strong man for a husband, was reminded of Sushila who too was of the same age. Sushila's nature was in total contrast. She was so gentle that she seemed scared that she might hurt the very words if she should utter them aloud.

Bhujangaiah got ready for the bathe yielding to his wife's affectionate insistence. When he divested his clothes the hairs on his skin stood on their ends in the biting cold. As Parvathy passed hot water from a vessel Bhujangaiah thought he had found heaven. "Is there a pleasure surpassing that of bathing in the biting cold?" he wondered. Bhujangaiah rubbed the soap with his hands not wishing to be late for the bus by spending time rubbing his body with stone. When Parvathy took the stone he said, "No, I'll be late for the bus." He asked her to pour water. Bhujangaiah who sat without a sound till all the water in the pot was emptied came to his senses only when Parvathy said, "Get up, the water's emptied." His body was steaming. As he hurriedly dressed to leave, his sister-in-law brought a plate of rice rotis and butter. The rotis were scalding hot. He could not eat them in a hurry. Bhujangaiah began to decimate them by breaking them even as the butter placed on the roti melted and started running all over the plate. He felt that the rotis prepared by Chinnamma were tastier by far than what his wife made. Controlling his desire to eat another roti, he walked hurriedly towards the hotel to catch the bus.

The bus had already arrived, Victor who learnt that Bhujangaiah would be traveling to Mysore had deliberately delayed his breakfast.The merchant and Sushila too left for Mysore with Bhujangaiah. Normally the merchant took the evening bus to Mysore. But that day he ran out of stock soon and he could not do business in the evening. The bus was crowded as usual. Bhujangaiah jumped on to the bus by the driver's door and sat next to Victor. Of late he never paid his fare. Victor who was by nature loquacious was glad to have Bhujangaiah's company. The pace of conversation exceeded the speed of the bus. The one news that Bhujangaiah learnt from Victor's talks was that there would soon be a new bus plying the route. It was called "Jayalakshmi Motor". It belonged to a man of the Urs community. It would leave for Kote from the big clock tower square in Mysore and return to Mysore for night halt. Henceforth people did not have to wait for Lingajamba bus alone. Victor who confessed he did not know from when the bus would start its run opined that there was no need for an extra bus on that route.

Bhujangaiah quickly finished his purchases and arranged to lift them to Madalli through Victor. He sent word of his intention to stay at Mysore that day so that he could get the tickets printed for the play before he returned on the following day. He placed the printing orders with Srikrishna press on Shivarampet Street through the shop keeper whom he knew and asked for delivery the next day. He decided to see "Karna the brave and benevolent", a play staged by the Gubbi Company in Jeevana Rayana Katte grounds. He also remembered to visit the bangle merchant's house before the play. He had asked for directions when the merchant had urged him to visit his home. He had agreed to do so in the evening once he completed his business. He went straight to the merchant's home after having completed his tasks. His house was on the road parallel to Nanjumalige. He did not have great difficulty in finding their house. The merchant and Sushila who awaited his visit welcomed him with much affection. The merchant's second wife did not seem to be around. Sushila served him snacks brought from the hotel and went in to bring coffee. In course of conversation Bhujangaiah said that he planned to see the drama and invited the merchant. As his wife was not at home, the merchant agreed to accompany him with his daughter without hesitation. His wife had left the key with the neighbour informing that she would be visiting her parents in Pandavapura for the next three days.

The merchant's home was small. The ventilation was poor. All the six or seven houses in that tenement were like small nests. However so, the merchant was relieved that it was his own house. Who knew how many centuries ago it was built? The Mangalore tiles were cheated of their ochre colour and had weathered black. All the houses were identical. The city municipality must have built them long ago. It was the only property the merchant possessed. Bhujangaiah let his eyes rove in all directions of the house. It was not really all that small. Sushila had a separate room. When he saw the comfort Sushila had in that house he wondered how Sushila even managed to sleep either on the *jagali* of Gowda's house or at his hotel.

Sushila served them coffee and stood drinking a cup herself. When the merchant told her of Bhujangaiah's invitation for the play she stood silent for a moment. She preferred a movie to a play. If she had voiced it Bhujangaiah wouldn't have ignored her wish. When the merchant asked his daughter who stood silent "Why Sushi, will you not go." She said "I will" and began to get ready. The merchant talked about the meanness of his neighbour. The entire tenement was made of people who were either engaged in some business or other, reared a couple of cows and sold milk. The wall of the merchant's house was decorated with handicraft. Noticing Bhujangaiah's attention the merchant said that his dead wife had made them all. There was a chariot, a swan, a peacock, made of colored beads. The merchant who had framed the art works in glass now began to unconsciously draw a picture of his dead wife for Bhujangaiah. He said that the present wife and the first were as different as a hill from the plains. Bhujangaiah felt pity for the merchant when he saw his eyes brimming as yet not free of his love for her, when he said his present wife was not worth the dust of the other's feet. Sushila who listened to the conversation while dressing came out in an eye - catching sari, wafting fragrance. It was the first time Bhujangaiah had seen her thus. He was distracted by her charm for a moment. The merchant was lost in the memory of his wife oblivious to what was transpiring. When Sushila prompted him he felt his wife had stood in front of him in the form of his daughter. That was the prime reason for the merchant's love for his daughter. There was always the guilt in a corner of his mind that he had erred by marrying a second time. Though the new wife had given him three children he had never felt the need for her as he had done with Sushila's mother.

When often her father was overcome by sorrow in the memory of her mother Sushila consoled him, though she herself cried. Whenever the merchant's new wife witnessed that, she felt as if a cauldron of hot water was being emptied over her and her natural envy and pettiness would grow twofold. The result was that Sushila would be subjected to an increased harassment. Though the merchant looked as thin as a rheumatic he would turn into the proverbial Benki Nawab, the gunnery nabob, when angered. As much as she raised her voice, she would get thrashed badly enough to be bedridden for three days caught in his ire. Of late Sushila would stand between her and her father not allowing him to hit her. But there would be some trouble or the other at home all the time. Sushila fed up with it, had chosen the gravelly path, the tree shade, and the *jagali* of Gowda's house for sleep. Though her body tired out a little, her mind was at peace.

Bhujangaiah stood up saying it would be late for the play if they delayed any longer. They hired a horse drawn Jataka from Nanjumalige. Bhujangaiah always found it a pleasure to ride in the jatakas of Mysore. It was unlike the bullock carts of their village. Sushila climbed on first. The merchant and Bhujangaiah followed next and sat at the back with their legs dangling.

When the Moslem driver of the jataka requested those at the back to move up front a little to balance the load, Bhujangaiah was forced to sit jostling against Sushila. Though he was uncomfortable at first when he felt Sushila's back touching his body he nevertheless found the warmth spreading through every atom of his body slowly. His blood seemed to match the pace of the horse. Bhujangaiah was unhappy when the far away Jeevanarayana Katte like misfortune was reached in no time. They paid the fare and walked towards the tent housing the theatre. The merchant insisted on buying the tickets for the chairs. It was quite crowded. The house was full by the time they went in. The people of Mysore were mad after the drama of Gubbi Company. Though Veeranna the owner of the company was billed to perform, Kotturappa who played the role of Karna acted superbly. One of the attendants found a place for them in a corner on seeing them searching for their seats. Sushila sat next to Bhujangaiah. The merchant sat on the other side of her. The drama soon began.

The play set in the Karuna rasa, of pity, melted their hearts. A villainous man awoke in Bhujangaiah when he felt the pulse of Sushila. The impudence that was aroused grew strident even as Bhujangaiah tried to check knowing that either to take the lead or to react in any manner was wrong. Sushila's thighs were moaning in the heat of youth spurring Bhujangaiah in the darkness to mischief. All the personal Gods to whom Bhujangaiah prayed perspiring in fear and in excitement to control his mind now deserted him. For all his efforts the body fed on salt and vinegar did not respond to any wise advice. His rough hand first in Sushila's hand and later slowly on her pleasurable thighs began to strum the strings.

When the play ended both Bhujangaiah and Sushila seemed to have descended from some strange world. There was no gulf between them. Caste, age and status had lost their stay pin to crumble. Both were shy. Sushila could not comprehend why and how she could desire Bhujangaiah who was far too much old for her, Bhujangaiah had been earlier subjected to a similar experience when he was very young. But that was in contrast to the present one. He had found a job in a big house in Mysore after he had run away from home and roamed aimless. It was the time when his youth gushed. The woman of the house must have been as old then as he was now in relation to Sushila. He suddenly remembered how he had become the tool to the middle aged mischief in spite of his tender age, the misfortune that was the result, and how he had narrowly escaped death. He shivered for a moment. Though he had forgotten all of that when he returned home, now and then, in weak moments, the desire for the taste of her body would overcome him and shake his being.

After the drama they had a meal at a hotel. Sushila had felt as though a wild beast had invaded her body. The urgency to have her body torn by sharp talons or for nails to be driven into every inch of her body grew strong. The beast that entered her seemed to remain dormant out of fear. Who knew when it would manifest in its bestiality? Why should they not run away this instant from all the sound and fury? Bhujangaiah hastily took leave saying he would meet them in the village the next day. Sushila found his behaviour strange. She wished that her father had asked him home. The merchant never thought of inviting him home to sleep. Sushila did not know how she reached home. The entire night she was assailed by dreams, as if a new universe had opened out for her, as if her body was encircled and churned by someone. She felt an uncontrollable thirst to have her untiring body churned forever, not getting wearied however long the churning went on. Fortunately, the merchant who snored did not feel the heat of sexual intensity that radiated from his daughter's body. Sushila was getting broiled within. It grew unbearable each moment. Though she got up and drank a whole vessel full of water, her thirst was not quenched.

***

CHAPTER - 17

There is no describing the gaiety on the day of the performance in Madalli. The tent for the audience was erected in front of the village court. The stage was raised high enough for the people to be able to witness the play even from a distance. Already a truckload of costumes had arrived from Mandya and every one had got busy. The elders of the village personally supervised such tasks as clearing the ground around the stage and the spectator area as well as making the pit for the musicians. Already the pamphlets for "Shiva Jalandhara" which Bhujangaiah had got printed from Mysore were pasted on the walls and pillars of every house in Madalli. They were also distributed in all the seven and odd neighbouring villages. More than that the pamphlets had reached all the villages where relatives of the folk of Madalli lived. This too was a festival for the people of that village. Since two days relatives and friends had begun to arrive in groups in Madalli. The homes of the actors especially, were crowded with their relatives and friends. As the summer Kharif crop that year was good no one found their visitors a burden. Relatives not only from Jakkalli and Kallalli but also from a couple of other villages had arrived at Bhujangaiah's house. Being a staunch devotee of Shiva, Ayya from Hampapura had arrived with his wife and children. Ayya, who praised Brunda for her staunch devotion to her husband, had brought his wife to be blessed by watching Brunda at least in the play. After Jalandhara, Brunda's was the most crucial role in the play. Two actors played Jalandhara's role. Master Govindaraju had divided the role into Jalandhara I and Jalandhara II and had apportioned the speeches and songs equally among two actors. Sannaswamy, who sang as melodiously as a woman, played the role of Brunda. In order to keep his voice from breaking no fried food was served at his home from three days before the performance. What if his throat sat as the performance day neared by yielding to his taste buds? Dhandhi alias Somappa played Jalandhara I, while Shivabasappa played Jalandhara II. Madalli's prestige depended on the success of these three roles. The stature of Harlequin Ajappa as well as that of Bhujangaiah too rested on it. Both of them had met the tribal, Kadukuruba of Hallada Koppal, to get him to ward off the spell that those who envied them in the village may cast.

Bhujangaiah had summoned each of the actors three days before the performance and had warned them to follow the diet strictly, impressing upon them the event's importance in bringing their village a good name. At last the anxious yet gay day of the performance had arrived. All the actors had conducted themselves with great restraint shunning both the snacks prepared in honour of the visitors and unnecessary conversation in their new clothes with visitors. Bhujangaiah's hotel too had turned busy as a beehive. Even Manja had worn new clothes and was lost in thought about the play since morning, which had forced all the work in the hotel on Shiva. But Urupa had reduced Shiva's burden. Shiva had by then gained enough expertise in preparing almost all the snacks in the hotel. He was capable of keeping the hotel from shutting its door in Manja's absence and ready to face the innumerable customers. He had this morning prepared enough of the spicy *masale vade* of lentils, as well as three large basins of *karasev* for the whole day. It was a day when there was no choice of snacks. These snacks could be served on pieces of paper too. The problem of washing plates had thus been solved. He decided to serve only tea and cancelled coffee. The relatives of the villagers who had arrived in Madalli a couple of days earlier were visiting the hotel almost every hour to drink tea. That day the rush of customers was unmanageable. Bhujangaiah had arrived early in the morning to leave instructions with his workers as to what needed to be done that day at the hotel. He had also told them to close the hotel before evening. The merchant and Sushila had already arrived from Mysore and the merchant shouldered some responsibilities of the hotel. The question who would watch the hotel if everyone went for the performance had bothered Bhujangaiah. Neither Shiva nor Urupa were the kind to check their desire to see the performance. Finally, the merchant who had seen many such village performances agreed to sleep at the hotel despite his desire to witness that particular play.

Madalli had begun to change its character as dusk advanced. Wherever the eyes turned one saw a throng of people. From where did all those children arrive? The sound of the dynamo run generator had added to the noise of the crowd, with the canopy of the theater already raised. The entire tent seemed to blaze forth. When the electric lights were lit people began to gather in groups. With the ground in front of the tent already full, people were sitting on mats all along the sides of the four streets that converged on the village court. Karigowda and the other elders of the village had taken upon themselves to control the crowd, The drama songs of some theatre company were blaring through the public address system. The women of the village too had finished their work at home and had arrived to sit relaxed, chewing betel leaves and eagerly awaiting the start of the drama. From Hundi everyone had arrived and was sitting in the front row, near the trellised stage on mats. The children of the village were full of unbridled enthusiasm. When all of them were jumping and hopping, giving vent to their immense joy by shouting, Raja alone looked downcast. He had wished to take part in the play. Bhujangaiah himself had fanned his desire. But the approaching exams like crashing boulders had smothered his desire. Raju sat disappointed next to his mother without getting involved in any of the activities. There was still time for the play to start. The musicians had not yet arrived. But their tabla, harmonium and other musical instruments were arranged on the tables kept in the pit. Bhujangaiah had organized food for those who were crucial for the drama at the hall of Karigowda's new house near the court. The new Mangalore tiled house of Karigowda built the previous year was not yet occupied. It had a vast inner courtyard of twelve pillars. On three sides of the house were the rooms. Each room could have housed a family. After Ugadi the eldest son had planned to move into the house. Today, even the new house was alive. The elders of the neighbouring villages and the musicians from Mysore sat on the *jagali* of the house after a sumptuous meal. The Petromax lamp from Bhujangaiah's hotel was burning bright. Master Govindaraju seeing Bhujangaiah still there sent him off immediately to get ready with his make up as his was the first entry. Bhujangaiah had to get through his part of the drama as early as possible in order to oversee the arrangements necessary to carry the rest of the play through safely. He hurried on to the stage. Already, most of the actors were ready with their make up and costume and stood wondering at their strange appearance. Pundri who was playing the role of a woman had dressed in a sari ahead of everybody. He tried to immediately put out the beedi, which he was smoking not being able to control his need for a smoke, when Bhujangaiah appeared. Bhujangaiah realized that the woman who had surprised him for a moment by smoking was none other than his dear friend Pundri. He felt like laughing.

As soon as Master Govindaraju arrived and tuned the harmonium the musicians too began to tune their various instruments. The vast crowd of people that was creating a terrible din suddenly fell quite. Sushila who had supped at Bhujangaiah's house had arrived with Parvathy to witness the play. Urupa finally succeeded in getting a place for those who arrived late on the mats spread by Muddegowda's family. Raja was irritated when they sat next to him. Sushila sat close to Raja and spoke to him. He had observed that very many eyes had watched Sushila when she arrived as if they would tear into her. He wished to get up and go elsewhere. All his friends were busy peeping through the palm leaf screen into the green room, and running here and there as if they played at "catch me if you can" troubling Sanna Thammanna the stage manager. He held a long stick chasing the children as he would a herd of cattle. Sanna Thammanna who always took upon himself the task of controlling children on any occasion in the village had been nicknamed for some unknown reason "Ashen Arse". The army of children teased him unrestrainedly, calling out his nickname "Ashen Arse". He provided an impetus to their natural monkeying. But when the play began, they had somehow appeared right in front of the stage slipping through the audience. Raja too wished to be with them. Sushila enquired with affection " When is your exam?" He pretended not to have heard. Was it not because of that horrible exam that he was cheated of the chance to act in the play? When Sushila said that she already found out the school and fixed a room for him to live in Mysore soon after he finished his present exam, Raja felt he had no reason to be unnecessarily angry and lent his ear to her.

The Invocation began. All the actors began to sing off stage. A young shrill voice very different from the others was heard. Raja could recognize it as that of Vasantha, the son of the village accountant, who was a year junior to him in school. He had boasted to Raja a few times that he sang better than all others in the drama. Raja out of envy had put Vasantha's brag down by using the language of the elders, "Shut your arse. Don't start your brahminical brag. Have I not heard you howling like a jackal?" Vasantha had gone away without another word at Raja's abuse. He had remained silent out of fear that Raja too like Swami the son of Kullegowda might say, " Hey shut up. I know what your elder sister did with our Narayana..............." When he heard that, Vasantha had grown furious enough to want to kick his sister Vanajakshi. But she was the only one who showed any affection for him. She gave him occasionally whatever money he asked for. Once as he walked with her, Narayana had met them and spoken to her with a smile. He had not seen them together ever after. On the day Swami had abused he had told his sister about it in the backyard of their house. After sitting silently for a while she had embraced him and cried. Vasantha too had begun to have doubts. Yet again he was comforted in the thought that his sister was not such a bad woman.

The curtain went up after the invocation. The entire village knew that Bhujangaiah played the role of Sutradhara, Sushila found his costume interesting. Though his voice was drowned in the terrible clamour of the musical instruments she found it pleasant. She fancied that he had descended from some strange angelic world of the Gandharvas and that she were floating away with him on the clouds. The audience clapped when a few went on stage after he had finished delivering his memorized dialogue and song and pinned on his brocaded shirt notes of five and ten rupees. When Sushila asked Puttakka, Raja's mother not comprehending why they did so, she was told by Puttakka that they were "returning favours", Sushila who had presumed that the ritual was observed only at marriages found it funny. As the play progressed the audience "returned favour" with money or silver framed pictures whenever a new character appeared on the stage.

The two speakers tied at both ends of the stage blared forth the speech of the character to split the ear. Bhujangaiah who had finished his role removed his make up and costume to come and sit amidst the audience to see if the play had gained in intensity. He later got up and went in by the side entrance to the stage. Sushila's eyes watched his movements. When the curtain was raised again the scenary dazzled the audience. It was the court of Indra. On every lip was an exclamation "Ah, there isn't another play where one had seen such a Durbar in the nearby villages". Even the throne of Indra was lit by red, blue, and green lights. He wore a sparkling crown, armlet, necklace, etc.. The large audience sat staring in wonder as if Indra in person had descended on Madalli. Sushlia did not find it novel. These scenaries were nothing compared to those of the Gubbi Company in Mysore. But for the people of Madalli it was a wonder which they had never before witnessed. On every lip was the exclamation "Aha! Nothing can be compared with this?" Raja was naming the character in the court of Indra to Sushila. He had already got over his anger at her. Whenever her soft hand touched him he was electrified. When she drew him in her embrace and asked "Raja, who are they?" He had grown all damp inside. Though he found pleasure in her embrace when Sushila had embraced him as if he were a baby he was also inexplicably scared. He named all the characters whether she enquired or not in an attempt to escape his discomfiture.

Doddathamma of Parivara played Indra. He used to sing the songs well. He sat on the throne with the air of a prince. The throne was surrounded by a few actors. As Raja was naming them, Harlequine Ajappa and the village accountant went up the stage with garlands. When the microphone announced, "Govindaraju the Drama Master and Bhujangaiah the Manager of the drama should kindly come on to the stage wherever they are". Master Govindraju who was playing the harmonium in the pit went up. Bhujangaiah was not to be found. He was not to be seen though they called out his name again. By then a couple of people dragged Bhujangaiah who was hiding among the audience on to the stage. As soon as Bhujangaiah appeared on the stage there was a rain of applause. Everybody knew that the drama was performed because of his effort. Rudrappa and Sannappa saw red at the honour that was bestowed on Bhujangaiah. Bhujangaiah humbly stood next to the master. Only Doddathammanna continued to sit on the throne in his princely arrogance. Cennamalla who was playing the role of the minister standing next to the throne said softly, "Hey, Doddathammana step down. How can you sit high when the master and Bhujangaiah are on stage!" his words were heard through the mike by all those who sat in the front row of the audience. Indra suddenly realized he was Doddathamma of Parivara and got off the throne hurriedly. Sushila laughed aloud. She found that all those humorous events such as the loud admonition, Doddathammanna climbing off the throne, and his ascending the throne again immediately after the garlanding ceremony had not brought laughter among the others. Puttakka not understanding why Sushila laughed explained innocently, "Should not Doddathamma at least realize that he belongs to the Thore community? When elders arrive how can he sit high?' Sushila was entertained by the manner of speech and the behaviour of the people of Madalli who intruded on the stage on innumerable occasions after that incident even as the play "Shiva Jalandhara" progressed.

The play ended by the time the cock crowed. The assembled audience left with praise on their lips. The children who were curled in deep sleep now followed unwillingly their mothers holding to their sari fringes. Raja had sat alert throughout the play though every now and then sleep threatened him. He found more pleasure in Sushila's proximity than in the play. When Puttavva invited Sushila who stood up, "Come home with us Sushila. She had replied seeing Urupa who waited to escort her to the hotel," Not now mother, I'll come tomorrow." She patted Raja's back, "Didn't you say the exams were next week? Study well." She left with Urupa.

All along the way, as Sushila and Urupa returned to the hotel, they met groups of people from Hosalli, and Kyatanahalli praising the play. Each one praised according to his preference the actors who played the roles of Brunda, Jalandhara, Ishwara, Parvathy, etc... Beard of Kyatanahalli had already arrived at the hotel with his family when Sushila reached there with Urupa. He enquired "Where is the merchant?" Urupa knocked on the door waking up the merchant before she could reply. Beard asked for a glass of water to quench his thirst as soon as the door was opened. He made his little daughter to drink water not forgetting her after having reprimanded the merchant, " What is this? You missed the drama...it was great. Bhujangaiah's efforts received their due. The acting was superb. Their acting cannot be matched." He left with his cohort saying," I will meet you again merchant; see you again Sushilavva."

Sushila rubbing her burning eyes spread the mat kept in a corner of the shop front as soon as she reached the hotel and slept. She had never been up so late. She fell into deep sleep as soon as she shut her eyes. The door of the hotel was open. Shiva and Manja had not arrived yet. The merchant couldn't find sleep again. Shiva arrived as the day broadened. Urupa was snoring on a bench by then. A few inquired if tea was being served seeing the hotel door ajar. The previous day itself it had been decided that the hotel would be closed for the day. Shiva prepared four cups of tea not saying no to the merchant. The merchant took a cup to his daughter. She refused to open her eyes. The merchant noticing the seragu having slid off her torso covered her with a blanket hanging on the clothesline in the room and drew the door shut as he came out to wake up Urupa. Urupa who got up as if he had seen a nightmare drank noisily the tea the merchant handed him without opening his eyes and rolled over to sleep. Except for the merchant the others found that the night had just begun for them.

***

CHAPTER - 18

It was almost a month since the drama had been staged but its memory was still green in the minds of the people of Madalli as though it were staged only the previous day. The play had grown so popular that all the neighbouring villages agreed that if ever there was a performance it was that of Madalli. Bhujangaiah's stature grew in Madalli because of that. Shivarudraswamy alias Shastri, the expert astrologer, had forecast his future saying that he would enjoy a King's fortune for the next 12 years and whatever he touched during that period would turn into gold. Parvathy who had nodded at his words had sent through Amase a basket full of ragi to Shastri's house.

Come summer, the people of Madalli hardly had any work. Everyone spent time indolently on his *jagali* playing *Chaukabara,* the game of squares and dice, or some other game. It was then that both Doddathamma and Pundri got busy with their cattle trading. As the cattle fair would be held successively everywhere they had to travel from one village to another with scant time to scratch their ass. They camped up to a week at each fair. The most important fairs for them were at Chunchanakatte, Bettadapura, Hemagiri and Mudukatore. As Pundri grew busy with his work the evenings in Bhujangaiah's hotel grew boring with little entertainment.

For the Tampura Ayya, summer was the right time for mendicant visits. He stayed for five to six days when he visited Madalli now. Bhujangaiah too not being busy otherwise used to sit lending his ears to his songs. Ayya would narrate the fortunes of the devotees of Shiva, apart from singing. Sushila too loved his tales. Each detail of the story of Akka Mahadevi heard from his mouth was imprinted on her mind. Ayya had sung in a heart rending manner Akka Mahadevi's plea to the plants, the trees, the animals and the birds if they had seen her master as she journeyed in Shrishaila's vast orchard of plantains singing and crying in search of God Chennamallikarjuna, after having left her husband the King. Sushila was surprised to hear that Akka Mahadevi had arrived at the crowded assembly to stand in the nude.

There were many changes effected in Bhujangaiah's room. There was a mirror with a stand instead of the one that looked afflicted by lukoderma. There was the razor he used, a big comb, a brush and other accessories. Half of the comb had large teeth to facilitate freeing the knots while the other had smaller teeth to smoothen the hair. In time Sushila began to find the hay-roofed, wattle-walled room dearer and a happier circumstance than her own home in Mysore. She would leave on business with her father in the morning and return only in the evening. Because of the summer heat people were always crowding at the hotel in the daytime. Sushila had got the gramophone repaired at Mysore and it was now in the shop front. She had kept it under lock in a deal wood box warning that all those who came would turn it and spoil it. Manja had felt his body burn at the proprietary manner of Sushila. Though he wondered at her 'arrogance' he felt like a serpent with its fangs removed when he saw her. He had not grown entirely without hopes though he knew of the friendship between his master and her. He took pleasure in stealthily watching her lovely legs through the gap in the kitchen roof as Sushila lifted her sari to wash her feet. Shiva too learnt of Manja's behaviour and did not approve of it.

As days went by Manja's will to work slackened. Though Bhujangaiah suspected that Manja was not properly accounting for the business as before, he consoled himself with the thought that Manja was not dishonest. But when he saw the difference between the business when he sat at the counter and when Manja sat he began to get perturbed. Of late, when Bhujangaiah saw Manja visit Mysore once every ten or fifteen days, he was unable to avoid being suspicious and felt a little unhappy with him. He had not abused him or put him down even a single day. He had taken better care of him than he had his son. Yes, why had he changed? Only Shiva had not changed. When he joined he was fit only to clean the plates and glasses but then had soon learnt everything. Only, he could not keep accounts. If he had known how to, he certainly would have by then found out how cleverly Manja had secreted money from the business. In the meanwhile, Manja had noticed Bhujangaiah's increased preference for Shiva. Manja had grown aloof much more when he learnt of Shiva getting a rise in salary when his father visited to collect the money and when he saw the father and son being happy the whole day. Yet Bhujangaiah never saw anything bad in Manja or seemed not to notice whatever misdemeanors Manja committed.

One evening Sushila returned from business. Her father had not accompanied her. The only two customers who were at the hotel finished drinking their tea and left. Shiva was chopping wood with Urupa in the backyard. Manja who watched them chopping wood in competition under torch light had pretended not to have noticed Sushila's arrival and as Sushila entered the room sidled towards the door on stealthy feet. Sushila had not bolted the door. It was her habit to change her sari after her return from her business trip. Manja who had known this suddenly pushed the door as if he was ignorant. Sushila, who had just then taken a fresh sari in her hand, screamed as the door opened and sat down. Manja who saw her naked body was stunned and pretended that he had opened the door unknowingly and walked back to the wood utters after shutting the door himself. Sushila who stood up with the sari held against her, bolted the door and sat down. She sat in shame and confusion not knowing if Manja had opened the door deliberately. Manja began to get scared seeing Sushila not opening the door. By then Shiva and Urupa had completed the task of chopping wood and sat down drinking a vessel full of water as soon as they entered the hotel. Urupa asked Manja to prepare a cup of tea. Manja who was busy preparing tea as if nothing had transpired said, "there is no water, go and fill the drum." Shiva immediately took the water vessel and called Urupa. Urupa lost his temper, "It is just now that we have rested after chopping wood. Can't it wait till we have had some tea and catch our breath?" Shiva sat down saying, "all right". When Manja asked Shiva to serve tea to Sushila in the room Urupa asked "Has Sushilakka arrived?" Manja stood up turning away sipping his tea as if he had no further interest in the matter.

When Shiva knocked on the door, Sushila called out, "Who is it?" Shiva replied, "It's me sister... Shiva." When Sushila opened the door Urupa enquired grinning, "Sushilakka, when did you arrive?" Sushila refused the tea and shut the door again. There were no customers. Manja could not bear it any longer. He went out saying, "Shiva I am going into the village for a while." He walked towards Madalli. Shiva was displeased with Manja's manner. Sushila used to go into the backyard to wash her limbs soon after her return. And she had never ever sat with the doors shut thus. She did not even drink the tea he brought. Shiva knocked on the door of Sushlia's room again. Sushila opened the door in rage, "What is it, are you suffering from a compulsion of knocking on doors?" Shiva stood stupidly staring with dead eyes. Urupa stood blinking not understanding why she was enraged. Sushila sat down, neither shutting the door nor speaking to them. Both Shiva and Urupa sat dispirited as if they had erred in not leaving Sushila alone. A little time passed thus. No customer arrived to break their silence, Shiva wondered if an argument had ensued between Sushila and Manja after her arrival and if she had raged at them because of that. Perhaps that's why Manja left for Madalli all of a sudden. He must enquire when Manja returned. He had grown very haughty. He behaved as if he were the owner.

Shiva wished to speak to Sushila. Though he stood up to ask what the matter was he could not pick up enough courage to address Sushila. He sat down as if his mind had grown blank. Sushila finally got bored sitting alone and came out of the room into the hotel. She saw them both sitting without uttering a word sighing as if they were undergoing punishment for some fault of theirs. Sushila felt pity for them. They were both nice boys. Not arrogant like Manja. There was no sign of Manja anywhere in the hotel. She looked out. He was not to be seen anywhere. Sushila once again looked at the two who sat without moving listening to the sussurrus of her sari. Urupa who was a fountain of enthusiasm sat with his long legs folded as if he were meditating. The milk on the stove was boiling. They both lifted their heads when finally Sushila who found the silence unbearable enquired, "Where is that rascal Manja?" Shiva relaxed his facial muscles feeling his spirit returning. "He went into the village sister." "Why are you sitting thus? What's wrong with you?" She asked and warned, "Look, the milk is boiling". Shiva suddenly got up and sprinkled water over the burning firewood saying, "He has turned into a gentleman. He purposely leaves things on the stove and disappears without telling anyone." Shiva justified that he was not at fault. He turned to her and asked, "Did he say something to you?" Though Sushila was uncomfortable for a moment she said without exhibiting it, "I'll slap him if he lets his tongue loose." Urupa was pleased. He opened his mouth like a frog, "Manja is very arrogant sister. He refers to you in the singular." He expressed his protest. Sushila invited them into the room as though she forgot all that happened and got them to remove the gramophone from the box and keeping it on Bhujangaiah's cot played two new film songs that she herself had bought at Mysore. Both of them more than listening to the song seemed to watch with blinking eyes the songs springing from the big horn. Urupa found it to be an insoluble mystery. He asked Sushila foolish questions. She too laughed. With the tension disappearing the three laughed happily.

When Manja reached the hotel he heard a song that he had never heard emanating from the room. Sushila had not played the new disc since she had brought it. The door was wide open. He stood at the door noiselessly. Along with the song their conversation too reached to his ears. Manja felt as if a cauldron of hot water was emptied on him. His losing control over the gramophone, Sushila looking upon him as a menial, and now her laughter with the two peasants, each incident made his bile rise to his brain. He called out to Shiva harshly, standing at the door, "Hey Shiva, what are you shaving there, instead of grinding rice?" Sushila stopped playing the gramophone at once. Silence grew thick for a moment. No one spoke. When Manja again said, "Why? Did you not hear? Have you got a dildo in your ears?" Shiva too was enraged. Sushila felt like puking listening to Manja's vulgar speech, Shiva who had never back talked to Manja came out of the room to confront him, "Why do you talk so brother Manja? Take care, or else my lips too will find such language" Though Manja was a little scared when Shiva stared at him sternly he said, "Hey, how come you are so bold? I'll kick you out." Shiva grew hot, "Enough now, shut up. You too have come here like me to eat the leftovers. It is not your father who owns the hotel. Do you think my feet will be eating Jaggery and chick peas while you kick me?" Shiva had never retorted thus. Manja's strength ebbed out. Realizing that Shiva would not keep quiet if he raised his hands Manja retreated into the kitchen simmering with anger. Urupa was hopefully waiting for a showdown. He burst into laughter seeing Manja reduced to a singed cat. Manja was further enraged by Urupa's laughter. To top it all Sushila played the song again for Urupa and Shiva as if to rub salt into his wounds.

Manja decided to leave the hotel that very moment. He presumed that the hotel would close down without him. He was under the impression that Bhujangaiah never behaved harshly with him because he couldn't manage without him, Manja felt like crying. Their talk, the ironic speech and the song in the room, everything began to torture him. Sushila herself must have been responsible for the dish washing Shiva putting him down. How else could he have plucked up so much courage? "The slatternly widow behaves as if she were very chaste," Manja went out of the hotel cursing and muttering obscenities at Sushila. It had begun to grow dark and the birds were already noisy in the tamarind tree. Manja straight away left for the village as if he were possessed by a demon. The others wondered at his going to the village in such a hurry. Only Shiva feared whether Manja would complain against them to Bhujangaiah. What if the master threw him out? Sushila promised to see that nothing happened to him. Shiva too believed that his master would not ignore Sushila's words for whatever reason.

Shiva got ready to take care of the tasks that were Manja's prerogative all these days. He did not have any difficulty in lighting the petromax. After asking Urupa to grind the rice he got the lentils ready for supper. Sushila too joined them to help. Sushila had belonged to a different caste. She had remained aloof all these days like an outsider because of a notion that she should not touch the cooking vessels. Sushila now joining them to help, chatting happily, spurred the enthusiasm of Urupa and Shiva. Though Urupa protested, "Why should you dirty your hands Sushilakka?" he wished that she stayed near them. The merchant too arrived by then, Though Ayya visited the hotel he never stayed there. If he had seen Sushila of the Bangle Sellers community touching the cooking vessel he perhaps would not have even touched tea. There was no sign of Manja though the night had advanced. Though Bhujangaiah remained at home whenever Sushila and the merchant slept at the hotel there were times he returned to the hotel as though by chance. Between the space where his cot was and the space where it was planned to set up the shop there was a short wall, dividing the room into two parts. Sushila slept with her father in the front of the room whenever Bhujangaiah too was at the hotel. Sleep eluded Manja on such nights. His head would fill with strange thoughts. Would Sushila be sleeping with his master? He writhed with suspicion. As much as Sushila rejected him so much his interest in her grew. Sushila too had subtly noticed it. Remembering his behaviour from the past she was sure that he had intentionally pushed the door ajar while she dressed. She decided not to tell Bhujangaiah after mulling over the incident for long. The fact of Manja disappearing without showing his face to her had strengthened her doubts. Though supper time was drawing to a close no one had arrived. The four sat down to eat finding it pointless waiting any longer. Both Shiva and Urupa found the rasam that Sushila had made delicious. After supper they sat chatting outside the hotel warding off the summer's heat.

The carts carrying firewood wended their way towards Mysore in a line. The only profession that the nearby villagers engaged themselves in when summer set foot was to chop firewood and take it to Mysore. If the carts managed to get past the Forest Gate of Madalli it was as good as having reached Mysore. If one warmed the palm of the forester or the guard Thimmanayaka they would turn the other way even if there were teak or sandalwood loaded in the cart. The movement of the firewood carts steadily flowed even after midnight. There were many even in Madalli who transported firewood to Mysore. As there were plenty of Beutea trees in the forests around Madalli the poor collected the leaves of Beutea, dried them and bundled them to send it to Mysore. Apart from cultivation, the other sources of earning that the very poor of Madalli had were such as these.

Sushila did not know at what time Manja returned. She had presumed that he had left for Mysore by one of those firewood carts. When she got up stretching her limbs she heard the loud voice of Manja. He had not brought coffee as was his wont whether she had asked for it or not. Shiva had brought tea instead of coffee when she had called him to get her coffee. Sushila never drank tea in the morning. There were very few customers who drank coffee. Everyone drank tea. Sushila contorted her face having sipped at it and called Shiva, "What is this, you have brought tea instead of coffee?" Shiva took the tea and threw it into the gutter as a slap on Manja's face and said "Sushilakka wants coffee." Manja had replied woodenly, "Tell her it is not ready." Shiva not wishing to retort in front of the other customers said gently, "Please prepare it brother". Manja shouted in anger so that every one in the hotel could hear, "See what I'll do to you if you go on behaving arrogantly instead of washing vessels with your ass shut" The ears of those present picked up. Shiva silently began to work. Urupa found Manja's behaviour intolerable. He decided to inform Bhujangaiah when he arrived. There was no sign of him that day, though he usually arrived by that time. He had not come the previous night too. He decided to visit the village. He was not answerable to anyone. As he was not working for a salary at the hotel Manja could hardly address him as he did Shiva. Urupa would not have missed a chance to get Sushila's accolades by slapping Manja's face if he had dared to speak to him.

When the merchant returned from the pond and asked Sushila for breakfast she had said "I finished mine." The merchant had his and left with the daughter for business. When Sushila said they should visit Hundi he acquiesced. They both took the path to Hundi. Both Shiva and Urupa were sad that Sushila had left not only without breakfast, but also without drinking a cup of coffee. Manja had never guessed that she would grow so stern. Apart from having showed his arrogance by denying a cup of coffee he too was perturbed at her having left without eating anything. Bhujangaiah who left for the hotel after breakfast at home called Cennamalla whom he found near the court. "Hey, Bakoti" Everyone who was close to Cennamalla called him "Bakoti" with affection. Who knew what it meant? None knew how the name stuck to him. Cennamalla looked like a Jangama with the yellow bell flower behind his ears and the ash smeared on his neck, near the ear, above the eyelids and in three stripes on his dark face. Bhujangaiah made fun of him saying "What is this Bakoti? Have you turned into a Jangama?" He took him to the hotel with him.

Bhujangaiah was taken aback when Cennamalla said, "Why don't you advise Manja? I have doubts about him. Your Manja will turn bad in Narayana's company. That he accompanies him to certain places means that they have found a hunt. Tell me, what does Narayana care about caste or community?" He informed him about his having seen Manja and Narayana, the son of Gowda, walking towards the Shrine of Basappa of the Pond. Though Bhujangaiah had seen the change in Manja he had not worried much about it. Though he wished to ignore the youthful misadventures, his companionship with Narayana was not something he could put up with. Sushila had told him how Narayana had eyed her and had attempted to ravage her like a vulture. Bhujangaiah couldn't tolerate the mention of Narayana's name. What Cennamalla reported must be true. He never lied. He should ask Manja and advise him. He had never admonished him even once. It was therefore that Manja was not scared of him. Ajappa was right in saying that servants should be shown their place. After having heard of all that transpired from Urupa, Bhujangaiah understood that servants sat on the head if given the scope. He was enraged when he learnt that Sushila had left without breakfast. Urupa who was at the door of the hotel jumped out as soon as he saw Bhujangaiah's arrival and had narrated all that had transpired.

Manja was full of misgivings hearing a short tempered Bhujangaiah stepping into the hotel. He buried himself in the task of frying *vades* hiding his trepidation. As the hotel was full of customers Bhujangaiah silently sat at the counter with his teeth clenched. But when he saw the empty tea glasses on the table he was enraged and called Shiva, "Can't you see the empty tumblers? Are your eyes suffering from cataract? Of late you have all grown too arrogant." Shiva immediately removed the glasses and took them to wash without lifting his head. Bhujangaiah addressed the forester who was eating his breakfast, "Do you see forester? When they come they are like mice, once they put on some weight on their buttocks they act as if they would try us." The forester smiled and began to narrate how Thimmanayaka the guard too had changed his colour. Manja's mind began to sour. He knew that Bhujangaiah's words were all directed at him. Though his heart sank for a moment when he saw Cennamalla accompanying his master remembering that he was seen with Narayana by Cennamalla he began to prepare himself to face the consequences.

When Manja re-entered the hotel after Bhujangaiah took him out into the backyard of the hotel as soon as the bus had left his eyes were full of tears. Bhujangaiah did not broach the issue again. He behaved as if nothing had happened. Only Manja acted as if he was paralyzed. When the merchant and Sushila returned after business as usual and went into the backyard for a wash Manja was waiting with his dead eyes to say something. Shiva observed through the gap in the wall a desolate Manja speaking to Sushila after the merchant went inside and behaving like a destitute. He was much disappointed when he saw Sushila's stern face breaking into a smile. Both Urupa and Shiva who had waited with the expectation of seeing something radical happen were disappointed when they saw everything cool down. They found it surprising that Manja began to speak with respect to Sushila from that very evening. They consoled themselves with the thought that at least his arrogance and proprietary attitude had been put an end to.

***

CHAPTER - 19

The news of Raja passing his eighth standard examination standing first in the school had created a festive atmosphere at Muddegowda's home in Hundi. Muddegowda who was privately pleased, having heard the news from others had in the end taken Bhujangaiah with him to Kyatanahalli and had heard straight from Master Govindaraju the news of his son standing first in the school. It was proved in the exam that he was the more intelligent of the three or four other boys in his class. Raja was liked by all the teachers in the school. They had all impressed on Muddegowda that if he were allowed to study further he would grow to be someone of consequence. Gowda felt proud of his son. Yet he was anxious about sending his son to Mysore for studies. More than the money that would be spent what if he grew to be like Narayana his elder brother's son? If children brought bad name to parents what did it matter if they were alive or dead? No. No. His son would not turn out so. Gowda consoled himself and sat up. His wife was already up and busy.

Raja too was up. It was just before dawn, The night in the rest of the house as yet slumbered, though the sun light had touched the well of the house. Gowda who woke up untied the oxen that were tethered inside the house and brought them out to secure them to the pillar of the *jagali*. The birds were noisy in the fig tree beyond the field adjacent to the granary. The clucking hens were busy in their morning routine among the fallen leaves under the hedge. Those were summer days. Gowda observed his tiny Hundi gently waking up as he walked towards the pond. Thamanna's father refused to yield to any of his advice saying, "There is no need for him to study to build a dam. I too am alone. I cannot work hard any larger. Sooner he learns cultivation better will he be able to manage at least what we possess." He had not allowed Muddegowda to speak further. Gowda too had not compelled him knowing his intractable nature. He had broached the issue thinking it would be good to have a companion for his son, Though Gowda wondered if he should ask him once more as he walked towards the pond he decided that no work would get done if he should see the scowling face of Boregowda early in the morning.

Gowda was filled with contentment when he saw that the pond was still three-fourth's full though it was summer, for normally in summer the pond would dry up revealing parched and cracked up bed, with no water even to wash one's buttocks. Thanks to God this time it was full. There would not be any trouble growing another crop. The pond between Madalli and Hundi when full was nature's boon to both the villages. For the children of Hundi, walking on the embankment of the pond in the rainy season was tantamount to performing acrobatics. If they should miss their step even a little on the soft soil of the bund they would fall. Muddegowda's desire to have the road metalled remained as yet a wish. Whenever he heard people say that it was his grandfather who had got the steps cut to the pond he felt proud and wished to do some such thing useful to people. He also wondered why he needed to worry when he had an elder brother in a person like Karigowda and got down the steps and cleared the water to wash his face. It was not yet dawn. The pond that was just then waking up to the warble of the birds had not as yet begun to feel the joy of life. Once the day progressed the four sides of the pond would witness one activity or the other; the clerk who dipped in the water chanting mantra, those who came to wash face, to wash their buttocks, to wash clothes, the women washing vessels, those who washed cattle, those who filled water in the carts, and those who made bricks to build new houses. More than anyone did the children from the street of Parivara Nayaka arrive enthusiastically holding fishing rods to catch fish. With them sported the egrets that seemed like festoons on wings between the two banks of the pond. They would end up in a sudden dive to catch the fish that surfaced in the tender sun. The entire pond grew lively inch by inch. Gowda wished the pond were full throughout the year. If the pond were full all else brimmed. His mind too seemed to brim over.

Bhujangaiah found Gowda so immersed in himself that he didn't even notice his approach. Gowda grew aware of things only when he was poked and spoken to. He blushed when Bhujangaiah asked, "Why? Are you worried that you should send your son to Mysore?" He told Bhujangaiah that he had got up early and had come to the pond because he wished to go to Mysore by the first bus. He talked to Bhujangaiah pleasantly wondering why he was dispirited. Bhujangaiah told him the reason that brought him to Hundi. Master Govindraju had agreed to accompany them to Mysore to seek admission for Raja in Maharaja's High School in Mysore. Bhujangaiah while assuring him that a seat was guaranteed as the master's relative was a clerk at the High School also informed him that it would be easy to rent a room at his acquaintance's home behind Halamma Choultry in Shivarampet as decided earlier. All along Bhujangaiah had repeatedly mulled over all the tasks to be taken care of that day. He was preoccupied with the responsibility of getting admission for Raja in Mysore and had walked without noticing anything on either side of the path.

When they reached home Raja had already bathed, dressed in new clothes and stood anxiously waiting to leave with two bags packed. Puttavva though was happy at the event of her son leaving for Mysore for studies was yet filled with the sadness of having to part from her son. She brought water for Bhujangaiah and her husband on seeing them arrive and sit on the *jagali*. They both washed and sat ready for a breakfast of steaming rotis of rice with large cups of creamy curds. Raja had already eaten his. Puttavva had packed some seven rotis and a packet of curds rice for her son. When they were about to leave she brought a palm full of castor oil and smeared her son's head with it, as was her wont. Raja felt uncomfortable whenever she did that. For the oil, saturating the head would trickle down his forehead and his cheeks. Raja would remember how he used to wipe it with the ends of his shirt only to find the ugly stains of oil and red dust. He was unhappy when his mother did not fail to apply oil on him even when he left for Mysore. However much he strove in front of the mirror the hair seeping with oil did not sit in a raised crown on the forehead. He left home trying to set his hair undeterred. Puttavva's eyes filled with tears as she took leave of her son. She took a vow to Kendagannaswamy that if her son should study well and grow to be of consequence she would wear a mouth lock. She tied a quarter coin in a piece of cloth dipped in turmeric and tied it to the stand. This bore many other such knots in the kitchen as reminders of various vows. Puttavva held Raja dear in spite of her three other children. Raja had been born after three years of marriage. It was only after she had served god every week without fail for three months in Gaddige that the divinity had blessed her with the fruit of children. After Raja not only had three children been born but their affluence too had grown. It was for these reasons that Puttavva found it difficult to part with Raja. The eyes watered and her tears flowed even as she stood at the door watching her son leave.

Though he had eaten well at home Raja was forced to eat again at Bhujangaiah's hotel. After eating steaming *idlis* and *vade* Raja refused coffee and went out on seeing many other boys like himself arriving under the Tamarind tree for the bus, ready to join school at Mysore. He talked to them. They all had studied with him at school for four years. When the bus arrived it was full. When conductor Subbanna refused to take on even a single passenger all the waiting passengers surrounded him not letting him have his breakfast. A helpless Subbanna asked them to talk to Victor. They then surrounded Victor. Victor went into the hotel saying, "Let's see, I'll carry all of you somehow." He packed the children inside the bus somehow and asked the adults to sit on the roof of the bus. Victor asked Bhujangaiah and Muddegowda to stand by his seat. By the time the bus groaned and spewed smoke making its way to Mysore it too had enough. Those sitting on the roof were made to get down near the tollgate, as agreed to beforehand. Bhujangaiah alighted from the bus and took them straight to Shivarampet. Raja who was hidden in some corner of the bus had felt stiff and musty. He was wet with perspiration in the heat. Muddegowda who saw his son's face smeared with oil gave him his towel to wipe. The house that Bhujangaiah took them to was behind the choultry. It was close to Raja's school, to the place where the bus halted, and to the cart square. The room was very small. But Muddegowda learnt in a very short time that the people of the house were good-natured. They took upon themselves the responsibility of cooking rice for Raja, while he could buy curry from a nearby hotel till he learnt to cook his meal. They also promised to get him milk from Cheluvaiah the milkman who arrived from Belavadi every morning. The list of things Raja needed was a mile long, a coal stove, vessels, cot, bed spread, clothes that were appropriate for High school, pen, slippers, etc.. By the time they finished shopping, Master Govindaraju had returned from his visit to the School. He had finished taking care of these. Raja was awed at the sight of the school and the innumerable students there. They all, like him, stood in a queue to seek admission. But they were seniors and old to the school. Most had arrived wearing pants instead of knickers like him. He was glad that he had asked the tailor to make pants instead of shorts. Bhujangaiah and Muddegowda stayed over at Raja's new room that night. There was a verandah attached to the room which could accommodate any one visiting from the village.

Muddegowda felt closer to Bhujangaiah when he thought how difficult it would've been to arrange all those things. Gowda who had been worried at the very thought of leaving a small boy on his own in such a big city was now relieved. Bhujangaiah not only promised to visit Raja personally once a week and inform Gowda of his son's welfare but also assured that if Raja required any thing in a hurry he could send a note through Victor. Bhujangaiah advised Raja throughout the night what he shall keep away from and how to comfort himself in the city, as he would teach a parrot. Muddegowda warned his son to bear in mind Bhujangaiah's advice and boarded the bus with his mind partially at rest. He did have his worries. Raja was a boy who knew nothing apart from his studies. How will he manage? The merchant and Sushila had arrived in

Madalli on the day Bhujangaiah had left for Mysore. Muddegowda who did not know what to say when they got off the bus said to Bhujangaiah, "When you are free do visit Hundi and inform my wife of all the arrangement made. She will be reassured if you should tell her." Bhujangaiah promised, "Why wait till tomorrow? I shall come now. Let us leave after tea." He asked Manja to serve them tea.

Shiva was disappointed when the master left with Muddegowda without staying even for a while. Shiva had since two days kept a careful account of how much business had been transacted, what the expenses were, etc... He was curious to find out how much Manja pocketed. He had given all the details to Sushila. Urupa had found out that Manja had gone with Narayana the previous night too. All the three had enough to complain about Manja. Though Manja was as arrogant as ever when the Master was not around, he was scared of meeting Sushila's eyes while addressing her. Moreover it had grown clear to him that the master took the side of Shiva and Urupa who had grown closer to Sushila than him. Though he had thought ten times to leave his job he had not been able to muster enough courage. Narayana constantly encouraged him to open another hotel in the village. However, Narayana could not help him financially. When the key to the moneybox had not as yet reached his elder brother's hand there was no saying when it would reach his. Narayana who had known that however much he may strive his cereal would not cook till his father died wondered many a time why his father was alive still. Therefore, Narayana had advised Manja to make enough money whenever his master was not around and Manja followed his friend's advice loyally. Though Manja would feel guilty at cheating Bhujangaiah who trusted him, an inexplicable jealousy and hatred burnt in Manja.

The Master did not visit the hotel again that night. Sushila and her father slept in the room. Manja as usual went out at the appointed hour. Urupa too followed Manja like the undeterred Trivikrama. Urupa's senses quickened when he saw Narayana joining Manja and the two entering the outhouse of Gowda's new house near the court. Soon after, a feminine shape arrived in a hurry and vanished into the outhouse. Urupa who had noticed the person who had accompanied the woman standing at a distance approached him as if he had not spied anything. When Urupa called out sternly, "Who is it?" the person froze. There was no mistaking Shivalinga, the younger bother of Puttabasavi who was the permanent customer of all the "elders" of the village. He was sitting like the very picture of innocence. Urupa had put his hand to small time thievery with him on a couple of occasions in the past. After his mother had made him take a vow he had left Shivalinga's company and had striven hard to earn a good name for himself. But Shivalinga seemed to have avowed to retain permanently the adjective of "thief" to his name.

Though Urupa knew the reason why Shivalinga sat there he pretended ignorance saying, "What is this Shivalinga, why are you sitting thus?" Shivalinga replied, "Have you finished your chores at the hotel?" Urupa said, "Not yet, I am here on the hotel's business. Come let us sit on the *jagali* of Gowda's house and talk." Shivalinga was caught. The *jagali* and the door of the outhouse were separated by a mere three yards. What is to be done now? Shivalinga couldn't lose Urupa whatever he did and Urupa began to talk with a raised voice forcing Shivalinga to approach the *jagali*.

Both Narayana and Manja were shocked to hear Urupa's voice. If they were seen by Urupa, the news would spread throughout the village by next morning. Manja almost felt his death. How could he escape? Puttabasavi felt like laughing at their predicament. She derided them "You are green lemons! If you are scared of Urupa the thief of my juices I do not know what great ecstasy you will embrace. It's getting late for me. I must leave now. Sannappa had said he would visit today." Narayana was enraged enough to want to push her on the floor and squash her under his foot when she forced them to hurry. Manja sat down without another word as if he were paralyzed. Puttabasavi who was not used to stealth went out without waiting even for a moment and called out to Shivalinga while abusing Urupa, "What is this Urupa, what did you want to lick here? Go and sleep you fool! I will spill my juice on your head." As she left with Shivalinga in a hurry, Urupa felt a scorpion move along his body at Puttabasavi's irascible abuse. Yet he did not stir from where he sat. He sat watching the half opened door of the outhouse. Were those inside sleeping? Manja had felt happy for a while when he heard Puttabasavi abusing Urupa.Though he bragged, "Look Narayana, the whore's son has followed us like a dog. I will pluck out his testicles if I should get to meet him alone somewhere on the road tomorrow." He did not find enough courage to go out in Urupa's presence. Urupa who waited till midnight returned to the hotel partly disappointed and partly victorious.

***

CHAPTER - 20

The loose mouths of Madalli which could not bear Bhujangaiah's good fortune were itching to wag, unable to fault him till now. But Sushila's issue had been found to be that sweet drink of *payasa* for those tongues. They now drank resoundingly on that issue for all to hear either on the *jagali* of the temple or in the village court or near the pond. It was by sheer accident that Sushila was acquainted with Bhujangaiah. Bhujangaiah was one among those who were known for their clean hand, clean tongue and tightly wrapped dhoti. Though his well wishers disbelieved what they heard, saying why would he who had a loving wife, three children and everything he wished for do such a thing, those who hated him began to vomit forth all that they saw and did not see in a manner that nauseated those who heard them. Most of those who talked were those who had been affected by Sushila's charm. Terribly thwarted in their desire they had all bean disappointed. They had given vent to their disappointment by accusing her of having cast a spell on Bhujangaiah.

Though Narayana who'd learn everything that went on at the hotel through Manja strove to forget his failure by spreading rumors in the village, he felt a burning desire to possess Sushila some day or the other. No woman in Madalli whom he had desired had ever spurned him as Sushila had done. He always felt like stripping her nude in the middle of the street to avenge his defeat whenever he saw her screwing up her face at his sight, as if she had seen something nauseating. But he was scared. What he felt in her absence turned into a fear in her presence. Now and then she still visited his house to either sell bangles or to converse with his mother and bring her betel leaves and nuts. One day he had waited for her to come out and when he uttered softly," Listen,..Sushila," wanting to say something, she had gone spitting with disgust without even turning towards him. It was as though she had spat on his face. From that day the desire to violate her had grown strong in Narayana's mind. If one should believe Manja, in what way was he inferior to Bhujangaiah who was the father of three children? What did she find in him? Or did Manja having failed like him in his desire for her deliberately lie about their relationship? Narayana's brain was tired thinking of it. He waited for Manja, abusing aloud, "Thu-..thu, the dirty widow thinks she is a great virtuous woman."

Manja too by now had futilely made all efforts whenever he remembered the adage he had learnt by wrote as a small boy, "Try and try again". Sushila began to address Bhujangaiah as if he were. her dear companion in front of Manja in order to make him burn with envy. Manja who was tired of putting up with all this finally went and told Parvathy adding colour to everything, on the day Bhujangaiah left for Kote with Pundri. Parvathy who had been shocked at hearing the rumours about her husband's fresh adventure now felt the very sky falling on her head. Each incident that Manja narrated made Parvathy livid. When news of what she had all these days prayed to the family deity to avert reached her she had felt a thunderbolt strike her. She sat for a while without breathing. She then began to hiss and sigh cursing the day Sushila was born as well as her class and community in words that made even Manja nervous. Manja began to have misgivings about his action. He folded his hands to Parvathy, "Please do not tell that I informed." Parvathy chased him out too saying, "You too are a fine man to have come now to utter all this without having said anything for this long." Manja took himself away from that place whining like a dog with a singed ass.

Parvathy was no mistress of her temper. She would turn the whole street upside down forgetting her status. There was no one at home when Manja had come gossiping. It had been a couple of weeks since her sister Chinnamma had left for Jakkalli. She would have sent her immediately to bring her father if only she were present. The only person she thought of under such circumstances was her father Parvathappa. The relationship between the father-in-law and the son-in-law that had gone sour because of the hotel had been set right when the Swami had visited. The control that her father had on his son-in-law had however been lost since then. Even if her father were to come now what could he ask? Was it something that she could confide to people requesting them to advise her husband? Who could be asked to advise him? What if she herself went to the hotel, plucked the hair off that temptress' head and threw her out? What if that outcaste were to stand up to her? Oh God! A bitch on the street had entered the house to cause her hurt! What evil force could have caused her this misery at the very moment when she found happiness in the village folk's praise, "What a responsible man is Bhujangaiah!" Parvathy sat helplessly in a corner of the room hissing and burning in anger. Jealous and intemperate, no action as yet had suggested itself to her mind. If either Bhujangaiah or Sushila were to be present she would have perhaps attacked them like an injured tigress, to drink their blood. Someone seemed to have taken aim at her sensitive part. She had not bothered her head about her husband's behaviour these past couple of months. He had not shown the earlier concern for either home or children. The neglect was there to see. She had not noticed any of it. It would not have gone so far if she had only paid attention. What if Manja's words were true? God, please see that it did not come to pass! She avowed to break ten full coconuts at every step of the temple of Kendagannaswamy in Gaddige. Amase's voice did not reach Parvathy's ears though he called repeatedly, "mother, mother" standing with a plate blinking at his mistress who sat smouldering in a corner. Amase was very hungry. He was scared at the manner in which his mistress sat without seeming to hear however loudly he called. Amase who had seen the daughter-in-law of Mada of the Wall on his street who sat thus felt that perhaps a ghost must have possessed the wife of his master like it had done the other. He shivered. By then Soma had come in running from outside and pulled at his mother in hunger, which brought Parvathy to her senses. She rose up suppressing all her misgivings and began to do the chores. Soma too found her silence which greeted all his speech strange. Amase sat on his haunches in the cattle pen and ate whatever Parvathy served in silence. He had never seen Parvathy in such a mood. Something must have happened. Deviravva too was not to be seen. She must have quarralled with her. Amase who had witnessed the occasional fight between mother-in-law and daughter-in-law surmised as much.

Amase left with the cattle towards the New Fields. The fields bought from Singari were referred to as New Fields by all at home. Though the grass had all grown dry in the summer heat there was still enough green cover on the bunds of the paddy field. The cattle would graze there. Apart from hay and the stems of ragi they had in store the chaff of horse gram too.There was feed enough for two years in Bhujangaiah's backyard. Pundri and Doddathamma who were on the lookout for a pair of medium sized dwarves since a week for Bhujangaiah had found them in Vaddaragudi village and had taken Bhujangaiah there for buying them. Bhujangaiah who normally informed home whenever he left the village had this time, risen, opened the box, taken the money and had left without uttering a word. Though Parvathy was busy in her task she had observed all that her husband had done. She had refrained from enquiring because it was inauspicious to do so when someone went out on good business. Parvathy opened the trunk as if she remembered something. Except for what Bhujangaiah had taken the money saved was still in the trunk. She sighed in relief. She left some money in the trunk and secreted the rest in a tin box in the attic. There was a ladder to climb the attic in the hall. It was normally stored on the rafter in the cow shed. Whenever needed it was brought in to climb the attic in the hall. The odds and ends stored in the attic were in neglect as Deviramma could not of late climb to arrange things. Pots were lined up there, as well as an odd box or two and a few baskets full of rare objects. It was a different universe altogether. Who knew to what age they belonged? All of them had incessantly inhaled the smoke and were shining black! Parvathy slowly removed the topmost of the stacked boxes, secreted the tin with money right in the bottom most of the boxes and rearranged the boxes as before.

Bhujangaiah returned with the dwarves before nightfall. When Amase was asked to feed them after tethering them in front of the door he began to run his hands over them as if he were examining their pedigree and quality. One of the dwarves shied a little. Pundri immediately said, "They will behave so till they get used to you. You need to train them gradually." He drank the water from the vessel, which Soma brought. A lot of people had already gathered. When Ninganna the son of the woman who sold *vade* asked, "They are a fine pair. What did it cost?" Pundri challenged, "Let us see you guess at the price." Ninganna examined the dwarves once more and mentioned a price. Though Pundri had purchased them at Rupees thirty less than the price Ninganna had mentioned he quoted a price adding twenty rupees more, which Ninganna approved. "One can give that price. The dwarves are very good." The dwarves were objects of estimation and evaluation till it grew entirely dark. Even after Amase took them into the cattle shed a couple of people visited to look at them.

Pundri and Doddathamma went to their respective houses even though Bhujangaiah invited them to stay over for supper. He called Amase and sent him to bring his father Shaggy Sidda, Amase left for his street. Bhujangaiah got up, washed his face and limbs with the water stored in the cauldron in the front yard and sat down for worship in the hall. The holy casket slung across his chest was from his father. The battered silver casket had grown black with dirt accumulated in the dents on it. Though he had thought of selling it by weight and get a new one made he had not done so as it was hidden under the shirt out of sight. Parvathy who directed her angry gaze at her husband who was lost in the worship felt like laughing reminded of the proverb she had heard on the lips of the village folk, "He plants the sacred shrub at home though indulging in acts of immorality". Bhujangaiah sat down for his meal after the worship. The daughter instead of sitting with him was busy trying to make her baby brother, sitting in her grandmother's lap, laugh. Parvathy who did not wish to broach the matter till supper couldn't hold back any longer. Standing with a burning face at the kitchen door holding the rice bowl she burst out, "Dont you have any morals that you play with a whore at the hotel?" The mouthful of food that was going down the throat suddenly got stuck. Bhujangaiah slowly lifted his face. Parvathy appeared ugly in the lamp light glowing near the kitchen door, Bhujangaiah did not speak. He struggled to swallow the food in the gullet and drank water from the vessel staring all the while at her. It was a problem he had to confront some day if not then. Unfazed, he retorted harshly, "What did you say you whore? I'll pluck your tongue out if you should open your mouth again taking me for a useless fellow". Parvathy did not yield, "Nothing will end if you try to use your anger taking me for a helpless woman. The entire village is disgusted at you." Bhujangaiah was further enraged, "Enough now, shut up. I too know who is what in the village. Let those bastards behave first before talking ill of me. Tell me which whore's son said all this to you?" Parvathy retorted as if she did not care for consequence, "It was someone who has seen everything. I am not born to my father if I do not worship her with my slipper when I meet that sharer of my husband". She banged the rice bowl in front of her husband. Bhujangaiah felt as if boiling water had been emptied on him. He lifted the rice vessel and threw it at Parvathy. Her scream as well as the rice spilled all over the house. The steaming rice fell on Bhujangaiah and Soma too. Soma too screamed at once. Bhujangaiah stood up and caught hold of Parvathy's hair and kicked her hard enough for her to double up. "You ... You want to let your tongue grow? Instead of staying in your place eating whatever is provided for do you want to try your Jakkalli manners on me?" Parvathy fell on her face screaming, "He is killing me. I am done." By now Deviravva had arrived running. The children were all screaming aloud, Bhujangaiah had not yet washed his hands. Deviravva who covered her daughter-in-law's bared chest with the seragu of her sari, sprinkled water on her face, abusing her son all the while. Bhujangaiah left home without even turning to see what had happened to his wife. When he saw Amase standing with his father as he climbed down the steps of the house he ordered, "Come to the hotel tomorrow" and walked away.

Though Deviravva had found her daughter-in-law sobbing since evening she had not asked the reason. She had not thought that husband and wife would go to such an extent. After the childbirth this time Parvathy had grown aneaemic. She would sit tired if she drew four vessels of water from the water cask. She had not helplessly collapsed thus when her son had hit her on other occasions in the past. Deviravva was scared for a moment. She prayed to all the Gods of the village. Though the mother-in-law and the daughter-in-law had fought over many a flimsy reason the daughter-in-law had not been a stranger to Deviravva. Of late even she suffered pain and tiredness. The daughter-in-law who had seen it had not allowed her to do any work. Deviravva took her daughter-in-law's head in her lap and fanned her. The yodel of the children was reaching a high pitch. By then Basakka, Nanjavva and a few more women from the neighbouring houses had arrived. When asked, Deviravva called Nanjavva near saying, "I do not know what she said to the man who came in from outside even before he could eat. He has beaten her like he would whip cattle." Nanjavva examined her by touching her body and hands and said, "Nothing has happened. She looks like having fainted. Come let us take her to the *jagali*. There is a good breeze blowing." They lifted her out on to the *jagali*. Parvathy who sat up moaning after a while began to spew forth her Jakkalli pearls. Deviravva slowly found her sympathy for her daughter-in-law waning hearing from her mouth at least ten times, "Let his feet be bitten by a snake". Those who had arrived also found her language obnoxious. One after the other they left. The children too grew tired of crying. The two little ones slept without eating. No one ate that night. Parvathy muttered whatever came to her mind as if she alone was injured and went to bed deciding, "I will not stay even for a moment after dawn in this house."

Bhujangaiah who arrived at the hotel simmering in anger had not noticed anyone on his way. When he saw only Urupa and Shiva he asked, "Where is Manja?" Urupa had replied, "Where does he remain in the hotel once it grows dark? There must be some mischief he is up to with Narayana, the son of Gowda. He has gone today too." He was some how shy and scared of informing him of how he had found Manja and Narayana with Puttabasavi in the outhouse of Gowda's new house. When Bhujangaiah finding the Petromax lamp dull took it down, stoked it till it burned with a noise, Shiva and Urupa were taken aback at the sight of their master's face burning with anger. Shiva retreated to the kitchen as if he remembered something. Manja had left asking Shiva to prepare rice for eight. He had already made the lentil gruel. Sushila and the merchant, four assistants of the timber man Ramaiah of Palghat and two more who were employees of Sabi of the whip had placed orders for supper.

Bhujangaiah went into his room without saying anything and lay down on his cot. Urupa had already lit the light there. Normally the merchant returned before nightfall wherever he went. But that day Puttavva had forced them to have supper in Hundi which had delayed them. Sushila had by then visited Raja's room once already. She had carefully kept in the basket the cloth bundle of eatables and money, which Puttavva gave her for her son saying his room was very close to the place where the bus stopped.

Though Raja was discomfited a little when Sushila came in search of him her affectionate speech made him pleased. Sushila who went to Mysore every week grew more endeared to Puttavva. Sushila laughed when Puttavva stressed that she should tell her son to be careful while crossing the road.

Bhujangaiah was alarmed when the merchant and Sushila both refused to eat their supper. By then Ramaiah's assistants and the Sabi of the whip were sitting around having finished their meal. Sabi warned the merchant "What is this merchant? The times are not what they were. It is not proper to roam around at night with your daughter." When Sushila entered the room Bhujangaiah had already gone to sleep. The merchant sat conversing with the timber man and Sabi. Sushila was surprised to see Bhujangaiah lying without a movement even after she entered the room. Bhujangaiah had really fallen asleep. He had lost his bearing. Earlier in the day he had walked talking humorously with Pundri and Doddathamma and had not realized the distance between Vaddaragudi and Madalli. But as soon as he sat at home his legs had stiffened like logs.

When he somehow managed to rise for supper he had faced his wife's horrible temper. And now, as soon as he arrived and stretched his body on the cot he had drowned in sleep.

Sushila pulled the mat and pillow under the cot carefully without disturbing Bhujangaiah's sleep and arranged it on the other side of the shopfront. Though Sushila normally changed her sari as soon as she came in she did not do so today because of Bhujangaiah's presence. Though she was certain that he was asleep she was scared of what the others who were outside may think and so slept in her grimy sari. Her father continued to converse in the hotel, Sushila did not find sleep easily. She called Urupa for a glass of water. Though Bhujangaiah stirred awake when she called, he again buried himself in sleep as his body was tired walking and his mind which was hurt by the terrible fracas at home desired nothing.

Sushila was in a strange ardour till her father arrived. She trimmed the lamp. She approached Bhujangaiah and straightened the cover that had slipped down to his feet so that his hairy legs were covered. She touched his forehead to find out if he had a fever. Bhujangaiah had fallen a victim to a sleep that did not allow him to react even to her touch. Sushila was much disappointed. She had walked from Hundi thinking of something all the way. The person who should give a form to any of those thoughts was now sleeping oblivious to everything. The endless night filled the open eyes of Sushila. The entire hotel seemed to have drowned in silence. The bosom of the thick night was impaled by the snores of a few. Sushila sat up once. She pressed her tightening breasts to the mortar floor, She felt a tightening that seemed to squeeze out life. She found each moment agonizing, Sushila found the night unbearable.

***

CHAPTER - 21

The life of Bhujangaiah which flowed calm like water from a brimming pond all these days was now disturbed by events associated with Sushila. Its waves touched not only those in the village who evinced an interest in his life but also those who were disinterested in him. For Bhujangaiah some magic had made the relationship with Sushila not merely a gossip in people's mouth but a tender bondage that had day by day strengthened deep within. Tampura Ayya of Hampapura had not visited since two weeks, Bhujangaiah had experienced the flow of a rivulet of ineluctable happiness in him when he occasionally lost himself in his songs. He had on the very first day felt the feminine touch of Sushila not merely on his hand but deep within his heart. Who knows why he desired her and when the seed of that desire got implanted? Day by day it had flourished to long for the day now when it would put forth ears and sway. Bhujangaiah's mind had not wavered even for a moment confronting the taboos of caste, creed and religion. He was by nature thus. Whatever he thought of he must achieve. He was not made to live in fear of those who might criticize.

Parvathy had turned into the awesome Rudri, the malevolent Goddess of destruction before Bhujangaiah could take the next step, knowing it was impossible to hide Sushila within his heart any longer. One day she arrived at the hotel. Luckily Sushila was not present. But her basket of bangles was there, Parvathy lifted it and threw it out on to the road; the glass bangles broke to pieces and were strewn on the road. Those present at the hotel found it strange. They did not find it right that a woman should break bangles. Both Urupa and Shiva watched Parvathy's rage in astonishment, but were scared to go near her. Manja who was in the kitchen felt the thought of his being the cause of all this sear him like a hot brand and grew apprehensive unable to guess what would transpire next. By then Ajappa arrived from somewhere and calmed down Parvathy enough to send her home. The news had spread like bushfire in the village. The incident became a feast for those who were on the lookout for some weakness of Bhujangaiah. They used on Bhujangaiah the proverb "When advised 'unlearn your trait shrew' she said, 'I may leave my husband but not what I learnt.' " And they began to parade once more all the events of his past life in the light of the new one.

Manja who had experienced Bhujangaiah's anger had at once begun to prepare to leave the hotel in fear of Bhujangaiah's wrath turning on him at any moment. He made efforts to leave Madalli forgetting his earlier plan of opening a hotel there. But what had surprised him was that Bhujangaiah had not even glanced at him in spite of all that had transpired. Parvathy had made a big scene only after listening to his words. But she may not have revealed his name to his master. If she had done so that day itself he would have found Bhujangaiah "worshipping" him properly. Shiva and Urupa had been thrown into confusion with all these problems. At Bhujangaiah's home once more evil seemed to have set foot. The hapless old woman had to once more bear the entire burden. Deviravva too was greatly pained at seeing her son once more treading the wrong path. Why did the vinegar have to sour the pot full of milk? Why did her son do so? Where did that irreligious whore come from to spoil her son's mind? Was he a newborn baby? Why did he become a victim of such an accusation? Once on that day when invited for a meal she had refused and gone like a whore. Let her be, why did not god give her son wisdom? Deviravva's head was full of worry. She mulled over the events for a moment. "What did her son do that no one else in the world had done? Was he past his youth? Parvathy need not have drummed the news of his having yielded to some sorceress at a weak moment to the entire village and the community. She had no sense. If she had would she not have known that her husband's loss of status would result in her loosing her status? Anyone may stumble. Would one amputate the leg because of that?" Deviravva saw Amase standing, served him food and said, "Amase after you eat go to the hotel and bring your master." Amase said "All right mother." When Amase arrived at the hotel it was empty. There was no body apart from Shiva and Urupa. Bhujangaiah had gone to Mysore. When a few people called the merchant and told him to his face Parvathy's act of throwing the basket of bangles out on to the road he felt terribly insulted. He had never even dreamt that either his daughter or Bhujangaiah would err. The news he heard had utterly consternated him. If it were true it was a great crime in his eyes. What was his daughter? And who was Bhujangaiah? How could such relationship be? Had his daughter erred? Why did she who spat on a youth like Narayana lose her heart to Bhujangaiah who was advanced in years? No, No, Sushila was not a woman to slip so easily. She was very much like her mother in her conduct and speech. These were uneducated villagers. If some one said a mouse scurried they would believe that a tiger had walked. Why should he be disturbed by their talks? Sushila was not a small child. Could she not distinguish between the good and the bad? Was she insane to fall into the well, which she had seen in broad daylight? He should enquire. She was not the kind of daughter who hid anything from him. He felt an urgent need to question her on the bus. What if she said that whatever he had heard was true?

Sushila sat calmly as if nothing had happened. When Parvathy had thrown her basket of bangles Sushila was in Hundi. It was enough to visit Hundi that had seven or eight houses once a month to sell bangles. But every time Sushila arrived for business she visited Hundi at least twice. She had grown close to Puttavva since Raja had moved to Mysore for his studies. Sushila had been stunned at the sight of the heap of broken glass bangles in front of the hotel, when she returned after lunch and a short nap at Hundi. Urupa had described everything that had transpired when she went into the room. Sushila broke into cold sweat. She shivered as she remembered the abuses that Parvathy had used quarrelling with somebody on a couple of occasions. What if she were to return? What if Parvathy were to insult her in front of every one? Sushila wished to return to Hundi at once. But as it was almost time for the bus to Mysore she decided to leave for Mysore instead. As the merchant too had arrived ahead of the bus he too gathered enough of the situation and both decided to leave at once.

Bhujangaiah who had been to Kote on some errand was surprised to see Sushila and the merchant boarding the bus from which he got off. There remained still two days for them to return to Mysore. When Bhujangaiah enquired, “Why?” the merchant turned his face away screwing it up and said, “I have some work.” Sushila was downcast. She looked at him once and bent her head down. Bhujangaiah who had got off the bus saw the broken pieces of bangles before entering the hotel. Sushila must have dropped the basket. Perhaps that’s why they were returning to Mysore. When Victor told Urupa, “Hey Urupa, look at the amount of bangle pieces. What if it pokes somebody’s feet? Sweep them up and throw them out,” Bhujangaiah added, “Why will they be concerned?” He asked him to clean it immediately and summoned Shiva under his breath into the kitchen and enquired, “Why? Did Sushila fall under the basket?” Because there were customers from the bus in the hotel Shiva said he would explain later and got busy with his work. The doubts grew sharp in Bhujangaiah’s mind.

Shiva took his master to the backyard once the bus left and told him of all that had happened. He also told him that it was Manja who had told Parvathamma everything that happened at the hotel and that Manja had left the hotel that afternoon with all his personal effects. Though it was certain that Manja would leave any day, his leaving that very day without informing him confirmed the doubt which Bhujangaiah had about Manja. It was now ascertained that he was the kind who would sniff at the place where Sushila sat. There was no doubt about the truth in what Sushila had said. It was good that he had left. Thank God he had left before he threw him out! Bhujangaiah immediately gave Shiva more responsibility and promised to give him not only the salary that was given to Manja but also employ Urupa on a permanent footing with a fixed pay. The new change stunned the two for some time. They immediately busied themselves in the hotel’s work as if they comprehended the responsibility given to them. Bhujangaiah who sat alone behind the door in his room found his wife's behaviour unpardonable. She had stepped out on the street with no compunction to put him to shame. What had he denied her? He had trusted all that he earned in her hands. He had brought everything she had wished for after opening the hotel. Not a single day had he made a fuss or abused her. When everything was running smooth what was this that happened? What was her problem if he desired Sushila, or even had kept her? Why should she behave like a mad woman? Weren't there many in the village with three wives? Sushila can never be his wife. She would only be a kept woman. If she were to be of his caste he could have married her. No bastard would then have opened his mouth. Why did Parvathy come to the hotel and create a scene by breaking and throwing Sushila's bangles on to the street in front of everybody? A woman must remain a woman. If she had dared so much, what should he, a man, dare then? Look at the arrogance of that woman, worth three kasu! Bhujangaiah went home immediately. As soon as he stepped in Parvathy welcomed her husband with a loud voice in the language of Jakkalli. She too had decided to put an end to it one way or another. If his mother had not intervened Bhujangaiah would perhaps have drowned Parvathy in the gutter at the back yard. Bhujangaiah gave a rest to his reason when angry. However much his mother restrained him he did not desist from beating her enough to make Parvathy sob with pain. Bhujangaiah had learnt from experience that under such circumstances more than words it was a beating that achieved the result.

Parvathy too left for her parent's village saying she was not born to her father if she stayed there even for half a second. She pushed away her mother-in-law who attempted to advise her and forced her children also to leave with her. Bhujangaiah disgusted with the ruckus left home. He walked straight towards the pond not knowing where to go. As he reached the spillway of the pond and turned his steps towards the shrine of Basappa of the Pond, Manja suddenly materialised in front of him on the footpath from behind the bushes. Narayana too was with him. Both stammered. Manja felt he would crap in his knickers looking at the burning face of Bhujangaiah. Narayana who had egged him on by saying he would take care of all problems had stepped away as if he knew nothing, having greeted, "What brings you this way brother?" Bhujangaiah caught hold of Manja's collar as he hurriedly tried to follow Narayana saying, "You son of a whore who husbands his mother! What had happened to you to be false to the home that fed you?" He had slapped him and kicked him violently, spitting at him. Manja had hollered and fallen into the bushes on the side. Bhujangaiah had walked away towards the temple without even caring to throw a glance at where he had fallen. Manja had suffered the fate of a dog. Narayana who had all this while stood without as much as a breath hurried to help Manja get up. Manja had now come to realize Narayana's valour was nothing but brag. Realizing he had lost everything trusting in his lies, he got up brushing off the dust and turned to look at the way in which Bhujangaiah had gone. He did not have courage to follow and accost him. The slap had left his face on fire. Manja felt like weeping when he saw Narayana standing without uttering a word even when he was kicked so badly. He decided not to stay in that horrible village even for a moment. He bent his head down and began to walk without even looking at Narayana. Narayana was very sorry at Manja's state. But he had found it impossible to confront Bhujangaiah. His father would not have kept quiet if he learnt that Narayana had raised his hands on Bhujangaiah who was respected and held dear by him. Karigowda when angered never discriminated. He wouldn't let even his eldest son, let alone Narayana, off the hook. Narayana had hesitated to intervene in his anxiety that the issue may reach his father's ears. But this insult to which Manja had been subjected who had of late grown close to him was quite unexpected. Bhujangaiah who had appeared suddenly had assaulted Manja without even enquiring. Manja was very angry with him. He would have been comforted a little if he had uttered at least one word, but, no, he had stood paralysed. But if he had intervened Bhujangaiah would not have hesitated to rain a few blows on him too.

Manja did not care for any of the comforting words, which Narayana offered, as he walked with his head lowered. Manja's soul cringed with the feeling that he had played false by the home where he had eaten and that he had erred. It was his desire for Sushila, which had made him hate Bhujangaiah who had taken care of him, as if he were a brother. Manja cursed her silently, "Why did that wandering widow appear at all?" He said to Narayana who was following close behind, "Narayana I neither want to stay in your village, nor open a hotel there. You hand over all my money. I will go to Mysore." Narayana felt as if a thunderbolt had struck him. He had promised to him the outhouse of the new residence for the hotel. Manja had given Narayana for safe keeping all the money he had of late saved without the knowledge of Bhujangaiah. Narayana had spent some of that money. He had not realized that such a situation would arise when Manja would demand his money on the spot. Manja now crowded Narayana finding it unbrraeable the very thought of living in Madalli even for a moment longer. Narayana said, "All right. I shall return your money", not knowing what else to do. They both covered a short distance silently. Manja would not have reached the decision he did if Narayana had confronted Bhujangaiah even for a second. If it was this bad today, tomorrow he would turn into a joke certainly. Why should he fall into a well believing him? He should either fall at Bhujangaiah's feet accepting his follies or he should leave Madalli. Those were the only choices he had. The maddening figure of Sushila, especially from the day he had seen her in the nude, had haunted him. But Sushila had not wasted a glance at him. She desired his master. Manja now found that he did not do right in having described to Narayana all that he had seen and not seen. She had acted familiarly with Bhujangaiah on numerous occasions deliberately in front of him; he had suffered without sleep whenever they both slept in the room. Thinking that it was better to die than stand with a bowed head in front of Bhujangaiah he began to hasten his steps, wishing to leave the village and distance himself from all those faces. Though Narayana tried to tell him that they could seek revenge if not that day at least in future, Manja's mind did not yield again to any of the temptations.

***

CHAPTER - 22

It was a week since Parvathy had left home. From that day on the home appeared like the house of the bereaved. Deviravva who sat disheartened in a corner sighing and wondering what could have struck the home that had constantly reverberated with the sounds of the cry, the laughter and the exclamations of her grand children came to her senses when Amase called out. Already darkness was pouring into the courtyard. Deviravva got up shrugging off the worry and the old age that enveloped her and lit the lamp of castor oil in the hall. She asked Amase to take the lantern down and light it. Amase preparing to milk the cow saying, "I shall free the calf mother", lit the 'lateen' and left for the cow shed without waiting for an answer. Deviravva washed her face and limbs in the courtyard, lit the frankincense to the pictures of deities in the hall and went to milk. No, she will not sit again thus paralyzed. She will not allow darkness to fill that house again as long as her limbs are strong. Why did she sit in forgetfulness? She only remembered having returned from the field. Her head was full of what Karigowda's wife had said. How can a woman drag to the streets what a man did? In her time such a woman would have been kicked into the gutter. Though God gave Parvathy three children he did not give her commonsense worth three kasu. She was mad enough to make a mountain out of a mole hill and run to her father's house to build God alone knew what! She had merely provided grist to the mouth of those who hated her son in the village. Those people still chewed the cud talking about it in whispers as if her son had done what no one else had. The heat of Deviravva's breath did not fail to touch Amase. Deviravva woke up only when the milk spilled from the vessel when the cow kicked a little as she went on milking mechanically even after the flow from the udder had stopped.

When she reached the *jagali* from the shed, she found somebody sitting leaning against the pillar. Deviravva asked, "Who is it?" She recognized her son who sat motionless, by the scent of his body. "Why, child? Get up, wash your face and pray first." She brought water from the kitchen. Bhujangaiah felt his limbs give way when he entered the house. His head throbbed slightly. The entire day had gone by with people arriving at and leaving the hotel. If he came home the thought of children would assail him. Soma lost a week of school. He had married a terrible woman. She left home at the smallest of pretexts. Let her go. Let her stay there as long as she chose. He will not go to bring her back this time. Even when Bhujangaiah sat down for prayer his mind did not grow one with the Linga. Of late it had grown impossible to lose himself in God when he sat down to worship. Ayya who had visited in the morning had not turned up again. He may have arrived at the hotel by now. It did seem that every thing - wife, children, property - was but an illusion. His desire to be active too seemed illusory. He wondered why Ayya who advised, "Lost in illusions do not distance yourself from Shiva" always was in a hurry to return to his wife and children in Hampapura.

Bhujangaiah finished worshipping and came out to sit on the *jagali*. The shadow of Amase who was as yet busy doing odd jobs in the glow of the lantern had taken a giant form and moved all around the house. Bhujangaiah was inexplicably scared of Amase's shadow, which looked demonic. Who knew when the house was built? The rafter was huge. The pillars were massive. So many events had been witnessed in these hundreds of years in that house. "Who knows? Probably they are now watching me too. Perhaps they are listening to what is going on within me. They may narrate tomorrow to my son or grandson the tale of my sighs." Bhujangaiah's head was filled with strange thoughts. They began to bubble randomly. He ate silently whatever his mother served and once again went out to sit on the *jagali*. Deviravva pitied her son. He seemed like an orphan sitting with his breath held. Deviravva approached her son and sat down without saying anything though she did wish to talk. Though his heartburn had scalded her too Deviravva asked without showing her pain, "Do you have a headache?" She touched his forehead. It was quite warm to touch. She immediately stood up to bring the eucalyptus oil from the stand where the gods were placed and began to massage her son's head taking it on her lap. Though Bhujangaiah was uncomfortable for a moment he felt he had regained a world that he had all these days lost. It was as if once more affection had filled his dried up being and put forth leaves. Bhujangaiah was everything for Deviravva from his childhood. She used to take a vow on her life to Hulikanthyappa whenever her son who was born of the very God's grace met with the slightest of problems. It had been ages since her son had thus laid his head on her lap. It was as if the dried up body of an aged Deviravva once more received a blood transfusion. It was as if once more the milk of motherhood had brimmed over in her heart that had been reduced to skin and bones. She went on massaging his forehead for a long time. Bhujangaiah dropped into a sweet slumber. Amase who sat watching in astonishment the love between the parent and the child stood up stretching after a while, saying, " Mother, may I go and sleep?" Deviravva woke up from her reverie to say, " Amase, If you wish to sleep here do so, or you may go home to rest." Amase, who was almost dozing, took his mat from the rafters in the shed, lay in a corner and using his arms for a pillow shut his eyes. Who knows how long Deviravva comforted Bhujangaiah patting him like she would a child? When Amase rose in the morning Bhujangaiah was still asleep. Deviravva had already sprinkled the dung mixture outside the house and was drawing the *Rangoli*.

Amase felt that the dullness that had descended since a week had now lifted and brought the cattle out to tether them in the street, with a new vigour. He had finished the job of cleaning by the time the master woke up and was sitting ready with his plate for the leftovers from supper for breakfast. He had to ready the plough after eating. He was using the newly bought oxen for ploughing. At each dawn Amase wondered when he would get help. He wished for someone to reduce his burden. Deviravva served a ball of mudde and poured curds on it. She also served red chili chutney. Amase would lift a mountain if such leftovers filled his stomach every morning. Bhujangaiah who noticed Amase's preoccupation with food got up and went out in to the back yard. The cow shed was already clean as a mirror. Praising Amase silently he enquired, " What field will you plough today?" After warning him with, " If you go on ploughing the new field the old one will fall fallow." He added, "In two week's time there will be another person. Then we will have two ploughs. All the fields can be tilled then." When he entered the verandah after a wash in the corner of the courtyard he too decided to eat the leftovers. Deviravva learnt of her son's desire after the worship with surprise. She served him too saying " Cold food cools the body." When she gave him an onion to go with it, Bhujangaiah felt no *idli* or *vade* could match the leftovers and ate one and a half mudde smacking his lips. He spoke laughingly to his mother as if he had forgotten everything. Finding it to be the proper time Deviravva cajoled her son to bring back his wife and children from Jakkalli after advising him. Bhujangaiah too wished to see his children. But he was not ready to give up his pride. Deviravva was scared when he said, "Mother you are mad. Let us see how long she will stay there, whom did she ask before she left? Let me see how she will step into this house again." Whatever she did her son did not retract. What enraged Bhujangaiah about Parvathy was her having secretly taken to her father's house the money he had saved, though Bhujangaiah had remained silent because to open his mouth would've meant losing face in front of his mother. He was nevertheless boiling within.

Deviravva who knew that her son wouldn't care for her words met Karigowda that very evening and requested him to urge her son to visit Jakkalli to bring back his wife and children. Gowda himself went in search of Bhujangaiah. Bhujangaiah was both scared and surprised to see Karigowda who never visited the hotel approaching. Gowda took him out under the tamarind tree and left after commanding, "You leave tomorrow at dawn for Jakkalli and bring back your wife and children to lead the life of a normal family man." Though Bhujangaiah was a little upset at Gowda's abrupt manner not caring to hear his side of the story he was still in a fix.

Finally he decided to go to Jakkalli. The business at the hotel went on as usual without any ups and downs. Though Shiva was highly trustworthy Bhujangaiah once more began to pay attention to money. He had experienced from Manja's incident that if there was money on hand however good a boy anyone was, he would tread the wrong path. He projected the entire day's income and expenses, explained it to Shiva and left for Jakkalli promising to return that very evening. Victor too had suspected that something was amiss when Sushila had not visited Madalli since a week. He had not inquired thinking it improper. Victor knew very well the story of the relationship between Sushila and Bhujangaiah. Bhujangaiah sat by the side of Victor. The Jakkalli gate was three miles this side of Kote. Bhujangaiah instead of getting down there went to Kote and bought snacks, flower, betel leaves and nuts and went to his father-in-law's house.

When Bhujangaiah arrived at the house of his father-in-law, who was fairly well known in Jakkalli all the children surrounded him happily, But not a single adult came out to welcome him. All were whispering within. Bhujangaiah who stood at the door for a minute before sitting down on the *jagali* felt terribly insulted. He wanted to leave instantly. But by then Soma brought the baby out and put him on his lap. The daughter stood sticking to his back. Though it was but a week since he was parted from his children it had already seemed like a month. When he asked him to go with him, forgetting everything as he petted them, Soma hesitated out of a fear of having to attend school. The daughter had already climbed his shoulder. She had missed her grandmother. Bhujangaiah noticed his daughter who had never left her grandmother had grown poorly because of her separation from her grandmother. Finally, as if a decision had been reached inside Chinnamma his sister-in-law brought a vessel of water welcoming him, "Brother-in-law, come in, wash your hands and legs, the food is ready." Bhujangaiah sat without stirring, "I have had my food, I ate in Kote." Parvathy called out to her sister angrily when she heard her cajoling him. Bhujangaiah's blood began to boil, He controlled his rising temper and stared at the peepul tree, which resembled a temple chariot in front of his father-in-law's house. The tree touched by spring was slowly transforming itself from russet to green. Bhujangaiah's burning body found cool comfort in the touch of his children who were clambering all over him.

Though neither his wife nor his mother-in-law, or for that matter any adult in the house spoke to Bhujangaiah he had sat as if in deep meditation though evening approached. His sister-in-law Chinnamma too had said in a distant manner that someone had been sent to call his father-in-law who was not at home. Bhujangaiah who had for a moment forgotten the insult he had suffered playing with his children could not hold his ire any longer when his wife came to the door dripping with sarcasm scolding her children. He entered the house to catch his wife's hair saying, "What did you say you whore?" When Parvathy hollered loud enough for the village to hear, her mother and sister fell on him in an instant like dogs. Chinnamma bit Bhujangaiah's hand. Wondering at their uncivilized behaviour Bhujangaiah went out in disgust and sat under the peepul tree saying to set foot inside that home again was as good as to die.

By then the people of Jakkalli had caught a whiff of the incident and the neighbours, especially Parvathappa's cousins arrived and compelled Bhujangaiah to go to their house. Bhujangaiah felt like dying with the insult. Bhujangaiah's ire and anger did not diminish however much the neighbours attempted to comfort him. They had stopped him from leaving immediately beseeching him variously till his father-in-law arrived.

Bhujangaiah recollected one after another the quarrels and disputes he had with his wife since their marriage. He had quarreled more with Parvathy than enjoyed happiness. Occasionally, when one almost decided to find in her an unmatched goodness she turned into a demon. Who knew if she really was possessed by some demon? He had not met any woman like Parvathy. None behaved like her, however angry one may be. Bhujangaiah now was certain that it was her father's house, which was the source of all such ill humour. His body perspired in the recollection of all of them surrounding him like wild dogs without a sense of shame, respect and decency. Bhujangaiah who thought it was better to live alone than live with a woman of such indecent house had lost all desire for bringing Parvathy back. Thinking that if the children grew up in such a house they would not even hesitate to auction him off he decided not to leave his children behind but to take them with him even if he had to seek the help of the elders of the village.

Parvathappa who had been to the neighbouring village to adjudicate on a dispute returned in the evening angrily when he learnt the news of his son-in-law's arrival. But he was disgusted to hear about all that had transpired at home even before his arrival. He found his wife's behaviour of joining her children ill advised. What was wrong in a husband giving a couple of blows to his wife who had left without permission? How can a woman insult a man, that too a son-in-law, who visited the house? Though Parvathappa wanted to go and call Bhujangaiah personally, he sent his eldest son who had returned from the fields as his pride stood in the way. Bhujangaiah did not stir. Finally when Parvathappa himself arrived to invite, Bhujangaiah was not fooled and told him sternly. "I will not climb the steps of your house even if I am born again. If I should step in you can be sure that I am not born to my father. I will somehow spend this night in these people's house. Tomorrow you send my children without any argument. I will take them with me. I do not wish to know anything about her who left without permission." Though Parvathappa was scared he hid it retorting, "Let us not talk of decencies, what happened did at an inauspicious moment; she left unable to bear it. If you should talk beyond your lips would I not know what to do?" He thundered. Bhujangaiah refused to be cowed down by his talk, "You may do what you wish to. Now you tell me whether you will send the children or not?" Parvathappa too was angered, "What will you pluck if I say I will not send?" Bhujangaiah lost his temper, he got up touched to the quick, addressing everyone who had assembled there, " All right keep them with you. If they are born to me they will come to me tomorrow if not today, if they are born to some one else, let them stay behind". "Parvathappa was enraged at his son-in-law's speech. Still he controlled himself with the thought that his daughter's life should not be ruined and that it should be mended. But his son had grabbed Bhujangaiah by his collar without a care. Everyone who was there had helped part them. Bhujangaiah left in the dark not heeding any one's words. He began to walk not looking back though he knew that he had to cross the forest. When he had walked quite a distance from the village, a few people arrived from behind. Parvathappa had sent them to bring him back. But Bhujangaiah did not retrace his step, whatever they said. They had accompanied him till they crossed the forest and reached the main road.

Bhujangaiah caught the timber truck, which arrived from Kote. Those who had come from Jakkalli returned to their village with the consolation that he at least left by a lorry.

***

CHAPTER - 23

When Bhujangaiah went in search of Ajappa, the only one in whose intimacy he could share either his happiness or his trouble, the latter had left for Mysore. Disappointed, he returned to the hotel and lay down on the cot, behind closed doors. His injured mind was pulsating with pain. The insult meted out to him the previous day at his in-laws was not to be forgotten all his life. Though he was anxious to seek revenge, not knowing how to he started seething within. He had told Victor briefly all that had happened when he returned from Kote that morning. Still, Victor thought things might have gone too far, looking at his sallow face. When Shiva called him for lunch seeing him lying in his room, though it was afternoon, Bhujangaiah had not felt hungry. He went home straight. He turned towards the pond finding the door of his house shut. The people of the village found his silence strange as though he was afflicted by something for a week now. He arrived at the floodgate of the pond disgusted by the nature of those who whispered behind his back. Already the transplantation of the summer crop was done. It was certain that he would have a good crop this time too when he saw the dark maturing of the ears, Though he of late had not paid much attention to cultivation, his mother had supervised Amase in getting the fields manured, transplanted, seeded and weeded at the proper time to get a yield of at least ten *khanduga*, almost two tons of rice paddy. There was nothing to fear as long as his mother was around, " But how long will she too live on? She is weakening day by day as was apparent to anybody. Perhaps she will live two more years at the most?" He walked towards Hundi thinking of it. As he reached Hundi his stomach began to rumble. He had not even had a cup of tea after breakfast. Bhujangaiah could live on tea and beedis even if he did not have food the entire day.

When he reached the house of Muddegowda that man was not at home. Puttavva was bolstering the new baskets and winnowing fans with a mixture of paper and dung in the cattle shed with other maid servants. She got up as soon as she saw Bhujangaiah. The unexpected visitor seemed very tired, "Why, are you not well?" He replied, "What disease can I have? Please give me a little buttermilk, it is quite warm." When he asked," Where is Gowda?" Puttavva answered stepping into the kitchen, "He has gone to the paddy fields in Puradakere." Though she had heard from workers about the village folk talking about Sushila and Bhujangaiah, she had exclaimed refusing to believe, "Can that ever be so?" She had assumed that it was a rumour spread by those who could not tolerate Bhujangaiah succeeding in life. When someone had said that Parvathy had left home because of the affair she had wondered in disparagement, "My God! What is this craziness of his? That too at his age!" Though she was curious, the discretion that such things are not to be enquired by a woman made her merely talk of her son. When Bhujangaiah confessed to his hunger Puttavva immediately lit the stove and prepared rotis. If only he would eat she could serve him rice and curry. She found the custom of Lingayats of Madalli strange. Apparently they could eat roti or *uppittu* at a house of her community but not rice. She served butter and chutney with roti. Bhujangaiah began to eat with relish like a child, sitting on the cot on the verandah. He had no hesitations in this house. After having eaten, he drank another glass of buttermilk and said he was leaving for Mysore the next day and that he would enquire of Raja if he needed something. He left. If it was not for servants in the cattle shed he perhaps would have told her about the quarrel in Jakkalli. He held back what he wished to say and left saying, "I'll visit again Puttavva, tell Gowda when he returns I wished to talk to him."

Though the earth had burnt black from Hundi to the pond the trees and plants were gurgling green. Above the head the sky filled with hot embers. Bhujangaiah found the creation of god strange.

He had not noticed it ever. The thorny tree of white blossomed Babool on the banks of the pond had not yet blossomed. It was almost the flowering season. One should witness when it flowered. Even the leaves could not be seen amongst the flowers blossoming on the tree as if the tree were covered in dew. The fragrance would reach from a distance. As long as the tree bore flowers all the women in the village adorned themselves with them. Even for the worship of god the flowers were used. Sushila had not known about the flowers. When he had told her once she had laughed and said " Let me see what sort of a flower it is." The funniest part was the tree never blossomed during certain years. It was said something evil would happen that year. Last year the tree had born flowers enough to break under that weight. People adduced the good harvest of the previous year to the tree in bloom. Though he had arrived on the banks of the pond and traveled quite a distance his mind was still full of that tree. He had climbed as a boy that huge tree and plucked large bunches of flowers and had given them to all those women of the village who asked him for it. It was as if it was only yesterday that he had heard the anxious warning of those standing under the tree when he had climbed the branch extending over the pond.

The bus from Mysore had left by the time he arrived at the hotel. Shiva gave the note from his knicker pocket as soon as he saw his master. Victor had whispered thrice over in his ear to hand it over to Bhujangaiah unbeknownst to anyone. Shiva had felt relieved of an onerous responsibility when he handed it over to Bhujangaiah. Bhujangaiah went into the room and began to read the note behind the doors shut. It was a letter written by Sushila. She knew how to read and write. But this was the first letter that she had addressed to anyone. Though the lines were irregular she had said whatever she wanted to straight. Bhujangaiah who had read the bottom line "Your own Sushila" ten times was as happy as if he had seen Sushlia. She had written asking him to meet her that very evening in Raja's room where she would wait. He hid the note in his knicker pocket and hurried home in anxiety as if the bus would arrive any moment though there was enough time for that.

Luckily the doors of the house were open not dampening his enthusiasm. Deviravva had already returned from the fields. Even as she laid a plate for a meal and served the customary tumbler of water, he sat down to eat though his belly was full. Deviravva realised he was leaving for Mysore only when he took out the dhoti and shirt kept for Mysore visit from the trunk. He had entrusted all the money from the hotel business with the mother since the day Parvathy left home. Deviravva gave him all the money before he asked for it. He left home saying, he would return the next day. He was surprised at Ajappa's presence in the hotel as if he would appear at the instant of a thought. He was away in Mysore that morning when he went in search of him. How had he returned? As soon as he saw Bhujangaiah, Ajappa came out and took him to his fields downstream, which was at a distance from the hotel. They sat under a tree and conversed for a long time. Bhujangaiah showed Sushila's letter to Ajappa. Ajappa had noticed her handing something to Victor at the bus stand and that her face had looked dark and tired. Though Bhujangaiah was a bit scared at Ajappa's advice, there was no other choice but to act accordingly. He had started as soon as Sushlia had sent the note requesting him to come. But he had not known what action he should take. They both once more decided on doing what they had to legally do and got up.

Bhujangaiah's terribly agonized mind since yesterday found some comfort now. It was as though a soothing balm had been applied on a wound burning with insult. Let those bastards speak after tomorrow. Let us see what my father-in-law would achieve. Let the entire village turn against me. He was not living under anyone's mercy, It was right to do what he pleased. Had he not seen the very people who bayed like dogs the first three days wagging their tail the fourth day?

It was as though the arms of Bhujangaiah which had fatigued swimming fruitlessly since morning had found the shore suddenly. He waited anxiously for the bus though it was not yet the scheduled time for its arrival from Kote, all the while praising Ajappa silently for having stood in his support under such exigent times. Bhujangaiah had felt that the bus was late that day in arriving and every moment was making him irritable. He had repeated to Shiva and Urupa the same thing over and over again. He had advised them to sleep that night in the company of Pundri or Cannamalla. Manja had vanished from the very day he had thrashed him. What if he arrived at the hotel in his absence in the company of Narayana, the son of Gowda? The bus arrived on time. Bhujangaiah inquired as soon as Victor got off the bus, "Why was the delay?" Victor looked at his watch saying, "Not at all, I've arrived on schedule." And he asked in whisper, "Did you get the letter?" Victor smiled for a moment and joked patting the back of Bhujangaiah who nodded in affirmation, "She is a lovely bird. You'll be lost if you let her go." Victor hurried the passengers after quickly drinking his tea as if he could sympathize with Bhujangaiah's urgency and started the bus. All along the way Bhujangaiah's mind was preoccupied with a hundred worries. At one moment if he felt that such an action was not right for someone like him the very next moment he felt that Lord Shiva would not approve if he withdrew the step he had taken already. For the insult that he had suffered at his In-law's home, to shut the lose mouth of the vagrant people of his village his plan was the appropriate one. More than all, the fact that Sushila who melted at his very touch was going to be his forever was the fruit of his previous births. It was remarkable that such a charming woman had desired him. What was he who knew nothing of gentleness and subtlety? Why did she desire him? What was common between them? He was already a father of three children. And she was yet a teenage girl. Yet she had desired him. She had decided to follow her desires, against the will of her father. Her heart should not be hurt any more. Who knows in what earlier birth they were related? It was all Shiva's play. Though Pundri's tales would make him very hot occasionally, he had never even fantasized about another woman's body. What was this illusion? Sushila had mesmerized him the moment his eyes fell on her. Even as she had wondered at the snake in his hand, he too had wondered at her comeliness. She had disturbed his senses as soon as she had appeared from nowhere as if she had descended from the skies. Her eyes, her speech, had all seemed to leave an expression of having smothered his rock like character. It must have been due to an earlier birth. Otherwise, how could she who never wasted a glance at those who came desiring her want him?

He was lost in himself. A hundred thoughts began to form in him about what he was about to do. He woke up only when the bus reached Mysore. He told Victor he would see him tomorrow and hurried to Raja's room. The people of the house where Raja lived were of a good nature. They were dear to Bhujangaiah, They had leased the room to Raja because of him. Raja had not yet returned from school when he reached there. Tayavva owned the house. As soon as she saw Bhujangaiah she called him in and gave him the key to Raja's room. Though Tayavva was at first irritated at Sushila visiting Raja's room, her behaviour and manner of speech had won her heart. Sushila had revealed everything to Tayavva later. Since two days her father had begun preparations to marry her off to somebody related to him. It was therefore that Sushila had come running in fear and handed the note for Bhujangaiah to Victor. Sushila had remained in Tayavva's protection after that. Her father had visited even that place a few times already in search of her. Tayavva had sent him back as if she knew nothing about Sushila. Sushila too was very frightened. She was anxious as to what may happen. She was happy that Bhujangaiah had come as soon as he had seen the note.

Sushila who slowly emerged from the house of Tayavva entered Raja's room. Her face was full of fear and anxiety. Bhujangaiah drew Sushila who was shivering like an escaped bird close to him, promised that he would not betray her, and gently caressed her back. Sushila not knowing what she should do turned to Bhujangaiah and sobbed aloud. Bhujangaiah comforted her again and decided to leave that place that very moment. There was still time for the bus by which he had arrived. He should depart by that. But he had told Ajappa he would arrive straight at Kendagannaswamy temple of Gaddige. But having decided it was not right to stay in Mysore that night he left after taking leave of Tayavva. Sushila followed him in the clothes that she wore. As he walked towards the stop where the bus to Kote halted he suddenly changed his mind, hired a jataka and drove to catch the bus near the tollgate. What if her father were to wait at the bus stop out of suspicion? When the bus stopped at the tollgate they boarded. Sushila sat in the ladies seat. Bhujangaiah boarded through the driver's door. When he learnt that Victor had seen the merchant waiting at the bus stand and had squirmed saying he was waiting for somebody Bhujangaiah knew that a disaster had been averted. Bhujangaiah stole a look at every body in the bus. Luckily there did not seem to be any one who knew him. The bus was not crowded. He sat with a sigh of relief. He did not speak to Victor too for a long while.

The bus seemed slow. He wished to urge Victor to drive faster, but what if Victor should laugh at him? When the bus halted at Beerihundi a couple of villagers of Madalli boarded the bus, Bhujangaiah who tried to avoid being seen by them was ashamed realizing his anxiety and fear emanating from a guilty mind. When the bus started climbing the hill of Saragur it started groaning. Victor began to speak to Bhujangaiah as if he had just then found tongue. In the agonized progression of the bus their speech could not be overheard by any. Bhujangaiah decided to reach Gaddige straight without alighting at Madalli. It would however be nightfall when they reached Gaddige. He had made up his mind to stay that night at Gaddige and complete his task as soon as the temple doors were opened in the morning before Victor arrived from Kote and then to return to the village by the bus. Victor had announced that no through passengers should get off the bus at Madalli as he had to reach Kote quickly. He started as soon as a few people disembarked when the bus stopped at the hotel. Those who were in the hotel were surprised. Such a thing had never happened. A passenger from Kyatanahalli had noticed Bhujangaiah sitting next to Victor. He told while drinking tea that he had seen Bhujangaiah on the bus and that he had gone without getting off. Everyone grew much more curious. Shiva and Urupa could not understand any of it. Once Urupa was permanently employed at the hotel he had stopped running to peep into the bus every time it arrived and so he too had failed to see Bhujangaiah.

Bhujangaiah had informed Victor of everything he proposed to do before getting down at Gaddige. Still Victor halted the bus for quite a long time in Gaddige and had personally called on the priest of the temple. Victor knew the priest well. The priest, who earned enough through donation by distributing the holy offerings and *arati* to the passengers everyday when Victor stopped the bus, had believed that though Victor was a Christian he yet took the holy offerings and *arati* of his God because of the power of his unequalled God Kendagannaswamy and told the people too. Whatever that may be he now happily agreed to Victor's request and took Bhujangaiah and Sushila to his house situated at a little distance from the temple. Basappa the priest too was a devotee of Shiva. He was very young. His father who had grown very weak with age attended to the temple only when there were special rituals. Basappa used to take care of the daily prayers and holy ablution. Basappa whose head was always adorned by a red piece of silk had a necklace of large rudrakshi beads and on his chest dangled an oxidized casket. The string that bore the casket had been cheated of its silver colour. He bought all the things that were necessary for the next morning's holy event. He also asked Gurulingappa who brought flowers to make two garlands and bring them early in the morning. Bhujangaiah who remembered that Ajappa had shouldered the responsibility of getting the gold *mangalya* made by the goldsmith Puttachari of Madalli told Basappa of it. Basappa instantly felt that it was impossible to conduct the marriage without the *mangalya* and began to worry. Bhujangaiah too felt he had erred. He should have called Urupa and told them when the bus halted at the hotel. He blamed himself for a bad job. Finally, when Basappa's father said, "It is all right if a turmeric piece is tied now, the gold *mangalya* can be tied later" The problem that had suddenly confronted him was thus resolved. They spent the night without worries.

It was Monday. There was a big crowd in Gaddige. Basappa opened the temple doors early and completed the important marriage rituals first and made the bride and bridegroom exchange garlands. As arranged, a wedding lunch for ten people was also served. A few who sat at the lunch were regulars at Bhujangaiah's hotel. By then the bus too arrived from Kote. Victor had brought two huge garlands of Jasmine. The couple exchanged garlands once more in front of the deity. Subbanna who had reserved two seats for them sat them down. A coy Sushila never lifted her head. Bhujangaiah was both scared and guilty. He perspired secretly. Everyone seemed to be watching him. If a few appeared to ridicule him the others seemed to whisper in disparagement. How soon would the hotel be reached? He sat without lifting his eyes in misgiving and anxiety wondering how soon he could escape from the eyes that seemed to pierce him.

Ajappa was one among the first to see Bhujangaiah and Sushila when the bus reached the hotel. Ajappa who had heard the news of Bhujangaiah going towards Kote with trepidation was happy as well as astounded on seeing them alighting from the bus. After the bus left he offered a prayer to the deity in the hotel room and made Bhujangaiah tie the *mangalya*.

***

CHAPTER - 24

Sushila accepted Bhujangaiah, surrendered all of her to him. She did not stop to reason; she did not doubt him whom she loved, even for a moment. She did not know if it were an ideal, or a love or a weakness. Bhujangaiah had filled her entirely. She did not nag or beg for any ornaments or clothes with a natural womanly desire either before or after she became his companion. The grass hut itself was a palace for her. His taste was hers too. His desire was hers too. All his likes and dislikes were hers. These virtues of Sushila were not learnt by reading any Hindu code for women or by injunctions of elders. They were naturally found in her. Seeing her behaviour from close quarters had surprised even those who said she had mesmerized him by casting a spell.

Bhujangaiah starting his new family in the hotel room was seen as a big challenge by the Verashaiva community. Though he had brought her after exchanging garlands in the presence of god she was his kept woman in the eyes of the villagers. If it had led to arguments, anger and rumours from one end of Madalli to another, it had been the cause of a great commotion in the house of Parvathappa in Jakkali. They regretted their neglect of him which forced him to do what he had, and cursed. Parvathappa roared loud enough to drown the village saying he would mete out appropriate punishment to his son-in-law. But again he was worried privately as to how he could once more patch up the shattered life of his daughter. He decided to bring with him a few elders to demand justice and decide one way or another.

At Mysore the merchant was stunned by Victor's news that

Sushila had become the wife of Bhujangaiah on the very morning she had left home. His second wife took her husband to task when he sat holding his head without a word, in a corner. She spewed all the anger she had nurtured against her husband for having supported his daughter all these days and for having quarreled with her and pummeled her. The merchant's nose flowed in a torrent as did his eyes. What had she found in Bhujangaiah to marry him ? Was he in the prime of his youth? Or would he place her on a feathery bed? He was neither of their caste nor of their community. He as father had not given her away with the holy water in the presence of his relatives. What could he say to those who might enquire? How could he show his face to them? What wrong had he committed? He had not accused or abused her ever. He had never wished that her feet be dirty. She herself had followed him. She had laboured following his steps not caring for the sun or the rain.

She was a strange girl. It was her youth that must have made her feel the desire. No, no, if she were to err so easily she would not have spat on Narayana to keep him at a distance. It was all the doing of Bhujangaiah. It is said that he who caught the snake also had knowledge of black magic. It was he, that evil man, who must have worked some spell. He had taken away the tendril of his gut. If god had eyes he would surely punish him. Whatever it may be he should visit Madalli once. His daughter's heart may melt at the sight of his agony. Whatever they may do they will never be husband and wife in the eyes of the world. She was a daughter he had looked after as he would a parrot. He could not live without her; he could never let her go so easily. What if he went to Madalli that day itself? People would laugh at his sight. How could they guess at his pain? They would not hesitate to say that he himself had sent her to Bhujangaiah. How many times had he not said, "No daughter, this wandering from village to village is not right". Even he had felt the heat from the fiery eyes that pecked at her in his very presence. He was a little scared too. He had watched over her without letting his guard down. Yet what should never have happened had transpired. He had acted as if he were an ignoramus. Where was he? And where was his daughter? Why had she tumbled into the well seen in the daylight? His wife was enraged seeing her husband getting ready as if to go to Madalli and then sit down in despair since that day. Though she had ridiculed, "It's a pot dented, it cannot be brought back and used again," the merchant had left for Madalli one fine day. When he confessed to Victor the agony of his heart before boarding the bus Victor had stoked the fire and had said that even god would not succeed in separating them. The merchant sank to the nether world. Finally, even after Victor assured him that he would convince her to go and visit them in Mysore the merchant had refused to listen and had boarded the bus adamantly. But Sushila did not yield either to his harsh words or to his self-pity. The merchant having reached the end of his patience kicked at his daughter, spat on her and took a vow that he would not set his eyes on her till his death and returned by the very same bus not even touching a drop of water at her home. He decided that it was a great sin even to sleep facing the direction of Madalli. The merchant's wife with much care consoled her husband who had returned home buried in agony. She was more happy than disgusted at Sushila's behaviour. What would be the fate of her and her little children if her husband spent all the money on Sushila's marriage? It was for the good. Let her be lost. Her running away had made her husband not to wag his tail any more. No more can any impediments confront her. The merchant's wife began to search for ways of keeping him under her control meeting her husband's sighs with her pretended sympathy. Parvathappa of Jakkalli arrived in Madalli with four or five people who like him believed that they were born to settle disputes. Rudrappa welcomed them with affection when Parvathappa arrived at Patel Rudrappa's house in the village straight away without even glancing at the hotel though he got off the bus in front of his son-in-law's hotel. The elders of Veerashaiva community met the visitors and discussed the matter. Finally they sent a servant and summoned Bhujangaiah.

Bhujangaiah asked why he should go to Patel Rudrappa's house and said that they could either visit his house or the hotel. His words brought the bile out in all the elders of his community.

But there was no consensus on what action they should take. If one said Bhujangaiah had ignored them, another said that since he had insulted the community he should be taught a lesson. The discussion heated up. The crooks who hated Bhujangaiah sought various ways to finish him off seeing in it an opportune moment. The talk of calling the Swami of the Mutt and excommunicating Bhujangaiah was also heard loudly. But Parvathappa's heart did not accept that. He who had assumed that all the elders in the village would summon Bhujangaiah and deliver justice in front of him began to silently sympathize with his son-in-law seeing the conspiracy afoot in his very presence. If he fell on misfortune would it not affect his daughter too? It would not stop before the heat touched him too. His own chances of marrying off his children would be endangered. Parvathappa thought hard. Why should he not talk to his son-in-law face to face and undo this skein?

The meeting was adjourned without taking any decision. They decided to meet again that night and find some solution. Sannaputtappa who was a mute observer in that group returned home silently and thought over the talk of excommunicating Bhujangaiah. There were many such incidents in the village. To excommunicate and to bring them back after purification were processes indulged in from a long time. He sent word to Bhujangaiah through his son. Bhujangaiah went to his house without thinking twice. Though he was poor, Sannaputtappa was respected by everybody in the community of the village for never ever double dealing. Bhujangaiah made explicit his forthright stance of not playing false by her who had come placing her trust in him. Sannaputtappa who appreciated his honesty subtly indicated what might transpire next. Though Bhujangaiah was afraid for a while he knew that no great calamity would occur as he knew the true color of his village, Yet, he bowed to the advice of Sannaputtappa whom he respected. He acquiesced when he asked him to go if sent words for by the elders that night. By then Deviravva who had learnt all that had taken place through somebody grew hot as a burning ember as soon as she saw her son, "You son born to my husband's second wife do you wish to drown us all in a well by losing your village, your community, your every fortune for that woman? Is she the beauty of Bidiralu? Hulikanthayappa, should I witness all this before I die? God call me to you soon." She started beating her chest. Bhujangaiah went straight to the hotel without another word at his mother's ranting.

Once more the Verashaiva assembly met at Patel Rudrappa's house at night. The holy ash specially smeared on their forehead shone brighter than the expression on their visage. The assembly agreed to Sannaputtappa's suggestion and once more sent a servant to summon Bhujangaiah. Bhujangalah arrived. Everybody looked at him as if they were seeing him for the first time. He too appeared a little strange to them. Arguments began. Nobody accepted Sannaputtappa's suggestion of solving the problem of converting Sushila to the faith by making her wear the linga. Each one said something to hurt Bhujangaiah. He sat through with great tolerance not lifting his head. Pundri, Cannamalla and other friends of his who had accompanied him were helpless in front of other elders. Sannaputtappa was hurt that he was responsible in calling Bhujangaiah only to insult him. Rudrappa to whom Parvathappa had whispered said arrogantly as if his was the final command which Bhujangaiah had to follow, "Look Bhujangaiah, no point in arguing till dawn. Our final decision is that whatever has happened has happened. You have besmirched our caste by joining one who belongs to god knows what lowly caste. The assembly of the community is like God. Apologize to it with folded hands and promise to abandon her before sunset tomorrow. If not we shall do what we need to." Bhujangaiah could no more control himself and he stood up staring at Rudrappa. "I am no vagrant to do what you order. You can shave what you wish to." Before he could leave Rudrappa jumped up like a tiger and said, "What did you say you son of a whore?" Even as Bhujangaiah retorted , " It's you who is a whore's son, and your father too" Rudrappa slapped Bhujangaiah. Before Bhujangaiah could lift his hand four others surrounded him and beat him up. Though Cannamalla and Pundri rushed to his rescue the other elders controlled the situation. Though Bhujangaiah felt further orphaned he went burning with rage. The words he uttered before leaving did not stop those who had touched his body from shivering in fright.

Rudrappa made everyone who had stood up in confusion to sit down again. What Bhujangaiah, who had threatened to bring the police, may do had already scared everybody assembled there. Once again the discussion was about what one should do in the matter as well as the event itself. The arguments did not end though it was late in the night. All this disgusted Parvathappa. He wondered why he had to come and smear salt on a festering wound. Sannaputtappa had already left. Though Bhujangaiah had suffered blows severe enough to fell him the latter's arrogant words as he left had scared Rudrappa who had caught in those words the scent of the support of the Gowdas of Madalli. He should not have lost his temper. But how could he put up with it? Though sleep was consuming everyone it was not clear what could be done. Rudrappa cast out a suggestion that would not bring a spot on his office as a Patel. It was to invite the Swamiji of Madapura's mutt and excommunicate Bhujangaiah, as well as for the community in Madalli to come together to raise funds for expenses if he should lodge a complaint with the police in Kote. But his words did not find a general acceptance. A few did not agree to raise funds. They dismissed it by saying, "Why worry about that now." The night of confusion was somehow passed.

With the coming of dawn, a few elders formed a new plan worried that the problem may descend on their head. They went to Karigowda's house forcing Rudrappa to accept their plan. They all knew that Bhujangaiah would never refuse to heed Karigowda's words. Though Rudrappa did not like going to Gowda he tagged along silently having known from experience that his own community would betray him in a crisis. Gowda was surprised to see them all. He spread a mat for them and asked them to sit. They told him of the reason for their visit and requested him to advice Bhujangaiah not to lodge a complaint with the police. Gowda had not known what had happened the previous night. He enquired in detail. He really felt like laughing. At the same time he was also anxious about Bhujangaiah being hurt. Why was he not informed? Who knows what had happened? Something serious must have transpired.

Otherwise these people would not have arrived so anxiously. He wanted Bhujangaiah too to be present. Who would bring him? Finally, Gowda sent his own man. He returned saying that Bhujangaiah was not at the hotel and that he had gone somewhere that night itself. Everybody was scared again. The people of Madalli shivered in their testicles at the very mention of the police of Kote. They had suffered enough problems at their hands here before, even over insignificant incidents. Those who had thought it a great insult to be taken by the police in front of the people of the village now wondered, " Why did we have to involve ourselves in such contentious business."

After everybody had left the servant whispered something to Gowda, He immediately went to the hotel. Bhujangaiah was lying down in the hotel room. His face had swollen, Sushila who sat with tears in her eyes in a corner stood up. Gowda who understood everything said, "Thieving sons of a whore! Let the heat touch them a little. It is only proper to go to Kote and make arrangements." When he enquired, "Who will accompany?" Bhujangaiah replied that he had sent word to Beard of Kyatanahalli. Gowda sipped the tea served by Shiva and asked Sushila who remained standing to sit down. He advised Bhujangaiah what needed to be done in Kote and asked him to send word as to the result through Shiva before leaving.

Parvathappa, Bhujangaiah's father-in-law, who intended returning with his followers by the morning bus, decided to stay back at Madalli for one more day in deference to Rudrappa's insistence. The police who were pleased by the offerings Bhujangaiah made along with the complaint incarnated in Madalli by the evening bus that very day. When they arrived Patel and the four accused had to be present and they were to be taken by them the next morning. A couple of them had disappeared at the very news of the police's arrival. Bhujangaiah had shown people that he was a person who did what he said. The village was full of the news. The police had partaken snacks and coffee at Bhujangaiah's hotel. They had agreed to dine that night at Gowda's residence. When Patel Rudrappa said he would arrange for their meal they straightaway told him that they could not go to his place, as he was an accused. More than anything else their mouths were watering by the imagined taste of chicken curry at Gowda's rather than by the rice and cereal at the Patel's.

Once again everyone met at Patel Rudrappa's home and finally decided to meet Gowda, as it was the only thing they could do. By then the police had finished their meal and were chewing betel leaf and areca nuts on the porch. They were secretly scared seeing the approaching crowd. Yet, Subbaiah the Head constable officiously asked "What is it Patel?" Rudarappa replied, "Nothing, we had to see Gowda." He walked in. Everyone entered Gowda's house and the door was bolted. Finally Gowda yielded seeing their trembling bodies, handed over the money they had managed to collect to the head constable, brought the complainant and the accused together and forced the followers of Rudrappa to stand in front of Bhujangaiah and seek his pardon for their crime. The police got both of them to write statements and left the village by the morning bus. Parvathappa too left by that very bus having nothing to show for the distance traveled. Even to those who had accompanied him all of this had seemed a bother. The elders of the community who had seemed to postpone the action to be taken against Bhujangaiah assured to send word to Jakkalli when the time arrived. Bhujangaiah knew very well the great job that those of his community who disliked him would attempt.

Bhujangaiah left for Devanoor where the cardinal mutt was situated, accompanied by Ajappa, Pundri and a few other elders like Sannaputtappa, three days after that incident.He got Sushila to wear the Linga by the immaculate hands of the Swami. He had performed special worship in the mutt on the occasion. After this the rage and the disillusionment doubled in those who hated Bhujangaiah in the village. Though it was promulgated that no Verashaiva visit his hotel those who had by then been habituated to drinking tea, eating snacks at the hotel did not heed the ban of the community elders. Sushila on no circumstance touched the vessels in the kitchen. By then Bhujangaiah had built another room with bricks adjacent to his own in the hotel. He had also fulfilled Sushila's need for an attached bathroom.

Though Bhujangaiah felt the course of his life begin to run once more smoothly the memory of his children began to haunt him. On occasion he felt a shame intense enough to think of suicide when he found it almost impossible to live away from his children. Back home he could not bear to see his mother's sorrow. She had found the house without children a veritable graveyard. She had grown surprisingly weak in the past fortnight. She thought of sending someone to her daughter-in-law's house. She finally sent Shaggy Sidda to Kallalli to bring her daughter and son-in-law. Though the daughter's children jumped and danced through the house the old woman did not find happiness, her eyes pictured Soma, his sister and the baby. Bhujangaiah did not counter his mother. His brother-in-law agreed to visit Jakkalli. His sister too accompanied. They returned that very evening. Neither Parvathy nor her children accompanied. They had sent word saying if the old woman had such affection she could visit them there. Though Bhujangaiah burnt with anger Deviravva left the next morning. When she returned the grand daughter had thrown herself on the ground and writhed crying, not wanting to be parted. Parvathy had snatched that girl child as if she had plucked Deviravva's intestine. From the sunken eyes of the old woman hot tears began to flow. She had no sense of the world around her even when Madalli arrived. Those who had accompanied her reminded her and helped her down. Deviravva who got off the bus walked home without even glancing at the hotel. The peace of her house was destroyed by opening the charnel of a hotel. When will Hulikantayappa open his eyes to the plight of her home? When will the problems end? Deviravva reached home in suffering. The son-in-law had already left. The daughter had agreed to stay for a few more days.

***

CHAPTER - 25

The calendar of Shastri, the great Astrologer of Madalli, had been ignored this time. Before people could go and ask him about the rains there was a heavy downpour. As there was time still for sowing, people were busy with their various tasks such as ploughing the harvested fields, cutting channels on both sides of the bunds so that the rain water from monsoon may not rush into the fields to erode. Rudrappa was greatly disappointed when the elders of the community refused to assemble, exhibiting a detachment asking why they should worry about the village, in spite of his having summoned them more than once for a meeting. Till then his word was the law for the Verashaiva community in Madalli. But today people deliberately ignored him. Apart from the anxiety that all the customs that had been handed down from ages would be destroyed Rudrappa had also an unshakable trust that those traditions would remain as long as the sun and the moon were in the firmament. When the community was disinterested why should he alone suffer this nuisance?

There were two servants now in Bhujangaiah's house, Along with Amase, Shaggy Sidda's nephew, Marikala too had entered bondage. There were two ploughs. They tilled the fields properly. The sowing would begin in a week. Bhujangaiah who had bought the fields from Singari had decided to plant sesame as Karigowda had instructed. He hoped that he would get half the money invested on returns if only God should open his eyes. He bought a compost pit, which would yield at least fifty cart loads of manure from Maragoni of the outcastes. It was excellent sheep manure. It was already well composted. He had used it on Singari's field. As soon as the rains began Deviravva was rejuvenated. The daughter left for Kallahalli. The aged woman would rise to cook before the cock crowed. Bhujangaiah also had found the hotel business less worrisome. Sushila herself began to manage the finances of the hotel. Of late she had begun to sit at the counter. Sushila had no anxiety or misgivings once people got used to her as an integral part of the hotel's ambience. Excepting a few puritanical Lingayats of Madalli everyone frequented his hotel. Even among the former a few would come secretly to eat. Due to this Bhujangaiah involved himself totally in the monsoon cultivation. Though it hadn't rained enough to fill the waterholes and ponds it had rained well enough to sow and deweed. The sign of a good yield was quite visible.

Bhujangaiah was free only on Mondays. But no one could hitch the plough that day. It was a day of rest for the divine bull. Though custom forbade hitching oxen to the plough on that day no such code applied to the bullocks that drew the cart. They in fact had more work on Mondays. They were hitched to the cart either to bring firewood, or thorny bush for the fence, or to hire out to Mysore. Though the dwarfs were good enough for the cart too they were not good enough to carry a heavy load. They were fit only for ploughing. Marikala was sharper than Amase. He had received good training in cultivation having served at Karigowda's for a couple of years. Even if Bhujangaiah did not instruct he did what had to be done in time. Marikala moreover appreciated the free hand of Deviravva very much. Because of the largesse of her nature wherein she served her servants whatever had been cooked at home without discriminating, the servants too worked with matching sincerity.

Bhujangaiah who normally bathed at home, worshipped and ate roti made by his mother every Monday, did not break his routine that day too. He later left for Mysore. This time, to his list was added a pickaxe, a shovel, a crowbar, etc. Bhujangaiah wishing that Sushila who had left her home in what she wore should not suffer for clothes if not for jewel and money visited a cloth shop with Raja. While making purchases he ordered a shirt to be tailored for himself. He bought a sari each for Sushila and his mother. However, he was apprehensive of his choice for Sushila. Whenever Bhujangaiah visited Mysore Raja took leave from his school.

He stayed with Bhujangaiah. He took Raja to Hotel Indra Bhavan at least twice in a day. He also gifted to Raja all the money left out of the visit. The generous nature of Bhujangaiah was one of the main reasons why Raja liked him very much. Subbanna the conductor told him that the bus would leave late that day when he had finished his purchases for the day and arrived to board the bus. Victor had not yet brought the bus from the garage after repairs. Bhujangaiah who had sat in the office had learnt that the new bus would run regularly from Monday. Though that was the rumor for long now no one had seen another bus apart from the Lingajamba bus.

The bus arrived late. Bhujangaiah had by then sent Raja back to his room after eating at a hotel on Gandhi Square. He boarded the bus. Victor's clothes were all dirty. He had left as he were, knowing that it would be late if he went home for a change. There was a big crowd. As Subbanna had already issued the tickets, the departure was not delayed. When the bus reached Madalli there were half a dozen people frantically looking for Bhujangaiah.When Bhujangaiah too overheard their words he jumped off from the driver's door with great trepidation. He ran towards the village forgetting even to instruct to unload his luggage. Those who had waited for him followed. Bhujangaiah went straight to the small room in his home, untied the gourd, hanging by the roof and rushed to Gowda's home. There was a big crowd at his house. Gowda had already fallen on the ground, the saliva was flowing from a corner of his lips. As soon as Bhujangaiah arrived everyone made way for him sighing breaths of relief saying there was nothing to fear anymore, One couldn't begin to describe Kalavva's agony, Muddegowda too had stood sobbing like a child. Bhujangaiah lifted Gowda's leg and inspected the place where the snake had bitten. The snake had sunk its fangs deep. Though they had tied his leg with a tourniquet to stop the venom from spreading it had begun to work its mischief. Bhujangaiah after sending out all those who had crowded inside the house asked for a blade and a copper basin. Narayana brought them. After asking all those who were present not to make noise he prayed to god and made incisions in a couple of places on the leg with the blade, put his lips to the wound and sucked the poison out and began to spit in the copper basin. It seemed as if Gowda stirred a little even as the poison mixed with blood began to fill the copper basin. Those who were watching with lifeless eyes too felt the stirring of life in them. Bhujangaiah had become a veritable god to Kalavva. Bhujangaiah also was scared at the outset with the doubt that the blood may have congealed. He had never ever sucked the venom thus with his mouth when the snake had bitten anyone other than people of his own caste in the village. But today he had put his lips to the wound unhesitatingly, not having a choice. The heart of those who saw the bloody venom thus sucked out fill almost half the basin shook. Gowda improved further. Kalavva sat wiping the frothing corners of her husband's mouth.

Bhujangaiah too was tired. As soon as he thought there was nothing more to fear he first washed his mouth with the herbal medicine from the gourd and sat down to administer Gowda the medicine by mixing it in a tumbler so that it would reach his stomach. Though the medicine noisily went down his gullet Gowda's eyes did not as yet register any sign of life. Bhujangaiah asked for some betel leaves, rolled them and twisted the roll in Gowda's throat to make him regurgitate the poison gradually. Kalavva and her sons felt that they should forever be obliged to Bhujangaiah who was nursing Gowda with great concern, leaning him against his shoulder and chest, as if he were reinvesting him with life.

As soon as he asked them to open the door of the house all those who had waited anxiously outside rushed in. Gowda was still leaning against Bhujangaiah, sitting with his eyes open. When Bhujangaiah announced that the danger had passed even as he was still making him vomit everybody cheered up. All the communities and castes had assembled. The rumours that Gowda died had shaken the village. They all thought that god himself had brought Bhujangaiah from nowhere in time. Bhujangaiah who had done all that he could went home saying he would return soon. Deviravva was not at home. It was already the hour to light the lamp. When he asked Amase who sat by the door, "Where is mother?" Amase had replied, "She asked me to wait saying she was going to the house of Gowda." Bhujangaiah sat down for the worship of Shiva washing his face and limbs in a corner of the courtyard, and lighted the lamp to gods, even as he enquired, "have you taken care of the oxen and the calves?" It was a wonder to him that Gowda had survived. He had begun to suck out the blood having taken a vow to god with the doubt that it may have already been too late. Gowda was not only dear to him but was also like the legendary Dharmaraya to the entire village. Bhujangaiah who had heard his mother say ten times. "The village still gets rains and harvest because there lives such a virtuous man" had the faith that whatever problems he had in the village Gowda would come to the rescue. When Deviravva returned she was scared to see someone having lit the lamps. When she found her son sitting in the hall at the altar forgetting himself in the worship of Shiva she was proud. All the antagonisms built up because of Sushila's incident washed away and the mind was cleansed once more. When Deviravva saw Bhujangaiah leave after worship she said, "you should eat first son." Bhujangaiah remembered his hunger only then. Ayya of Hampapura arrived even as he gargled with salt water and sat down for a meal. As he had already come the afternoon and had informed he would come supper for meal Deviravva gave him water to wash. Bhujangaiah proceeded with his meal, as he knew Ayya would take time with his worship. When he said he was going to Gowda's house, Ayya said, "I am returning from there now. He is all right. God is great. A good man is saved." Bhujangaiah sent Amase to the hotel instructing him to ask Shiva to go to the house of Gowda. When he asked Ayya whether he would sleep at the hotel or at home the later replied, "at home". However much he liked Bhujangaiah he had thought what Bhujangaiah had done was not what Shiva would approve of. He had been filled with sorrow hearing all that had happened as soon as he stepped into Madalli. His mind had grown bitter at the news of the Swami of the Main

Mutt having adorned Sushila with the Linga. Whatever it was he had not grown disgusted enough to not set foot in his house.

Bhujangaiah walked to Gowda's house. Though the crowd gathered in front of the house had thinned out the flood of visitors was yet unabated. When he entered the house Gowda had been made to lie down in the verandah, Bhujangaiah immediately knew he had erred. He had forgotten to instruct them not to allow him to sleep. Gowda was drowsy and tired having vomited repeatedly. It was said that those bitten by a snake should not sleep. Bhujangaiah woke up Gowda and made him sit. He made him drink the medicine again. Gowda was in no condition to speak. He told Kalavva that he would stay there that night as Gowda should sit throughout the night without sleep for the effect of the venom to wear off. When he suggested that if the Tampura Ayya who was at his house was brought they could all keep vigil listening to bhajans or Tales of Shiva throughout the night, Shankara the eldest son of Gowda personally went to bring Ayya.

Everyone from Hundi had come learning the news of Gowda having been bitten by snake. None of them stirred from the place where they sat. Muddegowda asked Puttavva to cook something for everybody. People still kept visiting to enquire after Gowda. When Sushila arrived with Shiva Bhujangaiah was surprised. Kalavva affectionately held Sushila's hand and made her sit next to her. It was the very first occasion that Sushila had stepped into the village after marrying Bhujangaiah. The eyes of everybody in the house turned to her. She looked new to everybody. Her eyes filled with tears looking at Gowda. She had come not caring what people may say as she could not control her anxiety to see Gowda.

Ayya arrived with his cymbals and tampura accompanied by Shankara. The tune of his tampura began to fill the house dispelling the anxiety and dread that had so far reigned in the house. Ayya who for a long while strummed his tampura lifted his face, shut his eyes and uttered "Om" losing himself for sometime in the resonance of "Om", before beginning to sing the verse he had learnt. The atmosphere made heavy by an impending death slowly lightened. Though he did not have a melodious voice he sang the verse with an unusual involvement making their meaning pierce the heart of the listeners. They were songs that the villagers had known for a long while now. Bhujangaiah too had heard them many a time. Though he had lost himself in such verses occasionally at his hotel, they had never cast their spell on him in such a manner ever. The hymns of Shiva had deeply stirred him. The Vachanas of Basavanna had made him introspect often. Yes, he had not conducted himself as enjoined by the Vachanas of the Virtuous. There had been no end to his desires. He had grown a slave to the needs of the body. He had performed the worship of Shiva without fail every day and still performed it. But nothing had altered within. His soul was full of desires. He also had revealed his pettiness revealing arrogance and hatred even at insignificant events. What could sweeten the bitterness in him as Ayya sang? "You may make a bed of jaggery, sprinkle the milk of cow and pour honey. But if you sow the seed of neem will the sprig ever be sweet and not bitter?" No, no, it can never be. He had never fixed his mind on the meditation of Shiva. When he sat down for worship though he concentrated for a moment, the next instant it leapt on to some other temptation. He too joined his voice silently to the tune of the song. "My mind leaps like the monkey on a branch! My mind doesn't let me be staid! Lord of Kudalasangama, have mercy and make me a bee that haunts the lotus of your feet"

Every song of Ayya was a mirror held to his character. True, he was a sinner. He had forgotten religion caught by iniquitous desire. He earned the money of sin. It did not merit good cause. It was only dog's milk and not *panchamruta*, the elixir of five purities. Whatever he had done had been done for his own bodily pleasure. Money and sex were not everything. He had succumbed to them knowingly. As Basavanna had said, his desires should be proper ones at least in future. He should free himself from the temptations that held him down. There was nothing that distinguished him from an animal and the mire called family. Can he never emerge from it? Will it be easy for him to kick away the desires that had troubled even Basavanna?

Bhujangaiah was touched by the verses of Basavanna about

caste that Ayya sang. Basavanna seemed to have dedicated himself to the service of Madara Cennaiah, Aidakki Maraiah, Madivala Machaiah without caring for their castes. When Ayya sang Basavanna's vachana,

"He who kills is a Madiga,

He who eats dirt is an untouchable.

What is caste? What is the caste of one's mother?

The devotees of our Lord of Kudala Sangama

Who wish the good of all alike

Are alone of true caste."

Bhujangaiah wished that Ayya should be made to sing that song a thousand times for his community in the village to hear. How dastardly had they all behaved because Sushila belonged to the merchant community. Bhujangaiah looked at Sushila with pride. The holy ash glowed on her forehead. She followed the customs of his community more faithfully than he did since the day she had worn the Linga. For a moment Bhujangaiah felt he had not done anything wrong. It was true he had fallen for her beauty. But his was not a momentary desire; he had held her hands in front of Shiva and brought her home. He would live with her in a manner that Shiva would approve of. He would not care for the anger of any one. What does he care if the entire village ignored him?

That night no one slept. Gowda who had been sitting leaning against the wall was very tired now, Bhujangaiah spent the night nursing him hour after hour. Death that had waited to swallow Gowda had taken to its feet. With dawn everyone was immensely happy. Gowda began to speak haltingly. In the house that had escaped a terrible disaster the joy of life began to spring. Bhujangaiah returned to the hotel in full sight of everybody with Sushila who had spent the entire night without shutting her eyes. The pearl like words of Basavanna was as yet inscribed as if on stone in the brain of Bhujangaiah. For the people of the Street of Gowdas Bhujangaiah was a veritable God come to save the life of Gowda.

Though he had saved many from snakebite, not a single one of those incidents had received such attention as this one. The news that he had put his lips to the wound of Gowda's leg to suck the venom out and save Gowda had already spread throughout the village. Though the question if it was right confronted the orthodox Lingayats none of them had opened his mouth for some reason.

***

CHAPTER - 26

The torrential rains of monsoon began. The life of Madalli revolved according to the season with people already beginning to forget Sushila's incident. No extraordinary event happened in the village. One day Deviravva was caught in the devilish rain and came home to lie in a corner. Either Ninganna's wife or daughter from the next door used to come and cook her meal. Parvathy had remained at her father's, unrelenting in her nature, however much her mother-in-law cajoled. Though the Pundit from Kyatanahalli, so titled in deference to his knowledge of medicinal herbs, visited regularly to treat Deviravva, the fever had not abated. Bhujangaiah couldn't convince her to go to Mysore for treatment. Her only desire was to see her grandchildren before she died. Muddegowda himself visited the Mutt of Madapura on Bhujangaiah's behalf with two others. Pundri too accompanied. Basavarajappa who was considered the most powerful in Madapura and Karigowda were friends from a long time. He too came to the mutt at Muddegowda's request. Pundri's son was "Junior" in the mutt. After meals when Bhujangaiah's story was brought to the Swami's notice he opined that as the Main Mutt had already presented her the Linga there was nothing more to be done and that Parvathappa was not wise to continue as he did, therefore he would summon him and advise appropriately. He had sent a servant that very day to ask Parvathappa to visit the mutt. Parvathappa had heeded the call of the mutt without a word. Because of a short cut between Jakkalli and the mutt it took just an hour for Parvathappa to travel the distance with his long stride. On his way Parvathappa had learnt the reason for the summons from the servant himself.

That evening, hot argument ensued in the mutt. In the end Parvathappa's attitude won the day. As the main concern was to somehow save Bhujangaiah from his agony of having to live apart from his children Muddegowda accepted the conditions laid down by Parvathappa. Muddegowda who had shouldered the onerous responsibility of bringing together a broken home and riven hearts agreed to Parvathappa's words, being more interested in re-establishing peace at home rather than argue. It was decided in front of the Swami that Bhujangaiah should will all the properties excepting the fields of Singari, which he had bought with his own earnings, to his wife Parvathy and her children. Bhujangaiah too without another word left for Kote at the appointed hour bound by Muddegowda's word. Parvathy was waiting with her father and children under the Papaya tree shade in front of the Sub-Registrar's office. Both the children leapt up as soon as they saw their father without any hesitation. Muddegowda's gut was wrenched as he saw Bhujangaiah shedding tears at the sight of his children. Bhujangaiah who gave all the details of the property, unable to bear company went to the market street with his children saying, "I will return at the time of registration after you finish drafting the paper." However much he tried the sorrow bottled in him couldn't help but spring forth. He bought every thing that the children wished for at Nagendra's Hotel. He too drank a cup of tea and sat smoking a beedi. The children ate as if they were starved. "Poor children! who knew how long it had been since they had eaten what they liked ?" He also got some deliciously sweet *Mysorepak* packed in paper for his little child Umashankara. Muddegowda arrived even as he was getting up, to say that the papers were ready for his signature. Parvathappa who was known for his shrewd business acumen had got all of Bhujangaiah's property willed in his daughter and her children's name leaving only the lands of Singari and the hotel in Bhujangaiah's name. As the land on which the hotel existed belonged to Ajappa it could not be hypothecated to anybody. Bhujangaiah signed all the papers as if he were performing the last rites of somebody, without raising his head. He did not look at Parvathy's face even by accident. He made Soma hand him the baby Umashankara and showered kisses on the child. When they returned Soma went with his father. He had felt that Madalli was better than Jakkalli even if he were punished at school; even the daughter threw a tantrum wanting to go with him. Though Parvathappa finally said he would bring all of them himself, Soma alone refused to be parted from his father.

Bhujangaiah narrated everything that had transpired to Sushila, after returning to the village. She reacted with a great detachment as if none of it had anything to do with her. She had no other desire except the love of Bhujangaiah. She would not have wavered even if he had given away all that he had to Parvathy. She treated Soma with affection. Though Soma did remember every thing that people said about Sushila in Jakkalli he did not find her to be a demon. He ran towards the village to see his grandmother. Though Deviravva was happy enough to move her limbs the memory of her other grandchildren grew sharper.

As promised, Parvathappa presented himself in Madalli with his daughter. Contrary to Parvathy's expectation no work at home had remained unattended to. Everything had gone on as it had when she were around. Deviravva, though she herself could not, through servants had seen to it that the order at home had never gone astray. Once more the house was lit. The gaiety of children reverberated. Deviravva sent word to her son thinking of her vow of breaking a hundred coconuts to Hulikanthyappa after her house were filled with happiness and wanted to fulfill the vow the very next day. He acquiesced and had it performed. The old woman who could not go to the temple sat at home and imagined all that was happening at the temple. That night she ate with her son and grandchildren, insisting on their company. She called her son separately and advised him not to forget his sister in Kallahalli. Bhujangaiah had found all of that rather strange. The entire night Bhujangaiah could hardly sleep. He sat up a couple of times. Sushila asked, "Why?" He went back to bed saying, "Some bad dream." At dawn he had yielded to a drowsy slumber. Sushila opened the door on hearing Amase's frightened call. He brought the news that Deviravva who had lived all those years a full life had closed her eyes without anyone to feed her a drop of water. She had detached herself from this world as if to assert she had no more desire to live now that she had seen everyone. She seemed to have held on to her life only to see her grandchildren.

Those who had hated Bhujangaiah too came to pay their last respects to Deviravva. Sushila too held the lamp of camphor to her dead mother-in-law. When the shadow of her husband's second wife fell on her, Parvathy who was rhythmically sobbing changed the tune to, "It is because of this ill omen of a woman that my mother-in-law died and we were orphaned." Sushila did not lift her head. She stepped away after prayers as if she were an outcaste. When those women who were by Parvathy's side themselves admonished her Parvathy altered her tune. This was the second death after his father's since Bhujangaiah was old enough to understand things. He was at a loss not knowing what was to be done . Kariappa and Pundri lent help in performing the rites. When the news of death reached Deviravva's parents' village Bilikere as well as Kallalli, Hampapura and Jakkalli, relatives had arrived from all over. The Tampura Ayya too returned from Hampapura although it was only the previous day that he had left Madalli. The burial took place and people returned home as the night fell.

The sorrow of having lost the only parent he had known this long pained him for a long while. Time was the only magician who could heal any sort of wound. Slowly Bhujangaiah recovered and got involved in his routine duties. Sushila's proximity dispelled all his worries. She was a true woman. His life with her made him forget all the pleasure he ever had with Parvathy for such long years. Sushila had been living as if she had none except her husband in this world, careful not to hurt him for any reason, yielding to his wishes, always being a shadow of his and serving her husband with all her being, in speech, in mind and in body. Bhujangaiah too found Sushila's proximity very dear. What kind of maya was he subject to? As Ayya had said, the maya of woman, money and earth would drown him. He should learn to live detached. The joy of family was not everything! Whenever he remembered the words of Basavanna he would grow inward. But when he was next to Sushila he would forget all else. He was not yet beyond his hours of happiness. He had not yet lost the strength of his waist. Even Basavanna had two wives it was said - Gangadevi and Mayadevi. Though Anna had all the riches, and wives who knew of his whims, he never lost himself in the mortal world. He developed the treasure of the inner mind and gave light to the universe. Tche, how great a sinner he himself was? Where was he compared to the other, the very God, Shiva? Yet how many were the troubles he too had to suffer like an ordinary human being? How many were the tests he was subjected to? When Ayya of Hampapura talked thus one felt like listening to the stories of the devotees of Shiva not just throughout the day, but throughout one's life.

Bhujangaiah confronted a question suddenly. Why does not Ayya follow all that he said? He says a true devotee has no caste. Basavanna was the founder of his religion. But he had been born in the caste of Brahmins. Finally he had founded the Verashaiva caste by collecting people from all other castes. Ayya himself said so. But why did he not accept his marriage with Sushila? Was it because she was lowly? Yes, he did not even touch the vessel which she had touched. He had not spoken to her even after so many days. Though he knew everything why did he behave so? Sushila bathed every day now. She never drank a drop of water without praying to Shiva. She was no less than any devotee according to Anna. Shiva loved all that his devotees did in their innocence. To him there was nothing filthy if performed with a true mind. He had got from Sushila in a few days all that he had not found in Parvathy in these many years. It was not just bodily hunger. If the bodily pleasure was what were important for him there were no impediments to satisfy that in Madalli itself. Sushila had given him more than that. He should not be scared or shy of experiencing anything for her sake, for her satisfaction. He should ask Ayya today. He should talk sharp enough to put to shame his soul.

Ayya who had come for Deviravva's death had camped in Madalli. He himself took the responsibility of gettng all the rites performed after death. On the day of the funeral, the Swami of Madapura had been invited. Till all the rites were done Ayya had not turned his steps towards the hotel. After completion of everything, on the day of his return to his village, when he arrived at the hotel to catch the bus Bhujangaiah did not compel him to enter. While he stood talking to Ayya under the tamarind tree Sushila came to touch Ayya's feet dressed in a sari covering her shoulders entirely. Ayya's mind was disturbed for a second. He blessed her out of habit. He was suddenly reminded of Mahadevi Akka's statue in the framed picture as he gazed at her who stood with her forehead shining with holy ash and the lucent quality of the pleasant face. Akka had left a king in Kaushika proclaiming that God Mallikarjuna was her husband and had left for Srishyla to join him. She was said to have divested her raiment to stand nude amidst the devotees of Shiva testing their self-control, making the world acclaim her devotion. Ayya's mind was further confused. Why should he be reminded of Akka at the sight of a mere merchant woman? It was his mind's weakness. Why did he yield to such a thought? His mind was caught in the whirlpool of right and wrong. He sat placing the tampura under the tree. He was silent without speech. Sushila walked back to the hotel.

Ayya felt a lightening bolt strike him confronted by the simmering doubt in Bhujangaiah, "Has he not followed faithfully the teachings of his religion for all these years? Why should he face such a test? There was meaning in what Bhujangaiah said in a sense. True! what if Sushila belonged to the merchant's caste? Was she not of his caste now, once she took the vows? Why had he seen her as a low caste? He had never thought along those lines all these years. A true devotee should not entertain such discriminations. Why did such meanness rise in him? No, no, he was as yet a wretch. He could never be a devotee till he overcame his wretchdness. He would never have ill treated Sushila if he had possessed the quality of a devotee. But, in the eyes of the society she was yet a merchant woman. No matter who gave the Linga or the vow to her she could never be one among their community. In his village even the untouchables sported the Linga. Can one establish marital relationship with them because of that? Someone named Mahatma Gandhi called them Harijan and insisted that they too should enter temples. He is supposed to have said that it was a grave sin not to allow them to draw water from the wells of the better born. Shiva! What has the age of Kali brought? Bhujangaiah had to bring and frame such a person's picture! He thinks him to be a god like the others. He lights the incense stick to him too along with those of his other Gods. When Rudrappa too had told him of that and asked if that was proper he had answered, " a grave sacrilege, a grave sacrilege." Bhujangaiah who had gone so far would not hesitate to call the untouchables and make them sit in his hotel. Look at his speech! He himself has no answer! All that he asks and says are proper. They were what Anna said. But how long is it since it was uttered? Perhaps those words were appropriate for that age. But who would accept if one said today there was no meaning in religion? Why does not the Swami of the Main Mutt who is thousand times superior to him think of such things? He presents the linga to everybody that goes to him. Will he adorn an untouchable with the linga and admit him to the victuals at the mutt? He should confront him with the question when he went to Devanur again." Ayya's mind grew into an anthill of doubt. Unable to answer Bhujangaiah at once, Ayya offered a lame excuse, " I shall find out what the scripture says" . He boarded the bus. The thought began to bore into him like an insect all along the way. He again and again saw Sushila's face in his mind, "How she had left in sorrow! He could have uttered a word. His tongue would not have grown filthy! How cruel he had been! But, each one to his fate. As one did so one reaped. Why should he be curt?" Ayya was drowned in introspection even when he reached his village. If he had felt the problem of Bhujangaiah to be that of a neighbour this conflict would not have been there. Somehow he had felt it to be the problem of his own house and so was lost deep in thought. "Forget duty and religion: why did Bhujangaiah yield to such a desire? His wife was like Goddess Gowri; he had three children who were like gold; what had god denied him? How charming Parvathy looked even now! Should one yearn for moonshine finding fault with the creamy milk at home? Oh, God! It is said that the horse laid egg to usher in the evil hour. I do not know what ill awaits Bhujangaiah!" Ayya was ashamed that his mind was assailed by such dark thoughts. All said, his brain was a burning cauldron of issues. He sat at home contemplating as nothing resolved. And he began to sing all to himself.

***

CHAPTER - 27

Bhujangaiah who had assumed that everything would straighten out as days passed by found Parvathy's behaviour intolerable. The home had grown into hell as she barked like a rabid bitch at the very shadow of her husband. There was a limit to his tolerance too though he went home at least once a day to check on the servants and to spend time with children. When that limit was crossed he would thrash her like he would an erring ox. The ember of hate for Sushila had not as yet burnt out in Parvathy. Day by day it smoldered. The harvested grains at home remained untouched. There was no want. The wife of Ninganna, from the neighboring house, could not understand why Parvathy behaved thus, instead of living carefree. She had advised her a number of times. She had tried telling Parvathy how she had never met a woman who prospered trying to wreak vengeance on her husband. No good advice ever touched Parvathy.

The mustard crop was good that year. Bhujangaiah decided to make good the loan he had taken from Muddegowda first of all. The short term loan he had taken from him while purchasing the fields of Singari had not been returned due to his extravagance. He had almost forgotten it as Gowda too had not asked for it. Ajappa's loan too had remained unpaid. Wishing to return all the loans this time he transported the mustard the very day it was harvested. He had got a good price for it. After accounting for their loan amount he decided to get a guinea necklace of gold for Sushila. He placed an order at the shop of a relative of the merchant from whom he regularly bought provisions. When God was munificent one should order all that one desired. He had married Sushila without even presenting her a new sari. Though Bhujangaiah went on to console himself that he had married Sushila with God as witness what stung him like a scorpion was the talk of the villagers that she was his "kept woman".

The news that Bhujangaiah had got a guinea necklace made for his "kept woman" spread from ear to ear and reached Parvathy too. It was impossible for any news to remain a secret in Madalli. Sushila herself had shown it to Pundri at the hotel one day. Though her husband always addressed him, "Hey Pundri" Sushila always called him full-mouthed, "Pudasamanna". At first Pundri too had been displeased by her setting up a hearth in the hotel. In time Pundri who had arrived at the judgment that there was not another woman to match her, had found the hotel, which had been the most appropriate place for the narration of his tales, out of bounds. He now spoke with a check on his tongue while at the hotel. Still when by force of habit the words he dearly loved accidently spilled out, he would be crestfallen. Though Sushila would turn her face away in shyness and disgust whenever such words fell on her ears she too could not help but laugh in secret. It was because of the loose tongue of Pundri that the news of Sushila's guinea necklace spread throughout the village. Pundri's wife had gossiped when she went to fetch water from the well and the woman who had heard had told another till the news finally reached Parvathy. There was a guinea necklace around Parvathy's neck too. Yet her husband having made one for his second wife had given rise to a terrible envy in her. She bemoaned that a scavenging bitch had now come to sit on her head. Of late, even the little love that Bhujangaiah had for his wife had been lost due to his wife's contentious nature and the very sound of her voice was enough to fill him with disgust. Bhujangaiah had not as yet left the custom of bathing at home once a week and performing special prayers. However much they were in disagreement Parvathy too had not hindered that. She used to heat the water, wipe, clean the framed pictures, and brought the flowers or Mukul leaves from the backyard. As the flooring had all been done up with mortar she did not have to use dung mixture to stamp the floor anymore. Today was the holy day of the week. Bhujangaiah had as usual arrived, bathed and performed his puja, and sat down for food with children. Parvathy who knew her husband's nature of even throwing the plate at her in anger if she should quarrel while he sat for a meal controlled all that she wished to say and served him food. As Bhujangaiah was getting ready to leave soon after his meal she confronted her husband, "How much did you get for the mustard?" Though Bhujangaiah was uncomfortable for a moment he asked "How does it concern you?" She answered,"' Why, should I not ask? I am not some one on the street who eloped. I came to you after a marriage that the village blessed. I too have the right to ask." Though Bhujangaiah was angry enough to slap Parvathy's ugly face, he laughed and exclaimed, "If you had at least a little of the loyalty of her who eloped!" Parvathy felt like screaming. She hissed, "What people used to say has come true. Where will the learnt habit go? Even if a dog is placed on a throne will it desist from jumping whenever it finds shit?" Bhujangaiah controlled his rage and left for the hotel, nauseated to speak to her.

Sushila who noticed Bhujangaiah's drawn face did not probe into the reason but informed him happily about Ayya of Hampapura's visit to the hotel, asking for water and drinking it from her hand as he sat in their room, and of his inquiring about her well being. Bhujangaiah too was surprised to hear of it. What a change? God himself must have changed Ayya's heart. How could a person who left without heeding his request only in his last visit change so suddenly? That event brought Sushila too the satisfaction of having climbed another step. She had decided to follow the practices of the Verashaiva religion much more faithfully and with greater purity of mind. That day Ayya who returned to the hotel after his alms round sang for a long while into the night. He narrated the story of Akka the devotee of Shiva as Sushila enjoined him to. Though Sushila had heard the story many a times she wished to hear it again. Akka who went singing soulfully enough to melt even a rock as she reached for Cennamallikarjuna of Srishyla, enquiring of trees, of birds, and of animals his whereabouts seemed to be etched in her mind. She looked at the picture of Akka in the light of the petromax lamp. Akka herself seemed to be stepping down pure from the blackened frame that had grown sooty because of the constant smoke of the hotel. Ayya too was extremely pleased at Sushila's involvement, and devoutness. Why had he taken such a pure hearted girl for a lowly woman? No, no she is no more lowly. She too is a devotee of Shiva. What she touched was not impure. What she served was not refuse. He too had grown small of mind having been a daily witness to smallness. Hereafter he would eat what Sushila cooked. Let the people of Madalli ask why. He would announce to the village that Sushila was a real devotee.

That entire week the troubled mind of Ayya caught in the conflict of various issues had finally grown placid. The story of many devotees of Shiva, the events in their lives, the feelings of difference that had bothered them even as they had in him, finally the paths they found had all brought a new knowledge to his simple mind. The Lingayat community was surprised at the faithful Ayya eating what Sushila cooked. A few did not desist from asking him hesitantly. When asked, Ayya praised Sushila's virtue and behaviour without any hesitation. Only those who hated her said,"That sorceress has mesmerized Ayya too." Ayya alone didn't care a cowry to their talk. One day when Puttavva herself enquired, Ayya convinced her how Sushila was in no way inferior. "Who knows if they weren't related from another birth? How can we either stop it or say it is wrong? Everything is Shiva's will." Puttavva too nodded at Ayya's words who said it was their duty to act as god willed. Because Sushila was not visiting Hundi every week as before Puttavva had felt she had grown distant. Puttavva desired to see Sushila and said so to Ayya. Sushila who learnt the news from Ayya when he returned to the hotel that evening was eager to visit Hundi. But that very evening they were visiting Mysore. Of late, Jayalaxmi bus had begun to ply competing with Lingajamba on the Kote-Mysore road, which was till then the only bus plying on that route. It was now easier to go to Mysore after evening, stay overnight, and return from Mysore by the first light of day. Mysore city had grown closer to Madalli because of the new bus.

Though the driver and the conductor of Jayalaxmi bus too were familiar to Bhujangaiah they were not as intimate with him as those of Lingajamba bus. Bhujangaiah kept them also happy with his tea and snacks to help his business. But their relationship had not grown strong enough to share problems and pleasures. Bhujangaiah had left for Mysore with Sushila for the very first time after marriage. They went to Raja's room after getting off the bus.

Sushila wished that Raja and Tayavva and her children at whose house Raja stayed all went to a Tamil movie currently showing at Rajkamal Talkies. Though Raja had already seen the movie he bowed to Sushila's insistence and accompanied them. Raja talked about the movie all along the way to Sushila. Bhujangaiah too nodded in appreciation of Raja's intelligence. Raja asked them to sleep in his room after the movie and went to sleep with the children of the owner of his room. From that day Bhujangaiah found Raja's room as comfortable as his own home. They began to stay overnight there whenever they were bored of Madalli. Raja too had begun to see in them his relatives. Occasionally when Bhujangaiah was very busy Sushila would visit Mysore by herself for purchases. She would stay at Raja's room without any hesitation. When Raja felt uncomfortable about sleeping in the same room with Sushila and said he would sleep at the owner's, Sushila would say as though she were an ancient, " Ah, you are a big male! Aren't you now shy to sleep next to me?" She would force him to sleep by her side making fun of him. He felt emotions that could not be explained. More and more he strove to sleep at a distance from her body some kind of a scent from her body seemed to inveigle him, and forcefully embrace him. Though Sushila slept unaware, he was scared that she may find out what was happening to him. Nothing could be seen in the room where darkness had settled thick. When an occasional lightening flashed through the open window Raja would feel like sitting up. Once when a thunder bolt flashed across the sky he had sat up suddenly. Sushila too had woken up asking "Why Raju?" He had replied, "There's a lot of lightening. It's thundering too. I think it may rain." She had said, "Then shut the windows". Raja was afraid of doing so. He remained sitting. Sushila got up saying, "How meek you are! I do not know how you manage to live alone!" She shut the window and pulled Raja close in embrace as she would a child and lay down patting his back. She was not troubled in any way. Raja's face was pressed to her bossom. He felt as if he had fallen into a furnace. His burning, hot breath did not touch Sushila. He was yet a child for her. She was unaware of a beast that moved even in his tiny body. Raja trembled as if he were scared. Sushila embraced him as though she would hide him in her. She began to comfort him as if she could dispel his fear assuming that he shivered because of his fright of thunder and lightning. Her every action again and again raised the heat in Raja and troubled him. Sushila who had slept insensitive to his body language woke up, when she felt something cold running between her thighs. Raja was in deep sleep. But she noticed that his hand was between her thighs exposed by the disordered sari. She removed it, and straightened her clothes. She was disturbed for a moment. A doubt pricked. But immediately she consoled herself and slept thinking, "Thu, what a thought to have? He is like a brother to me." She went back to sleep. Though there was a feeling of nothing untoward having happened, Raja was secretly shy. He felt guilty to speak to her. he decided never to sleep next to her ever. Sushila was unaware of any wrong on Raja's part. She found a greater affection welling up for him in her. If only she had a brother like Raja! She had never felt close to her stepmother's children. She had never held them against her heart even a single day. Her anger against her stepmother had distanced her children too from her. She could never put up with her stepmother's face. when her mother died her father had said that he would be both her father and her mother. All who had come to counsel him to remarry had returned silently after hearing those words of his. One day finally, she had arrived to occupy her mother's place. Where was the comparison between this women and her mother? Once realized the woman's countenance had grown fiery instead of showering love and affection . It was because of the desire to distance herself from that heat that Sushila had begun to roam through the villages with her father, not caring how hot the sky was. It was because she did no wish to have even its shadow falling on her that she had eloped with Bhujangaiah in spite of her father's strong opposition. Sushila suddenly remembered her father. With a desire to meet him she sent word through Raja. Raja was mad after riding bicycle. He rushed away as soon as Sushila asked him to. But the words he returned with stabbed Sushila. She returned to Madailli with a sigh not uttering another word.

The rain fell in time that year without waiting for the "Para" to be performed and once more the signs of good harvest were to be seen. In the old fields of Bhujangaiah the summer crop of ragi was good. As soon as the mustard was harvested in Singari's field he had got the stubble fields ploughed thrice and manured them again. He had decided to have the premium ragi transplanted in that field. If the returning monsoon too should bring good rains his long cherished desire would be fulfilled, which was to grow enough ragi to fill the pit in front of his house. It had been filled once when his father was alive. How long had it been since? Though every year it was intended to grow enough to fill the pit, that had not been possible. Even if he harvested enough to fill half of the pit, within the week he was forced to remove it to sell. It was not merely his story, but that of almost everyone in the village. Bhujangaiah had an insuppressible desire to somehow fill the pit that year. He had paid much attention to the cultivation. His mother's demise had shifted all the responsibility on his shoulders. He personally had to get the servants to do every little thing. Parvathy merely pretended to take great care of the fields and home in the eyes of the village folk. She had almost grown faint when her husband had sold the sesame crop to buy a guinea necklace for her successor. She was scared that he would give all that was earned to the one who had eloped. Parvathy had felt herself on fire since the day she heard that Sushila's periods had stopped. Her head was full of what Sannappa had said. Parvathy had known from the very beginning that son of a prostitute Sannappa was a breaker of homes. He had been the one who had spread rumors envious of her husband's good fortune. The entire village knew he was evil incarnate. Yet she had found his words dear. The future of her three children was hers to think about. If she trusted her husband who married that whore as if he had just come to heat, her children would never eat palms full. What Sannappa said was true. She herself must sell the children's and her share of crop from that year and keep the money. She must send word to her father before the harvest. Everything would go smoothly if her father were around. Otherwise her husband would not hesitate to sell the ragi tomorrow to get something made for her successor as he had sold the sesame and got the guinea necklace made for her earlier. The poisonous seeds that Sannappa had sown in the tiny brain of Parvathy had now begun to foliate one after another.

***

CHAPTER - 28

The villagers of Kyatanahalli and nearby villages not only held in affection and respect Madalli's Drama Master Govindaraju, the headmaster of Kyatanahalli Middle School, but also had their suspicions about him. Though a Brahmin, he dressed in Khadi and propagated the Gandhian principles in an effort to erase the ignorance of the villagers, and rid them of their discriminatory attitudes. With the desire of making the Harijan children attend school he went to their lane to convince them. When he insisted that no one should be addressed as "Holeya" and "Madiga", which were part of the common parlance in the villages but to address them as "Harijan" in the manner of Mahatma Gandhi, people looked at him with confusion and doubt. When the high caste villagers saw him making the children of that street sit "touching" their own children they wondered, "What kind of a Brahmin is he?" Though Govindaraju followed the principles of Gandhiji conscientiously, he too had a few vices. Playing cards was one of them. Those addicted to the game and long exiled from Bhujangaiah's hotel began to meet at the shed of Madalli Forest Gate. Bhujangaiah too visited occasionally. The teacher's esteem for Bhujangaiah was due to the latter's love for and loyalty to Sushila unaffected by what the others thought of it. Govindaraju had never sneered in disapproval at their relationship. Bhujangaiah too had great respect for him. Bhujangaiah had been greatly surprised and some what scared when the master, having seen the Harijans being made to stand under the tent behind the hotel to drink tea and to wash their glasses had condemned it as a great sin and a wrong. Though of late he too had felt that his words had truth in them, his heart wouldn't approve of it, "Who could ever say from how long the custom was in vogue? No one had ever said it was right. They would never enter even if he urged them to. All this was caused by god. Did we make the distinction between high and low? All the five fingers are not equal. Then how can one accept Gandhi's words of looking upon everybody as equal?" Bhujangaiah entered a conflict whenever he introspected. Yet he would grow excited at the mention of Gandhi. Having read Gandhi he proudly said that if there was a brave man it was he. The Parangis who had owned the nation had shivered in front of the old man. He had not relented till they left the country. There were times when Bhujangaiah wondered if Basavanna had not been reborn as Gandhi. whatever were his personal problems the addiction to reading "Tayinadu" paper, which had grown in him since the day he opened the hotel, had not left him. A few visited the hotel only to read the paper he subscribed to. They talked about the world events. Many doubts and curiosities would either get resolved or grow intense as Bhuiangaiah listened to their conversation. What had touched him to the core was a conversation between Ayya and the Master. When the master asserted Gandhi's ideology of the caste system as a curse, a blight, Ayya had not accepted it. The master had said that Basavanna too had opposed caste, he had never tolerated it, and that among his close followers there were people from all castes. He had illustrated his argument with the *Vachanas* of Basavanna making Bhujangaiah nod his head. Sushila who listened to the argument from behind the doors, in great concentration, had liked his words. Though they had heard Ayya sing the very same Vachanas many times it had not affected them as it had done today. Ayya too had been affected by the experience. But Pundri who had sat silently for a long while, listening to everything with his body and mind, not being able to hold himself, asked, "What are you saying Master? Did Basavanna offer the Linga to all those beef eating widows' sons?" The master immediately mentioned a few names of devotees. Pundri looked askance at Ayya. Ayya said, "True, true, but Basavanna was verily the God Shiva. Will what happened in his times happen in ours? Our Elder Guru may give Linga to anyone but would he go and eat in the house of an untouchable?" The teacher said with the finality of breaking a stick, "In the eyes of Basavanna even a Jagadguru is a charlatan and untrue in devotion if he does not act as he says. He would be a mere wretch like you and me and not one who could show the path to us." It was as if those words pricked the mind of Ayya. Bhujangaiah intervened before a momentarily silenced Ayya who would never tolerate the abuse of a Guru could begin an argument : "Ayya, it is blood that flows in every one's body is it not? Does something else flow in those who are called 'Oleru?" Pundri had immediately countered, "Will you then allow the untouchables enter your hotel?" Bhujangaiah had felt as if someone had stopped him from breathing. He grew inward without answering. The sound of the approaching Lingajamba bus cut short their argument. Ayya's trepidation grew suspecting that the teacher may further addle Bhujangaiah's mind.

Days went by without the hungry tongues of the Lingayat elders of the village finding anything to say against or accuse Bhujangaiah afresh with. But, both Sannappa and Rudrappa, albeit in an indirect manner, encouraged Parvathy to intensify the contention at home. In Parvathy's mind too day by day poison began to well up. She had in the meanwhile visited Jakkalli a few times with festivals and ceremonies for excuse. Though many days had passed since she had spoken to her husband she would send Soma to the village to bring home whatever money she needed. Soma never felt Sushila to be a bad woman in spite of what his mother said. Why did mother rage at the very mention of Sushila who greeted him with such affection whenever he met her, and who gave him money unasked, brought him the colourful top and cap and for his sister Gowri, tapes and dolls from Mysore? Sushila was better than mother who said he should not eat anything that Sushila gave. Since the day father introduced her as his "Chikkavva", he addressed her as "Chikkavva." But one day when he had replied to his mother's query "Chikkavva gave me", his mother had roared, "Thu! What sort of a Chikkavva is she to you, that casteless widow? If you call her Chikkavva again, I shall cut your tongue, take care!" Soma was scared from then on to call Sushila "Chikkavva". When Sushila found Soma stop addressing her in his normal full-mouthed manner "Chikkavva", she suspected things and cajoled him. Soma innocently revealed what his mother had uttered. Sushila felt her guts wrench when she heard Soma. when he saw her eyes brim Soma was troubled and regretted having revealed what he had.

Sushila was in the last stage of her pregnancy. She who was dreaming of her parent's house for the birth of her first child sent word to her father through Raja who had come from Mysore, the merchant he had sent him back saying, "She is dead for us. Tell her we won't even visit to see her dead body." Sushila began to forget her parent's house from the moment she heard those words. Nothing had posed an impediment to Bhujangaiah thereafter. He had thought to bring the nurse from Kyatanahalli. It was rare that Sushila left her room in those days. If she came out carrying her large womb she felt everyone was staring at her. She would feel disgusted at times. Again the uncontrollable desire to be a mother would overtake her, Sushila felt all that had transpired so far to be a dream. How fast had everything happened?

As Sankranti approached the village began to gather the crop with great joy. Bhujangaiah too was getting ready. The two huge stakes of ragi seemed to be displayed as if Bhujangaiah's long held desire had been fulfilled and struck the eyes of the villagers. One day Sannaputtappa said to somebody, "Even though the entire village envied him, see how Hulikanthyapa has blessed him!" That worthy transmitted those words to the ears of all those who nurtured a dislike for Bhujangaiah, including Rudrappa and Sannappa. It was as if salt had been rubbed into a festering wound. Parvathy who had remained as if she were an ignoramus till the crops were all harvested arrived at the threshing ground with her father on the day ragi was to be winnowed and filled in the pit after the ritual of "excess". Amase and Marikala had brought bundles of the Cadamba flowers from the pond's banks and decorated the threshing ground. The fragrance of the Cadamba flowers surpassed the strong scent of the proliferating Jerusalem pea plant. Parvathappa arrived and contended the right of Bhujangaiah to fill the granary pit in the presence of the peasants assembled for threshing and the poor who stood waiting to collect from a generous Bhujangaiah the gift of grains after the ritual of excess. When he said that excepting those grown in Singari's field all other crop should belong to his daughter and she would transport it to her house under her own supervision and that Bhujangaiah could take his portion and fill the pit or whatever else he wished to do, Bhujangaiah felt that the sky had fallen on his head. He never in his dream had imagined that such a thing might happen. He tried to win over the heart of his father-in-law and his wife in many ways curbing his welling anger. But his every word increased their doubts and they refused to relent. Though Karigowda in person had come to plead on Bhujangaiah's behalf, Parvathy had not stirred from the ragi heap. She sat like the fearsome Goddess Bhadrakali. By then Parvathappa had summoned all those who had conspired. Gowda too now learnt of their interference. He said sternly, "All this is not proper, no one has succeeded in life by breaking homes." "Did we come to listen to such words? Gowda, this is a matter to be settled amongst our community. Why do you want to interfere?" Gowda answered, "See Parvathappa, I had taken you to be wise. Do not forget that Bhujangaiah belongs to the village more than he belongs to your community. Your community is not more important than the village." Though Parvathappa too felt the truth of those words he unyieldingly argued that he was only asking for what rightly should belong to his daughter. Gowda before asking Bhujangaiah to let them have their portion asked Parvathy for the last time. Parvathy sat in confusion not knowing how to answer Gowda's words that touched her conscience. In the end she said with much difficulty that she would go by her father's words. Gowda was thoroughly disgusted by now. When he asked Bhujangaiah to immediately give them their share, Bhujangaiah felt he was lost. His eyes that had dreamed of witnessing the realization of an age's dream filled with tears. He walked away from them saying, " I do not want a single grain. You may take everything," Gowda too walked towards the village. The others who were there stood with sad faces not knowing what to do. The servants on hire who had been silent witness to all that transpired, and those who waited for the "excess" of ragi slowly left one after another in disgust. None of them cared for Patel Rudrappa's words. Finally Rudrappa went to the village, sent a few servants to transport the ragi from the winnowing field to Parvathy's home. Bhujangaiah lay down on his face overcome by grief. His burning stomach did not cool even at Sushila's words of comfort. The news spread throughout the village. A few said it served him right. The others opined it was not for the good. However, those who hated Bhujangaiah twirled their moustache with the complacency of the victorious.

The very next day after the incident a cart loaded with ragi arrived at Bhujangaiah's hotel. When enquired it was learnt that Parvathy had sent word saying that it was Bhujangaiah's share from the field of Singari in Bhujangaiah's name and that henceforth she would cultivate herself what belonged to her. Bhujangaiah unloaded the ragi in his room without another word. He carted the ragi to Mysore that very evening to market it. Parvathy's father too kept what she needed for the house and sold the rest. He left saying he would send one of his sons from Jakkalli to oversee everything till Soma came of age, Parvathy did not fail to repeatedly ask her father to account for the transaction of ragi and thus ensured the amount she should get from the sale. Though Parvathappa was glad at his daughter's business acumen, he was a little unhappy wondering if she distrusted him.

However, the incident severed all obligations that Bhujangaiah had towards his ancestral home. He was an outsider in his own home. A person born to a stranger sat as the master of his house. Bhujangaiah who thought that he should ask Gurumalla, his brother-in-law, when he met him next, "Are you born to Parvathappa or my father?" consoled himself saying, "Thu, I should not stoop so low." However, the agony in him did not wane. Parvathy too who learnt of her husband's illness was pained by the knowledge that she was the cause of all that happened. She merely sighed not knowing what to say. Of late Bhujangaiah had stopped paying attention to the affairs of his hotel. He had lost all interest. He began to spend his days in total disinterest, listening to the songs of Ayya, mulling over them.

That year too Shivarathri, the most important festival for his community arrived. He wore new clothes, but without any celebration or pomp. He had brought new clothes for his children from Mysore.

He sent them home through Shiva. But Parvathy had them sent back. This was a matter of extreme insult and rage for Bhujangaiah. He went home burning with anger, carrying the clothes. Gurumalla hid himself in the small room seeing his terrible countenance. Soma and Gauri who came fearfully at the call of their father donned the clothes that Bhujangaiah brought with him after their father stripped the clothes that Gurumalla had presented them with. Parvathy who saw all this without a murmur sat silently, knowing well that he would bash her up if she should open her mouth. Bhujangaiah led his children away. Parvathy sat blindly without moving, afraid that some thing that should not happen may happen on that day of the annual festival.

****

CHAPTER - 29

The verse of Ayya that used to disturb Bhujangaiah most was the one titled, "None has anyone." Bhujangaiah used to grow inward whenever Ayya sang that verse. Ayya had sung that song that morning before going for his round of alms. Bhujangaiah who sat at the counter in the hotel was not in control of his mind. Observing him err in returning change a couple of times, a couple of customers said, "Why, Bhujangaiah's mind does not seem to be in this world." He felt ashamed and got off the counter and went to his room asking Shiva to take care. Sushila had just had her bath, dried her hair in the backyard, and was freeing her hair of knots. Her face glowed with the charm of pregnancy. He stared at her. Sushila said smiling, "Why do you look at me as if you had never seen me?" The sorrow that had enveloped him all this while had suddenly melted. He shut the doors of the room. He lay down on the cot and pulled Sushila to his side and made her sit. He gently ran his hand over her smooth swollen stomach. Sushila's body shivered. She ran her hands on her husband's stubbly chin and said sitting close to him, "What is this? Why don't you shave?" He said, "Who should look at me?" and gently lifted her and laid her next to him anxious for the child in her womb. Though Sushila found her husband's behaviour pleasant she pretended to move away saying. "Thu! What is this at this time of the day?"

Bhujangaiah felt there still was someone who loved him. He was not alone. Though Sushila was the one who had eloped she was a hundred times better than she who was his formal wife. Though that one left him suddenly he had this one to call his own. Why should he be morose when he had Sushila who would give up her life for him? He should live. Why should he be ashamed because dogs yowl after caste? Let them bark. Some day or the other everyone would realize what kind of a woman Sushila was. It did not matter if they failed to. They did not have to visit anyone's home. His belly needed nobody's obligation. Sushila too was proud like him. She managed any eventuality. Sushila who relaxed in peace in his arms was put to thinking by Bhujangaiah's question, "What shall we do for the post-partum care?" Bhujangaiah made up his mind, to bring his sister from Kallahalli. The next day he went to Kallahalli, sure that his sister would not refuse.When his brother-in-law, unable to say no directly began to offer excuses saying there was a lot of work at home, therefore he could not send her at that time, Bhujangaiah took the hint and had left without a word, not even staying for a meal, however much his sister tried to compel him. Finally, when Shiva saw Bhujangaiah's difficulty, he volunteered to bring either his sister or his mother from his village. Bhujangaiah gladly sent Shiva that very day. Shiva returned to Madalli with his sister.

As if to test Bhujangaiah, who had staunchly believed that even if everyone betrayed him God would not and that if he had at any time, or in his previous birth, stayed by his faith, it would lead him by his hand, a very ordinary incident took place in an extraordinary manner. It was the issue of Govindaraju and the new teacher drinking tea at the hotel before the morning bus arrived. When a villager from Kyatanahalli saw them emerging from the hotel, and told people in the hotel that the teacher was a Harijan, they were discomfited. Urupa had already washed the cup in which he had drunk his tea and had kept them with the other cups. Dyavanna of Madalli felt disgusted enough not to drink even a cup of water in the hotel and said pointedly, "Was your tongue dried up not to enquire his caste before hand? Do you intend to spoil our caste and distance us from our Gods?" Bhujangaiah lost his temper. How could he ask his customers their caste? Who knew the caste of everyone who arrived by bus every day? Why did not anyone question that? As soon as his caste was known did his spittle stick to the cup? Was he not tidier than those of his own community? How neat he appeared dressed in a clean white dress like Master

Govindaraju? If Govindaraju had thought of him as low caste why would he have himself brought him in? Did he not sit close to him? Does this fellow have a purity that he as a Brahmin did not have? Bhujangaiah looked at Dyavanna again. Who knew when the clothes that Dyavanna wore had been washed? How many times had he not seen him sitting on his haunches without a shirt, getting his lice picked? Bhujangaiah felt like laughing imagining that picture of Dyavanna. "Let it go Dyavanna. In Mysore don't we sit and eat with the untouchables of our own village?" Dyavanna was enraged, "You have neither caste nor religion. Do you want to reduce us too to that?" Bhujangaiah felt the bile rise in him, "Enough now, shut up. Don't I know you? Living as you do with a body full of lice how come you are sharpening your tongue?" Dyavanna took to his feet saying, "My clothes may be dirty but I am not low like you in caste.' Sushila watching through the gap in the door was pained as Bhujangaiah had to listen to Dyavanna's parting shots because of her. Sushila found on the face of her husband, who came in, disgust, helplessness, anger and several other emotions.

Dyavanna began to spread throughout the Lingayat Street the rumour that a harijan teacher from Kyatanahalli School had come boldly to Bhujangaiah's hotel and had eaten food and drank tea in front of everyone and that the plate and cup that he used was mixed with the other plates and cups.

That very night all the elders met. They summoned two others of their street who were with Dyavanna. One of them said, "Bhujangaiah had not known the caste of the person. He drank only tea, but did not eat snacks as Dyavanna says.' Dyavannna not wishing to be caught in a lie asserted, "He had eaten his snacks before you came."

Rudrappa, Sannappa, and other breakers of homes who had already won a victory by egging Parvathy on and through her seeking revenge on Bhujangaiah had not known they would find another opportunity so soon. They immediately summoned from the Lingayat Achar lane Urupa's mother and relatives and threatened to excommunicate them if Urupa should wash vessels at Bhujangaiah's hotel from the very next day. They promised not to send him. It was also decided that if even a single human being of their community should step into the hotel the same fate should be meted out to them. The assembly unanimously decided never to invite him for any function of the village and to teach him who was bent on destroying the castes and creed of the village a fitting lesson. His having allowed a low caste into the hotel had not gone well with even his close friends and they too did not open their mouth.

The very next day as part of bringing the decision of the previous night's assembly in to force they sent Urupa to the temple for purification. He felt nauseated at their behaviour. Yet he had to bow his head to the compulsions of his relatives. By ten in the morning people went towards the hotel as if they were on war. Karigowda who learnt of their going, also went there. Bhujangaiah,when he saw the crowd in front of his hotel though scared for a moment, delved in his work not showing his fright. Sushila shut the room in fear and sat with abated breath. Sannappa raised his voice and called Bhujangaiah out. Bhujangaiah came out without caring and asked, "what?" When Rudrappa asked, "Did you invite the Harijans inside and serve the upper caste too in the same plate in which they had eaten?" Bhujangaiah asked ironically, "Oh! Who is that high caste man?" Dyavanna who was in the crowd jumped and shook his neck like a lizard uttering, "I am he." Though Bhujangaiah felt like spitting on his dirty face asked, "What is to be done now?" Rudrappa said hotly, "What is to be done now is you must close the hotel with your ass shut." Bhujangaiah too was enraged, "Oh! You seem to speak thinking that the hotel belongs to your father? I too know you. Shut up and leave.' He re-entered the hotel. Rudrappa in a terrible anger shouted, "Hey, what are you looking at, standing? Kick him and throw everything out and teach him a lesson." No one dared to enter the hotel. Only Rudrappa's nephew entered the hotel wanting to pull down the photos on the wall. But scared to touch the pictures of his Gods he removed Gandhi's picture and smashed it on the floor. All those at the hotel came to the door. Karigowda who had followed the crowd pushed his way to the front and stood across the door, "Who is it that is shouting so much? Are you not ashamed to say you will gobble him because he is a bit gentle? Do you think Madalli is made of only your street?" Rudrappa said, "Gowda this is a matter of our caste, you do not interfere in this." Gowda did not pay attention to him, "Instead of dealing with the dos and don'ts of your caste in your street is it proper to want to close the hotel?" He looked sternly at Rudrappa.

Though Rudrappa did not have the courage to talk lightly in front of Gowda who thus supported Bhujangaiah, he found courage somehow that day to abuse him in unspeakable terms. Those who had accompanied Rudrappa also were disgusted by his words. Though Gowda's blood boiled, he did not stir from his place and said, "Rudrappa, do not bark all that your mouth finds because Gowda is old. Hold your tongue." Rudarappa said in arrogance, "I too have seen things, let me see what you can pluck from me joining hands with that casteless son of a whore." As Rudrappa neared him, Gowda unable to control his rage slapped him. Before Rudrappa who pushed around Gowda could raise his hands Bhujangaiah caught Rudrappa by the collar. The force of the push by a well built Rudrappa resulted in Gowda's bald head catching the corner of a plank leaned against the door's edge and began to bleed. Those who came with Rudrappa were scared seeing the blood. Some went away at once. The others who remained tried to pacify the quarrelling groups. As Rudrappa was being pulled away Bhujangaiah pressed his hand to Gowda's wound and gently took him to his room. Sushila felt like crying aloud. She felt paralyzed not knowing what to do. As instructed by her husband she brought the talcum powder, applied it to the wound and tied a piece of white cloth. Sushila's eyes too started filling with tears when she saw in a short while the blood oozing through the cloth. Shiva brought the broken picture of Gandhi into the room. Though the glass had broken into pieces Gandhi's smile had not faded.

The news that Rudrappa had hit Karigowda and his head broken was tantamount to throwing scolding water on the Gowda Street. The three sons of Gowda came running to the hotel, not even noticing whether they tripped. Behind them followed the crowd from Gowda Street. Sannappa who had already guessed at the reaction had taken Rudrappa with him and slowly progressed hiding behind the hedge towards the village through a different route. Urupa who noticed it gave the hint as soon as he saw Gowda's children. He too had been terribly enraged at Rudrappa since the previous day. As soon as he learnt they were being followed, though Sannappa fearing for his life urged Rudrappa and began to run they were caught before they could reach the village. Narayana first struck Sannappa with the cart stake he held. Sannappa fell like a dog with a broken hip and began to crawl dragging his waist howling, "I am lost." Though Rudrappa attempted to defend, the blows with the cart stakes softened him. By then, people from the nearby Untouchables Street arrived to save their lives. Otherwise who knew what would have happened?

If the people who went from the Gowda's Street helped walk Gowda gently from the hotel, those who had accompanied Rudrappa from his street, having listened to him, carried Sannappa and Rudrappa who had lain near the compost pit of the Untouchables Street, not even possessing the strength to stand up. The others in the village found it ludicrous that two major communities had come to blows on an insignificant issue. That evening with the signs of a major fight between the two streets growing stronger a sort of fearful atmosphere began to overshadow the entire village. As the evening arrived, people from Hundi too had come making it certain that something or the other would certainly happen. Though whispers and collections of weapons in both the streets went on, the unity that was there in the Gowda Streets could not be found in Rudrappa's. Very many among them advanced the principle of neutrality, "Why should we go and fight because Rudrappa paid for his arrogance?" As all of them had affection for Bhujangaiah and were unhappy with Rudrappa's arrogance, none of them set foot outside their houses. They did not get fooled by others' inciting talk about caste.

Each side, Rudrappa's and Gowda's, waited for the other to attack first. None was ready to take the initiative. Karigowda who had dropped into sleep knowing nothing of this got up and went out as soon as he learnt what was happening. Seeing Gowda arrive the arbiters from other castes too came and met. They all advised both groups to return home. They also promised to assemble the village that very night itself and decide the issue. Rudrappa, eager to take revenge was more hurt when he saw the people of his street falling silent thus. He abused them roundly, “Unmanly sons of whores”. His shout filled the street, “If I do not get them skinned tomorrow by lodging a complaint with the Kote police, I am not born to my father’s seed.’ But that night with the entire village assembled at the court Rudrappa refused to come, no matter who said what. It upset the leaders of all communities. None approved the path that Rudrappa as the Patel of the village trod. If he himself ignored the justice of the village who else would comply?

***

CHAPTER - 30

What Bhujangaiah never wished would happen because of him in the village had come to transpire. Even though he had left the village, the village had not left him alone. Why does it trouble him with conspiracy and baseless accusations, not allowing him to live by himself? What wrong had he done by that village? Let alone wronging others he had never even thought ill of them. Then why did they harbour such enmity towards him? Even as he was about to reach the shore breasting the floods of constant troubles engineered by them, there appeared another misery. The village has once more invoked the evil forces which he thought had given up. The people who had stomped the earth for a fight were hot with arrogance. An adamant Rudrappa had lodged a complaint with the police in Kote. The children of Gowda too had lodged a counter complaint. The distant police from Kote were getting closer. The act of rising hands against Gowda who was like a father to the village had destroyed the peace of the village. The people of the village were scared. They shuddered in fear. The anxiety led unsure times ruled the village. The danger of a blast was imminent.

Sannaputtappa warned Bhujangaiah against keeping the pregnant Sushila at the hotel as the times were bad and the wheel of misfortune was turning. Girija the midwife from Kyatanahalli too had said it was better to take her to Mysore, as it was a first pregnancy. Finally, a way was now found to dispel the fears and the secret anxieties of Bhujangaiah. He left for Mysore with Sushila that very day. He took Shiva's sister too so that Sushila could be looked after at the hospital. Urupa who had broken the restrictions imposed on him by the village had presented himself at the hotel.

Apart from the passengers not many visited the hotel these days. The people of Kyatanahalli stared angrily at the new harijan teacher for having entered the Madalli hotel. Ayya who had visited the village the next day was scared seeing the heaving air of the village and returned at once. "It was all Shiva's will. They had to act as the fate in his hand dictated. What was to happen had to happen. You ascend once and then fall next. God had bent his eyes towards them the last two years. The crop had been excellent. So began to unfold the unbridled behavior of mortal man. How long will that too last? However much one waxed one had to finally break and fall. The evil wind had now begun to rise. The suppurating summer beat down from the very dawn as if to drain the earth. Oh God, there is some danger awaiting! Why should these people not remain content eating what you have provided? What's wrong with them? They are willfully rushing towards their destruction. They are impatient to bear an unimagined calamity. The times are bad. This time round the shadow of a terrible fear is enveloping Madalli. The hearts that should have united are asunder. I do not know what's wrong with these people who are welcoming calamities of which they know nothing and which they can hardly face. Is it that misfortune is knocking at the door as foretold in *The Wisdom of Ages?"* Tampura Ayya had felt as if he had stood on sandals of spike every moment of his stay in Madalli, hearing of every single event that had taken place. He sang verses that would bring wisdom to both the streets. But can the songs of a poor devotee join the hearts that had already fragmented? Gowda, the elder of the village, who should have led the village by the hand had himself lost patience. Tampura Ayya felt that Madalli couldn't be saved anymore when he saw the flame of revenge burning in him. Again at Rudrappa's end one heard speech beyond reason. Ayya who had boarded the bus felt he should not have left the village. He could have done something by staying back. He could do what was in his hand to stop people from destroying themselves. Even now it was not late. He should get off at Madapura and take the Swami of the mutt with him tomorrow. He got off and went straight to the mutt hoping that people may heed the words of the Swami and realize that the path they trod was wrong.

By the time Ayya reached Madalli by the morning bus with the Swami of the mutt what should not have happened had happened. People had fought in the village like demons. Once again Bhujangaiah's hotel had been gutted. With Ayya and the Swami all the others in the bus too got down to see the hotel. The entire hotel had been burnt down leaving merely the ruined walls. The cloud of smoke still hung. It was as though Ayya's body had been torched. The heat of the fire singed those who dared approach even a step closer. The petromax and a few vessels that even the God of fire could not melt lay orphaned. The people of Madalli stood at a distance scared to approach the hotel. Mercifully, no life had been lost. Shiva and Urupa alone had slept at the hotel. The hotel had been torched only after waking up Shiva and Urupa by knocking on the door. By the time they came out of the hotel opening the door the flame had raged forth and the two had scampered towards the village shouting with fear. The scene appeared terrible even to the Swami. He was disheartened having left with nothing to set right at the village. No one had really noticed his arrival. Everybody was in a hurry to either leave for Mysore or for Kote. Even the sky stood in anger against Madalli, spewing balls of fire. Sannaputtapa took the Swami home. No one appeared to have the patience to listen to the talk of peace by the Swami in a village filled with wolves. Hatred and envious nature had finished demonstrating their strength. Very many were injured in the night's skirmish. Envy was the fire of hell that would crush and swallow, let alone people, the entire village. It had admirably fulfilled its role in Madalli, which remained innocent, oxidized with centuries of ignorance. A very inane matter had split the village into two. What was right? What was wrong?

There was no peace in the homes of Madalli. There was no peace on the street. People were afraid of stepping freely. The earth itself seemed to sigh. It was as if the wind had forgotten to blow. Perhaps, someone had stopped the village's wheel of life from rolling. In the minds of those who only yesterday lived like brothers had now risen vague doubts and unfounded fears after living through that one night. In the dark night that had swallowed the village. it was a mystery who took part in the fight and who had not. Parvathy in spite of her ire against her husband now gave into the feeling that her being taken in by the words of a vile man like Rudrappa was a great sin. Soma and Gowri too joined the crowd which visited the burnt hotel. Soma's eyes filled with tears. Though of late his mother had strictly forbade him from visiting the hotel his heart was drawn towards the place. He carefully inspected every part of the burnt hotel. He gazed with curiosity at what had happened to the gramophone stored under the cot of his father. Along with the cot it had been burnt with only its horn sticking out of the ashes. It appeared as if the hotel wept through it. Soma wanted to remove it from there. But the adults did not let him enter. As the walls were made of split bambo and mud the danger of it collapsing any moment was imminent.

Because of Ayya's relentless efforts people of all the communities of Madalli assembled at the court in the presence of the Swami. By then a big force of police had descended on Madalli from Kote. Bhujangaiah had sat in a corner of the hospital holding his head when he heard the news, not knowing what to do. Sushila had not delivered as yet. She was in labour too. His heart would not allow him to leave her alone. Muddegowda who had brought news had himself got a signature from him on a complaint and lodged it with the police in Kote. The police who had decided that the act of torching the hotel where people lived was an attempt to murder, refused to yield to any temptation and had handcuffed Sannappa and Rudrappa who were at the village court. Everybody on Rudrappa's side got up by saying that nothing else remained to be patched up from the arbitration. Nobody paid attention to the advice of Swami. Ayya returned home with the Swami in grief that none of his efforts bore fruit. The assembly dispersed.

Bhujangaiah on the other hand was greatly worried about Sushila, who was his only fortune. When the delivery got delayed unduly, the doctor said that the only way out was to do a cezarian. Bhujangaiah had felt as if his life was ebbing out. Raja had assured him that the operation would bring no harm, as if he knew all about it. They cooked in Raja's room. Shiva's sister, Saki, was all the time in the hospital taking care of Sushila. Raja and Bhujangaiah could visit only at appointed hours as it was a maternity hospital. If they tipped the attendants at the hospital they would allow them at all hours. When Bhujangaiah had thus gained entry once, a matron had appeared like a whale and had chased him out, shouting at him. He had never ventured to enter at odd hours from then on. The operation was scheduled for that morning. Bhujangaiah and Raja had breakfast at a hotel, packed some for Saki and arrived at the hospital well before time. Sushila had not yet been moved to the operation theatre. She was scared, Bhujangaiah stood near her head and comforted by reassuring her. Raja too felt sorry at her condition. Shortly Sushila was transferred to a wheel chair and taken away. Saki waited at the ward. Raja and Bhujangaiah went out. Raja did not go to school that day. Bhujangaiah who sat under a tree outside the hospital was chain smoking beedies and taking vows after vows to all his gods and spent each moment in increasing anxiety. Raja would get up every now and then and peep in through the big doors of the hospital. They had asked Saki to come to the main door as soon as the child was delivered.

When Raja went to see if Saki had come out, she was standing there with a downcast face. Raja was scared looking at her face. When enquired, Saki repeated verbatim what a nurse had told, that the child was dead, but the mother was alive. Though Bhujangaiah was sad that the child died, he sighed a breath of relief that Sushila was alive. They allowed them to visit Sushila after a long time. She seemed to be sleeping. They were all sent out with instruction to visit in the evening. Bhujangaiah rushed in as soon as the doors opened in the evening having spent the time god knows how. Sushila had now opened her eyes. But she could not talk as yet. They were told that she had to remain at least ten days at the hospital. That night Raja's father arrived from Madalli. he described all that had happened in the village. Some how, Bhujangaiah was not pleased by the news of the poiice handcuffing Rudrappa and Sannappa in front of the entire village after they conducted the *mahajar*, the crime scene investigation, the crime scene investigation, of the hotel. He began to mull over the torching of the hotel, which was all the property he possessed, the reason of his affluence. Though there was nothing of value there, as Bhujangaiah had willed over all his property to his first wife and children, there was now not even a roof for him to stand under if he returned to the village. He had to start anew his life. He had for the time being handed over all his money to Muddegowda. Otherwise even that would have been reduced to ashes and he would have been thrown out on the street. They talked about what was to be done next. When Bhujangaiah talked of rebuilding the burnt hotel and running it as a challenge to those who had burnt it down, Muddegowda did not approve of it. When he said not to think any more of the hotel but to live on the fields of Singari or to open a shop in the village if he so desired, Bhujangaiah saw sense in that advice. Though he had wondered how he could live with Sushila alone outside the village he had never dreamt that the villagers would stoop to such a base act. What if they had torched the hotel when he and Sushila had slept? Bhujangaiah's body broke into sweat at the thought.

Bhujangaiah did not even look toward Madalli till Sushila recovered completely. In the meanwhile those who were close to him in the village, Victor and Subbanna had visited many times. Though Sushila had grown strong enough to smile at her visitors she had not entirely recovered. Her stick like hands and anemic face made those who saw her pity her. When she was discharged from the hospital Bhujangaiah took her to Raja's room. Tayavva looked after her with great care. When he said he would go to Madalli that evening to arrange things and return the next day, Sushila urged him to stay that day and to leave on the next morning. Her manner had changed. She would suddenly tremble in fear. She slept holding her husband's hand tight. Bhujangaiah spent an entire morning and night by Sushila's side as she wished. He fed her fruits, made her drink coffee. He comforted her throughout the night with his arms for her pillow. Sushila found her husband's nursing pleasant. Bhujangaiah promised Sushila he would return that very evening and went to the village as soon as he got up in the morning.

Raja was shy speaking to Sushila, meeting her eyes. He had returned only in the evening, having left in the morning after meals. Saki had personally cooked the rice and had gone with the little boy from the owner's house to buy curry from the hotel. She had found it easy to cook with the coal stove. Bhujangaiah too returned from Madalli before nightfall. Urupa had accompanied him. Shiva had left for his village a week before. Bhujangaiah had sent words through Beard of Kyatanahalli that he would send his sister later. Beard was the only one who had really sorrowed at the injustice meted out to Bhujangaiah. He had cursed the people of Madalli as worthless, comparing them to the stubbles in the field, to their face in the bus. He had already caught the scent of conspiracy that was being hatched by the Lingayat elders of Kyatanahalli to bring peace between Bhujangaiah and those who had torched his hotel in Madalli. Though Sannappa and Rudrappa were released on bail, Shivalinga who had torched the hotel had not been released. Shivalinga, who had been tortured, was wild enough to drink Rudrappa's blood as soon as he was let out. Urupa went to a movie with Raja that night. The next day, they shopped till late evening buying all the necessary things for a new home. Sushila who could not move about had given a list of things to be procured. Tayavva had promised to help purchase. She brought two new saris for Sushila. Sushila once again boarded the bus to Madalli. Victor halted the bus at the forest gate instead of at the hotel. After the hotel was torched he had not felt like stopping there even for a second. Subbanna who helped remove all the luggage of Bhujangaiah enquired after Sushila's health with affection. He could not carry the luggage, as there were too many. Bhujangaiah asked Urupa to take care of them and walked towards the village with Sushila. He had already decided to start his family in the outhouse of Gowda's new building and it had been freshly white washed and mortared. With the first son of Gowda Shankara occupying the new house the two other sons were living in the old house. Shankara and his wife Mallavva were a decent couple. The first night Sushila and Bhujangaiah ate at their house. The next morning Sushila, though she could hardly do so, began to organize things. All those who had been helped by Bhujangaiah visited him. Bhujangaiah who was living on the outskirts of the village having now come into the village to set up family had made all his community people disgruntled. The new house of Gowda was adjacent to the Lingayat Street. Parvathy grew much more desperate by this event. She complained of having to see her successor's face at every step. Soma and Gowri had run to their father on the very first day to embrace and cry unknown to their mother. Bhujangaiah had petted his children for a long time. He sent words to Saki's village saying that he wished to have her help till Sushila grew better. Saki herself took care of sweeping, washing vessels, lighting the hearth and drawing water from the well, etc... Bhujangaiah found it highly irritable to sit without doing anything the entire day. He began to subscribe to the paper he had stopped reading all these days. Ajappa and Pundri encouraged him to open the hotel again. But Gowda did not approve of it. He had built a shop attached to the porch of the new house. Having decided that Bhujangaiah should run a shop there, the very next day Bhujangaiah began to get the woodwork for the shop made. The summer that year was harsh. In the burning heat of summer it was an effort even to perform the slightest of tasks. When a shirtless Manchachari was planing the planks and joining them perspiration flowed on his dark skin like rain. A crowd of children had already gathered in front of the shop. Close to where Bhujangaiah planned his shop a Moslem, commonly addressed as "Kaka", from Manadavadi already had his shop. He had a settled business already. Though he was disappointed at another shop coming up near his he had put up a brave face, "His business is his and my business is mine. We both will have our customers."

Among the people of Madalli who had assumed that Bhujangaiah's game was up, his opening the shop as a dare, brought joy and pride to some while others were envious. Sannappa and Rudarappa who had to run around to the court twice in a month gnashed their teeth. Sannappa's money from his loan sharking was dwindling. The palm of the lawyer was expanding day by day. Sannappa who bemoaned that he had drowned in a well by listening to Rudrappa began to explore a means of striking peace through Sannaputtappa.

***

CHAPTER - 31

The people of Madalli who depended on the clouds for a living had reaped good harvests for the past two years. They had performed marriages, festivals, etc. with a fair amount of extravagance. If they had then found those days to pass by quickly they now found the days lengthening. The summer had pitched its tent with no intent to leave; the clouds that should have frightened it off were refusing to plant their feet on earth. The wind that blew carrying only the dust from the ploughed fields seemed to have forgotten to bring the rain clouds that quenched the thirst of earth. The people of Madalli had begun to remember the forgotten days of suffering. The heat of summer that spewed fire seemed to have sworn to make them lose the lard of arrogance. The pond, which was the life spring of Madalli, had dried and the bed had cracked to appear like the lined face of an ancient. The people of the village had dug a well in the tank behind the pond for the cattle to drink water. They drew water from it to fill a stone container on the bank. The cattle would then rush to drink. Their bellies too have stuck to their backs. The haystacks in the backyards had also dwindled. Some had used up their hay pile and ran after Sabi of the whip. He was happy. He fixed the price whimsically. He bunched the cattle he bought and transported them to Kerala through Manandavadi. Every one knew that the cattle sold to him ended up in the slaughterhouse. But there was no other go. Was such to be the fate of their ox, Basavanna who couldn't protest, who they had fostered like their own child? Because Basavanna the protector of the village had grown into stone each day they performed a different ritual of ablution. Whatever they did, Basavanna refused to get up and open his eyes. Because of the feed available on the other side of Kote people who had relatives there drove their cattle to them. Parvathy too sold a pair and sent another to Jakkalli. What hay remained in the backyard was enough for the milch cows. She wondered whether to sell or to drive them to her parents, if the feed should get over. Bhujangaiah had no such worries. He read the daily every morning on waking up. But the list of borrowers had grown long of late. There was trouble at the end of the week bringing stocks. If he went in search of his borrowers they vanished from sight. When accosted they shrunk their yard-high body to an inch and grinned helplessly. Only Kaka refused to lend grocery even if one were dying. He did not care if he had no business the whole day. He never wavered from his principle of to survive meant not lending. Only Bhujangaiah, obdurate like the legendary King Trivikrama, invested all his money in the shop. In the end he bought stocks by hocking Sushila's guinea necklace at the Marwadi shop. Whatever he did the drought of Madalli did not end. He had opened the hotel when he had caught a whiff of such bad times. But that had turned out different. Leave alone having as good a fortune as he had in the hotel business, it had now grown difficult to survive. People who couldn't pay back spoke as if he who lent was the villain, if he were stern they escaped offering lame excuses. Only Tampura Ayya visited regularly for alms even if the village were burning. Whether his bag filled or not he went through the village singing. He camped now in the outhouse of Bhujangaiah. He had not yet found the food served by Sushila's hand a taboo. Sushila looked better now. She went to fetch water with Mallavva, Shankara's wife. Even the village women had stopped passing remarks and had begun to converse with her. The hearth was lit twice a day only in those houses, which did not spend extravagantly or sell all the grain at Mysore because it was a good harvest last year. The Harijan Street had half emptied. Even the people in the village had migrated either to Kodagu or to Gaddebayalu. Bhujangaiah sighed helplessly watching life in Madalli turning worse. "Paras" were performed till they could not afford any more. They took out in procession the "Vana", the chariot, of the God who rode the tiger. Though there was hardly any water to drink they had drawn water from the well in the pond, filled the pit of *Okali* in front of the shrine of Basavanna of the pond and played *Okali*, the festival of rainbow, and yet Devendra the God did not open his eyes. The chariot of Indra who was the God of rains for the villagers seemed to have forgotten the existence of their region. Who had ever imagined such bad times would come? Those who were sharpening their knives against Bhujangaiah too had grown soft. Sannappa had begged Muddegowda of Hundi Sannaputtappa and finally succeeded in having Bhujangaiah agree to peace. After consulting Karigowda, Bhujangaiah signed the settlement paper in the court one fine day. From that day those who had torched the hotel found relief from running to the court. Even the newspaper that Bhujangaiah read reported that there was drought in many places. When Bhujangaiah who read about the steps that the government took to provide relief in those places, voluntarity asked people to accompany him to meet the authorities in Kote they went without a word. They spoke of the difficulties that their village faced to the Amaldar in Kote. The Amaldar promised to personally visit the following week to inspect and provide suitable relief. He also stressed on how they could improve their lot only when they sank wells in their fields and installed pumpsets instead of merely depending on rain for cultivation. No one agreed to Bhujangaiah's suggestion of approaching the banks for loan through hypothecation. Bhujangaiah kept thinking about it though they nipped his enthusiasm by saying taking loan from the government was tantamount to climbing the stake. The village had been united by an unwelcome drought. Even after returning to the village he mulled over digging a well. He read in *Tayinadu* one day, an article on digging wells. Bhujangaiah was completely preoccupied by it after he read about it. He talked about it to everyone whom he met. Let alone others, even Gowda who paid much attention to his words laughed at him, "You are mad." But the desire of digging a well and lifting water for cultivation held fast in his mind as a monitor lizard would in spite of what anyone thought. The business in the shop went down day by day and finally not having enough capital to replenish the stocks he had to borrow twice from Muddegowda. Finally because of the government undertaking a few relief works in the village the poor found a way to earn two meals a day. The various municipal works like getting the roads of the villages repaired, which were full of potholes from long ago, laying an unmetalled road to Hundi and the bus road to Madalli, lifting the silt from the village pond, clearing the undergrowth from the banks of the pond and increasing its height, etc.., were undertaken. In Madalli where half the population had already migrated, Narasimhaiah from Kote had given jobs to many of the men, women and children from the village who had stayed on. He now sent for more people from the neighboring villages in order to complete the works fast.

For Narasimhaiah the contractor those works were like Kamadhenu, the divine cow which yielded perennially, especially such drought relief works as these. Since the Taluk Board had come into existence he had taken care of its officials and had earned well. Narasimhaiah who said he could manage even a hundred works had grown close to Bhujangaiah on the very day he camped in Madalli. The taste of tea prepared by Sushila apart from Bhujangaiah's language and behaviour had turned the large porch of Shankara's house the temporary office of Narasimhaiah. Narasimhaiah was happy to hear Bhujangaiah's story. Begur, abutting the forest of Kakanakote, was Narasimhaiah's village. His family lived there. He had a mistress in Kote for whom he had built a house. It was common for people to refer to her as Narasimhaiah's second wife. Narasimhaiah was proud of Bhujangaiah's macho character in having "lifted a bird" from Mysore and set up the family in the very village where he was born and grew up. Sushila was unlike his woman, Siddalingi. Siddalingi resembled a baby elephant. He had his job cut out for him in making her cry "enough". But this woman? She was like a doll. She was as delicate as a mustard plant, lean and fair. Narashimaiah's romantic nature would spread its wing whenever he saw Sushila, But whenever he opened his mouth his real colours were betrayed. His harsh voice nauseated those who heard him. His incessant below the belt speech brought disgust to the listeners. Shankara had once warned him not to speak thus on his porch. His ambrosial words had fallen on Sushila's ears too disgusting her. She had called out insisting Bhujangaiah serve him tea.

However, the friendship between Bhujangaiah and Narasimhaiah grew fast. Narashimhaiah began to sit for his meal at Bhujangaiah's house. He found whatever Sushila cooked delicious. He distributed salary every week on the porch of Shankara's house. Week after week there would be a crowd in front of his house. Narasimhaiah used to get loan for the workers standing surety and would distribute their salary after deducting the loan. Bhujangaiah was happy that his shop's business would gain respectability and he too could save money from the shop. Now that people gathered all the time in front of his shop he was never bored. He used to sit swatting flies before now. Bhujangaiah's natural desire to be amidst people all the time received a conducive atmosphere now. Sushila never opened the door of the house because of the noise. Whenever she was bored she spent time with Mallavva or her children in Shankara's house. Those who were irked by the sudden flood of business at Bhujangaiah's were the Kaka from Manandavadi and his permanent customer Narayana. Though Narayana had thought of asking his brother and father to send Bhujangaiah out of the house and the shop, though he had enough encouragement in that direction from Kaka, Narayana was somehow scared to open his mouth. Bhujangaiah had been a veritable God to his family since the day he had saved his father. He was in no position to harm such a person now. But the wound in his mind caused by the insult that Sushila had meted out to him had festered. The thought that he would one day or the other try a hand at her was taking deep roots in him. Of late Sushila had visited the home to meet his mother when she had lost weight, grown pale and very weak. She did not exhibit anger at his very sight as before, nor did she turn her face away in disgust. Narayana remembered that he had run away scared to see her face. Sushila had once more grown full in her body. He couldn't control the desire to watch her from the cover of milkhedge as she went down the Well Lane carrying a pot of water on her head and a pot of water under her arm as other women of his village did. She disturbed him to the core as she swayed under the weight of the pot. He felt that the charm she had possessed while carrying the basket of bangles had once more returned. Even so his desire was growing. Narayana was squirming in confusion over the propriety of his desire. The rumors that someone had brought had shocked him greatly. They had linked Narasimaiah with Sushila. The gossip had disturbed his innermost being. Was it true? Or was it false? Would she who whouldn't raise her eyes and look at some one like him ever be attracted by Narasimaiah's ghastly face? The beaded saliva on both sides of his lips, the hair standing like that of a porcupine and the black, hairy legs of an elephant revealed while he walked with his dhoti lifted. Narayana himself was nauseated by Narasimaiah's appearance. He was disturbed when he heard from others too that Sushila flirted with such a man. Does Shankara know she whores in their new house? If not he must see that Shankara learns of it through somebody. Father believed Shankara. Narayana's brain was muddled with thoughts. Nothing was clear. He swore and turned towards the house of the Village Clerk, wanting to see his daughter Vanajakshi, for whom he had regained his love which had of late burned with intensity. After fruitlessly going past her house a few times, he learnt through her brother that she was at her uncle's place in Kote. Terribly disappointed not caring what people may say, he had in broad daylight gone stright through the ever open doors of Puttabasavi's house shamelessly and put his mouth to the rotting meat.

Assume that somebody farted in a corner in some house in Madalli, its stink would prevade the entire village. With the failure of rains and absence of fresh breeze, Madalli's air already polluted by the rising dust from the picks and crowbars of those who repaired the road, had been further polluted by the stink of this fart, making many in the village suffer from dry cough. The stink that had spread to the village did not fail to reach Bhujangaiah's nose. Even a single skein was not visible to the eyes of him who for a moment pinched his nostrils at this stink, in spite of having examined strand by strand everything that had transpired from the day Narasimhaiah set foot in the village to the present. It was the mischief of one of those whore's sons who broke homes. His Sushila's behaviour was like gold. The people who wished to tarnish it would themselves be destroyed. The reason why the village suffered was because of so much inequity. It is because he saw such uncleanliness that God

Devendra had sat without turning towards them. He had never seen a time when there was dearth for even drinking water in the village. Let these vile people be destroyed. Let the tongues that spoke untruth be paralyzed. Let their mouths be maggot ridden. Bhujangaiah once more grew sorrowful, murmuring unawares all the curses that would flow freely in the mouth of the women of Madalli, growing uneasy unknowingly at the shadow of Narasimhaiah, subtly suggesting to Sushila not to come out in the presence of Narasimhaiah for any reason.

If Bhujangalah was thinking up ways of distancing himself from Narasimhaiah, even as his mind was beset with false accusations and suspicions, Sushila was involved in her own business, unmindful of anything in her ambition of rebuilding her burnt house. One day as she went to bring water, a few women who were discussing her had suddenly changed their talk at her approach. Yet she had not failed to hear her name uttered with that of Narasimhaiah. From that day it had become a thorn in her mind.

The business at the shop had improved well enough. The borrowers began to visit without avoiding. They had all developed a new strategy of assuring Bhujangaiah that they would return his money tomorrow or the next week, next month or some time. he had returned the money borrowed from Muddegowda for the shop. Even as he was wondering, with the business continuing to pay as well, if he could one day redeem Sushila's guinea necklace which had been hocked, all of a sudden the clouds had one day gathered above Madalli like a heard of elephants and emptied in force. Come night the village resounded with the croak of frogs. The sleeping village sat up. The ploughs in neglect were repaired overnight. For the people who had thought they had forgotten the art of cultivation everything had turned around. There was not a single human being in the village, come dawn. Narasimhaiah and his mason realized that they would not be able to see through the works undertaken if they should depend on the people of the village and decided to bring the vaddas from Andhra who had settled in Kote to build the dam of Bidiralli. He returned to Kote that very morning requesting Bhujangaiah to take care of their equipments.

If the fields of the village were all filled with the noise of the sowers, the fields of Singari owned by Bhujangaiah lay as though it had been cursed, not even being ploughed to remove the stubbles. Bhujangaiah desired to till at least with the help of hired hands. But where could he hire ploughs at such a time? At his house Amase alone was retained with Parvathy having dimissed Marikala. Parvathy's brother had brought another pair of dwarfs from Jakkalli to plough. Bhujangaiah was terribly sorrowful. He wished to begin farming by buying a pair of oxen on loan. But he may have to sell his shop for that. What could he do? Finally as suggested by Gowda it was decided that he should give the fields to Chikka the washerman on weekly lease. He merely ploughed for growing vegetables and sowed horsegram. If it had been prepared earlier by fallow ploughing, ragi could have been sowed. Bhujangaiah did not feel like stepping towards his fields. Even though it had rained heavy the water in the pond of Madalli stood only knee deep in a corner. Two more good showers were seen within the week. By then Narashimaiah's contract too ended. The people of Madalli were astonished at the expertise of the Telugu-speaking people with the pick. The pay Narasimhaiah gave them was also good. Their work matched the doubled pay that they demanded. On one fine day Narasimhaiah left Madalli with all his equipments, having completed his task. Of late, he too had learnt of Bhujangaiah ignoring him and had distanced himself voluntarily. But on the day he left he had taken leave of him intimately, which had melted Bhujangaiah's heart and put him to shame. He had affectionately invited both Sushila and Bhujangaiah to visit him if they should bring themselves to Kote. He finalized the bill, which his workers owed Bhujangaiah without deducting a single paise. He got Shankara's children sweet and peppermint enough to fill their pockets. Though he left speaking cordially to everyone his heart did not desist from stealing a look at Sushila. With the exit of Narasimhaiah and the rains even though a fresh breeze had blown, in the darkness filled homes of Madalli which had no windows or which never opened the windows, among the many rumours that rotted in the folds and corners, Sushila's was the most pungent. The people did not desist from saying that

Narasimhaiah had lost his wealth for Bhujangaiah's shop to flourish. Of late Sushila sat in the shop in her husband's absence. A few youth visited the shop only to talk to her. When she spoke to them smiling affectionately they would grow confused. Sushila would secretly laugh at their plight. Bhujangaiah was worried that he had not ploughed his land and cultivated it properly. It burrowed in him like the borer insect. Though none had seen a single grain of crops during the Monsoon they grew a little horsegram and ragi during the North-Easterly. Who knew how long that may last? If the Monsoon crop had succeeded they would've kept jowar for food and sold mustard for other recurring expenses. No one had got a grain of mustard even for ritualistic necessities. They had somehow seen through the days. What could be done now? Till the next Monsoon, till the rains come putting an end to the drought how would they live? The village people were worried. A few had as soon as the North-Easterly had brought rains, planted split gram and coriander that would grow in the winter's dew. Parvathy too had planted split gram in her half-acre. The people of the village were worried thinking of the days of hot weather ahead.

Days went by without a change. Festivals arrived and went. Those who had money observed them perfunctorily. Those who had nothing washed their hands in mere tears. Though Soma and Gowri visited Bhujangaiah's house and shop they did so without Parvathy's knowledge. Whenever they came they were not allowed to leave without eating stomach full. The glutton, Soma could not rest without eating at least once in Sushila's house in secrecy. When someone informed Parvathy she had thrashed her children abusing, "Thu! You refuse eating dogs, you have no caste or religion. What happened to you to eat at that whore's house? Shiva, what will happen to me if that widow should poison you?" The desire of the children to eat never abated under any of her punishment. One day, in the end, Parvathy became as ferocious as Mari, the Goddess of destruction. Amase felt his entrails spilling out watching her branding them with a heated iron. After that incident the children did not go towards Bhujangaiah's for a week. One day when Amase met Bhujangaiah on the road, he told him of what had happened. Bhujangaiah went straight home as if he were taken hold of by a devil. Parvathy was sitting in the verandah like a burning Mari. She turned her face away as if she had not noticed her husband's arrival. In front of her was a vessel filled with the mixture of dung. She had sat down to stamp the baskets and the winnowing fans. The children who wished to rush and embrace their father as soon as they saw him stood in the verandah blinking their eyes, controlling their desire. Bhujangaiah asked sternly, stirring the stifling atmosphere, "Why did you brand the children?" The children who held back till then now stood up crying aloud. Parvathy did not stir from the place where she sat. Bhujangaiah approached his children. He embraced the children who had begun to cry as if the sorrow controlled all these days had now burst out, and saw the burns. Someone seemed to pierce his entrails. He said, "Thu ! Why did your hand not get bitten by a snake? Are you a human being or Mari of the graveyard? How could you brand children thus?" Parvathy retorted like an enraged tigress, "I'll do whatever I please with my children; I may brand them or strangle them to death." Bhujangaiah left his children and stood up, "What did you say whore? Did I give birth to them or did you call some body else to give birth to them?" He faced Parvathy. Though she was scared she uttered, "Are you a very honourable man? For an idiot who lies tied to a prostitute what care of children and home?" Bhujangaiah kicked her in great anger. She fell on the dung filled vessel. Her body was smeared with dung. Though her eyes misted by his kick and felt that she had died, in a trice she recovered and began to shower curses on him. By then people had gathered and dragged Bhujangaiah away consoling him. The children sat in a corner sobbing like orphans having got tired of crying. Parvathy who saw them felt as if she had touched fire and kicked them around on the ground till she satisfied her rage shouting, "Thu, why did you have to be born in my womb, you worse than dogs."

Bhujangaiah who was disgusted by this scene walked towards the pond. The trees and bushes in the woods, which used to be thick enough to hide a tiger behind the temple of Basappa of the pond, had lost their foliage and stood grinning naked at the sky. He couldn't understand why he came there. Who knew how long it had been since the temple doors were open? There was a heap of dirt in front of the door, and cow dung. Bhujangaiah felt a terrible anger against Muddu Basava, "Horrible man. I do not know what keeps him busy in the village. Why can't he come to the temple once a day and light the lamp? He goes about all the while gossiping." Bhujangaiah who thought he should warn him crossed the woods and walked towards his new fields as if he had thought of something. Last year at the same time what an excellent crop had stood there! Looking at it now wrenched one's entrails. The horse gram plants too had grown lumpy with the fields full of weeds. The arrogant and thorny caltrops stood with their heads held high. He had, as a farmer, never allowed even a single thorny plant to mature in the fields to let their seeds fall. Bhujangaiah stood in the field and began to weed them out with an insane urgency. The roots of the weeds that had grown stiff without rain began to break in half not yielding to his strength. Bhujangaiah realized the ineffectualness of his act only when his hands began to burn. His hands that were always calloused by constant work had of late grown soft with easy life, unused to such hard work. Bhujangaiah who learnt that even if he plucked them the whole day not even a small corner could be cleared, stopped clearing the thorns and stood mutely on the bund.

***

CHAPTER - 32

As if it was the forerunner to the end of rains the entire of Madalli was covered with dew. The dew had not lifted in spite of the day having advanced. One couldn't see what was ahead. It had never been so. Bhujangaiah wondered what ill it foreboded as he opened the shop as usual. His experience said if the dew fell then there wouldn't be even the scent of rain. Far from the village pond filling up, there was not even water half-full. What was to be done till the Monsoon? Let alone the people, what sin had the dumb cattle committed? The cold was biting. One felt like sitting idly at the hearth. The villagers had no other job except to sit in front of the fire from dawn. Since last summer life had grown unbearable for people. They had performed the festival of the village deity to cool her anger. After performing the fire procession, the people of the village had faithfully fulfilled all that God had ordered during the visitation on Veerappa of Devaragudda. For all their efforts, though the clouds floated in, they grew white and transparent resembling heaps of wool, and rose higher and higher but never made up their mind to descend. The dew kept falling. When it stopped falling entirely the burning summer heat would start. The face and limbs of people shrunk due to the cold and began to crack due to the chill.

The face of every one had cracked. Chapped lips began to bleed. Bhujangaiah's business too was dull. If the summer heat should reign thus for four more days even the water in the pond would dry up. Fear and anxiety about their future were thickening in the hearts of the people. The leaves on the trees and plants in the village had turned yellow and begun to fall. In just a few more days they'd all have fallen and the trees would stand like skeletons.

The idea of sinking a well which had flashed on the mind of Bhujangaiah, who stood on the bund of his new fields yesterday, like a streak of light in the dark, had now begun to find arms and legs. He had no wish to live like others in the village adhering to the social codes and customs. He had distanced himself from the fear of what people may say about him. Having sat in the shop for a long while after opening it, he called Sushila and asked her to take care of the shop and went towards Hundi. As he crossed the village and walked on the road to the pond the plants and trees all along stood naked having shed their leaves. Though he was deeply preoccupied with some important idea, the lizards that sat moving their necks in the hedges along the path to the pond without a care and the salamander that made a creepy sound on the fallen dry leaves did not fail to draw his attention. A mongoose rushed past him as he went by observing them.

Bhujangaiah at once thought he would gather some herbs for snakebite, dry them and powder them to store in the gourd remembering he had not as yet done so. He must also reveal to somebody what he alone knew in the village. He was not immortal. Those who lived today were tomorrow no more. If He called suddenly one must leave everything and go. He must at least reveal it to Muddegowda. It had been many years since he had learnt it. Why had he not taught anyone the medicine? Bhujangaiah wondered. It was not an easy task, one must have faith. If he taught it to frivolous people the medicine would not work. He had not taken a single paise from any one after learning this knowledge. The one who taught him also believed in that. He too must reveal the plant to such a person and teach him the mantra. Bhujangaiah thought that Muddegowda was the only proper man and reached Hundi to find him at home.

Gowda's threshing ground was next to his house. They were gathering the horsegram. Muddegowda who said they could speak at the harvesting site went there after asking his wife to get them buttermilk. They sat in a hut erected in a corner of the threshing field. Bhujangaiah sang the prelude, “if we sit depending on rain our life will be that of a dog’s.” Muddegowda laughed, “ Why should you worry? The business of the shop will produce harvest even if the rain fails.” Bhujangaiah appraised him of how even his business was failing day by day and how he could make money only if he dealt strictly as did the Manandavadi Kaka refusing to lend. When he broached the subject of getting a well sunk, Muddegowda laughed wondering from when Bhujangaiah was suffering from the new madness. “Such things are not for us Bhujangaiah. The rain won’t fail every time just because it failed this year.” Bhujangaiah sowed quite a few temptations in Muddegowda’s mind not letting go of his arm. Finally he said, “Why don’t we visit Padukote once? It is said the people there have sunk well in the termite ridden earth and grow crops nine months in a year. Even if rains fail they grow whatever they wish.” Though Muddegowda was tempted to say yes, he said he had to first ask his brother, disappointing Bhujangaiah. By then Puttavva brought a vessel full of buttermilk and two glasses. They began to empty the buttermilk garnished with onions and coriander. When Bhujangaiah said the coriander crop would be good that year Gowda told him that he had planted the entire of his fields down the pond of Pura with it. As the conversation digressed from the subject Bhujangaiah clean forgot his intention of showing Muddegowda the herb for snake venom.

Sushila sat in the shop whenever Bhujangaiah was busy. None asked for a loan when she ran the shop. Even if they did, she refused to give credit. Instead of having her say no to their face the creditors waited for Bhujangaiah. Of late, even in Mysore sugar and jaggery were not easily available. With it being very expensive, Kaka alone managed to some how bring it in illegally and sell for a high profit. Those who had been habituated to tea in Madalli found the going tough. When Kaka of the shop asked Ajappa the place after Bhujangaiah’s hotel had been burnt down Ajappa had sent him packing. He still felt sorry for the injustice meted out to his dear friend. He wished that if anyone would open a hotel there it should be Bhujangaiah. The walls of the hotel hadn’t collapsed either, as the rains hadn’t come in force. One could see children playing, occasionally among the walls as they passed by on the way to and from the school in Kyatanahalli. For the passengers commuting by the bus once more the tamarind tree had become the shelter. One fine day Kaka of the shop thought of putting up the hotel on the other side of the road in Chandanna's fields just in front of where Bhujangaiah's hotel had stood. On the very day he told Chandanna that a Brahmin from his village was planning to open a hotel, Chandanna took the advance money from him. Though in two weeks Kerala Hotel had opened it never had the same fortune as that of Bhujangaiah's. Finally one day while the villagers from Madalli were sitting in the hotel, a few untouchables entered the hotel. The villagers suspected Ajappa's hand behind this as they were all drunk. But they couldn't do much. Gopal of Kerala who had roamed around the country knew very well that if he should throw them out of the hotel on the words of the villagers he too may have to go to jail. He who had come to Kote to work in a hotel owned by a fellow villager had himself become an owner just now. He served tea to all those who had entered without a word and threw the cups out. But Gopal was totally bemused when they started coming everyday. The villagers did not enter the hotel even for a cup of water. With only the passengers from the bus and those who did not know of things visiting the hotel the business had slowly begun to reach a level of comfort when a large scale fight took place between the Verashaivas and the Harijans of Madalli. The hotel closed its doors as a sign of having completed its term of life on the very day the police arrived to drag Gopala with a few other elders of the village to Kote. People once again accused Bhujangaiah of the misdeeds. Bhujangaiah had never even stepped in that direction, busy with his own worries. Of late the newspaper too had stopped coming. He would bring it only when he visited Mysore occasionally. He would go to the forest shed when he wished to speak to Victor. The bus halted near the gate too. Bhujangaiah began to present himself at the cards company when he found it difficult to spend time in the village. Though the game did not have the same charm as it did at his hotel, he could somehow pass time amidst his old cronies. Sushila did not take long to learn of her husband's relapsed addiction to cards. He would return home at dawn on certain days having played the whole night. Though Sushila begged him repeatedly, his madness for card games did not abate. The meager profit that was there from the shop also was lost in the game to finally put at stake the very capital. Sushila sent words through Shankara. It was of no use. One day she herself went to Hundi and informed Muddegowda through Puttavva. Though Bhujangaiah promised that he would never ever touch the cards, he would close the shop and leave at nightfall. However much Sushila cried Bhujangaiah did not make up his mind to save a drowning family. Finally, on a day when he abused Sushila in front of the Tampura Ayya, Ayya too sat down not knowing how to advise him. Though he wished to tell him how a few in his own village had become destitute because of this game, Ayya had held his tongue looking at the burning face of Bhujangaiah. How to make him understand that the path he took was wrong? Ayya comforted Sushila praying that god alone should save him.

The situation in the village was pathetic. Apart from a few homes, it was hard put to light the stove once a day in most homes. For the people who had just one meal a day, fasting was becoming a habit. One day Rudrappa on his own came in search of Bhujangaiah. When he learnt he was not at home he met him at the forest shed and followed him like the legendary Nakshatrika, took him to Kote, met the Amaldar, appraised him of their village's dire strait, when the later said he had already sanctioned all relief works that he thought was necessary to be undertaken at Madalli. He said that as most villages suffered from the same fate the contractors available were not enough and therefore the works were getting delayed. Bhujangaiah immediately mentioned Narasimhaiah's name. They stood mute when the Amaldar said he had already his hands full of works and therefore they should find a contractor from their own village. Let alone Madalli, there was none who could fit the bill in any of the surrounding villages. The Taluk Development Officer and the Amaldar seemed to understand their predicament and promised to make some arrangement in a week. Bhujangaiah went straight to Narashimaiah's second wife's house. He did not take Rudrappa with him. As soon as Narasimhaiah saw

Bhujangaiah he invited him with his raucous voice. He asked Siddalingi to prepare tea. She brought tea and opening her mouth like a frog enquired, "Is this the Bhujangaiah you talked about?" Narasimhaiah answered, 'Yes this is he, do you know how charming his woman is? One should touch her only after washing one's hands. You look like a rice bag in comparison." He laughed aloud. He turned to Bhujangaiah and asked, "What do you say Bhujangappa?" Bhujangaiah blinked. Siddalingi blushed at her husband's words and flirted, "You think you are like Komaraswamy? I wonder if a better woman than me would have come to you looking at you" She threw a smile at Bhujangaiah as if he had appreciated her repartee and went in. Bhujangaiah who lighted up at their conversation raised the matter of contract in his village. Narasimhaiah immediately said, " I cannot do that under any circumstance. I have undertaken more than what is in my power. If I can complete those it is enough." Finally when Narasimhaiah suggested that Bhujangaiah could work as Mestri, overseeing the workers and that the profit could be equally divided, Bhujangaiah agreed without a word of protest. Narasimhaiah agreed to put in the required capital himself and accompanied Bhujangaiah to meet the authorities. When Rudrappa learnt of it after all the discussions were held he was put out a bit. Though he no more hated Bhujangaiah as much as he did earlier, he certainly could not digest Bhujangaiah improve again in life through contracts. Yet not revealing his emotions he said, "Ayyo! contract works are not for us, If something goes wrong we would be as good as a land where dathura grows," Rudrappa's words did not deter Bhujangaiah.

In a week's time the public works began in Madalli. All the labourers were from the village. Apart from seven or eight houses the labour was drawn from every house. Parvathy had dismissed even the one servant she had. She had sent all the livestock to Jakkalli, and was getting whatever she needed from her parent's house. Sushila was greatly surprised at the sudden change in her husband's behaviour. He would oversee the workers from dawn to dusk. Even those who hated him from the very beginning came now to work under him without an alternative. He first took up the work of desilting and deepening the well in the village. He himself went down the well to oversee the work.

At last from the kitchens of Madalli smoke began to rise both times. Even so Bhujangaiah's shop too was stocked again. Sushila went to Mysore for purchases. She would meet Raja every time. Though she was healthy once more the vigour of her early days she did not regain. Narasimhaiah himself visited once a week to inspect the progress. Sushila would cook something special whenever he visited. His hungry eyes had not ceased to glance unobserved by Bhujangaiah at Sushila as if they would peck at her. Sushila did not fail to get embarassed whenever she felt his eyes. The days began to roll. The repair work of the two dams neighbouring Madalli itself took care of the villagers' hunger for a long while. It had been many days since Bhujangaiah had touched cards.Whenever his companions called him for a game he refused saying he had not a moment of leisure. He now found it strange that he would not even recall his madness for gambling against the advice of all. He was now busy with his own work. The entire day was spent overseeing the labour. At night he had to keep a record of what was their due. Once the week was up he had to submit the details of labour to Narasimhaiah. Though the villagers derided him as Narasimhaiah's mason, Bhujangaiah didn't pay attention to that. He took care of the work loyally, not cheating Narasimhaiah even for a single paise. Shamanna the Engineer who came for measurements had praised Bhujangaiah in the presence of Narasimhaiah once. Shamanna had asked Bhujangaiah while having meal at his place, "Why should you not take up contracts, there is always enough work in our Taluk Board." Bhujangaiah too wondered why he shouldn't try his hand at it. He went to Kote with Shamanna and registered his name in the list of contractors undertaking jobs for the Taluk Board. He had already realized that the education he had was adequate for such jobs. When Narasimhaiah who was much less educated than him could manage such large works it should be easier for him. The important thing was he needed capital. Who would give him that kind of money? He decided that he could borrow a little money from Gowda, after seeing what he got from Narasimhaiah.

That very night he explained to Sushila the blueprint of his plan. Sushila, though she couldn't understand the workings of it all, happily encouraged her husband when he talked about ways to improve.. Though she had not enjoyed any great happiness after marrying him she had neither regretted it nor thought what she had done was wrong. Sushila who received everything that came in her life with a smile felt she was being stabbed with a knife whenever she heard those who hated her gossiping about a nonexistent relationship between herself and Narasimhaiah. She was disgusted by the behaviour of the mean people of Madalli who spoke lightly of her, taking her for someone who would spread a mat for anyone merely because she had come loving Bhujangaiah. But she had to live amidst them! When she had once hinted at that to her husband in an indirect fashion he had laughed at it, "We are not born to gain people's appreciation. It is enough if we live to gain God's appreciation." He had removed the doubts in Sushila's heart. What bothered Bhujangaiah most was the fact that he had to live with Sushila under someone else's roof. God would never let them suffer thus for long. He had faith that one day or another God would open his eyes and turn his merciful gaze towards them. The Monsoon would begin with the summer ending soon. What should be done if it rains early? He shall see to it at least this time that his fields do not fall barren. There was no dearth of servants. But cultivation was not easy. He had to gather everything afresh. Though he had nothing at home he yet had almost all the implements that should be there in a farmer's house, but where to bring it? Even if he collected them where was he to store them? Within a week of having completed the job agreed upon, Narasimhaiah had come and had given his profit after accounting for it properly. Bhujangaiah was truly surprised at Narashimaiah's honesty. Only Muddegowda in the village knew apart from Sushila how much Bhujangaiah had earned from his supervisory job.

***

CHAPTER - 33

Bhujangaiah and Sushila who had wished to visit Yediyur went there one fine day knowing that once it started raining they could find no free time. Tampura Ayya who visited that very day accompanied them without hesitation avering that one couldn't be tardy where serving god was concerned. After spending the night at Raja's room the three left for Yediyur in the morning. Ayya narrated the story of Siddalingeshwara of Yediyur all along the way. He had already been there more than three times. They had been to Nanjangud and Devanur too after their stay for a day at Yediyur, where they filled their eyes with the sight of God, had the holy ablution done, gave money for feeding ten people. Before they returned to the village what Raja told them came as a bolt of lightning. Cholera had broken out in Madalli. The rumor had it that someone had bought bamboo seed cheap at the Darga market or Kote market and eaten it, which resulted in the spread of Cholera. The village was being inoculated since three days. All of them got inoculated in Mysore on Raja's advice and then left for Madalli. Tampura Ayya said he would return to his village.

Bhujangaiah was shocked to hear that already seven or eight had died in the village. He enquired who they were. He learnt that three of his own community had died. All those who were in the bus too attributed it to the bamboo seed. Sushila asked her husband when she failed to understand what "bamboo seed" meant. Though he wished to tell her, somehow his soul trembled. He with much difficulty explained, " Once in many years the bamboo flowers, dries and splits to form the seed, when its life span ends. It then has to be born anew to grow. When again it blossoms, the seed grows and dries up." Sushila found it all very strange. She asked innocently, "Well, don't people know eating it would bring the disease?" Bhujangaiah replied, "I do not know who said so. How did they associate the outbreak of "chorela" with the bamboo seed? No one had even seen anything of bamboo seed eight years ago when chorela had broken out." Though Sushila had felt like laughing when her husband said "chorela" instead of cholera she suppressed herself and began to worry about how to live in a village where the contagion had spread. All along the way she felt strange emotions.

As they got off the bus and reached the village a terrible wail was heard by Bhujangaiah from a couple of directions. It had been just a few minutes since Shaggy Sidda had died in the Untouchables' Lane. Even as Bhujangaiah entered the Lane the cry of the people intensified. The wife of Shaggy Sidda wept aloud recollecting the past as soon as she saw his face. Bhujangaiah walked into the village from there. The entire village was in the grip of fear, as if death was knocking on every door. Those who lived in the morning were no more in the evening. Those who had left after talking in the evening had not risen in the morning. When Bhujangaiah entered his street he learnt that Sannaputtappa had grown one with the Linga that very afternoon. He went there. His body had been laid on the porch, the sound of bhajan mingled with a heartrending keen. Bhujangaiah felt like screaming. Death had no preference. It had begun to drag away whomever it found, whether good or evil. From every house food was carried to the village deity to calm her temper after performing many prayers. First the drought had ravaged the village and now death had rushed into the village in broad day light and hunted the poor people who weakly lay prostrate, with their stomach sticking to their back ready to be blown by a mere breeze. None had the strength to stand against death, let alone fight it. Even before the hunter could fire his arms a few victims had voluntarily come as sacrifice to fall at his feet.

Bhujangaiah went from one end to another of the village the entire night. That very day four people had died. The wife of Gowda,

Kalavva too had apparently fainted after having had diarrhea and vomiting a few times. She had not yet regained consciousness. Who knows whether she would last till dawn? Cruel Death was beckoning her who was the goddess of justice. The entire village was reeling under attack. Many years ago plague had attacked them too. Bhujangaiah remembered that they had all evacuated the village and had put up huts in their respective fields to save their lives. The sight that they saw in the village having climbed up the tree near their huts was still frozen in front of his eyes. Countless vultures and crows had descended God knows from where as if to swallow the very village. People had returned only after a month. Who knew if they needed to leave the village this time too? Why hadn't any one thought about it? Bhujangaiah walked towards his home as if he remembered something. The door had been locked. Ninganna's wife said that Parvathy had left for Jakkalli with children four days ago. As the travelers on the bus informed cholera had spread to the villages around Kote too. The markets of Darga and Kote had been closed. For a brief moment fear flashed on Bhujangaiah's mind if this deadly disease had visited Jakkalli too. Bhujangaiah prayed, "O God, let nothing untoward happen to my children!" He went to Rudrappa's house. Rudrappa who was sitting on his haunches on the porch, was lost in thought not knowing what to do, as if he were paralyzed. He had locked his family indoors ensuring none of them would stir out. Rudrappa told in a dead voice that only those who failed to get themselves inoculated when the paramedics from Kote had come suffered from the disease and that for all his efforts a few had escaped getting inoculated out of fear. Bhujangaiah too began to grow scared looking at Rudrappa shivering in fear of the raging death. They decided after much discussion that the town crier should be asked to announce the village to evacuate and live in huts in the fields outside. With Shaggy Sidda dead who would announce? They walked to the untouchables' quarters. None seemed to sleep though it was midnight.

It was an impenetrable night with the encompassing black shadow of death. The atmosphere was strangulating. Bhujangaiah was scared of the sound of his own footfall. The hoot of the owls rendered the appalling night yet more terrifying; somewhere nearby were the howling jackals. The very earth on which one stood was sighing in disgust. The village trembled in deadly fear wondering about the future. Speech had died between Bhujangaiah and Rudrappa. Both of them went from one quarter to another as if they were approaching the gallows, and approached the Gowda quarters comforting themselves that they could do nothing more till morning when they heard a lament from Karigowda's house that lifted the roof, unsettling them. Death in the end had swallowed Kalavva. She had succumbed to Death's design which did not wait for a second, and she was no more from that very moment. The one soul of affection that shed tears at the village's sorrow had closed its eyes. The hand that patted oil on the crown of destitute children so that their forehead wouldn't dry in the summer heat now lay paralyzed. Death had now sucked the sap of mercy, which had fed what it ate to all those who, squeezed dry by the iron hand of the hunger of drought, approached. Bhujangaiah stood silently in a corner. A sword seemed to hang over his head. Bhujangaiah did not have the courage to stand. The house was full of shadows that shifted in a ghasty manner. The deformed shadows were throwing into confusion his inner being. O God! Shouldn't this terrible night end soon?

Bhujangaiah went alone from there. The fear of getting bogged down in the mire of darkness forced him to lift one foot after another with effort. The new house of Gowda echoed with emptiness. The door of the outhouse was shut firmly. Bhujangaiah opened his mouth to call Sushila. No sound emerged. It was as if his tongue had shriveled. He knocked on the door gently, scared to do so loudly. The door did not open. Sushila had shut and bolted the door firmly. She had barricaded against death from entering. She must be sleeping comfortably, safe in the thought that death can never rush in. Sushila opened the door when Bhujangaiah after knocking repeatedly called aloud shaking in fear of someone approaching him. Darkness had curdled in the house. Sushila was scared by her husband's incoherence. Sushila who sat with the doors bolted, afraid of the misfortune that churned the village, trembling at the voices of agony and ear splitting pain as she felt someone knocking at the door, had moaned and slumbered in perplexity. She had opened the door only after ascertaining the identity of the voice that called after knocking on the door. If she had lighted the lamp she would have not failed to notice the chilling shadow of the fear of death on the face of her husband who was braver than her. Even under such terrible situations she had asked with her habitual sense of duty whether her husband would have lunch. He replied in a tired tone " No". Sushila lit the lamp when he with effort uttered, "bring me some water." She secured the door and brought her husband boiled water, which simmered on the hearth. Bhujangaiah remembered their drinking boiled water whenever a contagion spread in the village. He lay down on the mat appreciating Sushila's precaution. Sushila slept next to Bhujangaiah after putting out the lamp. The waves of sorrow kept rushing through the chinks in the roof of the outhouse. Any sorrow has an end to it. But as if there was no end to the sorrow of Madalli, the voices of those weeping expanded from moment to moment. Sushila felt the bolt of thunder strike her after Bhujangaiah sobbing, informed her of the death of Kalavva. She had been to visit her on returning from Mysore, but later had confined herself to the house scared of stepping out on the street again. Now that her dear Kalavva was no more a knife seemed to pierce her innards. For Sushila who had never known love and affection of a natural mother, even if she had known now unremembered, the pure love, which Kalavva had showered on Sushilia remained perpetually green. How could such a soul be lost forever? Sorrow began to drip silently from the heart of Sushila. Bhujangaiah enclosed her in his heart who would suddenly sit up in fright every now and then and put her to sleep warding off her worry.

The village began to preoccupy itself with the task of burying the four who had died yester night once the dawn broke. Rudrappa and Bhujangaiah had striven constantly to convince the majority of the villagers whose eyes had dried weeping everyday to leave the village and go to their respective fields. By then a van had arrived full of people from Kote. There were two doctors and the rest were nurses. They too were taken aback on hearing of the death of four people on a single day. On enquiry it was learnt that three of them were not inoculated. Those who had avoided inoculation earlier now arrived voluntarily to get inoculated. The doctors treated those who already suffered a couple of times from dehydration. Every house was informed that none should drink water without boiling it first and not to eat leftovers. Trusting in the doctors' assurance that none would die from then on the villagers shelved the idea of evacuating the village. As the doctor said, only two had died in the next one week. In the end as a sign of death having decamped from Madalli, the shop of Bhujangaiah and Kaka opened doors. But selling of sweets, fried edibles like *chakkali* and *mussore* made of rice flour were banned. The villagers took special precautions knowing that the contagion would not pass entirely unless the rains arrived. They got used to chlorinated water from the well.

The cholera that suddenly appeared to shake the people's heart in Madalli was responsible for a variety of change amongst them. Sannappa who had sucked the blood of people to attain prosperity had begun to speak philosophically of retreat. The disease had claimed his grown up son in the very first round. Those who had hoarded the grains opened their granary or the pit to lend the grains voluntarily realizing that the visitation of cholera had been due to people eating anything, unable to withstand hunger. Sannappa alone had not given anything without either the signature or thumb print of the borrowers. The pain of those who had lost their dear ones was still green. By then, Ugadi, the festival of New Year too had arrived and gone. No pomp greeted it. No ceremony saw it off. The agony of people had abated as days passed by. Once more the people of Madalli anxiously waited with endless hope, this time too as always, the arrival of rains that could wash their frozen sorrow along with the dirt of Madalli.

***

CHAPTER - 34

The shadow of rain clouds began to darken Madalli only when the first rain star of the new year, Ashwini entered the second house. But as soon as the Bharani star rose the sky seemed to regurgitate all that it had held back since a year. Whether the villagers had food for their stomach or not, as soon as the rains arrived, they brought solace to the children of the soil. The people squeezed dry by the cholera and the drought forgot the moment's hunger and pain, with hope for tomorrow's happiness they staked their little strength and put themselves to labour with vigour, once more filled with sap. Though time was known to heal any wound their present tolerance was the result of their getting used to pain and pleasure equally over centuries. Who could be accused if the rains failed? Who could they complain to? To those who believed that all their events were ordained by God the cause of their troubles was either their own misdeed or God's anger at them. As if to make Bhujangaiah's sowing the seeds of desire for new ways of living and new methods of cultivation in the heads of the villagers remain a mere desire, the rains this time around passed well. However, the desire to sink a well, install a pump set and grow crop began to take deep root in the mind of Bhujangaiah.

When the entire village began to sow mustard and jowar in their fields with the rains of Bharani, Bhujangaiah began to plough the stubble fields of his. He too could have sowed if he had fallow ploughed his field in the summer. He had already organized a pair of oxen, plough, etc... for cultivation before the rain. He had arranged to pen the oxen at Gowda's cattle shed. Bhujangaiah decided to close the shop feeling that the business was not good. Sushila opened the shop whenever she was free. As soon as the sowing was completed he hired two ploughs and got his field tilled properly. As the clouds covered the sky, he had hired a couple of female labour to remove the scattered leaves and sticks as they would not dry and readied his field as smooth as a mirror. Bhujangaiah's mind found ease only after all this had been achieved. He could now sow whatever he wished. Wanting to plant ragi when the Rohini star was born he procured the seeds of ragi by measure from Gowda's house. Sushila was a stranger to that life. She had newly learnt how to prepare *ragi mudde.* The work on the field was an entirely new world to her. She however made an effort to learn everything by seeking Mallavva's help every time. On the day of sowing, Shankara too had sent his plough to facilitate sowing in one go.

Bhujangaiah strove day and night so that he could once more live with his head held high among the people of Madalli. The festive happiness once more reverberated in the village. With Monsoon crops succeeding people had a little money in their hands now. The rate of mustard had reached a new high. Bhujangaiah rued for not being able to raise the mustard crop that year. But then the mustard collected in exchange for goods sold instead of money at the shop had itself resulted in three sacks full. Sushila had not agreed to close the shop. She was now managing the entire shop. The one desire of Sushila who carefully saved every single paise was to own a house. Though Bhujangaiah too had an intense desire to build a house in the heart of the village and set up family with Sushila in it to the envy of those who hated him he yet wished to buy a pump set first after sinking a well. He cajoled Gowda and went with him to Padukote to learn how the Tamilians were growing sugar cane and banana by digging hundreds of wells. He met Narasimhaiah and accompanied him to the agricultural hypothecation bank. The bankers knew Narasimhaiah. They took the share amount from Bhujangaiah and asked him to apply for a loan. All the relevant documents such as revenue tax papers, sale deed, etc... were asked to be submitted so that the loan could be sanctioned in a month or two. Bhujangaiah returned happily. Bhujangaiah who did not inform anyone but Sushila, visited Kote three or four times in the meanwhile. One day a stranger arrived in Madalli looking for Bhujangaiah. When a person resembling a government officer enquiring the whereabouts of Bhujangaiah even before entering the village, arrived at last at the shop, Sushila said her husband was away in the fields and would send word for him. She laid a mat on the porch of Gowda and sent a dawdling boy to inform her husband promising the boy some puffed rice and chickpeas. Bhujangaiah arrived somewhat anxiously. The Bank had sent the visitor. He had come to inspect the water source on his field and to show a proper site for digging the well. After going round his field with the stranger Bhujangaiah marked the spot shown by him with a stone. The news, that Bhujangaiah would sink a well on his field spread throughout the village. Everyone began to enquire. If some wished him well others opined that by taking a government loan he was going to end up auctioning off his properties. Bhujangaiah refusing to heed any one and without retracting his step one fine day brought a group of voddas from Kote who were considered experts in sinking wells. Shivarudraswamy performed the prayer selecting an auspicious hour. The work on the well began. The cropping of ragi by now was over in Bhujangaiah's field and he had yet to transport the heaps of grain to the granary. Every day people arrived to watch the sinking of the well. Whatever Bhujangaiah did the village saw as a novelty. Even those who had property ten times than he, did not have his courage. Karigowda himself visited every day and stood for long hours. In four days the earthwork was over and rocks were exposed on all sides. From that day began the task of drilling a hole and blasting the rock with dynamite. The entire village would come to watch that wonder. Gavaraiah of Vadda's group was in charge of blasting. Everyone desired to speak to him and ask him about it. Gavaraiah scared them who were already afraid, saying it was no ordinary skill and that even a little carelessness would result in tragedy. He succeeded in having them stand at a considerable distance from the well. They stood under trees at a distance and watched with wonder the blasted stones flying in the air from the well. In a fortnight water was struck. That day there was a major worship. Bhujangaiah had invited all those who were close to him. Even those uninvited had come. Pundri was busy. Water had been found in the North East corner of the well. A stream of water as thick a a finger was springing from the rock. The villagers looked at it with wonder. The workers themselves praised Bhujangaiah's good fortune. When Shastri who was present for the worship too said with a loud voice in order to safeguard the importance of his knowledge, "Look ! The water sprang in the North East as I had predicted", people looked at him with surprise. The rainy season was not yet over. The work progressed even on days it rained heavily. As it was a stone well there was not much of a problem. Even as the well deepened so the water began to fill. Two more pulleys had to be added to the existing one in a corner of the well to empty the water to go on with the work. In the end the water in the well refused to allow them to work. On Gavaraiah's advice Bhujangaiah hired a diesel pump from Kote. Only after draining the water out could the well be deepened. The noise of the diesel engine could be heard in the surrounding villages. The entire village was talking about the well. Bhujangaiah's name was on all the tongues. It had been thus when the hotel was opened. But now people praised him ten times more. If some uttered "Aha! Mother Gangavva is springing unceasingly" the others said "The water of fragrance is rushing up cutting through the rock. Nothing can equal this."

Sushila too went to witness a couple of times. Parvathy who heard of her husband's adventure throughout the village though desired to visit the spot desisted because of her pride and raged within. When Rudrappa's wife accosted her while bringing water, "Parvathy, did you see your husband sinking a well?" Parvathy had digressed as if she had no interest in it. Karigowda alone praised Bhujangaiah wholeheartedly, not caring what any body may think. He had said for all to hear, "If one keeps faith, Gangavva will spring through the black granite. Even if you sink a well in the pond you may not get as much water." When people saw the water flowing through Singari's field drained by the diesel pump, they exclaimed, "Aha, the land was fortunate to have come to his hands. It will now find water all the nine seasons of the year." They had praised the fortune of the land itself.

As the work on the well neared completion the hypothecating bank came for inspection and agreed to sanction a loan for a pump house and did so in a week. When Bhujangaiah wished to buy bricks from Karigowda who had a kiln he had given him bricks refusing payment saying he could return the bricks when he built a kiln. The bank supplied the pump set and the diesel engine through their own employee, who also was an agent for pumpsets and diesel engines, Tirupathi Raju. Dasappa the mason worked day and night to build the pump house. Bhujangaiah once more received accolades for undertaking a task successfully, in a manner that made people nod their head. He engaged the labour that either went to the plains of Yedathore or to the new paddy fields of Gaddige plains from Madalli and got them to make the runnels for water to irrigate the field, to level the bed, to prepare small squares of wet plots, etc... A surprised Madalli watched him with its finger on the nose. Apart from the wet plots of rice paddy prepared during some ancestral times below the pond, this was the first time when such transformation had come over the burnt earth of Madalli. The business of converting the dry fields dependent on rain into wet fields was seen as a miraculous event by people. Though everyone was busy in the tasks of readying his field for the returning monsoon, people did not fail to visit Bhujangaiah's field at least once a day. Bhujangaiah had used his brains to collect the stones and earth from the well and had them removed to one side of the field so that it acted as a wall. On Karigowda's advice he had already planted the fence of milkhedge, though he had wished to fence his plot on all sides once the North-Easterly offered respite. Before the rains abated the milkhedge would have grown into a thick bush. Gowda had made the job of building a fence easy when he suggested that thorns could be used to plug holes and gaps in the hedge row. People let their cattle stray all over the village on the day of the Sankranti festival. Nothing could be saved from the mouth of the cattle without a fence. Bhujangaiah was preoccupied day and night with what crops he should cultivate through irrigation. He called Amase who had worked for him before but now laboured on contract. He sold through Pundri the dwarfs he had as they were unsuitable for work on wet fields and bought a pair of excellent oxen. The pump house of Bhujangaiah turned into a place where once more his friends could meet. Pundri, Cannamalla, Nagaraja, Kariyappa everybody began to either unfold the purana of their adventure or steal jackfruit or bring the split bean to roast. Sushila began to get bored as Bhujangaiah rarely came home now. He had decided to close the shop, not being able to pay attention to the business. With good rains from the returning monsoon, the village too had grown sappy. The new field of Bhujangaiah had enough papaya trees, vegetable plants and a few coconut trees to be now called a garden. The bank had promised to give "coconut loan" if he would plant coconut trees on his field. But Bhujangaiah had found the loan of Rs. 10,000/- already a mountainous burden on his head. Of course it was a long-term loan. But the annually growing interest? Rudrappa went around saying if he did not pay the instalments and interest on time they would come and attach his property. Having seen Bhujangaiah's adventure those who had lands in the downs also wondered why they too should not hazard. But Rudrappa's warning confused them.

Raja who visited the village for the summer vacation felt Bhujangaiah's achievement to be a miracle. He cajoled his father too to sink a well. Though Muddegowda had a burning desire to sink a well his elder brother Karigowda had not consented. After hearing his son his desire took wings and he asked his brother one day. Karigowda agreed without hesitation. He too said that he would sink a well. Raja was glad to hear of it. He had already decided to join college after high school. By then seven or eight boys from Madalli had joined school in Mysore. Bhujangaiah's well was a "cooling off" place for the summer heat. Sushila who was in the garden occasionally was surprised to see Raja swimming like a fish. Though there were steps in a corner to descend into the well Raja would jump from the top of the well in a splash. Raja had learnt to swim as a small boy when the pond of Pura was full. He had laughed at Sushila's warning. "The well is too deep, careful" and said, " It's good to swim only if its deep. Ask Bhujanganna if you wish." Bhujangaiah had supported Raja's word in the manner of an expert. "Deeper the well easier to swim." Sushila who had observed Raja's regular visit would bring a little extra when she carried lunch for her husband. Raja too shared the meal on the platform of the well not refusing when compelled. Sushila would cook a different meal every day. She never knew how time went by as long as Raja stayed in the garden. Bhujangaiah's heart would brim when he saw them laughing and shouting in play like uninhibited children. His eyes would fill with tears when the memory of his own children seperated from him assailed him. When the drought had hit Parvathy who had sent Soma to Jakkalli had admitted him to school there. Bhujangaiah's desire to see his son intensified. He wished to send somebody to bring him. The school had closed for vacation. He might pay a visit. Parvathy was a shameless woman. What fort did he need to campaign against being adamant with her? They were his children after all. Whatever he earned was it not for them? Though his eyes were gazing at the excellent summer crop of ragi that stood, his mind was immersed in the thought of his children. Bhujangaiah grew aware of his present only when Raja and Sushila approached laughing at some joke.

The people of Madalli who had assumed that Bhujangaiah's story was finished when his hotel was torched were astounded to see him once more raising his head. Those who did not like him said, "Who knows what he will achieve having raised loan from every where? He thinks making a garden is as easy as earning a few paisa by washing dirty dishes." A few others praised, "He is a man with pluck!'. Bhujangaiah was once more the cause of mixed reactions among the villagers. He had created a desire in the hearts of a few, especially in Muddegowda and Karigowda, to sink wells. A few approached him, let alone he asking them, and compelled him to take them to Kote where they applied for loans for well. The lands of Gowda which had not been registered since ancestral times got registered in the process of applying for a loan for wells. The Village Clerk of Madalli himself went to get the lands in Madalli and Hundi registered in the names of Karigowda and Muddegowda respectively according to the register of Panchayat. The clerk who would never climb the steps of Taluk office before his palm was warmed had made the Gowda bribe adequately the clerk at the office too, knowing he could afford the money. Though Karigowda commented harshly, "This Brahmin is a bit greedy" he also added,

"Though he eats he gets the job done faithfully." The clerk never got put off by Gowda's words. He ignored the criticism of everybody in the village. No one from the village even boarded the bus to Kote without him on such errands. Even Patel Rudrappa who talked boldly with the Amaldar was unable to make out the dealings of the clerks. Rudrappa who knew of their ability to subtly stymie things if he were to lose his temper at them finally surrendered to the Village Clerk saying, "The brahmins are by nature corrupt. Let them eat what they will." The Village Clerk would unhesitatingly take bribe and help bribe the others too. Bhujangaiah always felt like he was watching dogs whenever he found the employees of Taluk offices, who looked at his hands before they even spoke. They wagged their tails and grew docile as soon as a piece of something was thrown at them. If not they growled. Finally, due to the constant effort of Bhujangaiah six or seven wells were sanctioned to Madalli. Two of them belonged to the Gowda. Gowda assigned the responsibility of sinking the well and the rest of the tasks to Bhujangaiah. Bhujangaiah had by then some experience in "contract" and therefore was forced to accept the task. He started work on an auspicious day. He brought a few more workers apart from those who worked on his well. He accompanied Gavariah to Mysore and himself purchased the powder, cape and the fuse for Dynamite. He saved quite some money because he bought them wholesale. Having stored them carefully at home he warned Sushila not to touch them. When Gavariah asked he would give whatever was needed keeping a careful account. The work on the wells began with good speed. Kulle Gowda who had borrowed money from Gowda and Nanjappa of the Lingayats who had gone on their own to sink their wells had brought labour from Jatti Hundi and had already grown tired of getting fleeced by them. Not even half the work had been completed. Karigowda's well was closer to Bhujangaiah's. But Muddegowda's well was located much beyond Hundi and Bhujangaiah would get tired running between the two places. But due to Bhujangaiah's irrepressible energy and the trust which the Gowdas placed in him, the wells were completed in three months. The depth that was reached in Karigowda's well for water was also the depth in Mudde Gowda's well at which water was found. On the day water appeared in Mudde Gowda's well Puttavva had brought her children for worship. When Gavaraiah said, "It is lucky that you found water so soon." Bhujangaiah immediately said, "Mother Earth's heart too is like that of Puttakka." He turned towards her and said, "Look Puttakka, because of your concern for the right and the good, this mother of mine Gangavva, opened her eyes so soon." Muddegowda was pleased at his words and looked at his wife with pride. From the day she had stepped into his house, it was as if Lakshmi herself had stepped into Gowda's house. It was also what the entire village said. In the entire of the Gowda quarters Puttavva was as well known for her kindness, generosity and affectionate speech as Kalavva had been.

***

CHAPTER - 35

By the time another summer stepped into Madalli, Bhujangaiah had grown popular as a "contractor" in the eyes of the villagers of Madalli, Kyatanahalli, Saragur, Shindenahalli, etc... He had completed the works on wells, and had convinced a few more to sink wells. He had also accepted the works on wells in the neighbouring villages. The Taluk Development Board of Kote had sanctioned a Primary School Building to Madalli and had entrusted the construction to Bhujangaiah. Till now the school of Madalli was run in the House of Para next to the temple. It was the only place for all community events, like for those who wished to rehearse, for community meals on festivals and holy events, for the visiting V I Ps to sit, etc. On those occasions Puttanna, who was the only teacher for the four classes, transfered the school on to somebody else's *jagali*. The villagers called the teacher Puttanna, "Black Putta", and he as the acronym suggested shone bright like washed ember. Of late one saw his hand behind many a mischief in the village with him carrying on along with his teaching the tasks of writing anonymous complaints, spreading rumours against one another, as if they too were holy functions. Pundri had nicknamed him "Mischief Putta" or "Kyathe Putta" as he was growing infamous by constantly marking time to the tune of Rudrappa, gobbling food at his house. He had begun to put on airs with Bhujangaiah by not only suggesting improvement but also criticising him from the day Bhujangaiah started work on the school: "The foundation is shallow, the bricks are not adequately burnt, the wood for the window and the doors are inferior." One day when he began to interfere in the presence of Shamanna who had come on inspection of works the latter had admonished him and sent him packing. After that incident when "Kyate" approached Bhujangaiah pretending cordiality, Bhujangaiah had shown him his place in terms that made him never show himself anywhere near the construction. From that day began the business of writing anonymous complaints. When even after the officers of the Board had come a couple of times with the President on inspection the complaints did not cease, they began to transfer them to the dust bin without reading. But Kyate Putta's job of writing went on unceasingly. Whether any official read the letter or not it was enough for him if Rudrappa and Sannappa who nodded their heads at his writing approved. Bhujangaiah did his job conscientiously, bound to the good advice of Gowda, "Tell me, which God loves to have you worry about the wagging of boneless tongues?" More than half the brick burnt for the school was left. He had also bought three or four neem and rain trees with the help of Beard of Kyatanahalli. There was no doubt he would have enough wood to build a house if he should have them sized. But Bhujangaiah did not have a place to begin with. He enquired wondering if Gowda had forgotten his promise of looking up a site for him to build a house. When he said, "Today itself you'll get a site. Tell me when you wish to begin constructing a house," Bhujangaiah was astonished. Gowda had already enquired Chikka about the latter's plot in disuse adjacent to his new house and the latter had agreed to give it up. Bhujangaiah found the site adequate as it was large enough for an inner courtyard. He bought it the next day. He began to collect all the essentials having planned to build a house of three *ankanas,* squares, resting on six pillars, with a verandah behind and one in front. Sushila was enthusiastic when work began on her own house. Bhujangaiah bought a bicycle to make the stomach of those who disliked him bileous. Sushila too had grown into a village woman since the day she began living at Gowda's outhouse. She bathed once a week, that too in the bathroom in the corner of the courtyard of Gowda's large house. Bhujangaiah of late bathed in the garden well. Sushila had to wait like other women for darkness in order to go to the field. She slowly got used to it though she was subject to terrible fear and discomfort. Sushila was not yet free from the fear that somebody may identify her voice while answering

Mallavva when the latter spoke. Now that the construction of the house had begun she insisted that a separate bathroom and a toilet in the backyard were also to be built. The bathroom was all right but Bhujangaiah did not find the idea of a toilet right. Though Bhujangaiah felt it improper to show the arrogance of a beggar when the others had no such facilities, he yielded to Sushila's desire and built a toilet. The news was one of astonishment and of joke in the entire village. Though the house was small it had all the facilities for a small family of two. By the time he completed the house Bhujangaiah had enough of that. Gowda's statement that it was no game to build a house had been proved right. Bhujangaiah who wondered how difficult it must have been for Gowda to build a large house with an inner courtyard when he himself faced such difficulties building a mere three square house, fixed an auspicious day for entering the new house. Bhujangaiah had planned to boil milk and invite a few people for meal without any pomp and then occupy the new house. But it did not happen as he planned. Parvathy deliberately left for Jakkalli on that day. His sister and her husband did not come though he went to Kallalli to invite them. Except a few people from the street of the followers of Shiva, people of all the communities in Madalli had come. Bhujangaiah's close friends Pundri, Kencha, Cannamalla, Nagaraja, etc.. who helped Kariyappa in cooking and serving the meal to everyone who came were tired at the end of the day. Everyone praised the sweet *payasa* of Bengalgram.Bhujangaiah had not yet got the house mortared. Sushila began to get all that work done one by one whenever Dasappa was free.

Tampura Ayya who came on the day Bhujangaiah entered his new house had not left even after a week. The room on the *jagali* of Bhujangaiah's house was now reserved for him. Ayya had managed to have Bhujangaiah's house always crowded by narrating the tales of Shiva or by singing bhajans in the night, on the *jagali.* People arrived from not only the Gowda quarters but also from the Lingayat quarters. Whatever the people of his caste may say Ayya never left Bhujangaiah's house. He praised Sushila's character in front of those who talked ill. People stopped speaking about her saying, "This Ayya is mad".

Though one might assume that the days of happiness returned once more in Bhujangaiah's life, he was in truth deeply hurt and troubled. The regret that he had to live away from the house where he had a right was coupled with the doubt if Parvathy would safeguard the honour and status of his family. Her lending an ear to the rumourmongers out of spite caused him anxiety. Who knew what those people who did not stop at anything may do tomorrow? But was what he did right? Wasn't the step he took for a woman of another caste at his age wrong? He had been told that no one had done such a thing in his caste. Though they had not one but four women, not one of them had abandoned their home or temple for a kept woman In the past a wife wouldn't ever lift her head while speaking to her husband. It was a time when women were proud of their husbands for having as many women as they would as it heightened their status in the society. Times were changing now. Since the time of his marriage he had conflicts with Parvathy. She was loose tongued. She said whatever came to her mind. Even so, how dear she was to him once! He had felt her to be a part of his being. But now? She had grown hard as flint to end the relationship between them. She won't ever soften. Is there a way to change her who believes her stance to be her pride? There is. But the price to pay was not ordinary: to give up Sushila. She left everything for the one whom she desired. She did not bow to any pressure or kinship. She did not fear any accusation or insult. Hers was so delicate a body that would singe if touched. He could never guess why she desired him so intensely as if nothing existed beyond that. He had got more from her than what he had given her. She never contorted her face at any difficulty that they faced. She never uttered a word that might hurt him. She swallowed intolerable pains and smiled. Can he betray such a woman? It was better he died. Even if the sky should fall on his head he should not ever yield to such a wretched thought. If only Parvathy had the qualities of Sushila he wouldn't perhaps have even lifted his eyes to look at her. It was because he was disgusted by a family life made intolerable by Parvathy's cantankerous behaviour that he had surrendered to the eyes of Sushila in which affection brimmed. Many were the chances for him to tread the wrong path. He had rejected them all with a firm mind. Only when he saw Sushila had he felt that it was a face he had seen somewhere - no, desired before. When he heard her talk, he had experienced that her speech were dear to his life, that he had heard them before. He did not think even for a moment whether it was right or wrong. She saw him, he too saw her. She smiled. He too smiled. She stretched her hand, without hesitating he too had stretched his. Thus soul mingled with soul. If she should cry now he too weeps. Her smile is his. Now and then he feels as if she is his everything. He feels shy when he realizes that the thought of such a feeling was a madness, was not natural, not what emerged from deep within. Bhujangaiah who had freed himself just that day from his weeklong busy schedule was going to Mysore with Sushila when all such thoughts came crowding upon him. The trees and plants too seemed to compete in a race with the bus traveling fast. The light green and russet coloured leaves of trees were clamouring the arrival of the New Year, As far as the eye stretched one saw the plains, mere plains, as though all secrets of Nature had grown plain. What lies beyond a field when the crop stands? Or what is hidden in the mature crop grown tall remains a secret. But now there is no such secret. Everything is out in the open. Bhujangaiah felt his mind undergoing strange experiences.

When they went to Raja's room wanting to take him too for a movie, he excused himself as he was preparing for his examinations. Bhujangaiah was pleased when he learnt that Raja would join college if he passed his present examination. He was surprised to see the boy who only the other day had not even known how to tie the string of his knickers, grown big enough to join college. Bhujangaiah spent the entire day in Mysore watching a movie, having lunch at Indra Bhavan and returning to his village by the evening bus after purchasing grocery. While returning he had bought two packets of sweets in the sweets shop in front of the small clock tower and as soon as he reached home gave one to Shankara's children and went to give another to his children. When he reached home his brother-in-law stepped off the *jagali*. Bhujangaiah asked him to call the children. Gowri flew out as soon as she heard her father's voice, Umashankara too followed her. Parvathy did not seem to be at home. If she were to be present she would not have resisted passing an ironic comment. Bhujangaiah removed a huge candy from the pocket and gave it to Umashankara and lifted the child. He gave the rest of the packet to Gowri. Soma was in Jakkalli. Bhujangaiah kissed and played with Umashankara and put him down, while he asked his brother-in-law to bring Somanna from Jakkalli. Gurumalla nodded.

Before Bhujangaiah could leave Parvathy arrived like Kali of Bevinahutti, burning. She snatched the packet of sweets from Gowri's hand and threw it. As her eyes fell on the sugar candy, the little child too realized what was in store and put all of it into its mouth. In the past Bhujangaiah would have struck her to the floor and stomped. But of late he had stopped raising his hands on her. He left her to howl whatever she pleased as if he were deaf. The neighbours stood blinking. They were all nauseated by Parvathy's behaviour. They whispered that she would hold her enmity till death. They were all tired advising her repeatedly like they would teach a parrot. Gurumalla too found his sister's behaviour improper. Dogs had eaten all the sweets that the children should have eaten, in front of his very eyes. Gowri had sat in a corner scared of crying too. Fortunately, Parvathy did not beat Umashankara on his back to make him cough up what he had in his mouth.

When Sushila saw Bhujangaiah, who had left happily, returning as if he had been to a funeral she assumed immediately that he must have quarreled with Parvathy and grew silent. Bhujangaiah sat disheartened on the *jagali*, as if nothing interested him. He did not speak properly with those who came looking for him. Pundri alone had sat down gossiping as if he had accepted a challenge to make him laugh. Sushila prepared a jug full of tea and brought it on to the *jagali*. Kariappa who sat in a corner without a sound got up at the fragrance of the tea and served everybody. Pundri began to abuse him as if he had not noticed him till then. "Look at that, God knows where this adiya was, he has presented himself in time for tea." Bhujangaiah could not help but laugh at Pundri's words. Bhujangaiah who by now had enough of useless gossip assigned both Pundri and Cannamalla new responsibilities.

Both of them accepted it without hesitation not caring for what the villagers may say. They were to work as masons for Bhujangaiah, helping him to organize and supervise the labour. They left after promising to present themselves for duty from the very next day, realizing it was better to work than spend time in useless and filthy talk, as they were free from cultivation for the summer. Bhujangaiah gave them each Rs. 5/- towards their smoking expenses, before they left. As Bhujangaiah's contract work was in progress in three or four places he alone could not supervise every work. He had sent word to Shiva through Beard. Shiva was an honest boy. He would find things easy if Shiva would come. He was not to be found yet. Who knows if Beard who was busy with a hundred little tasks remembered to inform him? Even the garden had not been of late attended to properly. If vegetables were grown properly the diesel expense at least could be met. Someone from Coimbatore had come to take a lease on the garden either on weekly or on yearly contract. He had said, he would like to stay in the graden with his family. Bhujangaiah who had asked him to come three days later remembered that he would be arriving tomorrow. He decided to lease the garden to him on a weekly basis. He went to Gowda's house to seek his advice wondering if it wouldn't be profitable to grow sugarcane or vegetables instead of ragi or jowar. Gowda too agreed.

Kalimuthu of Coimbatore spoke Kannada peculiarly. He built a hut on the very day he arrived in the garden, brought his family from Ratnapuri where they lived earlier. His wife's name was Bannari. He had two children. One of them was Muthuvelu who was eight years of age. In a week's time Kalimuthu had altered the very look of the garden. He had taken the help of four labourers with Bhujangaiah's permission. The runnels were straight as a taut wire, the paddy beds were level enough to fill equally from whichever corner the water was let in. He had prepared the beds for eggplant and capsicum and had manured them. The men of Madalli were astonished at Bannari who worked like a male with Kalimuthu wielding a pick. Bannari grew dear to Sushila. Bannari never sat idly even for a while. She had prepared beds for fenugreek, coriander and cole leaves next to the well for use at home. Sushila cooked vegetable curry rarely after she left Mysore, that too only when Bhujangaiah brought some vegetable from Mysore without forgetting. Normally they had curry of cooked peas every day, both times. She would get the leaves of drumstick from somebody's backyard to cook for a change. Bannari promised Sushila that she could eat vegetables all through the nine seasons of the year. Sushila realized when she ate the food prepared by Bannari one day that though they were all labourers whatever little they ate they did cook deliciously. Bhujangaiah was disturbed when he heard from his wife that she who had got the Linga from the Swami of the Main Mutt had in ignorance eaten at the house of Tamil Gaundas. Bhujangaiah had warned when he saw Sushila regretting her mistake, "Forget now whatever happened, but from now on watch carefully what you do." But he used to gobble up without any qualms the tea and snacks that Bannari made. Men could do whatever they pleased, but what would happen if women at least didn't remain strict? With days passing by quick, Muddegowda noticed Bhujangaiah putting on weight. He joked, "If you put on weight thus you will grow fat." That day Bhujangaiah had taken a bag full of cole leaves and tender eggplant, which he himself had chosen from the garden for Puttavva. Raja had come after his exam and was now with his father all three times of the day near the well helping him in various tasks.When Bhujangaiah brought the vegetables everybody was at home. Muddegowda said nothing when Raja said in a week's time his result would be out and then he could join college. Muddegowda who thought his son who was already praised by everyone in the village was wiser than him said nothing that his son may not like. In Hundi every home invited Raja for a meal and spoke cordially to him. Raja honoured all invitations with humility. He was shy to horse around with Sushila as before. It was as if he had suddenly grown in to an adult. He had been to Bhujangaiah's house a couple of times during these holidays, that too perfunctorily. Mallavva the wife of Shankaranna too liked him as dearly as her life; she liked his addressing her respectfully as his siser-in-law, "Attige". Sushila was a little put out at the change in Raja. She had found a vast difference from his present behaviour to the manner in which he had behaved with her in the garden when he had visited during the last holidays. It was as incongruent as the distinction between a snake and an elephant. Yet she had desisted from inquiring the reason for his attitude. She too had been distant.

The incident of Raja seeking admission in a college was a matter of pride for Madalli. None from the village, which had a good population, had ever stepped into a college. Bhujangaiah was extremely pleased. Raja had now rented a larger room in the Alamma Choultry finding his earlier room too small. He had begun to eat at a mess instead of cooking his meal. He had bought a kerosene stove instead of the coal stove, in case anybody from the village visited him. The vessels were all old, though. Bhujangaiah and Sushila visited occasionally but never stayed back as before and returned the same evening by bus. Even if the couple did stay behind they slept in Raja's room without any reservation. Only Raja found such occasions discomforting. This time when Bhujangaiah visited Raja's room he had told him that he had undertaken a big contract and therefore he found it difficult to visit Mysore or his home in Hundi. Raja was proud of Bhujangaiah. His childhood belief that Bhujangaiah was a stupendous person had turned out to be true. How many of his villagers used to speak ill of Bhujangaiah in his own presence? Those very people now sucked up to him shamelessly, extoling him as the moon, the very Indra. Bhujangaiah did not understand any of that. When Raja faulted him for taking all that looked white for milk, Sushila too concurred. Bhujangaiah laughed, "Look Raju, if someone is destroyed it is because God destroys. What can a poor mortal like me do? You tell me." He had spoken in a philosophical manner recollecting Ayya's words that the life on earth was as temporal as the bubble of water, "How does it matter what others say about us? It is enough if we spend the four days of our life as our soul would approve and then discard this sack. Who can live forever?"

***

CHAPTER - 36

The static life in Madalli, which followed merely the cycle of rain and crops, was unduly anxious and scared to do any thing new. Bhujangaiah alone was different from the villagers who staunchly believed that all the pains and pleasures of their life were due to their fate and that none could alter what was written on their forehead. He alone who was always energetic had to be constantly preoccupied with some act or another. As soon as something came to his mind his soul squirmed and would not rest till he acted upon it whether he succeeded or not. The villagers who had made fun of him seeing in his adventure of sinking a well and raising crops the ultimate extent of madness were now astonished. It was now a situation where when there was a festival in the village they went to Bhujangaiah's garden for plantain leaves and vegetables. Now, the person who wished to grow close to Bhujangaiah was the Village Clerk. Bhujangaiah used to give something to him when he managed every time to appear at the garden with a bag whenever Bhujangaiah was in the garden. Bhujangaiah believed in his ancestoral customs, "Never send empty handed a brahmin who comes to your door."

Madalli which boasted of a single well earlier now possessed as many as eight. To those who lived waiting with anxious eyes for the rainy days to come from time to time, knowing they would have food only if it rained or else it was dirt in their mouth, the possibility of raising a crop by irrigating from the well, even if the rains failed, seemed a new miracle. There was a time when people had no memory of cultivation in summer. But now, for those who had the well, summer and rainy season were one. The year round they were engaged in transplantation, weeding, harvesting, etc... The fields of those who had a well were called gardens. All those who had lands in the downs had desired to sink a well. But a few were scared of failure. Finally, a few more made up their mind to sink wells and approached Bhujangaiah. Bhujangaiah was not free. He had accepted the works on the pond of Shindenahalli. As it was a big "Contrat" for him and finding it difficult to manage he had taken as partner a Vadda known to Gavaraiah. His name was Venkatadasi. He looked trustworthy. All the permanent workers were living near the pond where the huts were erected. The workers on daily wages would arrive for work every morning from Shindenahalli, Madalli, Saragur and Katthehundi. Venkatadasi would submit the accounts every week. Bhujangaiah was a little unhappy that he had to disappoint those who approached him from the village to sink a well because of the huge work undertaken. He promised, "Please wait for some time. Once the work ends I will myself get your well made." If some said, "That's all right," others said, "He thinks he is the only Ganenayaka in the village, let's go. We can get the well sunk ourselves", and boarded the bus to Kote.

A new wind began to blow in Madalli. They had reached a stage where they stopped thinking whatever was novel as evil as if they had just then risen from an age long slumber. Gowda had planted sugarcane not finding it right to grow vegetables. Bhujangaiah too had a mind to plant sugarcane this time. But the desire growing in his heart was to plant coconut. The seven or eight plants bordering the garden had already put forth leaves and were perpetually gurgling green. Kalimuthu had said it would do to bring plants of good breed from his place. But Bhujangaiah believed that there was no plant as good as that from Tiptur in the entire country. Gowda who heard their argument decided that the seedlings could be brought from both the places.

Though Bhujangaiah's house was small it was well organized. Sushila strove to live as villagers would, but she could not forget all that she had learnt from childhood. She made breakfast in the mornings and lunch in the afternoon. No one else had the custom of lighting the hearth in the afternoon in Madalli. However rich they were they prepared meals only twice a day. The custom of breakfast, "Nasta", had not yet set foot in Madalli, Though a few visited Bhujangaiah's hotel those days for breakfast if they went to plough or to work in the paddy fields without eating two *muddes* the next instant, their stomach would growl in a short while. Bhujangaiah had lost the habit of eating a meal in the morning. Wherever he worked he would cycle home in the afternoon for his lunch. He went to Mysore with Sushila at least twice a month and had a good time, visiting hotels, cinema, etc.... He forced Karigowda to accompany him to watch Dussehra even though the latter was reluctant. With them went Karigowda's grandchildren and Mallavva. Sushila and Mallavva had found it a bother to look after those children. Raja's room was not big enough for all of them. Somehow they managed to stay there and went sight seeing. Karigowda's eyes welled up when he saw the *Jumbo Savari* of the Maharaja. The king was verily a God. Gowda believed that the Congress people wearing Gandhi Topee ruling the country a grave injustice. Raja found it comical that his uncle and the others stood with their joined hands in respect as soon as they saw the Maharaja's *Jumbo Savari.* When Gowda urged that they return home soon as the Dussehra was over Bhujangaiah replied, "Who knows if we will be alive to see these again." He had decided to show him the fair on the hill, the flotilla festival, etc... before they left for the village. Raja too accompanied them, however much uncomfortable it was. Sushila was joyous. She had felt her blood warming in the proximity of Raja. Raja was distant with her. He spoke familiarly with his sister-in-law Mallavva and whenever she asked anything inanely, he controlled his welling laughter at her rural simplicity and happily explained everything to her.

The fact that Karigowda, who never stayed even a single day away from his village whatever happened, had this time seen Dussehra, the fair atop the hill, the flotilla etc.. had pleased all the members of his household. When he returned he bought a large sack of puffed rice, savories, as well as the holy offerings of God and distributed it amongst everyone at home. Karigowda praised Raja as soon as he saw Muddegowda, "If there is a son who will bring honour to our family it is Raja." Muddegowda was extremely pleased to hear such praise from the lips of his brother. He told his wife that he had got the value back for having sent his son to Mysore on the advice of Bhujangaiah. Though her son had invited Puttavva to visit Mysore for Dussehra, she too had not gone because she was too shy to accompany her brother-in-law. She had sent her last son deciding to go herself the next year. Puttavva too was pleased that her son had deserved such praise by her brother-in-law. When his wife asked, "Why did he not come when he had holidays now?" Muddegowda said, "He is going on what he said was a tour. Bhujangaiah has paid Rs.100/- towards that. His uncle too has given him some money. When I asked why I was not asked, Bhujangaiah said, I have given him money. You need not give anything." Puttavva was scared. "No! what is this tour? That too paying so much money?" Muddegowda answered, "I too asked him like you did. He said that he is going round the country, visiting Madras, Bombai, etc.." Puttavva immediately recalled the picture she had seen through the chink in the coloured tin box a long time ago in the Gaddige fair. She could still hear the words uttered in a sing song voice. " Take a look at Bombai, at Calcutta. See the city of the God of death and justice." She was both pleased and scared that her son had gone to visit such towns. When she asked, "When will he return?" Muddegowda who had no answer replied, "stupid me! I too did not ask." Muddegowda dreamed of the villagers arriving to visit his son returning to the village as an important officer after studying in college, and he talked about it with his labourers. They too nodded their heads with pride, blinking at him.

The excitement of having seen Dussehra had not yet dimmed in the eyes of Karigowda. Someone had said when he went this time that it was the last Dussehra. "The Maharaja was not to sit on his throne or on his golden Howdah. What had the times come to? Had Kalikala, the age of Kali arrived? If the king was no longer there what would happen to crops and rains? How can all and sundry come and rule? If they should have such power let them sit on the throne with their Gandhi cap. They will not escape getting sizzled to ash! Is that a throne on which ordinary mortals sat and ruled? It is the throne on which Pandavas ruled. Kaurava himself got destroyed sitting on it instead of Dharmaraya. I wonder what these useless people will turn into sitting on it?" Karigowda had seen many a time the Maharaja who had died and the present one. They arrived once a month without fail for Tiger hunt and stayed in Gaddige. The forest of Gaddige was a habitat of tigers those days. If one entered that forest having lost one's way one would become a victim of some animal. But now? There were dwarf trees as a sign of their having been a forest. All of it is now a clearing with the irrigation canal going through. They cultivate all the nine months of the year. The water of river Lakshmanathirtha irrigates the paddy fields. Wherever you see it is green. The plains of Gaddige now appear to be better than the plains of Bannur, which was famous for the saying that there was not a time there when one could not get fresh rice and hot jaggery. If only such a canal would reach their villages too! If only the water should flow through to dispel all the destitution of this land! Who knows what generation will see that? Because of that noble soul Bhujangaiah who walks here the wells came. Still, so much of oil for that machine, repairs, who can manage all that? If they had the canal water such troubles would not be there. Karigowda's head was full of thoughts. He had felt anxious since morning. He talked to himself. He was worried about his last son Narayana. It was all right as long as he was alive. Who would look after him next? He would tread whatever path he found. Who knows what would happen? He went to the well in the garden, from there he visited the Pura's pond fields and Hundi. He sat on the *jagali* of his brother's house and talked, as he had never done. He talked to his brother of many things recalling them. When as he saw Puttavva he warned her that the family's future was in her hand. When she asked her husband why her brother-in-law had spoken thus it was a riddle to him too. Karigowda who reached home in the evening sat in the verandah complaining of chest pain and lay down asking Narayana's wife to give him a pillow. She lifted her father-in-law's head and placed the pillow under. She was scared. Would her father-in-law ever sleep at the hour of lighting the lamps? Even when he was down in sickness he would sit up when the lamps were being lit. Why was he thus today? No one was at home. When she came out after lighting the lamp she called the servant Pakali who was tying the milch cow and buffaloes to the pillars and asked him to go to the new house and inform. Mallavva, as soon as she heard dropped the vessel in her hand on the *jagali* and rushed. By then Narayana too had arrived. Gowda who was moaning with pain holding his chest suddenly attempted to sit up and failing fell. When his wife who had stood not knowing what she should do began to cry aloud, Narayana sat down in utter confusion as if paralyzed. In a moment the home was filled with people. Bhujangaiah and Shankara too arrived. Gowda attempted to say something even as his eyes opened wide. By then his tongue had paralysed and he couldn't speak. Before the great scholar Shivarudraswamy, who at Madalli apart from predicting the stars treated illness with some roots and juices, could administer the juice of his Sanjivini root Bhujangaiah had officially announced the death of Gowda by saying he had reached the holy feet of god. The dam that checked the sorrow of those who had sat holding their breath broke and the flood flowed at once to drown the village. People rushed towards Gowda's house from all quarters. Nobody believed until he saw the body himself. How can it be believed if told that the person who was going around like a rock was no more in a minute? Where had such a death waited? How can it come and deal a sudden blow? Is it not merely a game of gods? He did not suffer for a minute, did not even see the face of those who cried. He slept as if he was overcome by slumber. Each one interpreted differently Gowda's death. A man who had won death when a serpent had bitten, when the cholera that shook the village had come, how could he die as if he simply rolled over to the other side? Did a snake bite him again? There was no wound anywhere. The tongue grows dark if bitten by a snake and poison flows. No, nothing has happened to the tongue. What if he was touched by magic? When Narayana's wife shouted in fear Doddalinganna's wife who was in the house opposite had come running and removed the "contamination" and had tied it to the fence. None knew what it could have been. As the death of Gowda was a great riddle for the village so did it feel orphaned now having lost an invaluable soul. Till then no one had prospered by not heeding Gowda's words.

Should death visit so soon upon such a person? Perhaps even death was scared of the evil people who were bent on destroying the village. People said that was the reason why death never went near such people but hunted good people.

Who knew how anyone was affected? But Gowda's death took away Bhujangaiah's inner strength. For good or for ill he was the only person that stood by Bhujangaiah in the town. He had not let go his hand under any circumstance and had ensured his existence as a person in the village. He was neither of his caste nor of his religion. Let alone relatives, even when his own wife deserted him, Gowda hadn't pushed him away even for a moment. He forgave him all his faults. Bhujangaiah felt now that he was really orphaned. He had not been as much bereaved even when his parents died. Now that Gowda who was a shelter for people like him was no more, the village will fill with thorny bushes. They have no escape anymore. Doesn't the God who rides the tiger guarding the village have eyes? Why did he not distinguish between the good and the evil? Why did he call them back who were parents to the village so soon? Bhujangaiah's mind sizzled like a caterpillar falling into fire, Even though it was a week since the death, Bhujangaiah's house was one of mourning. Ayya sang Bhajans on *Oppa* the eleventh day, on the twelfth day when milk and honey were offered and on the thirteenth day when, *thithi* was performed. In Madalli when someone from the Gowda community died they followed almost the same rituals as that of the Lingayat. The only difference was if the Lingayats sat their bodies in the grave the former made their bodies recline. The funeral rites of Gowda was like his own parent's for Bhujangaiah and he did not turn towards Shindenahalli even once till all the rites were performed. When Venkatadasi came a couple of times to submit the weekly account he had told him, "not now". Muddegowda was another soul who had weakened much by the death of his brother. He had never crossed the line that his brother had drawn ever since he could think. It was perhaps because he had known of his end that he had visited Hundi that day and sat so long and spoke all that he had spoken. Even when he left he had done so as if there was something more to say which he would when he visited the next day. But he never returned.

He had gone without turning back to look, taking the path which never returned. When Muddegowda was narrating his brother's visit before death and what his wife had told him, Ayya who was there had explained in his own manner as if Gowda had known of his impending death, "True, true, what can't the honest ones see? That too how would they fail to see him who arrives to take him once and for all?" He consoled the sorrowing Bhujangaiah and Gowda. "One should come by such death. No illness, no one's help was asked either to lift or to sit, he went as if the water he drank did not ripple. One must deserve such death." He took his tampura and began to strum singing songs that talked of this body of clay as not real. What was real was the soul that could not be destroyed, what emerged from dust must return to dust, it was not proper to cry over such a body. The truth of his songs gently percolated into Bhujangaiah's soul.

***

CHAPTER - 37

Before Bhujangaiah who was deeply hurt by Gowda's death could recover another incident pushed him to a corner. Venkatadasi who was a partner in his Shindenahalli pond project had cheated him. He who had been taking care of all the accounts had absconded with his family along with the money from the bills submitted. Venkatadasi. who had never behaved in a doubtful manner even when Bhujangaiah had not paid attention to the works since Gowda's death had all of a sudden cheated him. Bhujangaiah had not known whom to trust and whom not to. Gavaraiah had promised to bring him back wherever he was and when he asked for expenses Bhujangaiah had raised a loan from Muddegowda and given him the money without hesitation. Gavaraiah had not returned even after many days. But his family was still in Vaddarapalya which had ensured Bhujangaiah not to lose faith entirely. As if to prove Muddegowda right who had said, "when problems come they come chasing one another, if we do not keep our advice in our hands we will be inundated", Narasimhaiah greeted Bhujangaiah with a bad news when the former met him in Kote. It was the news of the handing over of the contract on the pond to some one else because the work had stopped for a long while. When Narasimhaiah suggested they could meet the engineer, Bhujangaiah had refused and had returned to the village. The money that Venkatadasi had absconded with was no small amount. He would not have run if he had not got so much money at once. If one felt he could do it, such a large amount would put the devil in anybody, however loyal he may be. He should not have believed Venkatadasi so easily. As Narasimhaiah commented people like

Venkatadasi belong to no settlement or village. Who knows what town they may have ransacked? Such a thing would not have happened if he were a local. Ultimately it was all due to his ill luck. He should have stretched his legs only as far as the length of the bed allowed. He was scared even as he undertook the work that it was not for such as him. Yet he had at some moment picked up courage to accept the work. He was all the time nagged by fear and anxiety from then on. Who knew this would happen? Because of that pond contract mishap a burden beyond his ability had fallen on him. He had borrowed money from Muddegowda and with his own savings he solved his problems and decided that he would never venture into "contract". But the works on a few contracts he had already accepted had been left incomplete at various stages. He decided to leave that profession after completing those tasks. Once the rains fell heavily even Pundri and Cannamalla of late addressed as Bhujangaiah's "mestri' would return to their normal profession of being farmers.

Venkatadasi's cheating of Bhujangaiah had been like drinking a cauldron of milk to those who were envious of his growing stature in Madalli. They thought that he was finished at one go. They were loud in their condemnation, "it burned bright only to go out soon!" In Gowda's death Bhujangaiah had lost his own hand. He had remained aloof not interfering in any of the village's events. He limited himself to his garden. Rudrappa who learnt that as long as Kalimuthu remained, Bhujangaiah had no worries about his garden, met Kalimuthu and tempted him with providing four acres of land under *Daskkat* along with weekly rent if he should begin to work on his garden. He thus shook the roots of loyalty to Bhujangaiah in Kalimuthu. Though Bhujangaiah had remained dispirited for a few days he once more stood up with his normal vigour in life. Bhujangaiah's life was one that had matured with such ups and downs. He who had from childhood been used to such fights was not one to sit with his arms folded today. Whenever somebody sympathised, "Tche, why did such a thing happen?" He would reply, "Ayyo! Let that be! Did we bring anything when we arrived? He who gave took it away. If he wishes to give again, he will." He would then think. "Yes what did he bring? All was due to the mercy of the God who rode the tiger. He lifted you and dropped you whenever he wished. That was his job. Who are we to question him? He was not drowned completely! His limbs were strong yet. He must swim. The shore would be reached today or tomorrow. How much had nobler people suffered! What had they become?" The stories and songs that Ayya used to narrate and sing would make him once more confront life head on. Sushila alone remained detached. Though she was shaken for a moment at the blow her husband had received, she had consoled him asking him not to worry so that he did not sit in defeat. She had also suggested that once he completed the work he had undertaken he need not worry about any of that but live on the garden produce in comfort. The Ayya of Hampapura visited rarely of late. He too had grown tired of roaming. If asked, "Why Ayya, you have not come for a long time?" He would reply "Do I regain youth to roam around thus every day? My time too is reaching its end. Somehow I have to struggle till my Father summons me. My children ask me not to leave the village. But as long as there is strength in the limbs one must perform one's duty. In Ayya's eyes even the blow, which Bhujangaiah suffered in the hands of Venkatadasi whom he trusted, was also a game of Shiva, a kind of test. Shiva was not satisfied unless he tested his disciple by beating and pounding, scorching and burning him. When Ayya said he should not lose courage because of that Bhujangaiah laughed, "Now, why do you say that? Am I sitting refusing water and rice because such a thing happened? What had to happen happened."

As the addiction to tea grew in Bhujangaiah, of late it had grown difficult to find sugar or jaggery. It was expensive at Kaka's shop. Since the sugar control came into existence Kaka used to sell sugar in black market. He would deny stocks occasionally even if he had. Ayya too was addicted to tea because of Bhujangaiah. Now and then Victor of Lingajamba bus used to bring sugar. All this would last only a few days. Gowda himself was installing a jaggery maker. Only the day before they had been to Bannur to engage the Jaggery makers. In two weeks they were to come with the mill. When Puttavva praised him, "Because of your footsteps Madalli now has a jaggery maker", Bhujangaiah was secretly pleased. He dreamed of seeing a jaggery maker in his garden too. If only he had planted sugarcane when he sank the well how much would he not have earned? Kalimuthu forced the vegetables on him. Though there was a good profit one did not find enough money to save. He too had not paid much attention to it. He should pay attention to cultivation at least henceforth. What all had he dreamed of when he sank the well! He himself should water the plants in the garden: raise them like children. But he fell to the temptation of "contract". He had been deceived so far as to forget the garden. Enough of such problems. He should live comfortably not taking up any more jobs after completion of what was on hand.Bhujangaiah sat alone and thought. By then Sushila had served tea at least thrice. As if to cut short the thought process of Bhujangaiah who had smoked a bundle of beedies. Sushila said she was short on sugar for tea. When told to sweeten it with jaggery she replied in the negative. It had been three days since sugar and jaggery were finished in Kaka's shop too. When he told her to borrow some from Shankara's house Sushila laughed at her husband's discomfort, saying, "what kind of extravagance is this of yours?" She went to Shankara's house.

Ayya, who had been to Hundi for alms, had returned in the evening with a block of jaggery from Puttavva's house. Bhujangaiah who got the tea made that very night felt his head swim when he did not get tea in the morning. Who else could be asked? Sushila refused to go to anyone's home to ask. Both ate breakfast. He was satisfied only if it were followed by at least a sip of tea. He said all of a sudden, "I will go to Hundi" and left. Even before Bhujangaiah who was a rare visitor these days could be spoken to he had said, "Puttakka make me some tea first, the rest can wait." When he began to narrate his problem because he couldn't have tea since four days, gowda laughed, "You are a man of comfort. You behave as if nothing has happened when you lost so much money. But now you behave as if the sky has fallen on you because you could not get tea!" Puttavva too laughed. Before Bhujangaiah left Puttavva removed all the five blocks of jaggery she had stored in the jar in the attic and gave them to him. He had run through them in three days, once more facing the same problem. That afternoon as if he had a sudden enlightenment he sat up. He called Sushila and asked her to boil water for tea. When Sushila complained about not having even a little piece of jaggery he said, "That's all right, boil the water." Sushila walked to the kitchen. Bhujangaiah called the neighbour's boy who was playing in the street and asked him to get peppermint from Kaka's shop handing him an anna coin. He gave the boy one. He placed the peppermint on the towel and powdered them with a stone. He went to the kitchen and added the powder to the tea. Sushila was surprised. "What kind of sugar is this?" She asked. When he poured it into two glasses and said, "You too drink it. She found the tea sweet. Yet it was a bit brackish. Refusing to answer her query he said, "I have discovered a new kind of sugar. We do not have to ask for jaggery from any one." Sushila was more curious. When Pundri's group arrived in the evening she understood the riddle of the sugar. She herself ground the peppermints from Kaka's shop and made tea. Kaka too was surprised to see Bhujangaiah buying so many peppermints. In a week's time when Bhujangaiah's adventure of "peppermint tea" spread through the breadth and length of Madalli thanks to the loose mouth of Pundri a few said, "What kind of an addiction is it?" while others expressed their appreciation. " If one thinks of brains it is this son of a fallow woman's!" a few who were also addicted to tea as Bhujangaiah had been, began to emulate his method increasing the demand for peppermint in Kaka's shop. Along with it the demand for his jaggery and sugar sold in black market diminished. Kaka now began to seriously wonder if he should stock peppermint.

Kalimuthu revealed what was on his mind all these days to Bhujangaiah that evening hesitantly, when the latter returned from the garden. Bhujangaiah tried to make him change his mind. But Kalimuthu gave him a week's notice and asked him to look for some one else during that time. Bhujangaiah who said, " as you wish" went home worried when Gavaraiah suddenly materialized out of nowhere. As soon as he saw the latter's face it grew evident that the job on which he had gone had failed. Gavaraiah narrated where all he had searched. Finally Bhujangaiah said, "Let it go, he will neither build a palace with that money nor will I become a beggar." He began to talk about beginning the work on the wells. He thought about how to get the labour and the money for them. He had taken some money in advance from the well owners. He knew it was not right to ask them for money and decided to hock the necklace of golden beads and the guinea necklace in Mysore and get money.

Of late, Bhujangaiah once more began to believe in the forecasting abilities of Shastri of Madalli. A doubt began to assail him, if he had not erred in beginning the work on the pond with Venkatadasi without considering the time's auspiciousness. He called Shastri before beginning work on the wells. The later was immensely pleased. Shastri's belief that man will take the name of God Venkataramana when the going got harder did not take much time to be proved right. As soon as he arrived he told Bhujangaiah that his planetary influences were detrimental and advised him to perform the propitiatory prayers. He also put forth the inevitability of performing the Navagraha puja, to propitiate the nine planetary forces that now exerted inclemental influence. Bhujangaiah who was already bent under heavy losses found this to be like the drought month with extra days. Shastri had painted the fear of planets vividly to him. Everybody in the village was surprised at him having performed the rituals as grandly as he did. Bhujangaiah shook himself up and once more began to work putting his faith in god.

Bhujangaiah had to take care of the garden as well as manage the works on the wells. Kalimuthu had moved to Rudrappa's garden. His wife was displeased at the development. They had never treated them as servants. Kalimuthu had not listened to her sensible advice of not to leave Bhujangaaiah. He who watered Bhujangaiah's growing desire to plant coconut, sugarcane, and make the garden the very eye of the village had left suddenly to work for one who was his enemy. Why was Rudrappa seeking revenge against him? Not only had he never done evil to him but he did not wish it too. He could not understand why they were waiting to fry him and gobble him up. He felt now and again that he should remove himself to a distant jungle from such persons. Perhaps animals are better than them? Yet, he needed people from the beginning. He needed to be in a crowd. Bhujangaiah's mind began to lose peace.

The festival of Ugadi arrived. The works that needed to be carried out now went on smoothly. He now engaged another servant with Amase. He got the wet fields of the garden manured and treated with silt from the pond. People still took his advice because they knew he was not as yet bankrupt. They could find servants in time. As soon as it rained the labourers coming from Madalli disappeared before dawn. Bhujangaiah who had known that such might be the case had taken care to complete the sections of works, which were under the supervision of Pundri and Cannamalla. They too had returned to their fields. Gavaraiah had brought a few more labourers on the very day after the rains from Kote. If the works on the wells were not completed before the rains there would be problems. The works would slow down. The urgency of the owners also had to be considered. Muddegowda had promised to give the saplings for sugarcane. He must ready the garden for that. The labourers had no knowledge of the crop. It would not do if he himself did not look after the crop. Bhujangaiah who had decided not to have those problems began to work day and night so that he could recover some of his losses. He had forgotten Mysore since Gowda had died. In the meanwhile the fact that he was unable to save a victim of snakebite from Shindenahalli had undermined his self-confidence. Sushila was making constant efforts to reduce her husband's worries. She was troubled by Puttavva's questions whenever she met her. Sushila's periods had not stopped since the death of the child in pregnancy. Sushila who never thought of that would be reminded whenever she saw Puttavva and blushed as well as worried. Would she never have children? For whom should she and her husband work thus? As Puttavva said, at least they should have a child of their own who would give them a drop of water at the death bed. Whenever she sat alone the question would suddenly rack her mind.

***

CHAPTER - 38

The rainy season made the job of sinking wells that much difficult. Yet, Bhujangaiah who had avowed to complete the task somehow worked single-mindedly on it. Gavaraiah's labourers worked tirelessly though they were bathed in slush. The work force from Madalli could not match their efficiency. Ignoring the occasional heavy downpour they toiled to remove the rocks from the well. Bhujangaiah voluntarily increased their remuneration when his woman-like heart melted at the sight of their toil. The workers gladdened by that strove with doubled enthusiasm. Bhujangaiah wishing to be free forever from the troubles of this "contract" in two months made them work without respite even for a single day. Muddegowda who saw Bhujangaiah's problem took the responsibility of having the sugarcane planted in his fields. Sushila who had to cook the lunch for all the workers on those three days had to begin before the cock crow. By the time she finished serving food after drawing water from the well, dish washing and sweeping the house, lighting the hearth and cooking the meal she would have had enough of it. Bhujangaiah would bring himself to the fields straight from his work spot at the lunch hour. He would sit with Gowda for the meal discussing things and once more return to his work. Once he returned home he would be busy with accounts. The anxiety of when he would be done with all this remained with him. Sushila having failed in every attempt of hers to keep him happy had grown disheartened at his increasingly strange ways. The entire day the clouds veiled the sky. To step on the village streets meant having the slush squeezing through the toes. One could only walk on the street if the sun shone bright. Though it was a normal experience for the women of Madalli, Sushila found it a hellish experience as she pulled her feet from the slush with each step she took while bringing water from the well. She was surprised to see the others walking normally talking casually on those slushy streets. She would take her steps carefully scared of slipping every time. As she climbed the steps of the house without slipping once, she forgot in her joy of victory to bend low as she entered. The vessel struck the doorjamb and rolled down on to the street. Sushila put down the other vessel on her arm and went to retrieve the fallen vessel. She was shaken for a moment remembering the superstition of Madalli, which believed it to be an ill omen to let fall a vessel full of water in front of the house. The vessel had got dented on one side. She lit the lamp in front of the framed pictures of Gods in the hall after pouring four mugs of cold water on herself before lighting the kitchen fire. She prayed God to save her husband from the inclemental planetary influences. Bhujangaiah had to have a cup of tea before he left home every morning even if there was nothing else. But that day Gavaraiah had come saying he needed to leave for Kote at once. Bhujangaiah had left murmuring without drinking his customary tea. Why was her husband who never ever knit his brow so perturbed today? He had never left home without taking leave of her. Today he had not even turned to look at her. Having given leave to Gavaraiah, he had left straightaway. Sushila had forgotten to enquire if he would be at the fields for lunch. Why was she so absent minded? Something bothered her since then. Nothing dispelled her sense of unease, some anxiety, and a fear that was subtly unfolding deep within. Sushila who sat in front of the hearth gazed at the blazing flames. She sat with a fixed gaze oblivious of the fire burning and the flames reaching out, without pushing the faggots in. She was unaware even when someone stood at her back and called. She woke up only when the person touched her back and called. It was Raja who stood as tall as her. Sushila blushed immediately. She straightened the top end of her sari and asked, "When did you come Raju?" dispelling the dark mood. Raja joked, "It is some time since I arrived. I entered after getting tired of calling." He sat in front of the hearth. Though she felt uncomfortable at his sitting thus in front of the hearth, she comforted herself with the thought that he was not a stranger. She asked, "Shall I make tea?" Sushila was taken aback when he asked," Let tea be. What were you thinking?" She did not know what to say. She sat next to Raja. She noticed him sitting on the floor, "your clothes will get dirty." She laid a plank for a seat. Raja asked her again, "What is wrong?" He looked at her. Sushila's face was downcast. The joy when she had come for Dusshera had disappeared. The frivolousness that made him happy had at once been replaced with sobriety. Sushila had sat silently. The flames that had died down a little when she pushed the faggots in had grown even as the flames in her eyes burned forth, seeing which Raja did not address her again. He got up and went out not being able to put up with the silence. Sushila's behaviour was a riddle to him. Something must have happened or Bhujangaiah must have said something harsh to her. But then why did she not confide in him? Sushila who brought tea in a little while was confused not finding Raja. He was not on the *jagali* outside. He had left without telling her. Sushila blamed herself for her forgetfulness. She went out and looked. There was no sign of him. When she went to Shankara's house on a hunch she saw him there speaking to his sister-in-law Mallavva. She felt relieved; she entered protesting, "Well, how could you leave without a word?" Mallavva laughed when she saw Sushila coming in with the tea. Sushila was not even aware of it. She too laughed as she gave the tea to Raja, "Ayyo! Look at my terrible forgetfulness. I've come with the tea!" Raja said, "Sushila was sitting as if the sky had fallen on her head. I was scared sister-in-law, so I came away". Mallavva enquired, "Why Susi, what happened that you should think so much?" However much Sushila strove to smile and said, "Oh, nothing." Raja did not fail to notice her hiding something behind that smile. Raja had already known of the terrible loss Bhujangaiah had suffered in the Shindenahalli work. He was sure that Bhujangaiah was not a person to worry his head over whatever had happened and sit idle. He looked at Sushila as if he were scrutinizing her while he drank tea. An indescribable pain seemed to have nested in her face. "What was wrong with Sushila who would grow into a spring of joy whenever she saw him?" Mallavva asked the question that Raja wished to, "Why is your face so dour Susi? What happened?" Sushila said, "Nothing Mallakka, I dropped a vessel filled with water at the door even before I could step into the house. I do not know on which side I turned before I got up today." Mallavva laughed, "Why do you worry so much? Did the vessel break?" Raja too laughed. Sushila justified, "No, someone said that if a full vessel is dropped at the door something bad may happen" Mallavva too remembered suddenly what her mother-in-law had said and fell silent for a moment before suggesting a solution to Sushila. That was to tie a quarter coin in a turmeric-smeared piece of cloth and tie it in the name of god to a plant on the edge of some fence. Sushila said, "Yes" and invited Raja home again. He promised to visit the next day and left for Hundi.

Sushila performed what Mallavva had suggested as soon as she went home. She prayed to her husband's personal deity, the God who rode the tiger, and tied a quarter coin to the solanum shrub fencing the backyard. The clouds had made them oblivious to the passage of time. The task of planting sugarcane would be completed that day. That was the last day when she had to carry food. Sushila who felt relieved that by tomorrow she would be free, finished cooking early and went towards the fields carrying food. Muddegowda was overseeing the planting that day too. Bhujangaiah had not returned from the well. Sushila placed the basket of food in front of the pump house and drew water from the well. There was no sign of Bhujangaiah though it was late. Gowda was hungry. The workers too broke off for lunch. Everyone sat for the meal near the well. Amase brought the plantain leaves. Gowda asked for food to be served, as the work would get delayed if they waited any longer for Bhujangaiah; he too sat down. Sushila served. She saved her husband's share sure of his arrival. After the meal they rested for a while and then began to work. Still Bhujangaiah had not arrived. Sushila was ill at ease. The smoldering fears inside her once more began to burn. Again she consoled herself taking the name of god, convincing herself that nothing untoward would happen. She went and stood near the workers thinking that worries assailed her only because she sat alone. But her mind did not find comfort. There was an indescribable anxiety.

The sky was still grumpy. The frozen clouds had not thawed even a little. The trees and plants stood without stirring as if they were in meditation. With no sign of sun one doubted if it were afternoon. Gowda exhorted the workers in an urgency to have the job completed in time. Gowda had not felt curious about Bhujangaiah's absence at lunch. He asked Sushila to go home wondering if Bhujangaiah was still at the work spot or had gone somewhere else. Sushila unwillingly went towards the village. She realised that it was evening only when she reached home. With the sun only then having peeped out a little she had guessed at the time watching the shadow lengthening on her walls. Sushila who placed the basket with her husband's share of the meal in the hall came out to the door. There was not much of a movement in the street. Sushila had not known whose well her husband was getting ready. Where to send word and with whom? It was not the first time that he had failed to come in time for his meal. She had never been this anxious even then. "So why thus today?" Sushila suddenly thought, "What if he should have gone to the fields then? She should have waited for some more time. What else could she do after Gowda asked her to leave? Would she not have waited till evening if he had not said so? If he should ask her she could tell him that.

Sushila's mind seethed with unnecessary thoughts. The mind that had bruised thus since morning slumbered as she sat in the hall. She had lost track of time. She woke up only when Amase had shouted. When he stammered out what had transpired in his gasping voice Sushila felt the earth on which she sat opening its maw. Was all the anxiety that she had felt since dawn a harbinger to such news? What should never have happened had come about. Even the offering made in the name of god had not averted it. Amase described everything before Sushila could ask for the details. Sushila could not even get up to stand from where she sat. She felt the wheel turn in front of her eyes. She moaned loudly with great effort and fell down as if robbed of breath. Amase ran to Mallavva's house and informed them. Mallavva came and sprinkled water on Sushila's face. By then the women from the neighbourhood had assembled. By the time Sushila regained her senses the workers arrived carrying Bhujangaiah. The blood was still seeping through the white cloth covering his face. Sushila began to cry loudly enough to lift the roof of the house even before those who brought him could put him down. A few began to fan and asked the others to leave. They saw to it that Sushila was taken out. A big crowd gathered in front of the house. Each one uttered an opinion. If one said he would be fortunate if he were to live, another said it would be like emerging from his mother's womb again. Shivarudraswamy who was Madalli's doctor too as well as being the astrologer arrived with his bundle of herbs and began to treat him. He shook with fright at his wounds. With his face crushed Bhujangaiah's face had been deformed horribly. None who saw him stopped shaking with fear. Muddegowda who rushed not caring whether he fell, pushed the cloth from the face, and stood with his breath held as if paralyzed at the sight. With nobody knowing what to do all began looking at each other's face. Finally, Raja who arrived from Hundi immediately arranged to transport him to Mysore. Parvathy arrived by then like Kali showering a hundred and eight curses on Sushila. Parvathy fell on the road kicking her legs and flailing her hands and began to abuse Sushila when Bhujangaiah was lifted on to the cart from the house. "Ayyo, my rival, why did you snatch away the fortune of my thali." Soma was not to be seen. Gowri was crying with her mother. Umashankara who watched the goings on of the world of his elders blinked at it and finally growing scared at his mother's howling began to cry too. No one paid any attention to Parvathy's behaviour. Sushila swallowed all her terrible anguish without exhibiting it like Parvathy and hurried with Raja to get Bhujangaiah admitted to a hospital as early as possible. No one believed that Bhujangaiah could be saved. Victor himself shook with fear when he saw Bhujangaiah's face lifting the cloth. Victor reached Mysore in silence in spite of his habitual loquaciousness. He took the bus straight to the Big Hospital. He helped to get Bhujangaiah off the bus and shifted him inside. Raja was secretly scared. Though he wanted to find out if Bhujangaiah breathed properly he was not able to lift his hand to shift the cloth from his face. He stood silently in anxiety waiting with Sushila outside the emergency ward. It was already dark when the doctor came out of the ward. The two were relieved a little when he said there was no danger to his life.

As soon as she reached Raja's room Sushila sank to the floor. As if all that she had bottled within had welled up once more she sobbed. Raja went out saying he was getting something for them to eat without waiting for her reply. Sushila fell down where she sat. Though the light burned it was as if darkness had invaded the room. She was terribly tired. When Raja arrived and called she was shivering and scared even to open her eyes. However much Raja compelled her Sushila did not eat a morsel of food. All sorts of nightmares assailed her the entire night. She sat up screaming in fright a couple of times. Raja did not switch the light off after waking. He too was disturbed. Both had sat for a long time. Sushila did not seem to be conscious of her body. Raja had never seen her thus. Scared of either looking at her again or speak some comforting words to her he faced the wall and slept. When he woke up again the light burned still. Sushila had curled where she sat. Her neck lolled to a side. Raja's heart shook for a moment. He neared her hesitantly. As soon as he felt her hot breath he consoled himself with relief and gently pushed her down on the mat. Sushila was in deep sleep. It was almost dawn. Raja did not shut his eyes again. Already the birds on the huge neem tree in front of the house had grown noisy. Sushila still slept. Raja was sad to see her curled up helpless like a child. As soon as Sushila woke up Raja enquired, "Shall I meet your father once and inform him?" She said no as if she were snapping a stick. She sat up as if she had decided something. She firmed up her mind to face the troubles ahead of her. She spoke to Raja about what needed to be done next, as if she had kicked off the perplexity that had seized her. Raja was surprised to see the sudden change and the self-confidence in her.

***

CHAPTER - 39

Though Sushila had hardened herself and had resolved to manage what was in store, the sight of the ward in which Bhujangaiah was admitted had shaken her at once. On both sides of the huge ward were arranged iron cots. On every cot was a patient with either his arm, or his leg, or his head in bandages. At the foot of each was a red blanket. Next to a few cots were stands carrying Glucose or blood bottles. Sushila walked slowly behind Raja, holding her breath. Raja approached the cot on which Bhujangaiah rested. A red blanket was drawn up to his neck. Only the arm to which the Glucose drip was connected was visible. The head and eyes were bandaged. The swollen lips were slightly parted. Even as Sushila saw him lying without motion she felt her entrails being wringed and head swim. She held on to a leg of the cot and slowly sank down. Raja too went out unable to bear the sight. He spoke hesitantly to a nurse who stood at the door. They had shifted the patient from the emergency ward only that morning. As the nurse informed it would take many days for a complete recovery, and then again, Bhujangaiah would lose his eyes. Raja felt a thorn lodge in his entrails. He stood outside the ward consoling him. He wondered why he was troubled so much and in what way Bhujangaiah was related to him. Yet, whatever front he might wear a terrible agony began to assail him from within. He continued to stand outside not having the courage to see again either Sushila or Bhujangaiah. There were many like him outside the ward. On every face was suppressed pain, helplessness. Knee-length shorts, half-arm shirt, stubbly beard , unkempt hair. The village women stood around with greasy handbags afraid even to speak. Raja who stood watching them felt a bonding with them. They begged the nurses going to and from the ward to allow them in gazing at them in fear and devotion as if they were goddesses. They who went about arrogantly dressed in starched skirts or sari said it was time for the Doctor's round and so would not let anyone in even though they did not stop anybody who wore trousers and shirts like him from entering. They would instead throw a sparkling white smile to match their dress. Raja found their behaviour strange.

All at once those who stood by the door made way and the nurses too stiffened like their starched dresses. A large group of doctors arrived. A senior doctor would examine the patient and the junior doctors who surrounded him would note things down and asked questions as they approached Bhujangaiah. By then Sushila had stood up. Raja had followed them and stood silently. They spoke for a long time in English amongst themselves. They called a nurse and said something to her. Raja could not understand their language. After they left Sushila approached Raja and asked what they had said. Raja was silent for a while and said, "Nothing, he will be all right, but it will take time." The nurse too had said the same thing to Sushila. Even as Raja wondered how many more years it would take him to learn enough English to comprehend their speech a nurse arrived and prepared an injection. Sushila help her. The nurse said she would try to feed him a little orange juice in the afternoon and allowed Sushila to stay near the patient. Raja went out. Sushila had given all the money that she had brought from home. He went to the market to buy oranges and the machine, whose name he did not know, that would extract the juice. He also brought a tall glass tumbler, and a spoon with which to feed him. By the time he returned from the market a group of people from Madalli had arrived. Raja's father, mother, and Parvathy with her children too were there. The surprise visitor was Rudrappa who spewed poison at the very sight of Bhujangaiah. A few who had given advances to Bhujangaiah for the well stood anxiously. Pundri, Cennamalla and Urupa who stayed apart from the group and were just coming in after roaming about, perked up at the sight of Raja. He organized them into three or four groups, as all of them could not visit at once. Parvathy who had thundered so much in the village now stood silently at her husband's feet and sobbed. Raja had warned that none would be allowed in if they should make noise. Puttavva's entrails too silently dripped in grief. Everyone went out to sit under a tree in the hospital premises. Whatever Raja said Muddegowda did not believe that Bhujangaiah would live. He had noticed the juice trickling out when Shushila and Raja tried feeding him. How can he live if he cannot retain even a drop?

Raja asked those who sat under the tree to go and eat something. Parvathy stuck to Puttavva. When everyone got up to go Muddegowda called Raja. Raja, who wondered whether to inform his father about Bhujangaiah's eyes or not, now whispered to him on the way out about his condition and warned him not to tell others. Muddegowda queried, "Well, there is no danger to his life, is there? Raja replied, "They assure that he will live. There is no doubt about it.....only, the eyes......" Gowda sighed deep, "it is enough if he lives, and God shall somehow show a way out." Pundri was disappointed. Muddegowda ordered snacks for everybody and paid the bill. When they came out of the hotel the clouds loomed overhead darkening the sky. A faint thunder, the heat of approaching rain. Raja warned that as it already was time for the bus they need not visit the hospital again. Everyone left for the terminus from where Lingajamba bus started. On the way Shivanna the son of Karikalappa called Raja and whispered. "Raja is Bhujangaiah's survival guaranteed?" Only later did Raja realize why he had asked thus. Muddegowda sternly retorted putting to shame three or four people who were as anxious as Shivanna. "Keep quiet, he will not go with your obligation on him. If that should happen at all I will still be around." Though Shivanna was put to shame at Gowda's words and bowed his head, he whispered in the ears of Dyavanna who too had advanced some money to Bhujangaiah, "Did you know Bhujangaiah has kept all his money with him?" Even as the bus started the rain drops fell with a patter. Puttavva who saw the rain drops falling on her son standing beside the bus cried. "Go home son, do not get wet in the rain." The eyes of everyone on the bus turned to Raja. Raja squirmed. His mother was always thus. She still thought he was a baby. When Raja took leave of everyone saying, "I will see you again," Parvathy called him as if remembering something and took out a few crumpled notes from her bag of betel leaves tucked in her waist and attempted to pay Raja for expenses.

Though Raja refused at first he had to finally accept it under pressure from others. His father too had already given him money and had asked to send a note by the bus if he should require more. Pundri's speech had dried up. It started raining heavily as the bus left. Raja remembered Sushila. She had eaten very little when he had forced her. She must be quite hungry, the poor woman. Though he wished to carry something to eat from the hotel to the hospital the rains wouldn't let him. Raja who sat on the bench in the office of the bus company felt that the rains might not let up soon. The old tyres were stacked up to the ceiling one on top of another in one corner. There was a table and chair in another corner. Behind the chairs, on the wall, was a large portrait. A similar photograph, small in size, was in Lingajamba bus. As on the bus, here too the photograph was garlanded with colourful tinsel. The portrait revealed a huge turban, the forehead smeared with holy ash, a golden necklace with a pendent. Under the portrait was written, "Dharmarathnakara Late Master Karibassappa, son of Doddalingappa." Under it was the legend, "Owner of Lingajamba Bus." Though Raja had gone many times to board the bus, he had never noticed any of it. There was nothing written under the portrait in the bus. It was possible something may have been written. With the tinsel garland covering the portrait it may not have been visible. He gazed out on to the road thinking he should remember to notice it next time he travelled by bus. The rain had slackened. The earth having drunk enough was regurgitating everything as if it did not want another drop. The water flooded the road. After a short while when the rain stopped entirely the roads woke up once more. Raja stepped out onto the road. A car passed by a hurrying pedestrian splashing him with water. Luckily, with all the mud on the road having been washed away in the heavy rains the water that splashed on him was not dirty. Or else he would have been forced to return to his room for a change of clothes before visiting the hospital. He began to step carefully consoling himself that his clothes would dry before he reached the hospital after getting some food packed at the hotel. For all the efforts of Sushila and Raja, Bhujangaiah did not retain a single drop of fruit juice that they fed him. The nurse put an end to their vain effort when she said, " leave it, you can try tomorrow. We are however giving him Glucose." The lights in the ward had already been switched on. Raja and Sushila sat in silence. though Sushila wished to be free from the nauseating smell of the ward and the painful moaning of the patients, she herself was moaning with the agony of being unable to leave Bhujangaiah, her treasure even for a moment. If only he were to stir a little it was like she having found an uncommon treasure. It would have brought sudden life to her sallow face. Raja went out bored with sitting idly. Already the night had enveloped the World. The rain clouds were moaning. Raja went in again, "It is about to rain, let us go." Sushila followed him with leaden feet.

As the two passed the hospital, a few raindrops fell on them. They hurried. The chill wind blew. When lightning flashed suddenly Sushila was startled. The trees and plants swayed under the force of the approaching rain. People hurried home. Though it was not late the shopkeepers were anxious to pull down the shutter. Sushila tried to keep step with Raja dragging her tired body. But whenever she lifted her foot it was heavy as if laden with an iron ball. They took the tonga that appeared in front of them. But, they could not escape the beating rains. Their clothes were all drenched. Lighting and thunder. The rain poured as if it knitted the earth with the sky. The horse undeterred by the onslaught of rain reached them to the room. The rain came down as if the sky had been rent. The trees and plants in front of Raja's room moaned, buffeted by the wind. Now and then lightning flashed and thunder sharded the thick night. As the roof of the room in which Raja lived was tiled they had to spend the night in fear and anxiety at the wild countenance of Nature.

****

CHAPTER - 40

When Bhujangaiah regained consciousness, for a long time he did not realize where he was or what had happened to him. It was as if he had just emerged from his mother's womb. He moaned "Avva" with a voice that emerged from the very depths of the cosmos. He could not move his limbs. It was as if his body had been secured tightly. He could not stir even a little. There was darkness as if his eyelids were permanently fused. Everything was dark. It was as if he were writhing in the womb of darkness, as if he had fallen flat in a strange world. Strange voices. Strange scents. He squirmed in his mind unable to comprehend. He wished to scream aloud. Yet he couldn't. He felt all sound was suppressed within. What had happened? O, God, what had happened to him?

Bhujangaiah's petrified consciousness had begun to thaw little by little even as a snail would timorously put out its damp body from its shell and move in its secretion. He began mentally to examine his own unfamiliar limbs, one by one. "This is the head, these are my eyes, those are the ears, and these were his own hands and legs. All of them seemed to have suffered, and seemed to have lost something." Suddenly Bhujangaiah screamed in terror. Sushila who was outside the ward was stunned for a moment before she rushed in. By then the nurse had already reached him and had firmly held the hand on which the Glucose drip had been fixed. Sushila stood near her husband's head blinking not knowing what to do. Bhujangaiah felt as if someone was deliberately sawing his body into pieces. A deadly pain. Bhujangaiah's moaning slowly increased in a measured manner. Sushila tried to speak to her husband bending near his ears as if the torpor she experienced had at once gone. Somehow the speech refused to emerge. The nurse laughed a little at Sushila's confusion and then said seriously. "Do not be in a hurry. Let him regain consciousness fully, you hold his hand so that he does not move it. I will call the Doctor." Sushila followed the nurse's advice obediently. She grew fairly composed. The soul that was writhing with green wound found a little comfort. The mind that feared a loss, waiting in anxiety, burning, had found a cool spray. Bhujangaiah began to mumble in his sleep. The lips of her husband that were dry all this while were damp now. Sushila who noticed the saliva dripping from a corner of his lips wiped it with her *seragu.*

Bhujangaiah after an entire week had begun to regain the world he had lost. That night Raja and Sushila stayed for a long time at the hospital. Bhujangaiah recognized their voices. But as yet he had not recollected all that had happened to him. The comforting words of Sushila and Raja and the smell of medicine, the sounds that minute by minute confirmed the fact that he was in a hospital, surrounded him. Somehow the night passed. The sky too had cleared. Because the palms of the ward boys and the nurses had been adequately warmed they had paid good attention to him. Sushila and Raja had arrived early. Tayavva at whose house Raja was a tenant earlier was with them too. On the doctor's advice Sushila fed him a little milk with a spoon. The milk was retained unlike the fruit juice. Sushila too felt a little relieved now. The nurse assured her not to worry, as he would recover fast now. Sushila who depended on such an assurance, only today ate her food without worry. She found that the snacks brought by Raja were not sufficient. But shy to ask for more she satisfied herself with whatever available. Raja remembered that his father was to arrive by the morning bus and went to meet him. Many people had come from Madalli that day. Parvathy's father Parvathappa too had come with her. All of them approached the hospital listening to Raja's talk. Muddegowda who felt that his son had grown into an adult and was more knowledgeable than all others was secretly pleased. Bhujangaiah reacted to the voice of Muddegowda who was very dear to him.

When he asked Parvathy why she had not brought the children she started crying in her usual voice, covered her face with the *seragu* of her sari, while her sobs resembled low whistles. Parvathappa alone enquired after his son-in-law in his proprietary tone. He saw Sushila face to face for the first time that day. As soon as he saw her, hate filled the folds of his face for a moment with the black thought that she had sullied his son-in-law's Verashaiva blood. But when he saw Sushila nursing him in a manner more admirable than what his daughter who had been given away with hands held to him, he was disgusted at his own daughter. It was because his daughter had created a scene over little things that things had gone bad. A woman had to remain a woman after all. Doesn't his wife shiver at the very sound of his foot fall, let alone talk to him with her face uplifted after all these years? If a woman does not stay thus what was the worth of a male's virility? As though to put an end to the attempts of all of them to speak to him individually the nurse pushed them all out saying, "All of you go out, the Doctor is on his rounds." Sushila alone remained behind. Parvathy who saw this was further agonized.

Before leaving for Madalli by bus they all visited Bhujangaiah again. He was sleeping. There were paper bags of tangerine and orange, in every one's hand. Sushila silently received the advice and the accolade of every one. By the time they all left, Beard of Kyatanahalli arrived with his Playing cards company friends. Muddegowda told Parvathappa as they emerged from the hospital ironically, "Look Parvathappa you distanced yourself from your son-in-law because he erred once, but not even a lakhier can boast of as many sympathisers as Bhujangaiah." Parvathappa felt ashamed. Only, Parvathy cursed loud enough for people around to hear. Her stance was that it was because Gowda had supported him that her husband had made up his mind to do all that he should not have. She would certainly have uttered loud enough for the village to hear if it were in her village, "It is because of such destroyer of families as you that my life was shattered." Yet, Parvathy was comforted in the fact that her husband had enquired after her and her children. Those amongst the visitors who were disappointed were the ones who had advanced money for their wells. Their efforts to at least bring to Bhujangaiah's attention their presence had failed. When they arrived to see him the second time the nurse had ordered that he was not to be disturbed.

When Bhujangaiah awoke again Sushila let him know of her presence. She nursed her husband with attention according to the doctor's suggestion. She went on whispering in his ears the hope that god would certainly do well by them. He had not been told the terrible truth that he would not get back his eyesight. There was the fear of what might happen when he realized that he was forever cheated of the world of sight. Sushila's totally dried up face was beginning to gain colour again. By now she had got used to the daily routine of the hospital. The moaning of the patients, the strange smell of medicine, the veiling shadow of death as soon as it got dark, the cries of the relatives of the dead which rent the entrails at times, all shook Sushila's very soul. Especially when Raja was not around she felt she was slowly dying. She stayed out of the ward when Bhujangaiah slept. She was scared and shivered to see her sleeping husband. Nightmares crowded her when she sat alone and gazed. Sushila had never thus confronted death in her life. She too had cried like everyone else when her mother had died. But, she had not experienced the cruelty of death. Sushila who had left everyone had found in Bhujangaiah her meaning. If he ceased to be she too would cease to be. The cruel fate was pricking her with a thorn in a game of death and life as if it were tugging at her life line. Sushila took vows to all the gods she could remember. If only he could escape from this one danger! She would never allow her husband to engage on such a dangerous task. What they had was enough. However much one earned there was no end to desire. Sushila's thoughts were cut short when Raja came and woke her up. It was late already. When Raja whispered in Bhujangaiah's ear that they would return the next morning Bhujangaiah said yes. Though Sushila did not wish to leave her husband and go she followed Raja having no other choice. She could not sleep in the male ward at night. Raja once more asked the ward boy to keep an eye on Bhujangaiah. The ward boy replied, "Do not be worried sir, I shall take good care of him."

With night Bhujangaiah's pain too grew. He was in an intolerable agony. The nurse too softened looking at the agony that tore at the entrails. Neither her affectionate words nor her good wishes lessened his terrible pain. Finally, the nurse called the doctor on night duty. Bhujangaiah's cry stopped only after a sedative was injected to make him sleep. Somehow another terrible night passed. Though Bhujangaiah woke up, the difference between morning and night meant nothing to him. He experienced lying in the silt at the bottom of the pond of darkness. No one was lifting him up. He too could not float up by beating his hands and legs. Earlier, however deep the well may be, he would dive. He would dive and rise. But now he was helpless. Bhujangaiah grew aware of the dawn by the speech of those next to him and the shout of the nurses. As he began to visualize the atmosphere of the hospital through his ears, the nurses' sugary words enquired after him. It was as if the pain he had been unconscious of a moment ago had relapsed. Somebody seemed to churn his entire body. What part of his body was without pain? God! Who has set his own body against him and making fun of him? For what sin is he suffering such hellish torture? What did he do that he should not have done?" He was, reminded of what Ayya used to say. "We must pay the penalty for all the wrong that we may have committed in our previous lives. No one can escape His gaze. One must eat what one cooks. Would He ever let go if refused? He had the ledger balancing the good and the bad of not only men but all the eight crores of life forms. Who had the strength to stop His wish of either inundating or setting afloat this world? One must act as He willed till throwing down this bundle." The nurse consoled him as if he were a child, asking, "Does it hurt?" while she gave him an injection and making him drink medicine. The pain of the needle she pricked him with was no pain. His limbs were suffering an agony hundredfold. It was as if someone was tearing out each part of his body. Bhujangaiah had for the first time experienced such hurt in his life. "Why did his body that had presumed on pleasure have to eat such hellish pain on earth? As Ayya said how illusory this body made of clay was! It had been forced to vomit all the happiness it had gorged upon so far. There was nothing inside. What remained was agony, which filled him each passing moment. Was there no end? God! Enough. I have had enough. Call me to you once and for all. I do not want to die bit by bit. I cannot tolerate this terrible agony, not another second." Bhujangaiah squirmed in terrible pain. By then Raja and Sushila too had come. Sushila who arrived hoping he would be better felt her entrails being tugged at looking at him writhing in agony. She had brought the holy offerings after prayers to the nine planetary forces in the temple. She placed it under the pillow without fail. She took out a little holy ash and smeared it on his exposed forehead between the bandaged eyes and head. She began to console her husband as if he were a child unaware of who may watch her, free of her shyness and hesitation. Raja went out of the ward unable to watch Sushila's pain. Sushila who learnt that an operation would be performed that day was worried. The nurse put her agitated mind to rest saying, "Nothing will happen, it is a minor operation." When her husband was moved to the operation theater on a wheel chair, tears streamed from Sushila's eyes. Raja who saw Sushila standing orphaned outside the ward felt tears welling up in him. Finally, he brought her out and as they sat under the tree in front of the hospital consoled Sushila with words of hope of solace. Speech seemed to die between them. They seemed to freeze in silence. It looked like raining again that day. Looking at the growing heat he was sure it was precipitating. Raja had learnt from childhood experience the secret of nature that it was certain to rain if the weather was hot thus. The tree was noisome with birds. Under the gigantic tree others too like them sat in silence. On each face was imprinted a variety of anxiety and agony.

Ayya of Hampapura materialized amidst them as if to break the vow of silence between Sushila and Raja. They never knew from which end and from where he arrived. As usual the tampura was attached to him as if it was an inevitable part of his body. He arrived straight by the morning bus after he learnt the news only the previous day. Ayya felt his sorrow break through on seeing Sushila disheartened. Sushila had grown wooden where she sat. The volcanic fire of sorrow smouldering under her silence touched Ayya with all its intensity. He too sat silently biting his lips saying nothing. Something cold seemed to crawl down his spine. He was scared of asking anything. There was the terrible heat. No breeze blew. The sunbeams filtering through the leaves of the tree seemed like rods of fire. He felt his body perspiring profusely. Raja stood up feeling pins and needles after having sat unmoving, silently, for a long while. Ayya too stood up. Sushila alone did not change her posture even a bit. Raja stepped towards the operation theater. Ayya followed Raja keeping down his tampura next to Sushila. Raja walked, explaining the situation to Ayya who hesitantly querried Raja. The nurse who recognized him asked, "Why are you waiting here? You have your lunch and get back. It will take time." The nurse watched anxiously Ayya who was with Raja dressed in a saffron shirt reaching up to the knees, his forehead smeared with holy ash, his head dressed in a saffron turban. Ayya queried with concern, "What mother, how is he now?" The nurse replied, "Don't you worry grandfather. He is fine. You may visit him in the ward after some time." She walked away in a hurry. They both returned to where Sushila sat, a little assured. They all went to the hotel compelled by Ayya. The sun grew into a fire. Sushila was still dead of speech. Her stomach burned. The city roared even in the scalding heat outside the hospital. Wherever one turned, there were people and racing vehicles. Sushila followed Raja as if in stupor. When they returned to the ward after breakfast the cot on which Bhujangaiah was laid was still empty. They waited anxiously at the door of the ward. By then the nurse whom they had met earlier said, "The operation is over. It was successful. It'll be sometime before he is brought into the ward." The three went out again. Ayya had no other business. He made them talk, He enquired who all had visited from the village. Only Ajappa had not come. Ajappa was one of Bhujangaiah's very close friends in Madalli. How come he had not visited? Ayya was surprised. Perhaps he was away from the village. Otherwise would his soul rest? Even as they talked dark, mountainous clouds began to crowd in from nowhere. The wind that had forgotten to blow began to rattle the giant trees in the hospital compound. They rose up and entered the hospital again. It was evening when they brought Bhujangaiah to the ward. The fretful sky finally cracked open to pour all that it hid within and it rained heavy. There was the din of thunder and lightning. The day turned into night. Whatever was in sight melted. The din of rain was heard even though all the windows of the ward were shut. Bhujangaiah regained consciousness a long time after he was brought to the ward. His eyes were freshly bandaged. He had felt a relief from the terrible pain that had plucked at his life in the morning. Bhujangaiah's mind livened up a little learning of Ayya's visit. He had thought of Ayya only that morning. Ayya had stood frozen in shock at the condition of Bhujangaiah. All that he wished to utter had dried up in his throat. Finally, Sushila herself asked Ayya to speak in her husband's ears. Ayya could not find words to speak. His philosophic speech had been paralyzed. He could utter nothing. Finally he held Bhujangaiah's hands and cried like a child. When he left the ward he merely said, "the God with the fiery eyes will do what is good." and hurried away without even looking back.

***

CHAPTER - 41

Bhujangaiah woke up to the sudden clamour of countless birds even before dawn, which had arrived the previous night to hide on the Royal Poinciana tree beside the ward to which Bhujangaiah was admitted.

Life quickened as something warm seemed to flow through the bones grown wooden all these days. The slumber had not lifted in the ward yet. The blindfold seemed to loosen by itself. It was as if the inertia of many days had ended. It was as if the slush of darkness that had smeared his body and limbs had been sloughed by the touch of light. Even as the sun rays split through him and plucked at the thickened night in the comers and folds of his being, the memories that were hidden in the deep recesses too were awakening. They were bouncing with joy and rising up. They were stepping forth foot after foot now softly, now rough, climbing the hill steeply, descending the valley to grow light and again growing heavy.

He was still very young. Father had taken him to the dyke on the pond to fetch the flowers of the Mountain Ebony for the worship of Shiva. It was as if vermilion had been splashed on the tree. He had felt his hands grow ruddy as he plucked flowers from the branches stretching over the pond sitting on his father's shoulder. That very evening was the "Konda", the event of walking on fire, near the Shrine of Basappa of the Pond. Father too was one of the fire walkers. In front of the temple was the blazing *konda.* When father stood with him on his shoulder to run the pit, his tiny soul too burnt with fear. Father was filled with a frenzy when the horns, the trumpets and the drums shook the soul with their sound, and had run the *konda* even before he could blink. He was filled with surprise when there was not even a blister on the soles of his father's feet in spite of his having walked on the blazing embers. And the sound of the drums sensitized his ears to the sound beyond meaning and filled him with the same ecstatic daring. The sound was transporting him once more to a world that was familiar. In the forest beyond the village, in the black granite hills of Karikallu gudda, the wars of Rama and Ravana or Karna and Arjuna that he played at with his friends, fashioning out of bamboo sticks bows and arrows, their swimming in the pond unspied by elders, the welts on the body due to blows received as if some one had branded them, caught while eating the Jackfruit stolen from the tree of Gowda, someone having found him out by pushing a long pole through the dam of stacked ragi, in which he had hidden scared of his home school teacher, the teacher punishing him by making a small girl sit on his bent back under the porch, the women on the streets giggling at his state as they passed by while carrying water. As soon as Bhujangaiah fell flat on his face into his childhood a few more memories from the depth of the soil began to assault him.

On the very next day after the Sankranthi festival the task of collecting grains in their fields had begun. He too slept with the workers on the winnowing floor. When he melted among the innumerable stars spilt across the sky as he lay on his back, someone had woken him up by poking at him and had run towards the village. He too had rushed behind them. The cry and the shout filled the village as if it had got up to run. Even as he approached the village, his heart had pulsated like the drum at the festival of Mari, the Goddess of destruction. When he pushed through the crowd the sight he saw on the *jagali* of Shivabasappa made him almost shut his eyes tight and shout. Cennura who was his relative had been chopped to death by some body. Though the neck had been cut it had not been completely severed from the body. The blood had still been flowing making a pool. He had felt dizzy and had run home. Father was not at home. Mother was whispering to the old woman next doors on the verandah. Though he wanted to tell them what he had seen he had not found tongue.

The old woman oblivious to his presence had loudly pronounced her judgement before she had left, "Don't they say that the wife of a whoremonger is any day a widow?" When he gently sidled up to his mother and told her of what he had seen, his mother had said in fear, "Why did you go to see all that?" He had questioned in innocence, " Who killed Cennura? Why did they do it?" He had slept without uttering another word when his mother had admonished, "Why do you need all that? Go and sleep". He had gone to bed without a murmur. But whatever he did, he couldn't sleep. The blood that filled the eye, the cries that pierced the entrails then, he could still hear them. After a long while, only when his father had arrived and described all that had happened to his mother he too had learnt. Cennura had been chopped up by Shivabasappa's younger brother, that too in front of his own house. The reason, Cennura had kept Shivabasappa's wife. It was a long time since that incident. The village had forgotten that. The homes of Cennura and Shivabasappa have become one through exchanging women in marriage. Still why did that incident recur in front of his eyes? He had absconded to Mysore a long time after that incident. That too, he had run away in the clothes he wore because his father had said something regarding a small issue. What all he had suffered having run away! When remembered all that his body shivered. Having roamed the streets for a job he finally found one in a bungalow in Vontikoppal. They had two cows. Apart from looking after them he had to take care of odds and ends that the woman of the house ordered him to. She took good care of him. She had showered enough affection to make him forget his home. She was as old as his mother. But she had not been baked and dried up in the fire as his mother was. Youth breathed heavy in her as yet. On that day when he caught sight of her rippling rosy thighs his senses were perplexed. From that moment he was afraid to look at her, he was guilty as if committing a wrong. The fear of grave sin assailed him. She was his mistress who fed him. He must see in her his mother. How evil was he? Why did he desire her so? No, no, it was not his fault. She had drowned him. It was a time when he too was attaining youth. The urgency to pierce the earth and draw out water was intense. However many times he avowed not to yield to such sin, even though he thought of his mother whenever such emotion assailed him, he would melt in the warm folds of her body at a mere touch. No fear or shame bothered him then. His dark, iron like body would become the churning rod for her. Oh! What pleasure he had found then! In the end, one day, her son with a tendril moustache, of his own age had arrived from somewhere. He had his doubts about him. He was not like his father. Always short tempered. She too was very scared of him. One day when they were caught in the act, he had blazed forth. He had rushed to the kitchen for a knife threatening to kill him. He had immediately jumped the tall compound of their house like a wild animal and run. He had never turned back to see. All along the road someone seemed to chase him, as if he were about to be caught. What if he too was dealt with the same fate as that of Cennura? The lopped head hanging, hot blood that welled. When Bhujangaiah screamed in fright everyone in the ward turned and looked at him. The nurse ran to him and held his rolling head asking, "What happened, what is wrong?" Bhujangaiah grew ashamed, aware of his situation. "What a terrible memory he had yielded to! Why did that incident pummel him now? He had not even slept in the direction of Mysore for a long time in order to forget that. Who knows what had happened to her? Why was he remembering it at dawn of day? He had never recounted it to anyone ever. That street, that home, that woman, her mesmerzing eyes. She must have grown into an old woman now. What if he asked Raja to go and look? What will he think? Even if she were alive would she remember him? Tche, why did he at such a moment be tempted into such an illusion? A lightning bolt seemed to course through his body from the sole of his feet to the crown of his head. No, he must ask Raja to find out. Till the nurse came and spoke to him Bhujangaiah's mind had strummed the tuneless string of a strange memory that shot through his entire body. As a sign of the morning routine having begun the nurse had read his temperature and informed him that he had no fever. The noise of the birds had abated in the Royal Poinciana tree. All the birds must have flown. As soon as it was daylight they flew away. They returned once it got dark. Who knows where they go? How long has it been since he had seen all that with the eyes open? He must ask the doctor when they would open the bandage on his eyes. He cannot anymore rot in the darkness. He must open his eyes. It is as if the line separating the light from darkness is erased. It is in the darkness that the memories, the strange evils bother him. They will vanish once he opens his eyes. Otherwise they would bite him and eat him up even in day time. How could he tell this and in whom can he confide? It is difficult for him to know now whether it is morning, or afternoon, evening or night. Even if he distinguishes them he has to do so through his ears." Bhujangaiah's mind suddenly turned to his village, his street, his garden and began to hanker after them.

Sushila was taken aback for a moment when Bhujangaiah suddenly confronted her with the question when the bandage on his eyes would be removed, as she fed him breakfast that morning. He had never been so abrupt. Why so today? Though she too was lost for an answer, she said, "Did not the Doctor himself say it will take a week?" Immediately Bhujangaiah lost all interest. Once more an inertia seemed to envelop him. Somehow today, neither the soft, sweet touch of Sushila, nor her caring words could dispel the smothering sorrow of Bhujangaiah. "Sushila offers lame excuses. He must enquire with the Doctor, "Open the bandage so I can see everything to my heart's content and you may put it back on me. That is all I want. You may then undo the bandage why after a week, even after a month. The Doctor would not say no. He can certainly feel my anxiety. He will oblige." Bhujangaiah consoled himself. Even as the time neared for the Doctor's approach, Sushila grew troubled. Should she tell the Doctor not to tell her husband the truth even before he entered the ward? Or should she ask him to tell the truth? How long can one hide the fact? If not today at least tomorrow he will learn. Let it be today. She took a decision and went out of the ward. The trees and plants were rain washed and shone richly green. Raja left in a hurry saying he was busy. It would have been nice if he had stayed. He appeared to have grown bored. He does not speak properly. When she went to Tayavva's house for a bath in the night he had not escorted her. Earlier he would himself force her to go. How kind a person Tayavva was? She herself smeared oil on her head, massaged and bathed her with a whole cauldron full of water. She had asked in a strange manner why Raja had not come. She had never asked thus. Who knows what she felt? Tche, Raja was like her younger brother. Only till day before yesterday he used to sleep beside her. He was like a child. He is different since he himself began to distance from her. He was not like that before. He spoke only what was necessary. Why was he not intimate with her anymore now? It was all due to their ill fate. Who knew what else was in store for them? Sushila's mind began to grow damp with strange feelings. The plants in the park facing the ward had shed their colourful flowers. Some of them had just fallen, and others had already fallen and had faded. When the nurse called her, "Look, your husband is calling you", Sushila realized that she had all this while stood unawares. Immediately she hurried into the ward as if she had erred. Bhujangaiah who felt Sushila approach and standing near his head called, "Sushi". Sushila gently smoothened the forehead with her hand. "Why did Raja not come?" Sushila was silent. She could not reply immediately. After hesitating a while she said "He is busy he said, he left even as I talked to him saying he will visit in the evening." Bhujangaiah wished to tell Raja something. He was recalling all kinds of things even as he woke up by the hour of cock's crow. He felt the need to see somebody and tell something. Bhujangaiah was disappointed that Raja would not return till that evening. "Sushi, you ask the doctor to open the bandage on the eyes today." He continued without waiting for her reply. " You also ask how long we are required to stay here." Sushila answered, "You ask yourself." She felt pain stabbing at her when she saw her husband speak helpless like a baby. He had never complained thus under any circumstance. How strange she had found his behaviour? He was always the same whether happy or sad. In a moment his face would crumple but the very next he would appear as if nothing had happened. But why did he behave like a child now? Sushila found it very strange.

She went and stood near the door as the time for the doctor to arrive approached. She went near her husband again. Anxiety pricked making one restless. She was confounded for a moment when the doctor appeared suddenly in front of her. The ever smiling doctor inquired, "How is your husband?" and stepped into the ward without waiting for her answer, "Sar, a moment." The doctor stood for a second and asked, "What is it mother?" Sushila could not find words immediately. The doctor who comprehended her problem came out of the ward and gently enquired. When Sushila said, "you inform my husband", the doctor replied unemotionally, "Is that all? It has to be told some day." He went in, Sushila stood at the door. Sushila did not dare enter till the doctor who examined Bhujangaiah and talked to him for a long time came out. The doctor said, "I have told him, he is not upset by it." Sushila stood not comprehending what he meant by "upset". If only Raja were present! She approached her husband hesitantly. She was scared talking to him. Bhujangaiah who found out by the measure of her breathing Sushila's approach, her standing near him and the battle within her called out with love, "Sushi." She moved nearer and softly placed her hand on his forehead. She was surprised to see her husband remaining calm as if nothing had happened belying her fears. Bhujangaiah's silence was the silence that was beyond sorrow. Sushila noticed him uttering to himself after a long time, "It's all Shiva's play!" The bandage tied over the eyes had been removed. The iris had been removed. The wide forehead, the tousled grey and black hair, the prominent eyebrows on a dried up face. The hand, which she had placed on the forehead, seemed to grow damp. Sushila could not guess if it were her husband's perspiration from his forehead or her hand's. She removed her hand and wiped his face clean with the *seragu* of her sari. She looked at the eyes of her husband that could never ever be set right. The eye lashes gently moved. When she remembered that they had been cheated of the fortune of sight and drowned in ever lasting sleep she found it almost impossible to hold back what seemed to well up from within. However much she swallowed, the intensity of pain grew. Her sorrow seeped out without sound. But perhaps the heat of her sigh touched Bhujangaiah, when he called again, "Sushi" Sushila in answer took his hand on the edge of the cot and slowly caressed his fingers. The fingers responded as if they would talk to her.

***

CHAPTER - 42

When Bhujangaiah was discharged from the intolerable atmosphere of the hospital as if he were freed from a terrible curse, the monsoon had ended. His mind and body tingled as he stepped on the soil of Madalli holding the hand of his wife. Even as he took the first four steps there was a gentle drizzle. The breeze wafted cool. All along the way little potholes were filled with water. Sushila went along leading her husband carefully. Now her eyes were not merely hers but also her husband's. She herself carried all the weight of Bhujangaiah and slowly but firmly stepped on. The eyes grew moist, which witnessed Sushila walking him down carefully as she would a child that has not yet learnt to walk. Where was that Sushila who only a few years ago carried the cloth bundle of bangles behind her father and pranced as if joy had found legs and arms? And where was this woman?

Bhujangaiah seemed to find an inexplicable comfort as soon as he realized he was now in a house which he could call his home. As long as he stayed at the hospital his situation had seemed unbearable. Each day and night seemed to stretch unimaginably. As soon as he stretched his body on the bed in his home, whether it was darkness or light, he seemed to at once forget all the agony he had thus far suffered. The pain of defeat that had spotted his face seemed to slip away and was replaced by a certain optimism. The entire day the village visited him. On every tongue was found words of sympathy. Sushila's singed mind was cooled by words such as "God saved him","It was the fortune of your *thali* which saved him". Parvathy too visited with her children relenting. Sushila remembered her vow and offered ten coconuts to Basappa of the Pond. Bhujangaiah could guess at the time by the speech of those who visited. He did not find time a curse. All the sounds heard inside the house or outside seemed to say something to him. They seemed to ask him something.

Sushila kept the lamp near the head when they slept at night. She trembled for a moment seeing her husband's sightless eyes fill with tears. She wiped it with her sari and asked, "Why?" Bhujangaiah did not answer. She brought her face close to her husband's and asked in panic, "Why?". Her warm breath caressed him gently. His lips seemed to quiver. The expression on the face seemed to show an urgency to vomit the suppressed pain. She raised the wick of the lamp higher. The light shone brighter from the clean, wiped glass. Seeing the tears filling his eyes even as she wiped them she felt her entrails being squeezed, "Why? Why are you weeping? I am still strong. I will see that nothing will happen to you as long as I live." She placed her hand on his forehead. Bhujangaiah held Sushila's hand and pressed it lovingly, "Sushi, did you love me only to eat the happiness of these tears?" He began to sob like a child. She gently lifted him and leaned him against her chest saying, 'Thu! Why do you talk thus? Did you not leave all your relatives for me and are now suffering what should not be suffered?" As if Bhujangaiah's fingers too found eyes, his hand felt Sushila's arms. They were the arms that he loved. They would never part from him. He brightened up with the assurance that they would for ever support him so that he would never dry up, the sap within him would never dry up. He began to lisp like a child in happiness. Sushila too felt unburdened seeing her husband's happiness. She raised the flame. She seemed to find the light inadequate. She held the lamp near her husband's face. She desired to see light in the eyes, where no light played. She pushed the cruel reality that as long as they lived those eyes would be cheated of the knowledge of day and night, darkness and light and began to regain an assurance that such strength had not as yet been lost in her husband.

From the chinks in the roof cold air entered. Slowly the minds of both began to find solace. Having put off the light and placing the lamp afar Sushila surrendered her body to her husband's warmth in the blanket, which she had bought having liked it very much. She was busy with the home since her arrival from Mysore. The house having been left empty all these days had wringed her life before it regained its earlier order. She washed and cleaned everything before lighting the hearth. It had been a long while since husband and wife had eaten from the same plate. Bhujangaiah had never found food as delectable as now. He had found each morsel delicious. All the rain clouds filling his head had entirely vanished with the thought that Sushila's body was more delectable than the food he had eaten. He did not feel any want. His body and mind tingled. The thought that he could no more see what he loved nor enjoy what he wished to seemed a mere illusion. All the sights he had seen and enjoyed in the past unfolded their coils; his fields, the yielding crop that swayed to the wind, the crop of sugarcane that must now be laughing gleefully in his garden. The frenzied green in the village that preened wherever the eye turned, the ponds brimming over, the shimmering cupola of the shrine of Basava of the Pond, all, all seemed to wave and call to him. He wished to say so many things. He whispered many things. He began to search with his hands. Sushila found it strange. She felt like laughing. The bodies that had shriveled seemed to at once blossom and grow fragrant. He seemed to drink her up by placing his lips over every inch of her body, as if he would drink up this very night her entire femininity. She had no memory of having ever been pleasured so much. She had never felt thus satiated. It was as if he had just found his youth, like the bull dedicated to god, She had grown totally tired under the onslaught. Sushila who was melting in such pleasure was suddenly, unconsciously, perturbed by the memory of her mind weakening when she lay close to Raja once. Tche! What sort of a woman was she? He was like her brother. That's why she slept close to him. Yet her mind had whined thinking of him as a male. It had remained as a bad dream not to be dreamt. Sushila felt that event growing into a thorn and pricking her flesh blossomed by pleasure. No, she had never been dissatisfied in her husband. But still why did it happen thus? Raja began to sleep separate from that very day. As if a barrier had grown between them. He was not intimate with her as earlier. He did not even meet her eyes while speaking. She too seemed to have a canker within. As if she was guilty.

The raindrops fell softly overhead. The entire village was sunk in silence. The plantain trees were rustling in the backyard. The plants that were tiny when they had left the village had grown tall now. None nursed them. They stood dark and arrogant drinking the monsoon water. Luckily no stray cattle had torn the fence and destroyed the plants. Now she must take care of them. As her husband's tight embrace losened Sushila's mind recalled many things. The chores that she had to do in the morning were many. She shut her eyes forgetting all. Bhujangaiah had melted in sweet sleep. When Sushila realized that a hand of his still remained between her thighs she entwined once more in her husband's nudity. It was an embrace which joined not merely their bodies but even the blood that coursed.

Though the sun had traveled three yards Bhujangaiah had not yet woken up. It was such sweet sleep. How long was it since he had slept so soundly? Sushila who woke up when the servant came knocking on the door, blushed at having slept for that long an hour. She looked at her husband. She doubted for a moment whether he was awake or asleep. The iris, the eyelashes were tightly knit. "No, no, never ever can her husband's eyes speak to her. He can never find dawn with his eyes. Tche, why has she begun to think such things even as she woke up?" She began to do the chores around the house leaving him to sleep longer. The servant brought the cattle from the outhouse to the front and secured them. Sushila swept the dust off the door, sprinkled the dung water, and drew the *Rangoli*. The sign of life that had been absent all these days once more shone in front of the house. As she had not forgotten to light the bathroom stove the previous night, the water was boiling in the cauldron. Sushila poured water on her body till she felt rejuvenated and light. She first wiped all the framed pictures of gods with a wet cloth. She then went and picked the bell flowers growing on the fence in the backyard. She arranged everything for her husband's prayer. She washed the kitchen utensils, kept the brew on and woke her husband up. Though Bhujangaiah did not wish to wake up early he did so compelled by his wife and managed to go to the toilet unattended. Sushila was a bit surprised to see her husband conducting himself thus normally. Though Bhujangaiah remonstrated, Sushila helped bathe her husband. She took out the shirt and dhoti that were not worn for long now from the trunk and helped him put it on before she sat him for the prayers.

Bhujangaiah immersed in the worship of Shiva, which he seemed to have forgotten for long, had no thought of time. The tea that Sushila had brought had grown cold. Even when she brought it again after warming it up his prayers had not been completed. Though she wished to remind him of the tea getting cold, she could not do so. Letting him complete the prayers in his own time she placed the tea near the hearth and began to make rotis. After having taken the names of all his personal gods, he called his wife endearingly. Sushila came immediately as if she were waiting for his call. Placing behind his ear a flower he removed from the *Ishtalinga*, the personal deity, he took the rest and offered them to Sushila. Sushila who accepted them with cupped palms touched them to her eyes and stuck them in her hair. She led her husband to the kitchen, sat him next to the stove and served him roti. The hot roti tasted excellent, with his wife's affection spicing it. They both found no want in their lives. They seemed to have regained what they had lost. Once more everything seemed to be full. When Sushila went out into the backyard to throw the wash, the sky was clean as if it too had been washed. She rejoiced looking at the plants and trees in the backyard dancing in the tender sun.

***

CHAPTER - 43

Bhujangaiah who had returned to Madalli carrying the heavy burden of blindness found it lightening day by day. Sushila began to ease his burden of dark night with her affection so that it did not seem a terrible curse to Bhujangaiah. At the outset he could not get any of his personal work done without her. For all things he needed to depend on one or other of her limbs. He could not leave her even for a second. The inability to see her had intensified his desire to be attached to her constantly. Sushila's eyes would fill with tears watching her husband's desire, his dilemma. He would grow intolerably anxious and emotional if she should leave him for any length of time and grow busy with her household chores. He felt bereft of sustenance. His was the sorrow of one who had lost everything. By then if Sushila should unexpectedly arrive he would relax with the feeling of having reached another shore, be comforted. He would be gratified with the feeling of having owned the heaven, and its indestructible fruit. If she should stand up his whole body stood up with her. If she should step forth leaving him it would be as if the spanning bridge collapsed creating a huge gulf. No, no, he couldn't live without her even for a second. His blind body grew paralyzed without her, stood with outstretched hand like an orphaned child. Yet now and then he felt, "Tche, I should not live. I should not live to be the terrible curse of her life. My desire is a terrible selfishness. Why should she too be imprisoned in this constant blindness paying for an act of some earlier birth? The burden of this blind man is an insupportable burden. Why do you make her too to carry the burden of my sin? Is there no end to my selfishness? No, henceforth at least he must bear his load. He should not be the pest that constantly troubles her in the future as he had done in the past. He resolved thus in a moment. It was truly a moment of decision. In a few days he began to win over his blindness through sound, scent and touch. He had built a bridge, all by himself, to the world he had lost through those things. It was a hardy bridge. It was one that no one could destroy. Whoever visited from morning till evening he identified them through their voice and talked to them. He began to take care of his personal tasks one by one all by himself. His senses had grown sharp enough to surprise him. He began to walk up to the court holding a stick without anybody's help. The people of the village who saw him walking along the street without stumbling were surprised; "He must have eyes on his feet". Ayya's words that there was nothing stronger than the power of will was now known to Bhujangaiah through experience.

That year, it was an unusual autumn that visited Madalli. Though the day broke and the sun ascended the height of ten people in the sky, the heavy mist that rose made it impossible to see even at a forearm's distance what was in front of the eyes. The chill was sharp and cutting, Every one's face and limbs went dry, cracked and bleeded. This autumn filled with poison the veins and arteries of Nature who under plenteous rain had proudly flaunted her green wealth only a few days ago, and turned her pale. Wherever one turned the trees and plants stood grinning at the sky shedding all their leaves turned yellow. The earth was burnt and seared. But Bhujangaiah was unaware of all this. Yet, his body told him that it was the cold of autumn. The sussurrus of leaves that fluttered down caught in the blowing wind when he sat conversing with those who warmed their bodies under the tender sun on the platform round the peepal tree did not fail to twang the strings of his memory of autumn, more so when his companions began to talk of gathering ragi or driving the oxen to the Chunchanakatte fair. He remembered that those were the pictures of autumn. His mind pierced him with the fact that he was no more fortunate enough to see all of them. As soon as Bhujangaiah arrived from Mysore those that had wanted to contend with him about the advances made for the wells had been held in check by Muddegowda of Hundi. He had told them that Bhujangaiah did not have a single paise on him. All the money he had saved had been lost in the "Contract" of Shindenahalli pond and whatever little that remained had been spent along with the advances from the wells on his treatment in Mysore. Sushila had somehow managed the house all these days taking care to see that the heat of their situation did not touch Bhujangaiah. She had never asked anyone for anything. Only when she had no other go had she been to Hundi to apprise Puttavva of all the facts. Muddegowda had himself sent across to them all the grocery and necessities they needed. Assuming that all his loans could be cleared if once the sugarcane crop should yield he stood guarantee and stopped the people from raiding Bhujangaiah's house under one pretext or another to collect their money. Sushila had begun to attend to his garden. She got the servant who still remained with them to plant some vegetables. Yet she could not stay away for long intervals leaving her husband alone at home. Occasionally, Bhujangaiah too visited his garden. He grew sorrowful, silently cursing his fate for having cheated him of the joy of seeing all that he had planned to do on his garden, not that it could ever be done now.

It was a Monday. Even as Bhujangaiah prepared for the prayer of Shiva, Ayya arrived strumming his tampura singing the praise of Shiva. His prayers went on and Ayya sang undistracted. He sang six or seven songs one after another. Each one of them filtered into his soul as experiences. They were the ones composed by Basavanna himself. "If he should continue to attach himself to the life of this world he too will rot as a wretch. This body made of clay must return to dust today or tomorrow. He should prepare the body to meet the feet of Shiva before it passed. He should become a devotee, for that he should win over the illusions of ego and possession. He must reach the feet of Shiva discarding everything. He must wash his mind of all the dirt. This home, the garden, the wife, the village were all illusions. He had assumed them to be everything. He had thought it important to flaunt himself before a few in the village. He had enjoyed everything the body wished for. What all were rejected by great people! Anna had treated the King's treasure as the dust of his feet. Akka had rejected the glory of

King Kaushika's empire. Why did he lose himself in such illusion? No, in future at least he must not waste this life. He must make it fit for a good cause." Though Ayya grew tired of singing, Bhujangaiah was deeply immersed in meditation. Though Ayya had stopped singing his fingers went on strumming the string mechanically. Bhujangaiah rose from his meditation after a long while and spoke to Ayya. They had breakfast together.

Bhujangaiah sat listening to the stories of the devotees for a long time and finally began to converse philosophically, seriously. Though Ayya had found in the life of a mendicant a profession, he was not free of the life of material world. But Bhujangaiah had appeared to have taken a definite decision. He was a person who would not turn back from a decision once taken, even if his life were at stake. Only Sushila sat blinking not grasping the subtle meaning of their conversation. Her mind was preoccupied with the garden. She wished to sow the seeds of Cole preparing the bed next to the well. Even as Ayya left saying it would be late for alms Bhujangaiah asked him to return early in the morning. Sushila too left for the garden saying she would return early. Bhujangaiah went out and sat on the *jagali.* The passers by addressed him cordially. He was used to that, of late. Those who were free would visit him and apprise him of the events in the village. Ajappa alone visited every day. He arrived that day too. While casually talking, he learnt in detail the extent of Bhujangaiah's commitments, how much he had taken as advance from who for the well, whose work had progressed how much, and what was owed to whom. Last evening a couple of them to whom Bhujangaiah owed money had spoken ill of him. When Ajappa tried to defend saying, "Everyone undergoes difficult times, hold on for a while, he will return your money", one of them had said, "Why do you support him? Because of him our well is not completed, what can we do if he does not return the money?" Ajappa had felt as if boiling water was thrown on him. He had not said another word but spat on the ground and walked out on to the street. He told Bhujangaiah of all that now. Bhujangaiah listened silently to every word without getting agitated. He had felt as if someone had flung him into a strange world. The world created with Ayya had at once been lost. All his debtors began to take shape one by one in his mind. His ears began to reverberate with all that they may have said or not said. They all seemed to have turned him into a churning rod. This too was Shiva's play. It was said he tempers, beats and pounds his devotees as a test. Let him test. There was nothing wrong in their blaming him. Would those who give refrain from talking? His was the mistake. He had sat unconcerned. No, no. he must himself go to their doors and inform them. He will not eat even a morsel of rice before returning what was owed to them. If he eats then by Shiva, curse be on him!". Ajappa forced him to sit down when he got up saying, "By Shiva! By Shiva!" "Ayyo! Sit down. Let's see. If not today we can return that money tomorrow." Bhujangaiah said, "Tche, tche, do not talk so. It's my mistake, mine the error. Let us go to Hundi now itself, come." He urged Ajappa. Ajappa promised to go and bring Muddegowda and left. Bhujangaiah's mind was a tree buffeted by the wind. What sort of an amnesia was he victim to all these days? Why did he not realize they would be troubled by him? It was his fate to suffer all this as the result of a crime he had committed. But why should they suffer because of him? Bhujangaiah went on talking to himself, punishing himself till Sushila returned from the garden. Sushila began to prepare the meal talking about the work done in the garden. Bhujangaiah seemed to be muted. Sushila, who found her husband strange since morning, spoke to him after getting the food ready and called him for the meal. Bhujangaiah did not stir from where he sat. When she was insistant he told her of his vow and sat like a stone. Though Sushila was hungry she too sat without eating. Both of them sat silently for a long time.

It was evening when Ajappa brought Gowda from Hundi with him. Both had spoken to each other on the road about the event. Bhujangaiah straightaway told them of his decision. It was to sell his garden and return the advances. He did not allow Muddegowda and Ajappa to speak another word. All their efforts were fruitless. He squirmed as if something had entered his body. Again he sat still as stone. Sushila informed them of his vow. Gowda found it all a bit too drastic. But Bhujangaiah did not retract. As if he had taken some decision Gowda said, "All right, we shall pay them all their dues, call them all today itself Ajappa." Ajappa went and brought them all himself. Excepting one or two the others felt strangely hesitant. But everyone sat with his head bent without looking at Gowda's face. When Gowda asked Bhujangaiah who he owed what, Bhujangaiah replied, "I do not remember well, they themselves should be asked." Gowda questioned seriously, "Have you not written down accounts?" Bhujangaiah replied, " I had written everything down in a Kalanidhi Pocket Calender. It was always in my pocket, when the accident took place I do not know what happened to it." Gowda enquired Sushila. She too had not known what had happened to it in the anxiety of that day. They were caught in a terrible situation. Gowda at the very outset took the name of the "God who rides the tiger" and said "He is now in a bad situation; mind your morals and tell us what is due to you." Each one mentioned the amount due to him. Bhujangaiah said, "The amount's right." Only two of them had told the truth. What was the basis on which to call the others liars? The amount due to all of them was quite big. Even Gowda did not have that much of cash on hand. Yet he courageously said, "You come tomorrow morning, when all your dues will be settled." Gowda said, "Now that it is resolved, eat your food. We shall talk about the rest later." Ajappa too joined his voice. Only Bhujangaiah would not yield. In the end he drank a glass of milk, thanks to the efforts of Gowda and Ajappa. They left saying they would call again that night.

The decision of her husband to sell the garden to return the loan was a terrible blow to Sushila. The dream of the garden was dearer to him than to her. But when he himself decided to sell it she was speechless. Tampura Ayya too was saddened to hear the bitter news when he arrived in the evening. Only Bhujangaiah with a divine attitude said in a detached manner, "Our claim on the garden was only for this long a period, forget it. Why should we sorrow when Shiva who gave it took it back from us?" Ayya did not utter any word of philosophy now. But he felt that Bhujangaiah's behaviour in the morning was perhaps an indication of what happened now. Gowda put whatever money he had at home and borrowed the shortfall from a few of his close acquaintances in the village and some how managed to clear the loan of Bhujangaiah the very next morning as promised. If one said, “There is none as honest as Bhujangaiah” another said, “Ayyo, all that he had earned from long years he had secreted with Gowda, he took it out now.’ They all returned happily. Before Gowda and Ajappa left after completing the transaction Bhujangaiah made them sit down taking a vow. He insisted on selling the garden that very day. Bhujangaiah had repaid only one instalment on the loan he had taken from the Bank on the garden. The rest of the loan stood as it was. Along with that the money that Gowda had given that day together was almost the value of the garden. Who would buy the garden in the village? Bhujangaiah did not wish that it belong to anyone but Muddegowda. But Gowda was scared that people may talk loose. Finally he acquiesced to it when Ajappa and Ayya forced him to. Even Sushila did not find the arrangements to her dislike. By then she too had grasped that it was not possible to retain the garden shouldering such heavy loan. When Bhujangaiah insisted that the sale be registered in a week’s time Gowda murmured his ascent and got up.

The news that Bhujangaiah’s garden had been sold to Gowda spread the breadth and length of Madalli that very day. If the event created sympathy among a few, it made the others glad. But Bhujangaiah’s Dharmic wife Parvathy was enraged. She cursed Gowda loud enough for people on the street to hear. Patel Rudrappa had stoked her anger saying, “Do you now realize why Gowda behaved in such a subtle manner? He seems to have bought the land very cheaply.” Though Bhujangaiah had confirmed the selling of the garden to Muddegowda he had not finalized the amount yet. When Bhujangaiah saw the loud heaving of breath in the village already, he urged Gowda to go with him to Kote immediately. On one fine day, in the end, they prepared the sale deed, registered it at Kote and Bhujangaiah’s mind found peace when he handed over his garden to Gowda. After all his loans were cleared there was still some money left on hand. He requested Gowda to safe keep it for him. He could ask the servant to leave after the Ugadi festival.

Gowda himself arranged for the sale of the oxen for a good price. The two milch cows at home were grazed by hired help. They decided to hand over the money left to some trustworthy person so as to take care of them both till the end of their lives. Whatever the rest may think Sushila and Bhujangaiah were glad of the arrangement.

The autumn had ended. Summer arrived. Day after day Bhujangaiah grew inward. Tampura Ayya camped in his house without fail whenever he visited. Bhujangaiah was never happy however many Songs of Morals he sang. He pestered Ayya to sing more. Having heard with total attention to the songs, many of them were now on the tip of his tongue. He began to sing to himself whenever he was alone. Only Sushila began to grind her body day and night like a piece of Sandal wood, as if her life's ultimate goal was to serve her blind husband.

***

CHAPTER - 44

As the days passed by the relationship between Tampura Ayya and Bhujangaiah grew intimate. He could live without him but not without the Song of Morals he sang. Whether he comprehended or not there was a magical power in them. He would grow free from the pain of the knowledge of being caught in the prison of this world while listening to those songs, thinking of their meanings, gaining whatever his experience was capable of, on many a night and day. Sushila would both be surprised and scared on seeing her husband immersed in the illusion of hearing, growing glad, smiling secretly, keeping a measured beat on his lap, for long even after Ayya had left. He would not wake up from his reverie however many a time he were called. At such times Sushila would really be frightened, scared to speak, and sit looking at her husband in stupor. Now and then she began to worry if some spirit had invaded her husband. Bhujangaiah's manner changed day by day. She could not confide to anybody, yet could not rest without telling anyone. Though cattle, calf, garden and the money saved all melted one after another, not even a single day had Bhujangaiah, let alone sorrowed, uttered a word about it to anybody. He never asked his wife how she managed provisions. Whichever mendicant visited the village he had to be offered hospitality at his house. He seemed to suddenly remember something he had forgotten and invited the Swami of Madapura home and performed the holy worship of his feet. Having sent words to Gowda for a cart he visited Gaddige along with his wife. He forgot himself in prayers, holy ablution, and bathing, for a whole day in Gaddige. The picture of the Lord with the fiery eye who buried himself alive was etched in his mind.

Gaddige was a thick and impenetrable forest once upon a time. It was said that the Lord with the fiery eye came riding a tiger there when it was the lair of terrible tigers. He sat in meditation on the bank of the large stream that flowed there. He did not stir in a week, a month. Whenever the Lord awoke, from somewhere a cow arrived to yield milk in his mouth. Many people had seen the cow going without fear even though there were many tigers. And the tigers too remained unexcited, ignoring its presence. Bhujangaiah felt that the people who had seen all that were blessed. On one fine day the Lord with the fiery eye opened his mouth before the people who visited him. Till that day he had never spoken to anyone nor had he allowed anybody speak. That day when he opened his mouth let alone people, even the beasts of the forest sat listening to him in surprise when he told them of his "live burial" next to the Bael tree. People sat waiting to witness that miracle. The hour assigned by the Swami approached. He sat in the pit he had himself ordered. The waiting devotees built a tomb with stones from the forest. From that very day that place had grown holy. The stream in front of it had become Pavanaganga, the river that washed away one's sin. The flood of devotees that began that day is as yet flowing. It is said a day never passes without a devotee arriving.Today there is a quaint temple around the tomb. It was built by the Maharaja of Mysore who went on a hunt to that home of tigers. He had also built a bungalow behind the temple to camp, whenever he visited. He never left on the hunt without first offering prayers to the tomb of the Swami. Even now once a year, the present Maharaja comes and offers prayer. However, he comes now not because of his addiction to hunting but with devotion. Even if he should forget, the Swami summons him. A hundred and eight such pictures slid before his inner eyes. Even now a Bael tree stands adjascent to the sactum sanctorum as if to bear live witness to all that transpired in the past. Each one has an opinion about the tree's age, and about the family of the priest. The family too lived in Kuttuwadi village near the forest from the time the Lord entered his tomb. Even now the ancestral home of the family stands there. Since the day the glory of Gaddige drew the attention of the Maharaja he has provided the priest with a home in the holy place, sent money from the palace for the worship and holy ablution. But of late all has changed. The Maharaja himself is no more. It is the spirit of the age. What has to happen will happen! It is all Shiva's will.

After Bhujangaiah returned from Gaddige he grew far more detached. He burned in regret that so much of his life's time had been wasted in the illusions of attachment to the family, and temporal happiness. At one time whenever he saw a comely woman the desire to possess her would unchecked, grow intense. He had experienced everything. One day he had felt that it too was enough. Yet again though he had never had an inordinate desire for money he wished to be singular among the many around. He desired to grab like the miserly beggar who would grab more than what his fist can hold when suddenly a heap of money fell in front. The desire for land was similar! How it had rendered him into an illusion! He had thought every inch of his field and his garden was all he wanted. He had taken that to be the essence of life. He had worshipped the temporal with single mindedness ignoring truth. He had not known that all belonged to the almighty. All his life had been spent in the night of "me" and "mine". It was perhaps due to that Shiva took away his eyes. He had punished him appropriately for his misdeed. If it was not for that his senses would still be hanging on to the mundane, forever. Every now and then, the body that eats salt and spice, moans for the pleasure. He has not yet been able to transcend it entirely. Whenever it hungers after small pleasures he feels how wretched he is. That too must be Shiva's play. He might still be flailing, tapping and beating at him. It is all a game of fun for him. Let him play. Let him be frivolous as long as he wishes. He is the one who caught him in all the skeins. Let him free him from them now.

It was Monday night. On the *jagali* of Bhujangaiah was held the devotional singing even after midnight with a mendicant from Devanur having arrived with Ayya. People were involved in the hymnals of Shiva, sitting on the *jagali* and on the street on mats. Pundri continued to offer his shoulder whenever there was a special event in Bhujangaiah's house. As there was still a feeling among some puritanical Lingayats of the village that what Sushila touched was impure, Pundri and Kariappa themselves distributed the seasoned green gram *Kosambari* and *Guggari* made of chick pea to the assembled people. Once in every two days Pundri's group visited Bhujangaiah and spent time with him. But they now found his company unexciting. The frivolity of the past had gone. The atmosphere, which certainly did not encourage lewd talk, would constrict them in a few minutes. Day by day they too began to grow distant as a result. Still, whenever they arrived Bhujangaiah was filled with some sort of energy and the anxiety to spring out from the suppressed depth would surface. But then he would be subject to a feeling of being reined in, an artificial reticence. The visitors too would leave silently. But today even after the hymnals were over, the distribution of the holy offerings ended, though the villagers had left, Pundri and his friends were gossiping with Sushila. The Ayya from Devanur sang well. The villagers had made him sing till he was tired. Bhujangaiah was happy listening to some more new songs from him. Pundri had noticed the Devanur Ayya stealthily glancing at Sushila though he appeared to be a morally upright person. Sushila did not suspect him who looked well mannered. She treated him as she would Ayya from Hampapura. But Pundri alone felt that this ayya should not have stepped into Bhujangaiah's home. However good a woman Sushila may be, in a moment anything could happen. Of late, any one who called himself a mendicant, wherever he may come from, invariably camped at Bhujangaiah's home. Pundri had not found it proper. In Hommaragalli, where his relative lived, there was a staunch devotee of God. His name was Cannabasappa. He was well known for his hospitality to all the mendicants who came by, providing them with bath, food and a holy meal. One fine day a mendicant arrived from God knows where, when the house woke up in the morning he had eloped into the night with Basappa's daughter-in-law. They had not been found yet. Pundri who remembered that incident wished to tell Bhujangaiah about it. But how to tell him? He did not enjoy the same familiarity with Bhujangaiah as before. Yet, Sushila was no easy woman. Will she who resisted all of Narayana's overtures waste a look at this man? Thu! Why did he have to remember such things? Though Pundri consoled himself, unable to stop himself, he called Sushila and gently whispered in her ears, a lie of good intent, that the mendicant had no good name, and that she should be careful about him. Sushila's face was stern for a second and she said, "Oh, let that be Pudaswamanna, if he does not behave well in our house we could ask him to leave immediately." Pundri left with his army as if he had achieved something of consequence. Sushila felt like laughing after Pundri left. The manner of Devannur ayya was suspicious. He had deliberately talked to her asking her for odds and ends. Bhujangaiah did not seem to be aware of any of these things. He was immersed in himself. He requested Ayya to bring him a book of verses by Nijaguna Shivayogi. Of late Bhujangaiah had someone or the other to come and read to him to pass time. Or Sushila herself read to her husband. Sushila was glad that her learning to read long ago had now been put to use. She read for her husband. She was satisfied even though she did not understand what she read. As soon as Devanur ayya heard his request for books he wondered, "How will you read if you get the book?" Bhujangaiah replied, "Ayya, though God took away my eyes he has given me two more." Even as the other struggled to interpret, "You mean..." Ayya of Hampapura answered, "Look, as long as mother Sushila lives Bhujangappa will not want for either his eyes or for anything." He praised her virtues. The ayya of Devanur was surprised at this, "It is good! This girl then knows how to read too!" He too praised her. But a detached Sushila, as though she had not heard any of their conversation brought the mat out for them and spread them on the *jagali*. The ayya of Devanur asked for water to drink before sleeping. Sushila brought a big vessel of water out so that he wouldn't trouble her again for water and bolted the door. That night passed. The ayya of Devanur who had wished to stay there for a couple of more days realized she was not a fish that could be caught by any of his hooks, and left the place the very next day. When ayya from Hampapura stayed for two more days and left he was stunned to hear another of Bhujangaiah's desires. He wished to have a tampura and cymbals like the ones Ayya had. He asked Sushila to enquire the cost and pay Ayya. Sushila looked at Ayya questioningly. Ayya did not speak for a long while. He too had not known their cost. More than anything, why did Bhujangaiah have such desire? Begging had been the profession of his family. Who knows of what age these tampura and cymbals were? Since the day he took to the profession he had possessed the very same instrument of gourd, only he had some times changed the strings. The scales were the same and same the tune. Why did Bhujangaiah ask him these? He did not understand anything immediately. Sushila asked, "How much money would you require?" Ayya seemed to wake up, "Ayyo! Will it cost a hundred? A gourd, a stick, a string that is all. But why does your husband desire this?" Sushila too blinked her eyes not understanding any of it. Finally Bhujangaiah himseif said, "Nothing, whenever I am bored sitting alone it helps to sing the songs. It would be good to have a tampura, that's all." Ayya said, without further queries, "Is that all? Then take my tampura and cymbals. I will make new ones for myself." He placed the tampura in front of Bhujangaiah and as if he was deaf to his protest left the place taking leave of Sushila, "I will come again, mother." Sushila did not know what to do. Bhujangaiah lifted the tampura, caressed it along its length once and moved his fingers over the string. He tingled to the tune of it. His fingers began to strum the string unconsciously. The sound that emerged from it began to fill his being. He began to sing to himself overcharged with emotion, beyond anybody's hearing. The songs of Ayya, in his own tone, began to reverberate within him. But Bhujangaiah began to shiver where he sat when he felt something stopping them from springing out from deep within him.

***

CHAPTER - 45

To villages like Madalli which only under rains spring into green gold there is not another month as fructuous as the month of Sravana. The ponds and tanks were all full. The rain clouds hung heavy overhead. Around the village, in the fields of jowar where the crop stands tall, the corn heads seemed like pompoms of coral on the green plants. They stand mature, full with milk. Even on paths worn away under foot the green was springing forth. The flocks of birds have returned having disappeared for this long. Whatever tree or plant you look at you find them warbling. Every inch of the village is imbued with energy that springs forth in the flurry and joy of children who shoot from slings and shout at the birds that attack their crops. On every face, irrespective of their class, is a kind of satisfaction. In every house in the village where one ate merely curried cereal, there was now some vegetable served. Snake gourd and luffa hang under the trellises in the backyard of every house. Sushila's backyard too had four or five varieties of vegetables. They were plants which Sushila herself had grown, preparing the bed, deweeding and loosening the soil around the roots with a small pick. The brinjal plants were heavy with bunches. Sushila who sat at the back door gazing at them was reminded of the garden. She wondered what the few plants she herself had planted were like now. She wished she could visit it once. If they had retained at least an acre of land she too could have gaily gone about amidst a crop of ragi or jowar like all others. Sushila's eyes filled with tears. Their life was unlike those of others. It had no change of rain, wind or sun. They were confined to their little house and themselves. Sushila could not pass time from morning till evening. Sitting around her limbs seemed to be growing heavy. No, she should not sit thus. She should do something. She too should move around like others. The day ended for her if she fetched water in the morning. She was confined to her house the rest of the time.Why should she not go for deweeding or transplanting like all the other women of the village? However well-to-do a family may be every one worked. But she had not lived such a life from her childhood. She had to learn everything afresh. She did not even know how to hold the sickle to cut the weeds. Moreover was it possible for her to lift and tie her sari up to her thighs and transplant in the slushy rice fields? At such times if one thinks of the eyes of men who bring the seedlings devouring the thighs of women, one wishes to be buried in the slush with shame. No, no. She cannot do that job. She grew up different. Yet, had she not roamed from village to village carrying the bundle of bangles behind her father? Then she had found roaming the stony, thorny paths of villages selling bangles behind her father better than the torture of her stepmother at home in Mysore. In a few days she too had learnt to slide bangles on women. Often she would break one or two. She still remembered her father praising her and patting her back seeing her expertise. Sushila remembered her father. How long was it since she had seen him? Why did he have to persist in his hatred for his daughter? The father who could not tolerate anyone saying a word against her had entirely forgotten her. Who knows how he was? If her mother were to be alive no such thing would have happened. Somehow things had came to pass. The entire village had now accepted her. It had forgotten her crime. She had behaved well enough to shame those who used to deliberately, in order to hurt her, talked lightly of her at first in the village as the "kept woman" of Bhujangaiah. Now they themselves talk to her cordially. Still her father's heart was like stone. When she was in such trouble it would have been enough if he had visited them once. He had apparently told that she was not born as far as he was concerned. In such a kind heart how could such harsh a word emerge? Her head had swum hearing that. Sushila woke up when her husband called her wanting something. Or else who knows how long she would have gyrated in the hidden whirlpool of memories? The Ayya of Hampapura who left that day had not returned. Now and then the sound of tampura would emerge in waves from Bhujangaiah's home. Sushila alone heard his songs that he intended to sing for himself. Sushila who sat silently in front of her husband who would strum the tampura whenever he was bored would be lost in thought. The money left from the sale of the garden had almost been spent. She too had spent unthinkingly on the puja of Swami's holy feet, the holy ablution of God, in the service of the mendicants visiting the village, according to her husband's wish. She had not thought of tomorrow. Because he gave could one go and ask at Gowda's house? Only the money left for caretaking was left. At least that much was saved because of Gowda's forethought. Or else that money too would have been spent by now. They should wait for Sankranti for the sustenance paddy or ragi to come. What would they eat till then?"- What if somebody arrived who was dear to Bhujangaiah? Sushila explained the situation at home to her husband after much thought. Contrary to her fears, Bhujangaiah was not disturbed by her words. He sat unmoved as if he had not heard his wife. Let anything come, whether wealth or fire. There was not another sharper test than winning over this world living in it. Whatever impediment was put forth one should not be deterred by it. Even that was His game. It was He who dropped him into the slush of this world of sorrow deliberately. The one who had to lift him out of it was also He. He had not wasted what he had earned. It was put to such good use as feeding the mendicants, which Shiva appreciates. Why should he worry then? Why should he lose the peace of his mind?

Sushila could not understand even one word of her husband. All her thought was of tomorrow. Though she was perturbed for a moment at her husband's lack of concern about the future, she tried to tell him at least what she had decided to do about it. Just then Bhujangaiah began to sing a song he had learnt from Ayya:

> "I forgot you, trusting a cur called gold!
> I have time for money and not Linga
> God of Kudalasangama
> Can the dog which loves refuse
> Ever know the taste of Amrutha?"

Sushila called him for lunch as soon as he finished singing. Of late Bhujangaiah grew oblivious to hunger and thirst if he sat singing. Sushila would not let go till she made him eat at least four mouthsful when it was time. When Sushila broached the matter of what she planned to do he did not say no. Neither did he acquiesce. Sushila who took his silence for permission left for Mysore the very next day. She went straight to the house of Tayavva and sold her guinea necklace at a Shetty's shop that Tayavva knew. That was the only valuable ornament which she owned. When the very eyes for whose pleasure she wore it were gone what use was it to possess? Sushila did not worry even for a second at the loss of her ornament. She first bought a basket and then went to the shop where her father used to buy stocks. The owner of the shop, Sethji, failed to recognize Sushila at the outset. When Sushila introduced herself he recollected everything gradually. It had been a long time since her father too visited the shop. The last time he had come he had wept talking about his daughter and then had never returned. He had not known whether the father had changed his business or had left the town. The Sethji who said that if he were in town he would have visited his shop at least once took out the bangles that Sushila needed. Sushila while selecting the bangles informed the Sethji of the tragedy that had struck her life. Sethji's eyes too grew damp. After having loaded the bangles into the basket Sethji offered her a better deal than he did to anybody. He also informed his son and other workers to give her bangles at the same price even in his absence.

The fact of Sushila having started selling bangles again resulted in a variety of reactions in Madalli. Bhujangaiah did not find his wife selling bangles an insulting work. He had believed from the outset that any job that was undertaken with a pure mind was not lowly. Sushila visited only the villages of Madalli, Hundi and Kyatanahalli. She would leave in the morning and return by evening. She earned enough for their food and clothing. As soon as Sushila began to sell the business of the bangle seller who used to visit the village went down. But as there were a few houses that did not care either for Sushila or Bhujangaiah they still bought bangles from him. Patel Rudrappa ridiculed Bhujangaiah sitting on his *jagali* with those who said yes to all that he uttered, "See how the drop of milk at the nipple dried up. I had already predicted this.I had said that Gowda was planning to snatch his garden, did that prove false?" One amongst them said, "Ayyo, let that be. Did Bhujangaiah's father earn that? Gowda of Hundi helped him buy it, now that he is in trouble he has given it back." Rudrappa got enraged, "Hey Kempnanja, you too are a useless son of a fallow woman! God punished him for leaving the house where he was born, for having left the wife he had married, and for having sat leaving his religion for a whore he has kept." Kempnanja too got livid. He could not put up with Rudrappa who injected venom in spite of the entire village sympathizing at Bhujangaiah's state. He got up and left without even looking at Rudrappa. The others too found Rudrappa's words displeasing and followed Kempananja. Rudrappa regretted his behaviour. He too had been grieved at Bhujangaiah's condition. He had not said a word against him since the day he had felt, "Tche! This should not have happened." But why did he have to speak thus to get insulted by his own people? Rudrappa sat in a stupor.

In a couple of weeks Sushila found the business easy. She would finish cooking after bathing her husband, sweeping and doing the dishes and bathing herself. After both of them had their food if she left with her basket she reached home in the evening before the sun set. Whenever she went to Hundi, Puttavva never sent her back without loading her with grains, etc. Bhujangaiah did not venture out much of late. Only when he was bored did he visit Hundi in the company of somebody. When Sushila was not at home Mallavva, Shankara's wife, would occasionally send him tea. Bhujangaiah was still addicted to tea. He could not leave this though he had left everything. This too was an illusion. An insignificant desire like this was enough to bind him to this world. He was not yet free of addictions. He did not know as yet what the right path was. The conflicts in him were not yet over. He had not succeeded in spite of his efforts to merge his mind, that still followed his senses, wholly in the Linga. If anyone slighted him he still got enraged. He had not been able to wash off the excrement called arrogance that stuck to his mind. How could he grow engrossed in the meditation of Shiva till he could entirely free himself of the desires that peck and eat at him? Bhujangaiah could very well understand his weakness. Whenever that happened his soul grew agonized and he experienced an intense sorrow. When such a moment approached the only implement of escape he had was the tampura. He would express all his heartburn in its waves of sounds, strumming its string,

One day Sushila returned home from her business. She stood with fear and surprise seeing a large crowd of people in front of her house. Some one seemed to pull at her very life. She reached home with her life held in her hands. Fortunately the tragedy that she had imagined had not transpired. The cause of so many people gathering in front of her house was her husband's songs. Bhujangaiah sat on the *jagali,* and was singing at a high pitch strumming the tampura. Sushila had never heard her husband sing thus. The bronze voice was unfamiliar to her all those days. As soon as Sushila arrived the crowd dispersed in half a moment. Sushila woke her husband up by touching him. He had not known since when he was singing thus as if some spirit were on him. When Sushila led him inside the house and told him, Bhujangaiah could hardly believe it in his surprise. Was his voice that melodious? Did really that many people stand and listen to him? Was it possible for him to sing? Bhujangaiah repeated his questions ten times. Sushila was tired answering him again and again. Finally Bhujangaiah believed his wife. He decided now to sing every day. If a few listened to what he sang and if in them grew the devotion to Shiva his life's work would be achieved. He must sing. He must sing well enough for Shiva to appreciate till there was breath in him.

***

CHAPTER - 46

Parvathy who had shut the door of her heart as she had shut the door of her house to her husband would find her eyes water when she felt a thorn pierce her soul whenever people spoke sympathetically of the situation of Sushila and Bhujangaiah, though she retorted, "If one does what one should not what should not happen will happen. If he says that he is happy with that wretched usurper, leaving his children, would not Shiva have eyes to notice? They eat what they cook. Why are you worried?" As the days passed by her stone like heart was mellowing. Even under the most enraged moment Parvathy had not grown susceptible to the flashy, colourful web of words that Rudrappa uttered. Though he had felt sorry for Bhujangaiah he had not had the satisfaction as yet of having wreaked vengeance on him. He had attempted all kinds of guiles with the thought that if he should have Parvathy for a mistress he would have succeeded in stamping under foot Bhujangaiah. But Parvathy had treated him worse than a dog in the matter. After all his plans had failed though Rudrappa had spoken hot headed on a couple of instances he had sat with his tail tucked under him without a word, scared of her loud mouth. Occassionly Parvathy did think about selling and throwing everything here and going to her father's house instead of witnessing and suffering all this. She had found it difficult to spend time with her younger brother Gurumalla who was an unwilling guest. Still scared of the accusation that she had gone putting out the light of a home where people had lived and prospered, she managed to lead her life. Now and then, somewhere in a corner of her mind, a thought that her husband may voluntarily come and knock on her door still smouldered. If that happened, her severed relationship may once more get mended, and then she too could serve her husband, not for people to appreciate but for God who rides the tiger to appreciate. In Parvathy's heart, which entertained such a desire, there was no place for Sushila, not even enough to accommodate a mustard seed. Parvathy would not forgive her not only in this life but in the next too. She had many times cursed that the fate that met her husband should have met her usurper. She had resorted to many black magic practices to hasten Sushila's death. When she learnt that in spite of her having called the Kadukuruba of Hallada Koppal on the new moon day and sacrificied a black billy goat to bring evil upon Sushila, not a single hair on her body had been harmed, she had grown defeated.

On the other hand Sushila's desires and wants were entirely in contrast to those of Parvathy. She had forgiven let alone Parvathy, even Narayana, who had attempted to rape her. She had herself spoken to him on a couple of occassions in Gowda's house. He had bowed his head in shame. She had no other world apart from her husband. She did not even remember that in Madalli lived some who disliked her. She was busy with herself and in her husband's services. Whether it was rain or shine when needed she went to the houses that called her, forgetting all her troubles, carrying the basket of bangles and decked them with bangles smilingly. She had learnt from her husband to swallow her misery. Though she had lost all she had not sat shedding tears over it. She earned enough for not only the two of them but also for those mendicants who arrived in the village enquiring of her husband. The blow that had struck her heart was the death of Tampura Ayya who had left without looking back from their house after giving away his tampura and the cymbals as soon as Bhujangaiah had asked for them. He had grown one with the Linga shortly after he had left. He had not got up from his sleep after having eaten in the company of everyone at home and after having spoken to everybody happily. If death visited, it should visit thus. Sushila had really lost an intimate friend in him. He was the only one with whom she could talk with an open heart of her sorrows and of her joys. He was of their own family, advising them, consoling them whatever happened. Sushila could not believe that he would never ever come strumming his tampura. When the news of his death arrived her husband had sat for a long time without stirring. Even as her fear and sorrow grew intense he had woken from his meditation and had spoken of so many things! She had not comprehended any of it. She only remembered well what he had said in the end, "Devotees have no death, he became the vast in the vast." Let alone the meaning, she did not get a whiff of its essence too. Of late, Sushila had grown scared of his habit of talking to himself. Those words too were like riddles. She could not dredge their bottom. Raja had come from Mysore recently. He had visited their house once. He too had not understood his speech. He who had come to speak happily had returned without opening his mouth. Not only he, anyone who visited had the same experience. That was why as days passed even those who were dear to him seldom visited him. He was unconcerned about who visited and who hadn't. It was enough to have the tampura. That was his everything.

The smile that bubbled on Sushila's face had now vanished. On her forehead had begun to appear a few creases one by one. A seriousness far beyond her age had resided in her face. Now and then when she went alone to Kyatanahalli or Hundi, memories of the past assailed her. Those were paths on which she had roamed happily with her father. Every tree and plant lining the path to Hundi was forever familiar to her. They all remained unchanged. The pond that one passed midway was familiar. Whenever she climbed down the steps on the waterside to wash clothes, Mallavva's words of warning reverberated in her ears even now, "careful dear, the stones are slippery with moss, you may slip and fall." She had not slipped, thanks be to god. She had liked the life of this village. Her father too had distanced himself because of that and she had suffered so much! Her coming to this village for the first time with her father, the nights spent on the *jagali* of Gowda, the black shadow of Narayana, her escape from it, Bhujangaiah's hotel, his image standing with the cobra caught suddenly, her being lost to his charm, all those scenes crowded past her eye. Even so there was that evil moment when she with Raja who was younger than her... Sushila had found that one incident a burning ember tied to her *seragu*. However much she strove to forget that, it was smouldering at the depths of her mind. Though, now with her hands full of work she hardly ever remembered what had transpired yesterday, that incident alone had remained in her mind.

When Sushila reached Hundi Puttavva was at home. Her affection for her was unchanged. She was a woman who had known no evil. There was the task of adorning bangles in four or five houses of Hundi. Still she could not part from Puttavva. After Kalavva's death Puttavva was everything to Sushila. The talk veered round to Raja. Sushila felt a thorn had pricked her mind. Puttavva who did not notice the change in expression on her face went on talking about Raja wanting much money of late, his father's unhappiness over that, etc. Sushila stood up saying it was late for her. When Puttavva said, "Ayyo, look at me; I did not ask you if you needed something. If you should want something ask without hesitation. If only we could take our wealth with us when we leave it would matter. Why should we sway hoarding everything for these few days we sojourn here?" Sushila did not know how to answer. She did not want anything. Still to satisfy Puttavva she asked for shelled peas. She left taking it. When Sushila turned back to Madalli after her rounds of Hundi the sun was setting behind the hill of Andana Mallappa. All along the path were the harvested fields. Yet, the rows of Jerusalem pea and Hyacinth bean were green. The cattle were returning to the village. The pond was still full. The paddy fields below the pond having just put forth the ears were a feast to the eyes. The little egrets that stood in a line on the bunds of the paddy field made Sushila wish to stand on the banks of the pond for a while. She put down the heavy basket from her head. Climbing down the steps she washed her face and limbs and wiped with her *seragu*. She felt good, with an indecipherable pleasure. The woods beyond the paddy fields that stretched along, the cupola of the shrine of Basappa of the Pond shimmering silvery amidst the trees that had grown thick on the spillway of the pond were all lovely. Chikki, the washer woman arrived carrying a bundle of clothes as she was getting ready to leave. She could not wash clothes at the stones where the others from the village climbed down the steps, because there would be menstrual saris to wash too. Both reached the village talking about their trials and pleasures.

When she reached home Ajappa was sitting with her husband talking about the village. Of late Bhujangaiah never showed any interest in matters of the village, even by mistake. He would turn an indifferent ear if some one came to tell him of things. But today he had opened his ears to Ajappa. Sushila knew well that Ajappa was a person who had really been affected most in the village by the state to which her husband had been reduced. His soul could not rest if he did not come to enquire after Bhujangaiah every other day. Of late his liquor business too had been in danger. The cause of that was Mahatma Gandhi who had occupied the mind of Bhujangaiah at one period as a great personality. He had said that there should be no liquor shops in the country as it was bad to drink. The rumours said that all liquor shops would be closed down shortly. Ajappa said that he had personally found out from the Taluk Office that the government was considering letting the landless farmers use for cultivation all the palm groves. Ajappa said, "Look, what bad times have come!" Bhujangaiah remembered his devotion to Gandhi, which he had seemed to have forgotten. It had been a long time since he learnt everyday what was happening in the country. None subscribed to the newspaper in the village. Even he had forgotten all that since he had lost his eyes. Master Govindaraju of Kyatanahalli had been transferred and apparently he was now somewhere near Yelandur town. At least if he were around he would have visited occasionally and brought him some information. How many were the changes that had occurred these couple of years! As the conversation proceded, Pundri and his gang arrived. Though many a person had changed they had remained the same. Only the place where they met had changed. They were all surprised to see Bhujangaiah leaving his tampura and talking to Ajappa. Pundri was in a great hurry to tell all that he had withheld these many days. The things he had to tell were not one, not two, but a hundred from the incident of Pilli having entered the house of washerman Manchaiah when he was not around one night and getting abused by his wife, to the event of the Village Clerk, on somebody's suggestion, having copulated with an ass to get cured of the venereal disease he suffered from. Ajappa who sat talking useless things had not allowed Pundri an opportunity to open his mouth. By then Sushila had brought tea. She too grew lively seeing her husband sitting happily with his old friends talking. When she also joined them in conversation, Pundri was miffed. Yet where was the impediment to his habit of gossiping? He began to narrate Pilli's thieveries. If Pilli stayed for three months in the village the rest of the days he went around the country. Though he was in Pundri's group as long as he was in the village, none of them ever knew of his adventures. Pilli who was known for stealing the Jackfruit did not bring it on his shoulder now as he used to earlier. If he walked ahead swinging his arms the fruit followed him behind. Sushila found it funny. Bhujangaiah opened his mouth in curiosity. "How is that?" Pundri challenged his teacher, "What do you mean how is that? You talk so much about philosophy, purana, etc... tell me how that's possible now?" Bhujangaiah not worrying about it laughed, "In my Songs of Morality the secrets of your thieveries are not written. All right, You have won. Tell us now." Sushila was greatly pleased. How long was it since her husband had laughed thus? She sat open mouthed for Pundri's answer. None could hold back his laughter when Pundri explained, "Ayyo, it's merely thus—he had borrowed a plough rope from us. He had tried one end to the fruit and the other end to his waist. When he walked innocently down on the other side of the field like Donnebetta even we did not see anything. How would Motamma who was guarding that tree know, tell me?" Bhujangaiah who realized that Pundri would not stop till dawn if he had his way pretended to remember something and said, "All right, come again when you are free. It's getting late for my meditation now." He stood up. When Pundri's gang left with Ajappa unwillingly Sushila found that she was strangely disappointed.

***

CHAPTER - 47

Bhujangaiah and Sushila's life had no binding of seasons. The wheel of time rolled forward without any ups and downs. Their journey progressed behind it silently. Sushila stepped gingerly, holding her blind husband's hand and guarding the lamp in the dark with her *seragu* so that it did not flicker out. Occassionally she was scared of taking a wrong step. In the next second she would be relieved on learning that the path taken was the right one. The light when she had lit and held, had guided her along the right path even under the most intense of cold wind. Sushila had no fears now. She had experienced enough happiness and sorrow in life. She had not trembled in anticipation of some grave danger; she had not sat down pining for yesterday and the day before because something like this had happened. Her equanimity and the equipoise had come to Sushila both from her husband's wise words and from the branding which time mercilessly inflicted on her from her childhood. Age had already begun its attack on Bhujangaiah. After having lost his eyes he had not agreed to shave in spite of Sushila's insistence. In the long beard and moustache that had grown there was an occasional black hair here and there. It was a wonder to all those who saw him, how quickly he had greyed. Before starting off on her business Sushila would sit at the back door and search for silver lines in her dark head watching in the tiny mirror. She would be disappointed not finding any. She looked at the thick dark hair of hers. Remembering what Raja had said about it on that day she felt some one had tickled her. For a moment her mind wavered. Tche, what memory had come to her? The days of her happiness were over. She had already reached the end of life. Yet, when Puttavva had said, "Are you grown very old? I had my third baby when I was like you now. If you too had a tendril now? There will be. Come let us visit the shrine of the chaste wife, Masthamma once. That mother of mine is very true. If she should open her eyes why one, you will have a house full of children". She had been abashed. She had also felt welling up an uncontrollable laughter. Puttavva's mind was as yet like that of a child. But what can she say? She too had felt now and then the desire for a tendril of her own. The want would fill her when she sat alone in her backyard with nothing to do, when the mind seemed empty. In the very next instant a wave of warning pushed her on to another shore. Though Ayya had died what he had told her once had not. She seemed to have heard it only yesterday. Though she were younger than his daughter he addressed her "mother". He had taken a vow from her sobbing, "Look mother, from now on you are everything to this eyeless sinner. Every thing will be all right if you see him as a child born of your womb. Otherwise his life will be worse than hell here itself." She could not yet comprehend. Why had he made her take an oath? Did he distrust her? He was no relative either to her or to her husband. Yet why did she find in his words the mantra? Why is it that she feels that it was what was guarding her now?

Sushila suddenly got up pushing aside the crowding memories as one would slowly push aside the blanket pulled on in winter before getting up. She was to visit Kyatanahalli that day. When she went in, her husband's prayer was done. Both ate together. Now Sushila too, like her husband would eat next only at night. Occasionally having walked a long distance even if she felt the pangs of hunger she did not touch a morsel. In time Sushila won over that hunger too. Before getting up for meal Bhujangaiah gave her the string of jasmine she herself had readied for prayer to wear on her head. The fragrance of the flower wafted throughout the house. Sushila who got up in the morning went out into the backyard before bath to collect flower and leaves for puja. The jasmine creeper encircling the Mukul tree planted in a corner in the backyard seemed to strike the eye bearing great bunches of white flowers. Sushila's attention had not been drawn to that corner all these days. Already the creeper had stretched up to the branches of the tree and grown unnoticed. She must make the bed and manure it with a little cow dung. It would flower well. The pearly jasmine was a flower she loved from her childhood. She had brought a cutting from the plant in the backyard of Gowda's house in Hundi, and had planted it. Her husband's, words, "This jasmine is so fragrant Sushi!", had Sushila thinking about it. She got up as if she remembered something and walked towards Kyatanahalli. Bhujangaiah wished he could ask her to stay back at home and not go on business that day. But Sushila had already crossed the door by then.

A week later it would be Deepavali. The village was festive. In every backyard were many flowers. The red and yellow colours of Chrysanthemums dazzled the eyes. On the bunds of fields, outside the village, in the Pudding Pipe tree the opulence of flowers hid the leaves. The cows had grown healthy as they had feed wherever they put their mouth. With one cow being pregnant it would drop its calf in a couple of months. With another black cow milking Sushila made tea for her husband and visitors in the one quart of milk and with the rest she made yoghurt or buttermilk. Before this cow stopped milking it was good if the other cow dropped its calf. Or else she had to go to the doors of somebody even for a drop of buttermilk. Tammanna of the carpenter community, who grazed the cattle for a consideration never lazed. She never forgot to warn him when every day he drove the cattle from the shed for grazing, " Tammanna it is a pregnant cow, take care, do not hit her on her stomach." She would return in the evening before the cattle did. She would promise to attend to the completion of adorning bangles if it were to be left incomplete. For another week there would be labour enough not to have time to scratch one's buttocks. She had to adorn everyone with bangles for the festival. However much she hurried the job did not get over. One day it had grown dark before she had returned. The cattle stood in the shed chewing the cud. They had not been tied. The milch cow had the habit of butting. Luckily it had not butted the pregnant cow. Bhujangaiah would know her every movement even as she climbed the steps of her house. Her placing the bangles basket in its corner, going to the cattle shed, washing her face and limbs in the bathroom, lighting the lamp, each one of them were images in front of Bhujangaiah's eyes without light. When her husband asked Sushila with a little irritation, "Why were you so late today Sushila?" she approached and sat near his head in answer. Her husband never slept this early. She was anxious why he who sat and sang till late evening slept so early. She touched his forehead. He did not run a fever. When she ran her fingers through his hair grown long speaking softly, feeling relieved, "Why are you sleeping still?" Bhujangaiah felt he was singing a song, which he had forgotten. It was a song he had somehow forgotten. It was one that could make him forget any pain. Why had he been disturbed at his wife's arriving late? Why do even the smallest of things raise a sound out of tune in him? How selfish was he? Why does the illusion that it was a soul living only for him still bind him? He had not thought of Sushila who laboured day and night for him, even once. He had received from her. He had given nothing in return. Not a single desire of hers was satisfied living with him. How many were the dreams she dreamt about their life? None of it got fulfilled. She had washed her hands in tears all her life. The days of happiness remained in future. In her remnant life of emptiness nothing but pain was added. Still she had never contradicted. She said nothing even when they had nothing. Hers was really the life of duty as Shiva appreciates, as the devotees say. Is there an end to the injustice he meted out in her case? He had made her tread the paths of stone and thorns at a time when she should have dressed well and frolicked. He could not return her favour even in another ten lives. Still knowing all this why had he grown uncomfortable at her returning late one day in her life? Bhujangaiah began to strum the tampura burning within from a contrition, which he could hardly express. Sushila got up and entered the kitchen. He tightened the strings feeling the tone imperfect. He began to sing loudly, strumming again, the Vacana of Anna, "Melt me and burnish the rust of my mind." In the house where everything had been drowned in silence a few minutes ago, life seemed to return. Each phrase of the song was a phrase uttered from the depth of his being. When his song ended his mind seemed to relax too. Light seemed to spread throughout his house. He too seemed to float in that light. Bhujangaiah returned to consciousness when Sushila arrived with tea.

Among those who arrived to hear Bhujangaiah sing was Gurusiddappa of the Little Lane. He needed the *jagali* of Bhujangaiah to spend time come evening. When he saw Bhujangaiah not sitting on the *jagali* and singing though it had grown dark he entered calling aloud. Sushila invited him in. He too was given a cup of warm tea. He drank noisily enough for those in the street to hear as he came out on to the *jagali.* Bhujangaiah too followed. As soon as Sushila tied the lantern to the rafter, some eight villagers arrived one after the other to rest their ass on the *jagali.* Bhujangaiah began to sing with intensity. The new style of singing the Songs of Wisdom, made the audience nod their head. Sushila had repeatedly read the verses from the book that someone had brought only recently. He had made her read six or seven of the songs till he had memorized them. He had begun to sing them with tunes he himself composed. Whether those songs suited the tune or the tunes suited the songs, when those who heard them appreciated, he felt immensely happy. He sang the very same songs again and again. Even to those who heard them they seemed for ever new. Sushila who came to call her husband for supper having finished cooking stood leaning against the doorframe, forgetting herself, unable to call. When they got up for supper after ending the song the food had grown cold. Sushila warmed it again though Bhujangaiah did not wish her to. She found the food tasty.

Sushila had slept wishing to wake up before the cock crowed, but when she woke up it was already dawn. If she visited Kyatanhalli that day then her task would end. The festival was tomorrow. She had promised to visit many houses. They never bought bangles from anybody else. Even if delayed by a week they waited for her. She woke her husband up so that she could finish her chores quickly. Bhujangaiah had finished all his daily routine before Sushila had finished cooking and sat down for prayers after bath. Raja arrived unexpectedly when they were about to get up for their meal. How could she leave when he just arrived? He does not eat meal early in the morning. Sushila lost the urgency to leave early, lit the hearth, made tea and brought it. Raja had without forgetting brought the books which Bhujangaiah had asked for. He read the titles one by one while drinking tea and wondered aloud, "who will read them to you?" Bhujangaiah said, "Why? Is Sushila not there?" Raja gazed at Sushila. Sushila felt shy and changed the topic. Raja who had come home for the festival got up saying he would visit again. Sushila too had her meal and left for Kyatanahalli. She told her husband she would return early and took the foot track instead of the cart road. She never took that path if she were alone. All along the path were bushes grown so thick even if a tiger entered one would not notice. It was rare that people took the path. Sushila was not scared of any body. She felt she had reached her destination quick. She decided to return by that path.

Sushila finished her business just before sun set and returned by the same path crossing the temple of Beeredevaru, adjacent to the pond of Kyatanahalli when she met Beard's mother. The latter expressed her concern, "Why are you going by this path dear? There is no body with you, it will be dark before you reach your village, don't go now. I will send somebody from my hut, you can take the big road." Sushila replied, "I am not scared grandma, there is God to protect." She walked without looking back. Sushila would not have entertained any doubt if Beard's mother had not talked thus. But now if a lizard should make a noise she felt her heart in her hand. By the time she arrived at the Pig's rivulet however fast she had walked, it was already dark with the sun having set. There was just water enough to wet the feet in the rivulet. If she should cross this point there was nothing to be scared of ahead.

Sushila crossed the rivulet without turning her head. When the bats in the ghostlike trees on the edge of the rivulet beat their wings and cried shrilly her breath seemed to stop. She hastened her steps. When she arrived at the fields she sighed with relief as if she had crossed a great danger. The ragi and jowar fields stretched bare after the harvest. She slowed down her pace catching her breath along the footpath winding across like a snake, thinking there was nothing to fear. The village was in sight. When she neared Ankaiah's fields hoping to reach home before dark she saw someone approaching from the linseed fields with the standing crop. When she enquired boldly, “Who is that?” there was no answer. Sushila was scared. She could not scream. She stood unable to lift her foot. When the person neared she forced her breath to her lips and uttered again, “Who is that?” The person who confronted her from the linseed fields was no ghost but Narayana. Sushila seemed to regain her lost life, “Was your tongue dead to answer back? I had almost died. Is that how you should behave Narayana?” Narayana was silent without speech. Sushila stepped forth without fear. Narayana stood in the way like a beast. Sushila stared at him. He was trembling as if he would faint. She perspired seeing the burning fire in his hungry eyes even in that dim darkness. Though she begged him in a hundred ways he took away from her her basket of bangles, lifted her up easily and walked into the fields. He began to satisfy his long awaited fruitless desire not letting Sushila go, however much she screamed and fought. She felt her bones almost break in his iron grip. She loosened her thighs sobbing, having no other recourse.

By the time Sushila reached the village carrying her body that nauseated her as though she carried filth that shouldn’t be carried, the village glowed with lights. It was the custom in Madalli to light lamps not only in front and behind the home but also in the manure dumps. Narayana had eaten her up, biting into her body as if he was taking revenge for a previous birth. There was nobody on the *jagali* when she reached home. The door was half open. The lamp was not lit. When all the houses were glowing with light only her house was steeped in darkness. Even as Sushila stepped in sighing, placing her basket on the porch, Bhujangaiah noticed a difference in her step. She began to weep, sobbing instead of speaking. Bhujangaiah was stunned. He stumbled across to her asking, “Why Sushi? What happened? What happened?” She did not allow him to touch her, “Do not touch it, it has lost the honour of being touched by you.” She moved away from him. He could not understand. She said nothing about what happened in spite of him asking her in many ways. Sushila had never behaved thus since the day he had held her hand. Why was she who had faced all sorts of difficulties behave thus today? Bhujangaiah’s mind was disturbed. He got up, walked holding the walls, removed the basket from the porch and bolted the door. He caressed the back of Sushila who lay on the floor and said, "Get up Sushila, light the lamp first." Her husband's words pierced her. What had she to see lighting the lamp? She too had lost the light now. How strange it was? When the entire village glowed with light her house was in darkness. Darkness adumbrated darkness. Sushila squirmed in an intolerable pain not wishing to live any longer. Bhujangaiah gently lifted her to his heart, caressed her body softly and comforted his wife who squirmed like an insect fallen in the fire, not being able to tell or hide what had happened, as if she were a little baby. Finally, Sushila not being able to bear it told him of how she had fallen into a pit of filth and though drowned had got up without dying. She sobbed and hid her face in her husband's heart. Bhujangaiah immediately felt that he had unknowingly embraced to his bosom a child that was smeared with excreta and for a moment wished to put her down. But the hands that embraced did not loosen. In the eyes that had lost light one after the other the scenes flashed past. The hands that embraced tightened around. He felt like screaming aloud his helplessness for the village to hear. But his voice too seemed to have died with his eyes. In the endless darkness both the sorrowing hearts began to melt in silence.

***

CHAPTER - 48

Madalli had sat up before dawn. Everyone in the household was busy with some task or the other- the women who drew *rangoli* and sprinkled dung water in front of the house, the servants who went shouting towards the pond to wash the cattle, the enthusiasm of children who brought loads of flowers plucked from gardens or from somebody's backyard. Sushila alone had not wished for the day to dawn. The body that had cried the whole night was tired, agonized. She had never been a victim to such weakness. She could not move her limbs. It was as if somebody had nailed her joints. It was as if she heard the sound of death in her pulse. That was all that had remained to comfort her. There was no other way. The wound suffered by her would not heal. The poison smeared on the wound would not allow it to heal. It had infected her blood vessels. Should not the marrow of her body be at once dried? What else remained? She had seen and suffered all pains and hell here. Who knows what awaits with dawn? It was as if some one had stripped her nude in the middle of the street. She must shut tight all the doors through which light enters. She had no need of light. She had already reached the state of no return. Nothing and none would ever lift her from there. Bhujangaiah's blind hands had opened the doors of the house as if to foil the desire of Sushila who had decided to hide herself in the night. Sushila was subjected to further torture as the light poured in to make the darkness vomit forth.

Sushila could not comprehend her husband who behaved as if he had forgotten everything in the morning though he seemed to have been stunned by the nightmare dreamt at night. Her husband's comforting words began to fill her empty cup slowly as the water dripped to fill the plate from the leaky roof in rainy season. His fingers that had grown wet in sympathy gently freed her lashes enmeshed with darkness. The light which Sushila had refused did not seem as terrible as she had assumed. All that she tremblingly feared might happen in her nightmare did not happen. She too mechanically sprinkled the dung water and drew the *rangoli* in front of the house. But the *rangoli* was not as usual the one which passers by stopped a moment to look at. The grazer himself brought the cattle washed. She sat down unwillingly to make the garland at his compulsion. He had brought a heap of flowers from the backyard. Sushila was enthusiastic about making garlands. All that had now dried up. She had no wish to do anything. Still she had to do. People would not remain silent if she did not. They would ferret out everything. Instead of subjecting herself to their torture it was better to swallow all for half a moment and smile. When everybody looked at her with envy she had built a house and lit it. She had taken up the challenge and lived in a manner that won the villagers respect. But now? Though however much Sushila consoled herself she did not find the liveliness of the past. If her husband lost his eyes she had lost her everything. Whether joy or suffering she had lived without cheating him whose hand she had held in front of God, in mind, in dream. Only once she had with Raja that too in dream or in real... she had washed it off from her mind. She had lit lamp to god both times of the day wishing to die before her husband did as a chaste wife. Is this too a game of god as her husband said? Otherwise why would He do this to her? How could she forget what had happened? What can she say when people asked her, why she was dull, whether she was not well? god, can such a mother produce such a son? Why should he be the one in whose hands she suffered? She did not even wish to curse him when she remembered the help that his parents had extended them. If she told her husband he fell silent for a moment, laughed suddenly, and as if he had heard nothing sang to himself some song. Sushila never stepped out on to the street for anything except to bring water even though it was four days after the festival.

Bhujangaiah who through singing had comforted himself from all his conflicts had found the past three months to be days of test of his spirit. Fire danced destruction in him. However much calm he were, Narayana's act had insulted his very character. But the songs of Ayya had saved him from drowning entirely, from losing his humanity even in the most decisive and crucial of hours. They had saved him from growing blind of intellect as he was blind of eyes. He even now felt his body suffer a shock at the memory of all the ills that had raged in him then. This body that someday would rot and stink was made of clay. Why was he attached to it so much? Why did he yield to the illusion that it had grown impure because a dog had licked at it? How many nauseous things had raged within him because of that? They had grown unknown to him and hidden in his own body. They had suddenly began to hiss. They had in a trice made a lie of all that he had achieved all these days. This event too was a game played by Shiva. He had tested him with this. He must be laughing at his defeat. Let him laugh; let him laugh to his satisfaction! Bhujangaiah who sat immersed in some thought, in silence, suddenly burst out laughing loud enough to lift the ceiling. Sushila blinked at him surprised. She shook in fear remembering something. She sat down in a faint as she cowered in a corner not daring to approach her husband to comfort him. After a long while even when Bhujangaiah called her with great endearment as if he had woken up from a deep slumber, Sushila had not lost entirely her fear. This behaviour of her husband affected her deeply. She prayed to all the gods she could remember.

It was a Monday, when Bhujangaiah woke Sushila up before dawn. He completed his daily ritual and sat down for prayer. Her husband had never sat this long. Of late every act of his was strange. Bhujangaiah who finally got through his long prayer stood up as if he realized something, called Sushila and asked her to bring the clothes he had not worn for a long time. Sushila brought everything without a word. Even as she watched, Bhujangaiah wore the dhothi with the bottoms tucked, tied a turban, smeared boldly the holy ash, lifted a bag on to his shoulders and stepped on to the street with his tampura not speaking a word with his wife as if

Ayya of Hampapura himself had returned. Even before Sushila who stood paralyzed watching him could come to the door to stop him he had left beating his cymbals, strumming his tampura, lifting his voice in song to melt the heart of those who heard him. He appeared to the villagers as someone who had descended from nowhere. Bhujangaiah had no conflicts now. His will was strong enough to ignore the laughter and criticism of people. His having sat without a word all these days had resulted in such misfortune. Even begging was a job. Did not the great devotee do it? Who was he? Why had he sat scared of blindness? No, no. He can never sit thus. He too must sing, must cross mortality singing, cross to reach the proximity of Shiva.

On the first day when her husband had thus gone out on the street to beg Sushila had felt her life go out. She wept in an unbearable agony and pain. She beseached him not to go again when he returned after begging. But his decision was unshakable. That day itself was the end of the bangle business. Before she could think of what next Bhujangaiah had begun on his new profession. Within a couple of days Bhujangaiah had sent Pundri to Mysore to get a necklace of Rudrakshi beads and Saffron robes. It was rare to find any one not influenced by the melodious voice of Bhujangaiah who went singing from one end of Madalli to another. Though at the outset people talked all sorts of things at his state they had all been put to shame in time. He had never wished ill by any, cheated any one. Now even the doors of those who disliked him opened to the sound of his song. The hearts of those who heard him grew damp either in sympathy or because of the tune of his song.

Sushila now sat at home all the time as if in stupor. She stuck to herself and to her husband's service. Only Puttavva visited her from Hundi without fail once a week. Sushila was disturbed enough not to talk to her with an open heart. What could she say? She had given some excuse when Puttavva had inquired why she had stopped selling bangles. She too had not pressed. She had been a riddle to her too. None in their house had liked her husband's decision. From that day Raja had never stepped into their house.

Gowda too. Only once had he himself brought the sugarcane juice. He had advised her husband as he would a parrot not to take up such a profession. He had laughed aloud. Gowda, poor man, had sat with his head bent without a word. He had not understood perhaps a single word of her husband. He had left silently. Her husband had gone on talking. When she herself could not understand his words, in spite of her having lived with him all this while, how could Gowda understand? As days passed by Bhujangaiah's profession of begging had grown to be a part of Madalli's life. None could turn him away from it whatever they did. Parvathy herself came home once, fell at his feet and requested him to return home. She got her father to come and try dissuading him; finally she surrendered in defeat and agreed to live with Sushila forgetting her anger, but to no avail. Bhujangaiah's mind did not waver. His answer to all those words was laughter. He laughed to himself even after they left. He either sang or laughed till he was satisfied. Now unlike earlier he went on singing to himself whether visitors were there or not. Sushila who would sit motionless, staring at her husband's face would forget all bitterness. She was engrossed in her husband's songs whether she understood them or not. She had heard many since childhood. But she did not remember anybody singing as well as her husband. On the day when the Swami of the Main Mutt had been invited to Madalli, a day before the Anniversary of Basava, the entire village was stunned to see the Swami sitting, listening to her husband's songs the entire night as if he were spellbound. When the Swami invited him to the Mutt to sing on the festival of the holy night of Shiva let alone others she herself could not trust her ears. But her husband had not grown proud at the invitation, at the accolade. He had just said, "The will of Shiva." Bhujangaiah who had won the heart of the Swami of the Main Mutt had become 'Bhujangappa' to the people of Madalli. Let alone the younger people even the elders talked to him with respect. Whatever function was held in any house of the village whether of Lingayat, Gowda or the Parivara they called Bhujangaiah and had him sing a few songs. Only recently, he had sung at the festival of the "elder mother" performed by the untouchables. Though it had discomfited the people of the Lingayat quarters none had dared open his mouth. Rudrappa who should have exploited such events to blame Bhujangaiah had changed. He had philosophically uttered to those who heard him, "What fort have I to win by seeking revenge on Bhujangaiah?"

Of late the Lingayats of the neighbouring villages had begun to invite Bhujangaiah for *binna* the holy alms. Though Bhujangaiah refused to go that far, they would come with a cart to take him. Though he disliked those offerings, not wishing to hurt their sentiments he would go. Even though there were still two more days to the holy night of Shiva, the Swami of the Madapura Mutt had brought Bhujangaiah to Madapura on the command of the Swami of the Main Mutt and had sent him on to the Main Mutt from there. Bhujangaiah who had taken Pundri with him had experienced no problems till he had returned. Pundri had felt it was his fortune that he was called on such a task. Though it was a week since Pundri had returned from the Mutt he had not yet finished recounting in detail all that had transpired there.

***

CHAPTER - 49

When Bhujangaiah got ready to visit Hundi as if he had remembered something Sushila found it strange. He had already finished begging alms. He had himself told that he had been to his house and spoken with Parvathy, played with Umashankara, and had asked if they would bring the children from Jakkalli. He had now started off in high afternoon to Hundi. It was hot and terribly sultry since morning. He wouldn't listen even when Sushila said she too would go with him once the day cooled a little. Like a truculent child he had refused to heed her words. He stepped out on to the street as if he were in a hurry. Sushila went to the door. The entire village was dozing under the heat. With the heavy showers of the day before, earth was intolerably humid. The earth, which had burnt under the summer heat had not drunk enough water to cool down. Sushila's face too perspired. To head out was to enter fire. She gazed at Bhujangaiah who unaware of all this, slowly progressed opening the path in front with the knock of his stick, stirring the congealed silence of the village street. Sushila who continued to stand even after he turned the corner was troubled by memories. He had never acted thus. Why today? Deep inside Sushila an anxiety began to smoulder. She went in. Inside too was an unbearable heat as if she had entered a boiler. She didn't feel like doing any work. She opened the backdoor. The blaze of the sun did not let her open her eyes. The trees and plants in the backyard too were frying in a terrible heat. The wind forgot to blow. Not a single leaf stirred. It was like the day before yesterday. That was why the devilish rain had come. Today too it must be the precipitation bringing rain. Sushila lifted her head and looked. The sky was a cleanly swept courtyard. Nowhere could be seen a sliver of cloud. He was at home when it rained the day before. He had sat like a child with his face held to the spray at the backdoor. There was an indescribable happiness and joy on his face. The rain had softened everything bringing comfort to her mind too. The life that had shaken under a similar unbearable heat was cooled. It may rain today also. He had left all by himself. What if he were to be caught in the rain on his way back? The mud on the banks of the village pond was clay. It grew slippery under the lightest of showers. Sushila wondered if she should visit Hundi at once. Yet, she seemed to remember something and consoled herself with the thought that Puttavva would not send him alone if it looked like raining.

Moment by moment the heat of the sun grew. The shrill cawing of the crow from a distance was disturbing the silence ever so gently. Sushila bolted the front door and sat under the banana tree in the backyard. The shade of the tree was better than the heat under the tiled roof of the house. The tender shoots of grass alone smiled joyously, grown thick and dark around the washing stone under the banana tree. Only that small plot which daily drank water ridiculed summer and bubbled with the joy of life. Sushila's mind, which had felt everything grown wooden, experienced a stirring of something. Around the banana tree that had stood tall were four to five secondaries with tiny leaves. The black worker ants constantly climbed up and down the smooth trunk of the banana plant, Sushila who was engrossed in their movement began to recollect one by one the events of her life, the pain filled moments, the moments that brought pleasure. Each one stirred her entrails. She had come with misfortune tied to her birth. Even as she escaped from one danger, another visited her. The rare moments of happiness she had, were they really happy? No, no. The terrible agonies hidden in their womb, each one was terrible - even imagining them brought pain! For what crime of hers was this punishment? O God what was her misdeed? Is there no end to her pain? All her pains are memories now. They remain sharp memories now. Is there no escape for her from those that pluck her life out and eat? She was never entirely defeated by any event. She did not sit ever in defeat. She had assumed that all was a part of His game as her husband had said. She believed that none of that would happen without His cruel intervention. What terrible curse had begun to haunt them? She had sworn to live without betraying him whatever happened, even by giving up her life, so that he would live in peace. But then, O God! Had she really conducted herself unblemished? Someone seemed to dip his hand deep within Sushila's disturbed soul and stir for a moment. Narayana had attacked her that day as if he were testing her absolutely. She had really lost when he held her with his brute force. Why did her mind too slacken along with the body that could not protest? Has she not felt as if she were carrying an unbearable burden of sin from that moment? Was it false that the waves of pleasure of the loosened thighs also loosened her mind? Was everything a mirage? If that was so then why does that incident seem a horrible curse? Once before she had herself with Raja ...? But why did that not seem such a sin? Why was that not nauseating? What was wrong? What is right? Should her life, which had almost grown rich enough for all the envy crumble so suddenly? Was this life?

Sushila had never indulged in such serious thoughts. Today, somehow, her entire body was filled with pain. She did not know how long she had sat thus. She woke up when the clouds overhead gently thundered. When she got up from under the banana tree and looked up, the devilish clouds overhead, black as poisonous rocks, had gathered. Where were they? How did they come? They had surrounded not letting even a hint of sun to be seen. The fight of prime bulls, the shout that shakes the heart, the lightning that seems to lift the village and throw, the terrible thunderbolt, the drops that pattered exploding before she stepped inside the house. The rain began to pour heavily within moments. The monsoon rains were always so. Sushila opened the front door. People reached home, drenched in the pouring rain. The children stood on their porches and held out their hands to the sleet. The rain was beating as forcefully as it started. Perhaps there was such heat only in order to bring such a rain. It seems to have taken up a challenge to at once satiate the long time thirst of earth. In a short while water began to flow on the street. Sushila came to the backyard. The backyard too had filled up and resembled the paddy field. The earth and the sky seemed one. The force of the rain did not ease. It had been a while since Sushila had witnessed such rains. The house was leaking in a couple of places. She kept vessels in all those places. She shut the backdoor. Her mind was worried, an inexplicable anxiety. She stood leaning against the door. She looked out on to the street without batting her eyelids. The rain passed. The day seemed to grow into night. Would there be floods? Sushila's soul writhed. The trembling which began since she gave in to the guilt of having committed a crime intensified now. She lit the lamp to the gods. She made an effort to fix her mind on gods to escape from the blossoming fear within. She could not do so however much she tried. All kinds of evil surrounded her. She had erred somewhere. She too should have accompanied him to Hundi. She had misgivings then. She had falsely consoled herself. What if he were caught in the rains? What if he stood under a tree and a thunderbolt should strike? Sushila trembled where she sat. The wind began to blow as if to lift the very roof of the house. The spray entered through the front door. It seemed as if the plants and trees in the backyard were snapping. As soon as the wind began to blow the rain stopped. The wind continued to roar. Sushila decided to leave for Hundi, But she could hardly move her limbs, as if her legs were caught. She opened the backdoor getting up with the support of her hands. The banana plant was completely bent and was leaning against the ceiling of the house. It would have fallen if the ceiling had not supported it. Only the Mukul tree stood without moving under such stormy wind. Sushila shut the door, came in and was undecided about going to Hundi. Finally having decided to go she shut the door and locked it. When she got down the steps on to the street it was still drizzling. The gutters on both the sides of the street were overflowing. Because of the heavy rain the street had not grown slushy but looked clean swept. But the stones stood grinning caught under the beating rain. Sushila covered her head with her *seragu* and walked quickly. Though the wind had scattered the clouds the sky had not yet cleared. Even as she passed the court the cattle were already returning to the village through the pond fields. When she reached the top of the pond's dyke it was growing slippery. She remembered that only when the steady rains began did it grow slushy and slippery. When she crossed the pond and reached the lane of Hundi, she saw Muddegowda leading her husband by the hand. Sushila was relieved. The clouds of anxiety that had crowded her mind since morning had melted in a second. Her soul relaxed. Both were approaching, conversing loudly. Sushila was ashamed at having imagined things and getting scared. Only when Gowda neared her did he notice Sushila. Even as Gowda said, "Why did you have to come? Would I not have brought him?" Bhujangaiah realized that Sushila had arrived in search of him and said, "You go back now Muddappa," and went holding Sushila's hand. When he asked, "Why did you come Sushi?", she felt like crying. He felt strange at his wife walking without uttering a word. He asked, "Why? What happened?" What could she say? How to tell him all that had happened since the afternoon? When he said, "I suddenly felt like seeing everybody at Gowda's house and so I went" Sushila said, "Wouldn't I too have come?" He replied, "That's all right, we could visit again tomorrow." He began to walk firm footed warning her, "The banks may slip, take care!" With fresh water in the pond already the frogs had begun their ear splitting music. All the fields below the ponds had been inundated by water. When they neared the shrine of Basappa of the Ponds after crossing the pond she saw a few people running in great haste from the village and moved aside in fright. They stopped seeing them and began to stammer. Sushila could hardly understand them. Finally Shankara, the son of the elder Gowda said haltingly, "Our Narayana, bitten by snake in...." he began to weep hard. They both fell silent at his speech. Bhujangaiah was lost in himself. Already within him a big battle had started over the survival of a life.

As they stepped on to the street of Gowda a huge crowd had gathered in front of their house. As soon as they saw them their sorrow seemed to break out. All those who had gathered made way for them. Mallavva sat leaning Narayana who was bitten by a snake, against her. Sushila did not wish to see Narayana's face. Even as she opened the door of the house Shankara placed in Bhujangaiah's hand the neem leaves, which he had already brought to caste a spell. Narayana's wife, who saw a confused Bhujangaiah sitting silently began to beat her bosom and weep loud enough to cut the entrails of those who heard her, fell at Bhujangaiah's feet saying, "I will be your daughter, please save the fortune of my *thali.*" The agonizing moan of others seemed like background music to her weeping. Bhujangaiah pressed the leg of Narayana, which was struck by the snake and examined it while learning from Shankara the changes that had resulted in Narayana. There was a stifling silence. Everyone stood scared to breathe fast. Bhujangaiah realized once more that there was no use casting a spell. The herbal medicine that acted as an antidote to the venom had been used up. The memory of that had made him feel helpless from the moment he heard the news. He put his trust in god saying, "Let things happen as Shiva wills" and asked Sushila to bring the gourd in which he stored the herbal medicine for snake bites. Shankara himself took the gourd and tried passing the medicine on to his palm. Not a drop fell on his palm. Shankara's heart sank. He comprehended Bhujangaiah's doubt and sat silent not knowing what to say. Bhujangaiah felt sure moment after moment that this was nothing other than the game of Shiva. One day, before he had lost his eyes, when he left to collect the medicinal herbs, he had thought of something suddenly and had gone to Hundi wishing to teach Gowda how to identify the herb. That day it had not been done perhaps because this event was intended. Let alone showing it to Gowda, he also had not collected it. Along with his eyes the medicine too had been lost. None else in the village had the knowledge. What could be done now? He somehow had to save the life that had approached his door. It was a test of character which Shiva himself had thrown as a challenge. Whether it was a loss or a win he decided he had to take it up and called for a new razor blade. Narayana's leg had not yet grown stiff. As instructed by Bhujangaiah, Shankara cut an incision on the leg of Narayana. Narayana did not stir. Bhujangaiah who prayed to his personal God who rode the tiger, put his mouth to the incision and began to suck the venom out and spit into the plate. The venom tinged blood began to fill the plate. The people looked at the scene wonder stuck. Bhujangaiah appeared to be a man of miracles. Narayana did not recover, however much he sucked the venom out. Bhujangaiah began to tire out. Such a thing had never happened in the past. He rested a little and began again.

Though the rain had poured well and cooled the village, Madalli was breathing hard once more. All the villagers had gathered in front of Bhujangaiah's house. It was getting dark. Sushila lit the lamp and brought it out. Some anxiety, emotion was playing truant with her soul. No one had noticed her. She went in and out of her house ten times trembling at the danger ahead. If she stood for a second she felt as if she stood on sandals of thorn. It was as if her heart had come to her mouth. It was as if what was crouching in wait since that afternoon was beginning its attack now. Finally, in the end, Bhujangaiah had won the war. Narayana writhed in pain. Mallavva wiped the saliva that flowed out of the corner of her mouth with the *seragu* of her sari. The people too who had assumed all was lost sighed in relief. Bhujangaiah who had plucked Narayana out of the mouth of death had grown absolutely tired. Yet, the satisfaction of having achieved something was brimming in his eyes. Narayana grew a little lively as people watched. Everyone who noticed the change in him said, "It is as if he is reborn from the womb of his mother," Even as Narayana who had escaped from a grave danger was opening his eyes, Bhujangaiah's stomach began to burn and writhe. Only Sushila's eyes had observed it. She grew much more anxious. She had comprehended the change in her husband's face. Bhujangaiah not revealing what was happening to him asked Shankara to break the gourd. Shankara broke it and scrapped the medicine sticking to its bottom. Sushila felt her life return. She brought a glass of water instantly. She mixed the medicine in the water and attempted to make her husband drink it. Bhujangaiah refused to drink and took the glass himself saying, "Wait a moment, Sushi". He knew very well if Narayana had to survive, the poison in his stomach had to come out. Without any hesitation he began to feed Narayana the medicine in the glass with the help of Mallavva. Though some of the medicine came out of the corner of his lips, Narayana retained most of it. Sushila who sat watching as if paralyzed felt the darkness strike her eyelids and

fell near her husband screaming aloud. The people were astounded, not knowing what they watched with their lives in their eyes. Bhujangaiah who embraced her who was screaming like a bird with shorn wings began to comfort her gently patting her back saying, "It's all his design—his design". Even as the people watched, Bhujangaiah's hands slowly grew stiff and slipped from the body of Sushila. The cruel jaws of death had now caught a life that had been victorious over death. There was no other man of miracle in Madalli who could save it. Madalli, which had all this while suffered the pain in silence and breathing heavily began to cry aloud as if it would throw up everything at once.

<<< >>>